ENGLISH RECUSANT LITERATURE
1558–1640

Selected and Edited by
D. M. ROGERS

Volume 354

THOMAS WORTHINGTON
Whyte Dyed Black
1615

THOMAS PRESTON and THOMAS GREEN
Appellatio
1620

THOMAS PRESTON and THOMAS GREEN
Supplicatio
1621

THOMAS WORTHINGTON

Whyte Dyed Black
1615

The Scolar Press

1977

ISBN o 85967 3995

Published and printed in Great Britain by
The Scolar Press Limited, 59-61 East Parade,
Ilkley, Yorkshire and
39 Great Russell Street,
London WC1

NOTE

The following works are reproduced (original size) with permission:

1) Thomas Worthington, *Whyte dyed black*, 1615, from a copy in Cambridge University Library, by permission of the Syndics.
References: Allison and Rogers 919; STC 26001.

2) Thomas Preston and Thomas Green, *Appellatio*, 1620, from a copy in the Bodleian Library, by permission of the Curators.
Reference: Allison and Rogers 677; not in STC.

3) Thomas Preston and Thomas Green, *Supplicatio*, 1621, from a copy in the Bodleian Library, by permission of the Curators.
Reference: Allison and Rogers 678; not in STC.

WHYTE

DYED BLACK.

OR

A Difcouery of many moft foule blemifhes, impoftures, and deceiptes, which D . Whyte
haith practyfed in his book entituled
The way to the true Church.

Deuyded into 3 fortes
{ Corruptions, or depra-
uations.
Lyes.
Impertinencies, or ab-
furd reafoninges.

Writen by T. W. P.

And Dedicated to the Vniuerfity of Cambridge.

*Hæreticum hominem, poft vram & alteram correptio
nem, deuita: fciens, quia fubuerfus eft, qui ciufmodi eft
& delinquit, cum fit proprio iudicio condemnatus. Tit.3,*

*Cathedra tibi quid fecit Ecclefia Romanæ, in qua Pe-
trus fedit, & in qua nunc Anaftatius (fiue Paulus quin-
tus) fedet? Cur appellas Cathedram peftilentiæ, Cathedram Apoftolicam? Auguft. lib.2.con.lit.Petil.*

Cum priuilegio.

1615.

Academiæ Cantabrigiensis Liber

THE EPISTLE DEDICATORY.

TO THE MOST CELEBRIOVS
and famous Vniuerfity of Cambridge.

Ingenious and learned *Academians*, I do not prefent this my fmall labour vnto you, intreating hereby your patronage thereof. For how can I expect fo greate a fauour fince moft of you diffent from me in that Religion which is here mantayned : neither as houlding this poore worke, for any art therein, worthy your iudiceons vew. For I am not onely confcious to my felf of myne owne weaknes : but do alfo grearly admyre your pearcing and cleare eyed indgmenres.

To you then I exhibite it, as appealing to the Mother (fuch is my confidence in your impartiall and euen cenfures) as Iudg betwene her fonne and my felf. For wheareas my defigned aduerfary at this prefent M. Whyte, (to whom your vniuerfity haith firft geuen his education for literature, and fince hath graced him with the inueflure of Doctorfhip) in anfwear to a Catholick Treatife (firft pēned by one of my fellow-labourers in the vineyard of Chrift) haith writen a moft virulent and fcandalous booke, entituling it, *The way to the true Church*. The which booke was fownde fo full of corruptions, vntruthes, and other fuch baiffe matter, that it was houlden in the opinion of many great and learned Preiftes, rather worthy of contempt then anfwear.

Neuertheleffe M. Whyte, not onely in the Preface of his faid booke, but alfo in diuers places of his fecond worke, vaunteth much of his fincere dealing in the firft, as particulerly pag. 129. where faying that it is the profeffion of Iefuites in their wryting, *to rayze bookes, counterfeat, forge, and lye :* he then thus ambiti-

oufly

ambitiously concludeth . *My aduersary can not present the Reader with one conclusion* (meaning of his first book) *one doctrine , one quotation , one lyne , or letter , to make him really see wherein I haue fayled .*

Now this idle venditation of ingenuity and vpright dealing , haith awakened my sleeping pen , and indeede haith geuen birth to this short Treatife , whearin I do vndertake to make good our former cenfures , that is , to demonftrate , that the very ground and burden of his firft booke , is mere corruptions , vntruthes , and other fuch impoftures , in the euicting of which poynt I am fo fecure , that I willingly make your felues Iudges both of him and me , being affured , that in a true and ferious perufall of this my accufatió , you fhall fynde no candor in Whyte , nor any of Gods fpirit in him who ftyleth him felf Gods minifter , but rather in reguard of your fruftrated hope , you fhall haue iuft reafon to fay of this your childe (who feming Iacob , proueth Efau) *Expectauimus lucem , ecce tenebra . Ef.* 59. which deformities of his , I am not of fo rigide a Iudgment , as to afcribe to your famous vniuerfity , for at this prefent , I do not wholly approue that comó pofition of the Ciuilians , *partus fequitur ventrem* : And we all obferue , that thofe faire heauenly bodies , fomtimes bring forth monfters .

It is certainly reported , that defyre of praife (a windy *Meteor* ingendred in the Region of felf conceate) firft inuyted M . Whyte , to fupport forfooth , with his learned hand , the threatning and falling piller of his new Church : and thereupon he inftantly ftept into the number of writers , hauing thereby already gayned great applaufe and approbation from the wauering vncertaine multitude , in whofe weake opinion , he feemeth to haue ouerpaffed moft of his tyme and ranck : but I doubt not , but by the affiftance of him , who *In veritate*

veritate educet iudicium, Ef. 42. and by the enfuing difcouery of his calumnious forgeries, fo to picke the
fwolne bladder of his pryde, as that all his frothy of-
tentation, fhall refolue to nothing : and that his wrytinges (lyke vnto new found wells, being commonly
of acompt onely for a yere or two) which heretofore
his fauorites haue fo highly eftemed : fhall for euer after remaine contemned and neglected : which euent
may well be expected fince it often hapneth, that he
who ryfeth fodainly, faleth precipitatly.

But as in this following Treatife you fhall be fully
fatiffyed of the want of his fincerity, fo here I hould it
not inconuenient, to geue fome touch of that oppro-
brious tongue of his, which cafteth moft fowle and
vndeferued afperfions of contumely and reproch vpon
all Preiftes and Catholickes. For euen in his Epiftles
of this his booke impugned by me, he wryteth,
that the, *Iefuites are the Popes Ianifaryes, that Priefts
are cunning feducers poffeffing mens wyues, &c. vfing their
goods to fwager, and ferue their owne luxurious vfe, &
that fince the Harpies were chaced away, and Bel was
ouerthrowne, neuer was fuch a greedy and rauenous Idol
as the feminary, and that friars, feminaryes, and Maffe
Priefts, are fo many beares and bloody Tigars, the fatall
enemyes of Princes, &c. that the Papifts laity, doth liue in
extreame ignorance, and finally that their religion teacheth to pay no debts, murther Kings, and tendeth cheifly
to all bloody confpiracies, &.* Our innocency in all which
pointes, one daye will difcouer, when the vayle of
each mans actions fhalbe drawne awaye, and when all
deedes and thoughts fhalbe plainly laid open, at what
time M. Whyte, for theefe and other his moft falfe,
iniurious, and vnchriftian reproches muft render a
feuere account ; only at this prefent our retaliation
to him fhalbe to faye with the *Apoftle c maledicimur* c 1 Cor. 4.

fed

fed benedicimus , blafphemamur fed obfecramus . and tel-
ling him , that by thefe his *Philippickes* and declama-
tory inuectiues , he haith worthily gotten the reputation of being counted a good rayler , and hath bene
carefull (as it fhould feeme) to warrant in him felf thofe
wordes of the Scripture : d *the tonge is an vnruly euill ,
full of deadly poyfon* .

d Iac . 3 . And now *illuftrious Academians* (whome God hath en-
dued with tranfcendent fpiritts , and vnderftandings
farr aboue the vulgar) fuffer me , before I remit you to
this following difcourfe to prefent vnto you touching our Catholicke faith , thefe few admonitions , the
which you are not to contemne , as proceeding from
me how meane foeuer , but rather herein to remember , that from the earth (the loweft element of all)
we beft obferue the motions of the heauens .

Make then particuler triall of the cheefe grounds of
our Catholicke religion , and looke backe vnto the
Continuall practize of Chriftes Church fince it firft
beinge , & affure your felf , that we fhall not be found
fuperftitious and blynd (as it pleafeth M. Whyte &
others to terme vs)for how can they be blind , who behould the articles of there faith with the eyes of all
antiquity .

Examine it by the rules of Gods facred word , & for
the true fence of his written word (as following e-
uen the iugments of the moft difpaffionat and fober

e Kemnitius
e cam. concil.
Triden. par . 1
pag . 74 .

Iewell in his
defence of the
Adology .
Proteftants) e recur to the ioynt expofitions of the primitiue fathers , who liued , when the church was moft
florifhing , and in her full orbe ; and know , that the
leaues of fcripture , without the intended fence of the
holy Ghoft , are but leaues without frute . & as touching his vnwritten word , call to mind that faying of
*Tertulian : Id uerius , quodprius , id prius , quod ab initio ;
id ab initio , quod ab Apoftolis .*

Remember

Remember, that the most markable Protestants f for learninge, do confesse, that those doctors are patrons of our Catholicke fayth, who liued when the Spouse of Christ was most spotles, chaft, and intemerat : Apoynt indeed so euident, as that from their learned monuments we are able to delineat, and draw the very Image and face of the present Romane religion; & as for the more obscure passages occurring in them, your ingenuityes may suppose them to be the sad colours or darke groundes, seruing onely to giue greater luster and life to the whole portrayture. Be neuer perswaded (since it is graunted, that the *Romane Church* was once the true church, and the time of her supposed reuolt cannot be knowne) that the daughter of Sion, could euer so vnespiedly become a *Babilonian* strumpet.

Deuide not your selues frō that most conspicuous church of Christ, which haith bene promised, g that in all ages it should gloriously appeare to the eye of the world, left so in lew thereof, as for the last refuge, you be forced to forge a *Mathematicall* and acry Church, consisting of certain imaginary inuisibilites, impugned by the fathers, h and your more iudicious wryters : i since it being, mearly consisteth in a not being.

Suffer not a *Heteroclyte* sectary, who reiecteth (though contrary to gods word k and his owne brethren l) all regular, ordinary, and mediate vocation (like an other *Melchisadech*, borne without father or mother) to plant in your soules a new kind of religion neuer heard of before, till a libidenous Monke by mutuall breach of vowes, had yoked him selfe with a lapsed Nunn: and be a certained, that such a nouelift must needs be one of those, *who say they are Apostles, and are not, but are found liars.*

finally Iohn . 10

f Luth. tom : 2. wittenb. anno . 1551 lib. de feru. ar bitr. pag .454

Beza in his preface vpon the new Testament, dedicated to the Prince of Condy anno . 1587.

Doctor Humfrey li. de vita Iewelli.

g Esa.2.60. Micheas. 4. psalm . 19.

Math . 18 . h Hiero . Epist. ad Pammach .

Athanatius. li. de decret. nicen. Sinod.

August. lib . 3 de baptismo contra Donatum. ca . 2.

iDoctor Humfrey in Iesui part.2.rat.3 pag.240.

k Hebru. 4. Roman . 10.

Finally relinquifhe , and abandon that fupreame foue-raignty of the *priuat reauealing fpirit* (condemned e-uen by *Chrifts* owne n *Apoftles*) it being firft cheefly erected, therby to decline the weighty authorityes of the auncient fathers in the expofition of Gods fa-cred wryt , & to reduce all thinges to the moft graue (for-footh) and inappealable tribunall of each illite-terate mans empty fcull and braines . Thus do the gof-pellers of thefe dayes , hould the fanaticall *reuealing Spirit* , as their mount *Sinay* from whence they receue their new euangelicall lawe , it being in deed fhadow-ed with a cloud , not wherewith to couer it owne ouer glorious infallibility , but with a cloud or mift of pride, ignorance , and vncertainty .

And thus worthy *Academians* , leauing you to the cen-fure of your vnworthy fonn , I take my leaue , expect-ing , that my good meaning herein , fhall ouer-ballance with you , my bouldnes , and wifhing euen in the bow-els of Chriftiane charity , that euery one of you weare ftrong armed with our moft aunciet Catholicke Roman faith ; for then you would eafily learne to contemne thofe poore and weake affaults , which euery firft ap-pearance of new doctrine doth threaten : it being an acknowledged , & experienced truth that *Harefes* o a-*pud eos multum valent , qui in fide non valent* .

Your well willer in Chrift Iefus

T . W . P .

l Doctor Co-uell in his de-fence of Hoo-ker pag. 86 .

Doctor Sarani-a contra refp . Bez . pag . 360 .

Cartwright in his fecond re-ply part . fec. pag . 142 .

m Apoc . c . 2

n 1 Cor . 12 . Petr . 2 . c . 1 Iohn . 1 . c . 4

o Tertul . li . de prefcript .

THE PREFACE TO THE READER

Good Reader, before I remit thee to the perusall of this enfuing difcourfe, I here thinke it good to acquaint thee with the occafion inducing me to wryte it, and with my methode houlden therein. And as touching the firft, thou art to conceaue, that the worthles efteeme, which we haue had of M. Whyte his booke (how foeuer his owne followers do magnify it) as feeing it fraught with fuch impurity of ftuffe, haith for theefe yeares paft preuailed with moft of vs fo far, that we weare determined to forbeare the anfwearing thereof, houlding it altogether vnworthy of fuch labour; yet feing in diuerfe paffages of his late fecond worke, he vaunteth in great exultation, and iolity of words, that this his firft booke doth not ftand chargeable with any wilfull corruption, falfification, or other fuch impofture, and that he confidently prouoketh his aduerfary (if any fuch be) to fet them downe : Therefore to controule this mans moft fhameleffe affeueration (as being one of an obdurat confcience, not caring how falfly he wryteth, or how impudently he iuftifieth it being wrytten) I do here charge his faid firft treatife with moft fowle abufes, falfifications, & other fuch fraudulent dealing, & will in theefe few fheetes following particularize to thee diuerfe of them, whereby thou fhalt haue reafon to affure thy felfe that M. Whyte, in reguarde of his calling in his new Miniftery, and his exercife therein, may truly be num bred amongeft them a *Qui Commutauerunt verita-* a Roman. 1. *tem Dei in mendacium, who changed the truth of God vnto a lye.* Now concerning my methode taken, in difplaying of his falfhood, and deceate, thou art to be aduertifed, that my cheefe proiect in this treatife being to proue M. Whyte in his wrytings a moft difhoneft, con-
                                                            fcionles

conſcionles, and faithles man: therfore forbearing to confute the whole courſe of his booke in reſpect of doctrine (which is already learnedly performed by my fellowe A.D. in his reply to M.W. ſaid worke) I do here reſtraine my ſelfe to three heads, reducing all theeſe impoſtures, in which hereafter I intend to inſiſt, to ſome of them. The heads are theſe Corruptions, Lyes, and Impertinecyes. By Corruptiōs, I meane thoſe depraued authorityes of the auncient Fathers, and our own moderne Catholicke authours, which this our Miniſter (thereby to make thē to ſpeake in his proteſtant language and dialect) haith moſt ſhameleſly altered, either by inſerting, or adding ſome words of his owne, as part of their ſentences; or by concealing of ſome part of their words, which do expound the reſt of the teſtimonyes, in a far different ſence frō that, in which M. Whyte doth vrge them, or laſtly (though ſetting downe their words truly) by ſtrangely detorting and wreſting them from the intended ſence of the authors.

By Lyes, I vnderſtand falſe aſſertions and vaſt vntruthes mantained by M. White, whom the more fully, and irrepliably, and for the greater compendiouſnes, to cōuince therein, I haue made choice of thoſe vntruthes, as are acknowledged for ſuch by the moſt learned Proteſtants, thus making his mother (to wit the *Vniuerſity*) the iudg, and his own *Brethren* the plaintifs, betwene himſelfe and me herein.

By Impertinēces, I conceaue his idle and fruteles aledging either of ſcripture, fathers, or Catholick writers, to diſproue thereby ſome poynt of our religion; where my meaning is, that allowing the ſenſe and conſtructions to thoſe authorityes, which the wordes neceſſarily and truly importe, yet they doe in no ſort diſable & weaken the catholicke poynt, for the impugning whereof they are there by our Miniſter produced, ſo that it followeth

followeth, that his illations drawne from thofe teſtimonies, to the queſtion intended, are moſt abfurd, in-
congruous, and inconfequent. Thefe three now are
the feuerall particuler deliueries of our miniſter, in his
fo much applauded worke, himfelfe in this his fcene,
fometimes acting one part, fometimes an other, agree-
able to the former heades, but wee leſſe maruaile,
fince eich man knowes that whyte is fucceſſiuely ca-
pable of feuerall tinctures. Now touching the number of thefe his impoſtures, thou art (good reader) further to vnderſtand that my meaning is not to difplaye
all thofe with which his booke is ſtored, for this would
require too painful a labour, and rifing to an ouer
greate volume, would be leſſe fitting to be printed
and diuulged. Befides, feeing my maine proiecte here
is to decipher the difhoneſt dealing of our miniſter,
euery cleere iudgment will acknowledg, that the
true charging him euen with a few wilfull and vniuſ-
tifiable corruptions, doth condemne and proue him
for fuch a man : and euery one knoweth, that who is
found out of malice to corrupte fome few places, would
in like forte depraue as many authorities as opportunity might licence him. Therfore touching his Corruptions or deprauations, I haue contented my felfe
onely with fourty, which fourty, are taken out of a-
bout fome twenty different writers, hauing in truth no
more bookes alledged by him, wherewith to examine
it : from which circumſtance thou maiſt thus conclude,
that if, reſtraining my felfe onely to twenty authours
more or leſſe, I can find fourty moſt notorious corruptions of theyr teſtimonies, how many fcores in all lik-
lihood of fuch like deprauations might be found in all
the reſt of the authors alledged by him, which amount
nere-hand to a hundred, if diligent fearch weare
made of them : & the rather confidering, that many
bookes produced by him, but omitted by me, are moſt
hard to

to be gotten, and therefore he might corrupte their
fayinges more fecurely, and with greater bould nes,
as prefuming beforehand, that fuch his corruptions
through want of the bookes themfelues, could not
eafely be efpied.

In like fort concerning his lyes, I haue made choyce
onely of fuch as are all of thē acknowledged for vntruthes by his owne learned brethren. From which
point thou maift alfo thus infer; if M. Whyte his
booke, doth minifter fundry fuch groffe lyes againft
our catholicke faith, as that the moft learned proteftants, that euer writ, are forced (though to their owne
difaduantage) to confeffe them for fuch: How many other vntruthes might be found therein, which
through fome fhewe, or culour of anfweare, and euafion, are fuch, (as though being lyes indeed) wil not
yet be fo acknowledged by our aduerfaries, who are
loth to confeffe more in fauour of our catholicke religion, then the vnauoidable euidence and clearenes
of the truth it felfe conftrayneth them.

Laftly all his impertinencies, or weake abfurd reafons
hereafter fet downe, are taken out of leffe then twenty leaues of his booke, from which thou maift in like
maner thus collect, that if twenty leaues, and theefe
in the firft part of his booke (deuiding the whole into three partes) do afford fuch aboundance of impertinent allegations, and authorityes, how many hun-
dreds then in all probability of like nature, are difper-
fed throughout his whole treatife, it contayning a-
boue two hundred leaues. And the rather, feeing
that diuers authours do commonly fortify and ftreng-
then the firft part of their wrytings, with more forcible
proofes and authorities then the latter part, both
thereby the fooner, and with greater fpeede toinuade
the iudgment of the reader, as alfo knowing, that
                                                    many

many do perufe the beginninges of bookes, who through a werifome carelefnes do neuer reade the latter part of them.

And thus much of my methode in this my treatife. Here now thou feeft (curteous reader) what I vndertake to performe, that is to make euident, that M. Whyte his firft booke is ftored with moft fhameles falfifications, lyes, and other fuch collufions: the which if I doe not effect, I am content to become a reproche, and fhame, not onely to my particuler profeffion (the facred function whereof I hould my cheefeft honour) but alfo to the Catholicke caufe in generall; for here I proteft in the fight of god, and as I fhall anfwere the truth or falfhood of this my proteftation at the moft dreadfull daye, that I neuer perufed booke of this quantity, wherein I did find more vnanfwereable corruptions, lyes, and impertinencies, then in this worke of M. Whytes. And if fo eminent a man (as he is prefumed by many to be) doth ftand chargeable with fuch prophane, and wicked deportments: what fhall we then cenfure of other inferiour wryters of his fide, Since b *if the light be darknes, how great is the darknes:* or what may we iudg of the iuftnes of their caufe feeing the faith of Chrift is of that force, as it fcorneth to be vphoulden with the weake fupporters of fuch deceatfull meanes, it being no better, then an impious deuotion, or irreligious godlines, to defend truth with falfhood, or to blaze forth the light of the gofpel, by the workes of darknes? And as touching his fecond booke, which is fraughted with all bafe fcurrility of wordes, and railing, I will onely fay, that feing there hath not bene as yet fufficient opportunity for the particuler examining of it, yet I am affured, that who fhall impofe that labour to himfelf, fhall find the fame to ftand chargeable with no lefe ftore

of

b Math. c 6.

of impoſtures, then this his other : for if this his booke impugned by me (being the ſtrength and firſt borne of his cauſe) be found ſo corrupt, how can we probably coniecture that this other ſecond feminine, and leiſe perfect labour of his, ſhould not pertake of the former blemiſhes and deficiences .

But now good reader, I will detaine thee no longer from peruſing this my accuſation, earneſtly entreating thee (euen tor the good of thy ſoule) that if thou vnderſtand latin, thou wouldeſt ſee the teſtimonies them ſelues, as they lye in the authours, the which I doe avouch to be here corrupted, which if thou doſt, doubtleſly thou ſhalt be forced to confeſſe, that M . whyte is a moſt egregious falſary, and howſoeuer he enameleth his cauſe, with the phrazes of *the waye to the true Church*, of *he enlarging of the Ghoſpell of Chriſt*, *of rooting out ſuperſtition and blindnes*, and the like, neuerthe leſſe thou ſhalt find that he is moſt conſcious, and guilty both of his owne weake cauſe, as alſo of his perfidious, and prophane mantaining and defending of the ſame, ſo as in reguard of his hipocriſy, and diſſimulation herein, thou ſhalt ſee the wordes of the apoſtle

a Rom . 9 . iuſtified in him a *all they are not Iſraell, which are of Iſraell*, himſelfe being one of thoſe b *which will not*
b Act . 13 · *ceaſe to peruert the way of our Lord* .

A TABLE OF THE CONTENTES.

The first Part .

Chapiter 1 .

Conteyning Corruptions, concerning woorkes and Iuftification.

The Firft Paragraph .

Chapiter. 2 .

Concerning the reading of the Scriptures .

The firft Paragraph .

Chapiter. 3 .

Concerning the Church, and the Pope .

The

Vincentius Lirinenſis Corrupted, in proofe that the Church may erre .

2 The Rhemiſtes Corrupted, for the Churches inuiſibility .

3 S. Auguſtine Corrupted, concerning the ſame ſubiect .

4 Doctor Stapleton abuſed, in behalfe of the proteſtantes markes of the Church .

5 S. Gregory *de valentia* Corrupted , concerning the ſame .

6 Bellarmine egregiouſly Corrupted, for the ſame .

7 S. Thomas fouly corrupted, concerning the Popes authority .

8 Doctor Sapleton corrupted , concerning the ſame ſubiect .

9 S. Ciprian corrupted , againſt appeales to Rome .

10 The Rhemiſtes abuſed , concerning the authority of the Church .

11 Cardinall Cuſanus corrupted concerning the ſame .

12 The canon lawe corrupted , concerning the Pope .

13 Bellarmine corrupted , againſt the Popes authority .

Chapiter 4 .

wherin are diſcouered ſundry corruptions , concerning the ſacred Scriptures and Traditions .

The firſt Paragraph .

Bellarmine corrupted , in behalfe of the Scripture prouing it ſelfe to be the word of god .

2 Bellarmine corrupted, in proofe that the Scriptures are the onely rule of faith .

Chapter. 5.

Concerning Faith and Herefy.

The 1 Paragraph.

Chapter 6.

Concerning mariage of Preiftes: Fafting: and Mira-cles.

The 1 Paragraph.

Chapter. 7.

Concerning the Sacramentes of the Fucharift, and Penance.

The ſecond part.

Containing ſundry notorious vntruthes or lyes, proued
to be ſuch by the confeſſion of learned proteſtantes.

And

And first is preuented a weake euasion, which may be vsed by M. Whyte against this second part.

The 1. vntruth.

That protestantes embrace that kind of tryall which is by antiquity,

2 Against Traditions.

3 In proofe of the protestants Church, to haue continued in all ages.

4 In proofe of the vnity of faith, and doctrine amongst protestantes.

5 In proofe of the immutability of the present English Religion.

6 In proofe of the Romane Churches mutability in matters of faith.

7 In proofe of the protestantes concord, in matters of Religion.

8 Against the vnity of Catholickes, in matters of faith.

9 Against the Popes primacy.

10 That Gregory the great, detested the Popes primacy.

11 In proofe that Catholickes are more viceous then protestantes.

12 Against auriculer confession.

13 Against Fasting.

14 In proofe that Montanus the herityke, was the first that brought in the lawes of Fasting.

15 In proofe that they make not God the Author of sinne.

16 In proofe that S. Bernard was noe papist.

17 Against the miracles wrought by S. Bernarde, and S. Francis.

18 In proofe of the protestantes Churches euer visibility.

19 In defence of Preistes mariage.

The Third Part.

Contayning diuers impertinences, or abſurd Illations, or reaſoninges.

The 1. Paragraph.

Wherein are diſcouered, ſtrange Illations or arguinges, in proofe that the Scriptures are the ſole rule of faith : and againſt Traditions.

2 Wherein are diſcuſſed certaine arguments drawne from Scriptures & Fathers, in proofe that the ſacred Scriptures & the true ſenſe thereof, are made ſufficiently knowne vnto vs, without any probation, or explication of the Church.

3 Wherein are examined ſome of M. Whites profes, againſt the viſibility of the Church.

4 Wherein are diſcuſſed, certaine proofes of M. Whytes, in behalf of the proteſtantes markes of the Church.

5 Wherein are examined ſtrange kindes of Arguinges, a gainſt the Authority of the Church.

Faultes efcaped in the printing.

In the preface to the Vniuerfity of Cambridge.

Pag. 1. lin. 10. for *iudiceous* reade *iudicions*.
Ibid lin 11. for *grearly*, read *greatly*.
Ibid. pag. 4. lin 27. for *Iugements*, read *Iudgements*.
Ibid. pag. 5. lin. 22. for *inuifibilites*, *Inuifibiliftes*.

Preface to the Reader.

Pag: 2. lin. 4. leaue out (faid worke.)
Pag. 4. lin. 15. for *culour*, read *colour*.

Chapter 1.

Pag. 4. lin. 25. for *Iuftiieth*, read, *infifteth in*.
Pag. 5. lin. 25. for *preadmonifh*, read, *premonifh*.
Pag. 18. lin. 21. for *great*, read, *greateft*.
Pag. 27. lin. 9. for *Quod*, read, *Quid*.
Pag. 31. lin. 23. for *Anolegie*, read, *Analogie*.
Pag. 47. lin. 4. betwixt druncke, and fhould, in-
ferte, one.
Pag. 52. lin. 16. & 17. leaue out thefe wordes, All
which your o niffions, are impaled and marked, in
the faid englifh authority.
Pag. 52. lin. 20. for *Emprour*, read, *Emperour*
Pag. 53. lin. 14. for *difopting*, read, *difforting*.
Pag. 53. lin. 23. for *perufing*, read, *purfuing*.
Pag. 64. lin. 14. leaue out the word, is.
Pag. 77. lin. 10. for *Chapiter*, read *Chapter*.
Pag. 87. lin. 24. for *maliuolent*, read *maleuolent*.
Pag. 138. lin. 27. next after the word (Maffe) infert
affirmeth.
Pag. 159. lin. 10. betwixt, authority, & the, in-
fert, in.
Pag. 73. lin. 30. for *fully*, read *fouly*.
Pag. 87. lin. 33. for *paralayes*, read, *parallels*.

Pag. 92. lin. 4. for differences, read discoueries.
Pag. 97. lin. 28. for musk, read musick.
Pag. 114. lin. 24. for proh dolor, read proh pudor.
Ibid. lin. 27. for clausure, read closure.
Pag. 118. lin. 33. for entertaine, read enteruaine.
Pag. 125. lin. 12. for concurre, read recurre.
For ingenious, read in sundry places ingenuous.

WHITE

DYED BLACK.

THE FIRST PARTE.

W HE ARE IN are difcouered Fourty moft foule & vniuftifiable corruptions and deprauations of Authors vfed by Doctor Whyte, in his
Treatife of the way to the
true Church.

Chapter. 1.

Conteyning Corruptions concerning
workes & Iuftification.

Paragr. 1 *Premonitions geuen to M. W. if he
intende to reply vpon this prefent
Treatife.*

WE reade (*Exod.* 13) that the firft borne of
the people of Ifraell, was euer confecrated
vnto god in regard of a gratefull acknowledgment of his innumerable benefites fhewed vnto
them: and by reafon of fuch his tytle thereto, god
(who had a fupreme intereft in all theire iffue) peculierly pronounced, *This is myne.* I feare that M. Whyte
(who vaunteth himfelfe for a true Ifraelite) haith not
fanctified vnto his diuyne Maiefty, this his child, the
firft borne of the wombe of his braine, for bookes

are *fætus ingenii*, carying in them felues an inward refemblance to theire parentes, and withall as perpetua-
ting their remembrance, doe extende their lynes beyond their liues : Nay I am rather perfwaded that he
haith particulerly deuoted it to Gods and mans ghoftly enemy. For to whom rather are lyes and impoftures
(the very burden of his Treatife) to be afcribed, then
to him who is the father of lyes? And fure I am that
God who is the truth it felfe can not be found herein
fince no man vfeth to gather *grapes of thornes, or figgs
of thiftles*. (*Mat*.7.) And M. Whyte him felfe confeffeth that *we can not learne truth in the fchoole of lyes*.

Now to difcouer that this worke of his is euen loaded with many moft foule vntruthes, corruptions, and
deceiptes, is my tafke voluntarily impofed by my felfe
and I hope with thy good patience (gentle reader)to
performe the fame.

And firft according to my former prefcribed Methode, his perfidious corruptions of fathers & Catho-
lique Authoures, rhereby to force them to fpeake in a
language and dialect of which they were merely ignorant, fhall begin the Scene.

But becaufe as M. Whyte is pregnant in deprauing of mens writinges, fo alfo he will no doubt fhew
him felfe ingenious in fynding fome fleighty euafions
and anfweares, vnder the tecture whereof to fhrewde
him felfe. Therefore I thinke good now in the front
and beginning of this my labour, to fet downe by way
of preuention, all what may be imagined that he can
pretende for his defence and Apology, and to difcouer
the weaknes thereof, that fo his impoftures may be obferued and perufed with greater benefite to the reader,
and more fhamefull guiltineffe to him felfe.

Firft then M. Whyte can not tranfferr the fault v-
pon the

pon the printer for heare he ſtandes for the moſt part
chargeable either with adding too , or detracting frō
the authority alledged(ſo abaſtarding it by this meane
that the true father thereof would not acknowledg it
for his owne) whereas the printers errour comonly
reſteth in quotations made by figures, or (by miſta-
king of ſome letter) in placing one woord for another , ouer-ſightes heare forborne , and indeede vnworthy to be inſiſted vpon by any iuditious penne .

Secondly he can not ſay that his intention in alledging ſuch authorities , was onely to alledg the ſenſe of
the Authour not tying him ſelfe to the authoures perticuler wordes . Of this euaſion he preuenteth him
ſelfe in that he euer vndertaketh to alledg the perticuler ſayings of the Authour , and for that reaſon doth
diſtinguiſh them in a different letter from that wherin his owne wordes are printed (a courſe amongſt
writers moſt certaine and vſuall to know when a man
deliuereth the preciſe wordes or ſentences of an other)
and which is more for the moſt part he thus vſhereth
his teſtimonies , *Bellarmine ſaith*, *Thomas Aqninas
ſaith*, *Anſtine ſaith, &c*. or putteth their names in the
mergent: whereby it is not to be doubted but that he
would haue his reader thinke, that the Authorities
ſet downe, are the very wordes of the Authoures them
ſelues, without any variation or chang whatſoeuer.

Now if he will iuſtify them to be the preciſe words
of the Authoures without any chang either of adding
or detracting: then is he to name the perticuler Edi-
tions of ſuch bookes which he foloweth, and wherein the teſtimonies (as they are alledged by him) are to
be found.

Thirdly where he is charged to corrupt any Authority by concealing for his owne aduantage any part

A   thereof

thereof, he can not iuftify it by replyinge, that he is not tyed to fet downe all which his Authour faith of that poynt, fince fo his Authorities would grow ouer longe and tedious : this is no fufficient anfweare. For although a writer is not bound to fet downe all that his alledged Authour faith of fuch a point: yet is he bound not purpofly to omitt any part of the beginning of the middeft, or of the ending of the faid fentences which he produceth, efpecially when the wordes concealed make for his aduerfary, and againft the drifte and fcope of that meaning wherein the refte of the fentence is by him deliuered. Aud this kind of omiffion (wherevnto M. Whyte ftandeth extremely obnoxious, and is in this part folowing fo by me charged) is in the iudgment of all writers, a wilfull, vnpardonable, & vniuftifiable corruptiug of mens bookes.

Fourthly it is no excufe to fay, touching fuch autho rities as M. Whyte truly alledgeth without adding or detracting (of which kind there are very few if any) that his meaning is onely to fet downe the wordes of Catholick Authoures without reftrayning them to any perticuler fence which he leaueth to that daungerous and inconuenient expofition which the wordes in the readers eye may beft feme to afford. This is moft falfe, for there is no Catholick which he iuftifyeth, but he perticularly reftraineth the fence of his teftimony either to the fupporting of fome point of proteftacy, or els to the manteyning of fome abfurde and fcandalous opinion which he obtrudeth vpon vs. And thus much, befides the often anfwearable entituling of the pages, his owne precedent or fubfequent wordes, do, for the moft part, imply.

Fyftly, if his pryde would fuffer him to defcende fo low, he can not plafter the marter in acknowledginge
that

that the teftimonies heare corrupted, are not of his
owne reading, but that he relyed therein vpon the an
notations and note-bokes of others of the miniftery(a
refuge wherunto fome of his profeffion haue bene here
tofore driuen) and fo as being ouer credulous and con
fident of his frendes fuppofed allegations, he was by
them miftaken. Of this fily & poore euafion, he haith
already precluded him felfe. For in his firft Edition
(which I here folow)after his Alphabeticall Table in
the end of his booke, he haith made an ambitious note
to the reader, that *he will (* to vfe his owne wordes *)*
mantaine the quotations for fubftance to be true &c . And
againe, *it is one thing if I haue wilfully falfifyed or forged*
a place, and an other thing if the printer onely haith mifta-
ken the quotation : the latter may be , but the former is not ,
as I will be ready to fatiffy any that will charge me with it .
Thus he. But how mantaineth he the point, or what
fatiffaction geueth he, if in anfwere to the corruptions
and deprauations wherewith he is heare charged, he
reply, that in good footh fo it is that he did not read
the teftimonies of the Authoures them felues, but
onely tooke them vpon the credit and affiance of fuch
of his owne brother-hood as he thought would not
haue deceiued him? A graue & fufficient anfweare.

And heare I am to preadmonifhe M. Whyte,
that I doe expect in his anfweare (if he doe intende
fincerely and truly to free him felf from thefe imputa-
tions) to anfweare all the corruptions and deprauations by them felues as heare they are gathered, and
fo the lyes and falfhoodes feuerally by them felues ; as
as alfo the impertinences in like fort, and not promif-
cuoufly to iumble aud fhuffle them together, now
feeking to falue a corruption, next a lye, and fo by af-
fecting an obfcurity, in methode, to bleare the eye of
the reader that he fhall not difcerne what corruptions
in his

in his reply he omitteth, and what he maketh shew
to iustify; wherefore I say if he make choice of this obscure course after this premonition, he but bewrayes
his owne guiltinesse. And though I can not by the
lawes of writing impose a methode vpon my aduersaries pen: yet seing the reason why M. Whyte should
affect an other course then I heare wish him, is seene
aforehand, and so him self hereby aduertised thereof,
to be onely (by answearing so confusedly) to delude
and wrong his reader: therefore euen for his owne honour and credit sake, he can not refuse this desyred
methode which heare I requyre, especially seing it is
wished onely for manifestation of the truth, as being
in it selfe most obuious, facile, & perspicuous.

Thus much I haue thought good (for his greater
caution) to instruct the reader with afore-hand; and
therefore now I will remitt him to the ensuing deprauations, still wishing him to haue his eye (whensoe-
uer M. Whyte shall vouchsaife to make answeare hereto) intent and fixed vpon the corruption obiected:
neither suffer him to turne the question (as before I
touched) from the corruption, to the sence & meaning of the Authour (a sleight vpon the lyke occasion vsed by Plessis against the Bishoppe of Eureux) &
so to entertaine the reader with long discourses thereby to diuert his myud from the point in question: but
let the reader alwayes remember, that the question
heare for the most part immediatly is, whether such a
sentence or testimony is truly and faithfully alledged
as it is to be found in the Authour him selfe, without
any addition or concealement of wordes in M. White
his behalfe, and so breefely whether M. Whyte corrupteth the place or not, still obseruing that whatsoeuer M. Whyte saith, if it do not conclude that the
testimony is in noe sort altered and changed from the
wordes

wordes of the Authour him felfe, is (in refpecte of
the point here handled) but idly, extrauagantly, &
impertinently fpoken.

Paragr. 2.

The Rhemiftes corrupted concerning merite of workes.

BVT now at the laft to come to M. Whytes deprauations the which (for more perfpicuity) I
will range to certaine heades: the firft whereof fhall
be fuch as concerne the doctrine of workes and iuftification And to begin with one which as it conteyneth in it felf many foule and ftrang corruptions: fo
the iniury thereby offered is not to one but to many
and thofe men for their learning and vertue, of wor-
thieft memory, to wit, the englifh Doctors of *Rhemes*
who (if we may beleue M. Whyte pag. 238.) feare
not to affirme that our *workes of their very nature, de-*
ferue eternall lyfe, the reward whereof is a thing equally &
iuftly anfwearing to the tyme and weight of the worke rather
then a free guift, fo that God fhould be vniuft if he gaue it
not. And for this he quoteth in his mergent. *Rhem.*
Annot. vpon 1. *Cor,* 3. 8. *& Hebr.* 6. 10. But for
the plaineft and moft certaine difcouery of this brafen
faced minifter, I willfet downe the true wordes of the
Rhemiftes, who commenting vpon thofe of S. Paule
(1. *Cor.* 3. 8) *And euery one fhall receaue his owne re-*
ward according to his owne labour, wryte as foloweth.
A moft plaine text to proue that men by their laboures &
by the diuerfities thereof fhall be diuerfly rewarded in heauen:
and therefore that by their workes proceding of GRACE,
they deferue or merit heauen. Here before I procede any
further, I muft charge M. Doctor with a dooble corruption, firft for omitting the word Grace, the true

wordes

wordes being *workes proceding of Grace*, *do deserue or merit heauen* : secondly, which maketh it more inexcusable and damnable, for inserting in steed of the word *Grace*, the word *Nature*, the which was not so muck as dreamed of by the Rhemistes, or by any Catholick Author, yea to defend that workes of their owne nature do merite, were to renew the heresy long since condemned in the Pelagians by the Romane Church.

But to goe forward, the Rhemistes in this ministers mouth affirme, that *the reward is a thing equally & iustly answearing to the tyme and weight of the worke*, *rather then a free guifte*. But in their owne wordes they auouch the contrary. *And indeede (* say they *) this word Reward which in our english tongue may signify a voluntary or bountifull guift, doth not so well expresse the nature of the latin word, or the greeke, which are rather the very stipend that the hyred workman or iournay mã couenanteth to haue of him whose worke he doth, and is a thing equally and iustly answearing to the tyme and weight of his trauels and workes (in which sence the Scripture saith* The worke-man is worthy of his hyre *) rather then a free guift: though because faithfull men must acknowledg that their merites be the guiftes and graces of god, they rather vse the word Reward, then hyre, stipend, or repayment. &c*. Now all that from hence can be gathered are two thinges, first that the Rhemists affirme that the word Reward, in latin and greeke, doth rather signify a *stipend or hyre then a free guift*. Secondly that because *faithfull men must ackuowledg that their merites be the guiftes and graces of god, they rather vse the word Reward then hyre*. But now all this whyle I can not fynde this sentence cyted by M. Wh. that *the reward of workes is a thing equally & iustly answearing to the tyme and weight of the worke rather then a free guift*. Indeede I fynd most of the wordes, but many of them in seuerall lynes, and vttered vpon seuerall occasions

occaſions, all which to ioyne and chaine together in one continued lyne or ſentence, and thereby to make the Authour ſpeake contrary to him ſelfe, is a thing eaſy to performe, but the performance is wicked, ſhameleſſe, and execrable.

And geue but this libertie of omitting, inſerting, & coopling to the Atheiſt (which your ſelf M. Whyte haue heare aſſumed and practiſed) and you ſhall finde ſtrange poſitions well manteined by him. For example, the Pſalmiſt ſpeaking of your ſelf and other ſuch like ſaith, *The foole haith ſaid in his heart, there is no god.* Now kindly allow him to blott out the word foole, (as you more the foliſhly did the woord *Grace*) & to inſert in ſteed thereof, the wordes *wyſe man* (as you according to the wiſdome of the world inſerted the word *Nature*) and then obſerue how eaſely he will defende from the ſcriptures that there is no god, ſeing according to your ſcriptures *The wyſe man ſaid in his heart there is no god.* But to conclude thus knowingly and deliberately to corrupt to the diſhonour of your owne & Catholick Religion, and to the ruyne of your owne & other ignorant ſoules, is to mean argument moſt conuincing, that you are one of thoſe fooles *who ſaid in his heart there is noe god.*

Paragr. 3.

Cardinall Bellarmine corrupted concerning Iuſtification.

IN the verie firſt page of his preface to the Reader (ſo loth it ſemed he was to looſe any tyme) he ſheweth vs an other trick ſomwhat like vnto the former. Where by the way I muſt aduertiſe him that I hould him a man herein impolitick and incautelous, that would not ſuffer the verie face or front of his Treatiſe to paſſe vnblemiſhed, ſince firſt he rather ſhould haue coueted to

winne

winne the eare of credulity with pleasing insinuations
of truth : and then (the iudgment of his Reader being
once possessed) after to haue vented forth his more im-
pure dregs : for we are taught (Io. 2.) that *omnis ho-*
mo primum bonum vinum apponit , & cum inebriati sunt ,
tum id quod est deterius . But to the deprauation pag. 1.
of his preface , M. Whyte falsly to intimate to his reader how much the Catholicks do disualew the passion
of Christ , thus wryteth . *The Church of Rome teacheth*
that iust fication is wrought by the habite of our owne righte-
ousues or not by Christes . Thus you see how peremptorily he affirmeth without any reseruation , that we reiect
the righteousnes of Christ to concurre to our Iustification . Now this he laboureth to proue from a testimony of Bellarmine *de iustificat . li . 2 . ca . 2 .* which he thus
setteth downe . *Our owne inherent iustice is the formall*
cause of absolute iustification , not the iustice of Christ impu-
ted vnto vs . That we may conceaue the true meaning of
that learned Cardinall in this place , I will set downe
his owne wordes in latine , who there discoursinge of
the causes of our Iustification thus saith . *Ad quæstionem,*
an vid . iustificamur propter meritum Fil i dei , an propter in-
choatam renouationem nostram ? Respondemus. Si illud prop-
ter significet causam formalem , nos iustificari propter noui-
tatem nobis inhærentem , non propter meritum Christi quod
inhærere non potest : si veró significet causam meritoriam ,
nos iustificari dicemus propter meritum Filii dei non propter
nouitatem in nobis hærentem . That is . In this question
whether we be iustified *propter meritum* , for the merit
of the Sonne of God , or for our owne renouation of
lyfe ? I answeare . If the word *propter* , doe signify the
formall cause , then are we iustifyed through our owne
newnesse of lyfe inherent in vs and not through the merites of Christ , because they can not inhere in vs : (and
these are the wordes alledged by M . Whyte) but if the
worde

worde *propter*, do here signify the meritorious cause,
then are we iustifyed *propter meritum Filii dei*, through
the merites of the Sonne of God, & not through any
inherent newnes or iustice in vs: And then presently
concludeth, *ita iustificamur propter vtrumq̃ &c*. So we
are iustifyed by reason or through them both, to wit,
through the merites of the Sonne of God, *meritorie*,
meritoriously, and through an inherent iustice in vs
formaliter, formally. Thus Bellarmine. Where you see
the question is not, as M. Whyte suggesteth, whether Christes iustice doth concurre to mannes iustification (which were a horrible blasphemy to deny) but
onely in what kynd of cause it concurreth: the Catholickes teaching that it concurres as the meritorious
cause, not as the formall cause, since if it did as the
formall cause, then, euen according to philosophy,
it should really inhere in vs, but so it doth not.

But now to obserue M. Whytes calumny & fraude
in alledging this testimony. First he purposly concealeth the latter part of the sentence which sheweth how
we ascribe our iustification to Christ, as vnwilling that
the reader should heare that in any sence we rely there-
on. Secondly that whereas this testimony of the Cardinales, euen as it is set downe by M. Whyte himself,
excludeth onely Christes merites as the formall cause
of our iustification and in none other sence: yet our
minister alledgeth it to proue that it is no cause thereof at all, & in this respect it is impertinently vrged,
for in his owne wordes immediatly before, without
any limitation of the cause, he saith, *The Church of
Rome teacheth that iustification of a sinner is done by the ha
bite of our owne righteousnes & not by Christes*. And then
as I said, alledgeth for proofe thereof such wordes of
Bellarmine as excludeth onely the formall cause thereof. But his sleight here was, that perswading himself

that the

that the igno rant reader not knowing what the word *formall cause* is, or how it is diſtinguiſhed from other kinde of cauſes, but thinking that it did ſignify any cauſe in generall, ſhould no ſooner ſee the wordes of Bellarmine, but then ſhould inſtantly conclude with him ſelf, here Bellarmine & the Church of Rome tea-cheth that *mans iuſtification is in no ſort or maner wrought by the iuſtice of Chriſt*. And thus much of our Doctors deportement herein, who through his ſubtill feaninge (at his pleaſure) what we are ſuppoſed to mantaine, doth in the meane tyme endanger and wrong the ho-nour of the worthy and illuſtrious Cardinall till more full ſearch and diſquiſition of the truth be made. And thus our poetizing miniſter (I meane our lyinge M. Whyte) doth intereſt him ſelf in the cenſure of the po-et (*Ouid. li. 2. faſt.*) *fraude perit virtus*. Heare now I end this deprauation, aſſuring my reader that Bellar-mine is ſo farre of from teaching that Chriſtes iuſtice doth not neceſſarily concurre to our iuſtification, that in the former alledged Chapter he thus writeth *Iuſti-tia homini a deo per Chriſti merita donata eſt. &c.* That is. Iuſtice is geuen by god to man through the merites of Chriſt. And then preſently thus repichendeth Kemni-tius for his deceipte vſed in this queſtion. *Kemnitius fraudulenter egit. &c.* Kemnitius dealeth fraudulently herein, in that to precure malice againſt vs, he oppo-ſeth on the contrary ſide our late begon renouation, or newnes of lyfe, to the merites of the Sonne of God, as if we prized more our owne change or newnes of lyfe, though imperfect and late begon, then the moſte perfect and the moſt abſolute merites of the Sonne of God.

The 4. Paragraph.

Bellarmine againe abufed againft
Merite of workes.

A Gaine to take away the doctrine of the me‑
rite of workes, M Whyte pag. 236, thus wri‑
teth. *Howfoeuer our aduerfaries contend for their merites,*
yet the learnedeft and moft iudicious men difalow them &c.
houlding that which I haue faid to be the founder doctrine;
and fo anfwearably entitleth that page, *merite of wor‑*
kes reiected by papiftes them felues. Now in proofe that
the Catholick Doctors condemne all merite of works,
he alledgeth among others the forefaid Cardinall thus
writing. *By reafon of the vncertainty of mans owne right‑*
oufnes, & for feare of vaine glory, it is the faifeft way to re‑
pofe our whole confidence in the fole mercy & goodnes of god.
But why think you ftayeth the man in that place & paf‑
feth no further? You fhall knowe, for the immediate
wordes folowing in Bellarmine are thefe. *Explico pro‑*
pofitionem. Non enim ita accipienda eft & c. I explaine
this propofition (meaning his former fentence) which
is not fo to be taken as that a man fhould not laboure
with all his endeuoure to do good workes, and that
there were no truft to be put in them, or as if they were
not to be accompted as true iuftice, or could not endure
the iudgment of god: but onely this we fay, that it is
more faife to forgeate after a fort our good workes, &
to caft our eye vpon the fole mercy of god. Thus we
fee how greedily our minifter takes hould of the texte
and yet concealeth the comment though geuen by the
Author him felf. And therefore I appeale to the cen‑
fure of the iudicious if the whole contexture of this tef‑
timony, which is vrged for the ouerthrowing of me
rites, doth not euen depofe the contrary, in pofitiuely
confirming

confirming and mantaininge the doctrine of merits.
Againe what impudency is it in M. Whyte to produce
Bellarmine as denying the doctrine of works, when as
the subiect of this very booke (from whence the former wordes are taken as also of diuers other bookes
in that tome) is onely to proue that works do merite.
Therefore I will onely say that this our Doctor in alledg-
ging his proofes and Authorities, carieth himself perfectly minister-like: I neede not further to expresse my
meaninge, since among some thinges there is such an
inwarde and inseperable association and nearenes, as
that but naminge the one, we are supposed withall implicitly to vnderstand the other.

The 5 Paragraph.

*S. Thomas notoriously corrupted against iusti-
fication by work.*

T O the lyke effect he deprauceth a saying of S.
Thomas Aquinas. For pag. 262. we thus find.
*Workes be not the cause why a man is iust before god, but
rather the execution and manifestation of his Iustice, for no
man is iustifyed by workes, but by the habite of faith infused,
yea Iustification is done by faith onely. (Aquin. Ro. 3.
lect. 4. & Gal. 3. Lect. 4.)* Wheare the reader is to
know that the place to the Romanes is onely spent by
S. Thomas against the Iewes, in coufuting that Iustification is wrought by performinge the ceremoniall
workes of the law, or morall preceptes: & therefore
he there immediatly before the wordes alledged thus
saith (which M. Whyte thought good to conceale)
Apostolus loquitur &c. The *Apostle doth speake in this
Chapiter both of all ceremoniall and morall workes, for
workes be not the cause &c.* to neither of which the Catholickes ascribe any iustification, but onely to works
                                                     done

done in ſtate of grace, and receauing their vertue from the paſſion of our Sauiour. In lyke ſort in his ſeconde reference of S. Thomas which is *Gal*. 3. *Lect*. 4., we fynde the lyke wordes in ſence which our doctor here alledgeth: for there S. Thomas comentinge vpon that of the Apoſtle, *I doe think that a man is iuſtified by faith without the workes of the law*, thus writeth, *Non autem ſolum ſine operibus cærimonialibus &c* Man is iuſtifyed not onely without the cerimoniall workes which did not confer grace, but onely ſignifyed it: but alſo he is iuſtifyed without the workes of morall preceptes, according to that to *Titus*, *&c*, and then preſently foloweth in S. Thomas, *ita tamen qnod hoc intelligat &c.* yet ſo that the *Apoſtle here meaneth, ſine operibus præcedentibus iuſtitiam, non autem ſine operibus conſequentibus, without workes which goe before iuſtice, & not without workes folowing iuſtice*, which is the doctrine of all Catholickes, who teach that workes done out of the ſtate of grace (which are thoſe that doe *præcedere iuſtitiam*) can not iuſtify, but onely ſuch as are *conſequentia*, to wit performed after oure firſt iuſtification, and ſo in ſtate of grace. Thus if M. Whyte had vouchſaifed to haue ſet downe this laſte parte of S. Thomas his ſentence (which he moſte calumniouſly concealed), the reader would haue eaſely diſcerned how impertinently theſe teſimonies are alldged againſt the Catholick doctrine of Iuſtification.

The 6. Paragraph.

S. *Auguſtine corrupted againſt Iuſtification.*

The doctor not content to depraue and corrupte moderne and more late writers, exerciſeth his faculty euen in the monumentes of the auntiente fathers.

For

For pag . 245 . the more to depresse mans iustice , he produceth S . Augustine *de Ciuitate dei li . 19 . c . 27 .* thus writing . *All our righteousnes standeth rather in the remission of our sinnes , then in any perfection of Iustice .* The Fathers wordes are these , which I will relate at large in latin for the more full discouery of M . Whites demeanour therein . *Ista nostra iustitia (quamuis vera sit propter veri boni finem ad quem refertur) tamen tanta est in hac vita vt potius peccatorum remissione constet , quam perfectione virtutum .* This our iustice (though it be true by reason of the end of the true good to which it is referred) yet it is such in this life as that it rather consisteth of the remissió of our sinnes thē of the perfection of vertues . Here first our minister addeth the word , *all,* for greater swelling and fulnes of speach against our doctrine , which is not in S . Augustine : but this we let passe as a smaller fault . Secondly he leaueth owt a parcell of the same sentence , to wit *(although our Iustice be true by reason of the end of the true good whereunto it is referred)* in which wordes S . Augustine acknowledgeth the very Catholick doctrine of iustification , to witt , that our Iustice is true Iustice , against which this very place is vrged . Thirdly he falsly translateth (for his owne aduantage)those wordes , *quam perfectione virtutum ,* then in any perfection of Iustice , where it shoud be , then in any perfection of vertues . This he did to make S . Augustines wordes sound in an ignorant eare more clearely against Iustice & Iustification mantayned by Catholickes . For he can not but know that a man may be truly iust , and yet not exercise all vertues in theire highest perfection.

Now that the reader may learne what is the true meaning of S . Augustine in this place : he is to conceaue that the drift of that father here is , to shew that a man cannot liue in this lyfe in that perfect and true peace
of mynde

of mynde as to exercyfe vertue and flee vice without
all fodain reluctatiō of our fenfualitie though we geue
no affent thereunto : and therefore the tytle of that
Chapiter is. *De pace feruientium deo &c. Of the peace of*
fuch as ferue God, whofe perfect tranquillity can not be en-
ioyed in this temporall lyfe. And according to this his tytle, fome fewe lynes after the fentence alledged by M.
Whyte, he thus writeth. *Nam profecto quanquam im-*
peretur. &c. For although reafon doth ouerrule vyce: yet it
doth not ouerrule without fome conflict of vyce. And there-
fore as longe as it is exercyfed in commaunding and ouerru-
ling vyce, man haith not perfect peace. But to ende this
fubiect of Iuftification, here you fee how dexteroufly
our minifter haith borne him felfe, who for the impugning of the fame, haith feuerall wayes abufed the
fentences of his Authors, fomtimes by infertions of
his owne as if they were the Authors wordes : fom-
times by taking away and concealing what is there
plainely fet downe : othertimes, though the Authority be truly alledged, yet by violent detortinge and
wrefting the place from the true intended fence, yea
often when the very place ftrongly fortifyeth that Catholick point or doctrine againft which it is theare
brought. Thus though M. Whyte in his deprauations vfeth feuerall fhewes and coloures : yet they all retaine in them one generall countenance and looke of
deceipt and falfhoode, fo as the Poets fentence here
houldeth *Facies non omnibus vna, nec diuerfa tamen.*

Chapiter

Chapiter 2.

Concerning the reading of the Scriptures,

The 1 Paragraph.

S. Ierome corrupted for the reading of the scrip-
tures by the vulgare people : where also upon
occasion geuen by M. Whyte , it is
examined whether S. Ierome
was a papiste.

IT being a certaine truth that from Scriptures euill
vnderstoode procede most heresies, M. Whyte (a
faithfull frend thereof) well knowing by dayly experience that no one thing in truth is more auaileable
either for the first beginninge or propagation of heresy
then generall libertie graunted to the vulgar people
of reading, and expounding the sacred Scriptures ,
doth thereupon much labour in sundry places in profe
of his supposed commodity and necessitie thereof : a-
mongst which he grosly abuseth the authority & person of that great and most Catholick Doctor S. Hierome in these wordes. pag. 22. *Hierome writes of Pau-*
la a gentlewoman how shee set her maides to learne the Scrip-
ture , and many of his wrytinges (saith Whyte) *are directed*
to women, commending theire labour in the Scripture , & en
couraging them thereunto &c. which he would not haue done
if he had bene a papist .

Heare Christian reader I must confesse I reste verie
doubtfull whether the malice of this minister is more
to be detested, or his greate folly to be admyred & pi-
tyed : for not contenting him self to corrupt S. Hie-
romes wordes and meaning, he will needes inferre
hereof

hereof that S. Hierome was noe papifte, which how true it is, I will onely for this prefent appeale vnto this Epitaph of S. Paula writen by this holy Doctor to the Virgin *Euftochium* and here cyted by our proteftant minifter: whereby if it do not plainely appeare by fundry pointes of religion there mentioned and practifed that S. Hierome, S. *Paula*, and the Bifhops, Preiftes, and people of thofe tymes were of the fame Religion or beleefe which Catholickes now profeffe, and proteftantes impugne: that then let me be enrolled in the black bill of lying minifters, or coopled in brotherhood with Whyte, as a legitimate fonne of the father of lyes.

First then S. Hierome vndertaking to fet downe the bleffed lyfe, and death of the holy woman S. Paula, in proofe of his fincere proceding therein, maketh this proteftation. *I call Iefus to witnes and his Sainctes, yea that very Angell who was keeper and companion of this admirable woman, that I will fpeake nothing in her fauour, or after the maner of flaterers, but for a teftimony, and that which is leffe then her merites, whom the whole worlde doth praife, preiftes admyre, quiers of virgins defyre, and troupes of Monkes and poore people bewayle.* Is the inuocation of Sainctes and Angells which of neceffity fuppofeth their knowledg? is the beleefe of euery mannes proper Angell to guard him? and quiers or companies of Virgins and Monkes, plaine proofes of Catholick or proteftant religiou?

To procede, S. Hierome defcribing in perticuler her pilgrimage to the holy lande whereunto he affirmeth that men of all Nations did come; fheweth how that *proftrating her felfe before the Croffe, fhe adored as though fhe had feene our Lord harging thereupon. Entring the Sepulchre, fhe kiffed the ftone of the Refurrection &c. & as one thirfting defyreth waters. fhe licked with her faithfull*

mouth

mouth the very place of the body wheare our Lord had laid.
Then hauing visited the pillour at the which our Lorde was
bound and whipped, and the place where the holy Ghost did
descend vpon the faithfull: she went to Bethelem, where entring our Sauiours caue, and looking at the holy Iune of the
Virgin, and the stable, after many other deuout speaches
she vttered these wordes, *And I wretch and sinner am*
thought worthy to kisse the marger in which our Lord a litle
babe cryed, and to pray in the caue in which the Virgin
brought forth our Lord an infant. After this amongst sundry other holy places, she went vnto the *Sepulchres of*
the 12 *Patriarches* where she trembled beinge affrighted
with many wonders, for she saw the diuells roare being dy-
uersly tormented: and before the sepulchres of the Sainctes she
saw men howling lyke wolues, barking lyke dogs, roaringe
lyke lyons, hissing lyke serpentes, and belowing lyke buls &c.
And is not all this with a protestant papisticall superstition? Will our Whyte allow of pilgrimage to holy
places? or will he with S. *Paula* prostrate him selfe before the Crosse and worshipe? will he kisse sacred Re-
liques? or will he attribute such sanctity to the Sepulchres of Sainctes that in presence thereof diuells are
tormented? I perswade my selfe he will not. And yet S.
Hierome (with him noe papist) relateth the premisses
to the commendation of *Paula*.

But to come nearer the maner of lyfe which S. *Pau-*
la led, her daily practise being best witnes of her beleefe, hauing visited with greate deuotion all the places of the holy land, intending to spend her lyfe in *holy*
Bethelem. she stayed there in a straite lodging for the space of
three yeres vntill she had built Cells, and *Monasteries, &*
Mansions for diuers pilgrimes: where she liued in such
humility as, being attended with many virgins, in her ap-
parell, speach, habit, and going, she was the least or baseste
of all. *After her husbands death, vntill her owne, she ne-*
uer eate

with any man though she knew him to be holy and a Bishope.
Bathes she went not to but in daunger . In her greatest a-
gues she vsed not soft beds, but reposed on the hard grounde
couered with hayre clothes &c. Thou wouldest haue thought
fountaines of teares to haue proceded from her: yea she so
bewayled litle sinnes as that thou wouldest haue iudged her
guilty of greatest crimes &c . Soft linnens & pretious silkes
she changed with a sharpe hayrecloth &c . Her loue of pouerty was such, as that she *desyred she might dye a beg-*
ger , and not to leaue one peny to her daughter , yea her selfe
at her death to be wrapped in an others sheete. And as for
her dyet, her abstinence was such, as that (*festinall*
dayes excepted) she scarce tooke oyle in her meate , by which
may be iudged (saith S . Ierome) what she thought of wyne,
of any thinges molted , of fish , milke , hony , egs , and the rest
which are pleasant to tast . If I should now aske Maister
Whyte whether his wyfe for example being no doubt
an Euangelicall sister of highest perfection, him self being often absent about preaching of the worde , whe -
ther , I say, in his conscience he thinketh her modesty
such, as that at such tymes (to speake sparingly) shee
doth not often both eate and drinke with his Clarcke
and other neighboures : as also whether for the mor-
tifying of the flesh and the quickning of the spirit , she
changeth a soft bed into the hard ground, or fyne linnens into hayre-cloth : and in breife whether without
all exceptions of dayes , not fish , milke , or egs , but
the daintiest flesh and most delicate wyne , be meates
most welcome to him and her ? I doubt not but he will
answeare me that none of these agreeth with the fashi-
on of these tymes . But thereto then must I needes reply , that therefore neither must he be much greued if
his foresaid yokefelow grow wanton in the lord , hard
bed , hayre cloth , and fasting (the best externall pre-
seruatiues against such impurities) being vtterly aban-

C 3   doned

doned . And yet if the lyke queſtion ſhould be pro-
poſed vnto me in regard of Catholickes , all Chriſtian
Countries would anſweare with me , that the ſaid auſ-
terities of B . *Paula* are not onely imitated & practiſed
by Religious perſons, but euen by wiues , widowes , &
Virgins which liue in the world .

But to touch yet one point further, wherein I ſup-
poſe all proteſtantes will diſclaime as being incompatible with theire new goſpels libertie , which was S .
Paula her Monaſticall lyfe , whereof S . Hierome ſaith ,
*I will ſpeake of the order of her Monaſtery &c. Beſydes the
Monaſtery of men which ſhe had geuen to men to be gouerned, ſhe denyded the Virgins &c. aſwell noble , as of the mea-
neſt and loweſt degree , into three companies and Monaſteries &c. After Alleluia ſong or ſounded, (by which ſigne
they were called to Collect or prayer) it was not lawfull for
any of them to ſtay &c. In the morning , at the Third houre,
at the Sixt , the Ninth , Euenſong , and Midnight , they
ſong the Pſalter by order or courſe .*

And now foloweth Whytes proofe of theire proteſtancy , *neither was it lawfull for any of the Siſters to be ignorant of the Pſalmes , or not to learne ſomthing daily out of
the ſacred Scriptures .* But what is this againſt vs , who
allow not onely Religious women ſuch as theſe weare,
(Whom M . Whyte moſt fraudulently calleth Paules
maydes) but euen the laity to reade the Scriptures , ſuppoſing they be knowne to be humble , diſcreete , and
vertuous . And yet in what maner S . *Paula* her ſelf , &
her daughter *Euſtochium* being both well learned, did it ,
S . Hierome a litle after expreſſeth in theſe wordes. *She
forced me that together with her Daughter , ſhe might read
the old and new Teſtament , I declaring it : (me diſſerente)
which in modeſly denying , yet throvgh her importunities
and often intreaties , I performed, that ſo I might teach what
I had learned, not of my ſelf, that is preſumption the worſte*
                                                    maiſter

maiſter, but of the famous men of the Church. And when in any poynt I doubted and ingeniouſly confeſſed my ſelf to be ignorant, yet ſhe would not reſt but with dayly intreaty enforced me out of many and diuers ſences, to ſhew that which to me ſemed moſt probable.

Would not any man think this miniſter diſtracted, thus producing againſt vs that which confoundeth him ſelf? Do not theſe Religious women in reading of the Scriptures requyre S. Hierome a Preiſt for their maiſter? Doth not he profeſſe to teach them, not what he had learned him ſelf, or from any imaginary ſpirit, but from the *famous men or Doctors of the Church*? Yea doth not he plainely and humbly acknowledg his doubting and ignorance in his explication thereof; none of which I am ſure is orthodoxall with proteſtants.

But to returne to S. *Paula* and her *Virgins in the monaſtery. They had all one habite alyke; Lynuens they vſed onely for wyping of their handes. Their ſeperation from men was ſuch, as ſhe ſeuered them euen from Eunuches. Beſides ſuſtenance and apparel, ſhe ſuffered them not to poſſeſſe any thing. Such as were talkatyue & vnquiet, ſhe cauſed (in penance) to pray at the doare of the refectory & to eate alone.*

I might recyte many other lyke, but theſe abundantly proue that *M. Whytes maides* were indeede Nonnes or Religious womē, whereof good ſtore to gods greater glory euen our Counrtie doth as yet daily afforde.

Now for a concluſion I will breefely note what S. Hierome relateth of her death. As firſt hauing offered vp many deuout prayers vnto god almighty, beinge almoſt ſpeachleſſe, *ſhe ſigned her lippes with the ſigne of the Croſſe,* a deuotion alſo vſed in her lyfe tyme, as imputing much vertue thereunto, which S. Hierome before, mentioned in theſe wordes. *When ſhe had ſigned her mouth and her ſtomake, endeuoring by the impreſſion of*

the Croſſe

of the Croſſe to mitigate her greife .&c . At her deathe were preſent the Biſhopes of *Hieruſalem* , and of other *Cities* , and an innumerable multitude of *Preiſtes & Leuits* , yea all the *Monaſtery was filled with Virgins and Mouks* , Some of the *Biſhops caried the Coffin* , and the reſt goinge before caried Lampes and C A N D L E S , and Led the Singers *.&c .* In the Hebrew , Greeke , Latin , and Syrian Language *Pſalmes were ſonge* , not onely for three dayes , but euen for a whole weeke . And in the end of all , this bleſſed Doctor as ſuppoſing her in heauen , inuocateth ſaying . a *Farewel o Paula* , and help with thy prayers the old age of him who worſhippeth thee : thy faith and workes doe ioyne thee with *Chriſt* , being preſent thou ſhalt obtaine more eaſely what thou aſkeſt .

a
Vale o Paula
& Cultoris
tui vltimã ſe
nectutem ora
tionibus inua
fides & opera
tua te Chriſ-
to ſociant :
præſens faci-
lius quod poſ
tulas impe -
trabis .

Out of theſe premiſſes I may eaſely inferre that not onely S . Ierome , but euen the Biſhopes , Preiſtes , & people of his tyme , did wholly agree with vs Catho-lickes in the pointes folowing . viz ,

(1) Worſhipping and Inuocation of Sainctes . (2) That euery one haith an Angell guardian or keeper . (3) Pilgrimage to holy places . (4) Adoration of the Croſſe : (5) and ſigning the body with the ſigne there-of. (6) Kiſſing and reuerencing of Relickes . (7) Tor-menting of deuils at the Sepulchres of Sainctes (8) Building of Monaſteries and profeſſion of Monaſticall lyfe . (9) Voluntary pouerty . (10) Wearing of hair-cloth and no linnens at all : and lying vpon the ground in ſteed of a bed. (11) Abſtinence from fleſh , wyne , & other dainty meates vpon deuotion . (12) Keping ſet houres of prayer , as in the morning , at the Third, the Sixt , the Ninth , Euenſong , and at Midnight . (13) The difference of litle and greate ſinnes . (14) The vnlearned reading the Scriptures hauing a learned mã for their Maiſter . (15) The learnedſt confeſſing their doubtinge and ignorance in their explication of the
Scripture

Scriptures. (16) Biſhopes and Preiſtes ſinging & carying of Candles in the day tyme at the burials of the
dead. (17) Church ſeruice ſong & vſed in the Hebrew, Greeke, Latin, and Syrian languages. And for
the Concluſion as including many thinges in one, remember S. Ieromes prayer made to S. Paula after her
death. *Vale o Paula, & Cultoris tui vltimam ſenectutem
orationibus iuua: fides & opera tua Chriſto te ſociant, præſens facilius quod poſtulas impetrabis.*

And now let any man iudge whether S. Ierome was
a papiſt; as alſo what wiſdome, learning, or honeſty
M. Whyte ſheweth in obiecting that which but truly
ſeene and conſidered, doth manifeſtly confound and
condemne him ſelfe.

The 2. Paragraph.

S. Cyrill of Alexandria abuſed for the ſame purpoſe.

It was the reproch (ſaith Whyte pag. 22) that *Iulian the Tpoſtata laide on Chriſtians, that their women were
medlers-with the Scriptures: and from him the papiſtes haue
borrowed it:* for which he cyteth *Cyril. Alex. Iul. 1. 6.*
If our Miniſter had cyted Iulian reprehending the auncient Chriſtians of his tyme for not *adoring Iubiter, &
adoring the Croſſe, and making the ſigne thereof in their for-
heades, and vpon houſes* (the lawfulnes and profit wherof S. Cyrill defendeth) he might haue truly ſhewed
what himſelf & other heritikes had borrowed from Iulian in impugning the worſhip of the Croſſe, and ſigning therwith: but in that which he obiecteth in the
behalf of women medling with Scriptures, him ſelfe
borroweth from Iulian the libertie of lyinge, for Iulian
onely reprehendeth Chriſt and his Apoſtles, for that

D

for that they propoūded the heauēly preaching vnto all
calling *vnto their doctrine men and women of baiser forte* ,
which S Cyrill defendeth , fhewing thereby the b:nig -
nity of our Sauiour , but as for mention of the Scrip -
tures or women medling therewith , he haith no word
at all : our black-whyte haith only inuented it to proue
him felf a true Apoftata.

───────────────────────────

───────────────────────────

Chapter . 3 .

Concerning the Church & the Pope .

The 1 . Paragraph.

*Vincentius Lirinenfis wilfully corrupted in proofe
that the true Church may erre .*

WE will now take into our confideration his
corrupt proceding concerning the fuppofed
generall erring of the whole Church , not remembring that in regard of Chriftes folicitude , care , & af-
fection to his Spoufe , it is faid *Cant.* 1 . *My welbe-
loued is a clufter of Cypre vnto me in the vyneyardes of En-
gaddi* . That the vniuerfall Church may erre he labo -
reth to

reth to euict from the testimony of old *Vincentius Liri-*
nensis whom our minister pag. 83. makerh thus to
speake *Advers. proph. nouit. ca. 4.* *Not onely some*
portion of the Church, but the whole Church it selfe is blot-
ted with some new contagion. Obserue the true wordes
of this Father, and then you can not but admyre to fynd
such *Blacknes in Whyte*, and such perfidiousnes in him
who styleth him selfe a minister of Gods word, for thus
the wordes doe lye in latin. *(Quod si) nouella aliqua*
contagio non iam portiunculam tantum sed totam pariter ec-
clesiam commaculare (conetur.) What is to be done if,
some contagion (shall endeuour) to blot not any one parte,
but the whole Church? then (saith he further) *must a mā*
be carefull to cleeue to antiquity. Now here our D. abuseth his reader in two sortes: one way in concealing
the word *Conetur*, and so *commaculare conetur* he translateth *is blotted*, and consequently making Vincentius to confesse (for our minister most impudently saith)
that the whole Church is actually blotted with some
contagion of heresy, whereas at the most he saith that
heresy may endeuour to blott the whole Church. But
who knoweth not that euery thing which is endeuored
to be effected, is not actually effected? An other way
in deliuering these wordes in a *Categoricall* and absolute
Ennuntiation which are *Hypotheticall* or spoken merely of a supposal as appeareth by the first wordes *Quid si,*
which M. Whyte thought good not to translate. The
difference of which two kind of propositions, is very
markable as euery yong Sophister knoweth : as for example if a man do say, what if diuers of Suffolk do report that M. Whyte is extremely geuen to his bely &
to *Epicurisme*, and to say. Diuers of Suffolke reporte
that M. Whyte is extremely geuen to his bely and to
Eicurisme : where we see the first is merely of a doubtfull surmise and suppofition, the second is a peremptory

rory and abſolute propoſition that they do ſo reporte: the truth or falſhode whereof (notwithſtanding any intelligence whatſoeuer) I here quietly paſſe ouer.

The 2. Paragraph.

The Rhemiſtes corrupted for the Churches inuiſibility.

Now to the next point which conſiſteth in the mantayning of a Mathematicall, aery, & inuiſible Church: for the vphoulding whereof among others he ſtrengthneth his cauſe with the ſuppoſed confeſſion of the Rhemiſtes, thus bringing the whole Colledg of Rhemes vpon the ſtage to ſpeake in the dialect of proteſtantes: and ſo ſorteably thereto he ſtyleth that page 88. and ſome other pages in this maner. *The Papiſts alſo ſay the Church is inuiſible.* The words wherwith he chargeth thē in this point are theſe, vpon the 2. Theſ. ca. 2. *It is very lyke (be it ſpoken vnder the correction of Gods Church and all learned Catholickes) that this great defection or reuolt, ſhall not be onely from the Romane Empyre, but eſpecially from the Romane Church, and withall from moſt pointes of Chriſtian Religion: for that neare to the tyme of Antichriſt and the conſummation of the worlde, there is lyke to be a great reuolt of Kingdomes, People, and Prouinces from the externall open obedience and communion thereof. For the few dayes of Antichriſtes reigne, the externall ſtate of the Romane Church, and the publick entercourſe of the faithfull with the ſame may ceaſe.*

Here good Reader let me entreate thee to areſt & ſtay thyne eye and iudgment a whyle, to obſerue what ſtrange corruptions he is forced to practiſe before he cā make an *Iſraelite* to ſpeake a *Babilonians* language. This place as you fynd it here vrged, beareth a faire ſhow to

proue

proue by the Rhemiſtes confeſſion, that the Church
may ſomtymes be inuiſible : and yet in this very place
being truly ſet downe in their owne wordes, they doe
affirme that the Church ſhall at no tyme be inuiſible .
Theire true wordes are theſe . *It is very lyke (be it ſpo-*
ken vnder correction of Gods Church and all learned Catho-
lickes) that this great defection and reuolt , ſhall not be one-
ly from the Romane Empyre, but eſpecially from the Ro-
mane Church, and withall from moſt pointes of Chriſtian re-
ligion (not that the Catholick Chriſtians either in the tyme
of Antichriſt or before, ſhall refuſe to obey the ſame, but for
that neare to the tyme of Antichriſt and conſummation of
the worlde, there is lyke to be a greate reuolt of Kingdomes,
people, and Prouinces, from the open externall obedience &
communion thereof. &c. when for the few dayes of Anti-
chriſtes reigne, the externall ſtate of the Romane Church,
and publick entercourſe of the faithfull with the ſame may
ceaſe (yet the due honour and obedience of Chriſtians towar-
des it, and Communion in heart with it, and practiſe there-
of in ſecret and open confeſſion thereof (if occaſion requyre)
ſhall not ceaſe, nomore then it doth now in the Chriſtians of
Cyprus and other places where open entercourſe is forbidden.

   Here now the parcels of this teſtimony which are
purpoſly omitted, do ſhow that the Rhemiſtes do euen
peremptorily affirme that gods Church ſhall neuer (no
not in the tyme of Antichriſtes greateſt perſecutions)
be latent and inuiſible . Thus doth our M. you ſee v-
pon a ſudaine breake of with the Rhemiſtes in alledging their wordes : yet after ſome lyne or two curteouſ-
ly ioyneth with them againe, and then after that once
more vnkindly leaues them to them ſelues : & all this
in one poore teſtimony . And here good reader thou
art to take notice of an other ſleight of our miniſter touching this particuler place . For whereas he in
the firſt Edition of his booke, which I here folow, ſet-

teth downe the Rhemiftes wordes, as thou feeft aboue,
in no forte intimating that any one word of their faid
teftimony is pretermitted : he in fome other of his E-
ditions (as it fhould feme being aduertifed that this his
egregious corruption was efpyed by his aduerfaries, &
thought therefore in fome fort to falue the matrer)
haith at the laft wordes where he breaketh off from the
reft of the whole fentence, added a virgula, or lyne
as this , ———— ingenioufly forfoth to acknowledge
that he omitteth fome part of the fentence . But this I
fay auaileth him nothing : for firft it doth not warrant
his fincerity in his firft Edition . Againe , though in alledging of a teftimony we are not bound to fet down e-
uery word thereof, yet (as I haue before premonifhed)
that which is omitted ought to be impertinent to the
mayne point for which the teftimony is produced .
But fubtily to pretermit with an &c. or fome fuch like
marck , that which punctually doth touch or explicate
the true fence of the fentence alledged , & that directly contrary to that conftruction there pretended (as
here it falleth out : it is no leffe then moft impious corrupting and corrading of other mens writinges . And
therfore I fay M. Whyte is nothing aduantaged hereby , but doth for the tyme plafter one euill with an
other euill : but no meruell, for it is a high miftery a-
mongft heritikes to fupport deceipt with deceipt, till
at the length all do tumble downe with it owne
weight , and fo *erit nouiffimus error peior priori* . *Mat* . **7** .

Thr 3 Paragraph.

S . *Auguftine corrupted concerning* the *fame fubiect
of the Churches inuifibility* .

In lyke fort pag. **103** . he alledgeth *S* . *Auguftine
de bap* .

de bap . con . Don . li . 6 . ca . 4 . thus to ſay . *The Church may be ſo obſcured , that the members thereof ſhall not know one an other .* S . Auguſtines wordes are theſe & none other . *Idem ſpiritus Sanctus ea dimitit qui datus eſt omnibus ſanctis ſibi Charitate cohærentibus ſiue ſe nouerint corporaliter ſiue non nouerint . The ſame holy Ghoſt which is geuen to all the Sainctes (or holy men) agreing together in Charity , whether they know one an other or not , remitteth the ſinnes .* But what is this to the inuiſibility of the Church ? or by what Sintax or Grammar can M . W . tranſlate thus the former latin lynes ? Finally by what ſublimation or art can he extract ſuch a refyned ſence from the bare minerals of the former wordes . Neither can he ſlubber the mater ouer in ſaying that he here gathereth onely ſome neceſſary Illation , prouing the Churches latency : for the ſentence alledged by him is ſet downe in a different letter or caracter frō his owne , and he there perticularly geueth them as the very wordes . Now S . Auguſtine in that place , doth not ſo much as glance at the Churches viſibility or inuiſibility , but there ſhowing how ſinnes are remitted as effectually by the bad preiſtes as the vertuous , proueth it by Anology of reaſon , to wit , that the power of the holy Ghoſt may aſwell be geuen to a wicked Preiſt , as to a good and vertuous , as it is geuen alyke to all the godly though they know not one an other . But M . Whyte fynding that parcell of the ſetence , *ſiue nouerint ſe corporaliter ſiue non nouerint* , to be ment of the faithfull and vertuous , thought preſently that he lighted vpon a bootie , and ſo hoping thereby to entrappe the incautelous reader , was the more eaſely induced to create the world of this his deprauation out of a mere nothing of a ſound of wordes . And thus farre of his corruptions touching the Churches inuiſibility : from the mantayning whereof we **Catholickes** do ſo far diſclame

clame as that euen in the most tempesteous and raging tymes of perfecution that either haue or shall happen, we acknowledg innumerable members thereof to be euer visible, and in faith permanent and vnmoueable : for we reade that the *beames of* the *house of Christ his Spouse are Cedars*, the *raftens are of firre*. *Can. 1.*

The 4. Paragraph.

Doctor Stapleton abused in behalfe of the Protestantes markes of the Church.

The next corruption which I here will shew shall be concerning the markes of the Church, wheare he to proue that we absolutely embrace the markes thereof deliuered by the Protestantes, to wit, the preaching of the word, as acknowledging it to be a more infallible marke to euery Christian, then our *C*atholicke markes are, *Antiquity, Succession, Vniuersality, &c* . all which notes he after endeuoreth to confute. To this end (I say) pag. 105 . he produceth Doctor Stapleton thus wryting. *princip. doctrinal. li 1 . ca. 22 . The preaching of the Gospell is the proper and a very cleare note of the Catholick Church, so it be done by lawfull Ministers.*
Mark heare how he declareth this authors meaning by concealing the wordes in him that there are immediatly subioyned, for thus that Catholick Doctor. *Prædicationem Euangelii . We graunt that the preaching of the Gospell by lawfull Ministers, is a very cleare and proper note of the Catholick Church (Hæc est enim ordinaria &c for by this is that ordinary and perpetuall Succession of Bishops, Preistes, and Pastors deryued in a continued order euen from the Apostles them selues to vs.)* From which latter part of the sentence purposly omitted by M. W. it is euident that D . Stapleton doth allow the preaching

ching of the Gospell by lawfull pastors, so far forth
onely to be a note of the Church, as it is included in
the Catholick note of Succession and in no other sence:
which point is made more cleare (besides his mayne
drift in that Chapter & diuers others of the said booke
being to cōfute the Protestants notes) by the said Doctors wordes also concealed by M . Whyte , which doe
immediatly precede the sentence vrged by him. For
there speaking of the preaching of the Gospell , and of
the ministration of the Sacraments , he saith . *Adiu-
menta & ornamenta. These are furtherances & ornaments
of the true Church , non ipsius nota & insignia , but noe
markes or signes therof.* Here you see how Iewefhsly M.
Whyte haith circumcysed this poore Authority in pa-
ring away both the first and latter part thereof . But
seing his inexcusable faultines not onely in this place
but in most of his deprauations , is to set downe one
part of a testimony and fraudulently to hyde an other
part : let him remember the greouous punishnent inflicted by the Apostle vpon *Ananias for bringing halfe,
and concealing the other halfe. Act . 5.*

The 5. Paragraph.

*Gregory Valentia corrupted in behalf of the Pro-
testantes markes of the Church .*

In proofe of the Protestantes markes of the Church,
to wit , *Truth of doctrine and administration of the Sacraments* , M . Whyte pag . 137 . alledgeth *Valentia Com.
Theol . Tom . 3 . disp . 1 . q . 1 . punct . 7 . parag . 18 .*
saying . *Among whomsoeuer the truth of Doctrine and Sacraments are houlden: thereby it is knowne the Church is
there .* But for the true displaying of this baise iugling
minister, I will set downe the wordes at large as that
E

learned

learned Author deliuered them him self. *Nos autem fatemur* (faith he) *neq, veritate doctrina neq, legitimo sacramentorum vsu Ecclesiam Christi carere posse: & apud quos hæc omnino sint salua, ex iis constare veram Ecclesiā. Sed negamus tamen veritatem doctrinæ, & legitimum sacramentorum vsum, idoneas notas esse discernendæ Ecclesiæ. But we confesse that the Church of Christ can neither wante truth of doctrine, nor lawfull vse of Sacramentes, and amongst whom these are altogether saife (or sincere) of them to consist the true Church. But yet we deny the truth of doctrine and lawfull vse of Sacramentes, to be fit markes of discerning the Church.*

Here M. Doctor first I must admire the profundity of your indgment, producing, by an vnknown kind of pollicy, a most famous learned man contradicting him self in one and the same sentence, yea not onely contradictinge the tytle of his disputation which is the *Marckes of the Church which the sectaries assigne are euidently confuted*, but euen the many and different profes which for sixe pages he continueth against the said markes assigned by protestantes. But becaufe this so great an ouersight is more then probable, let vs examine brefely your demeanour towardes him. You alledg in a different letter as though they were the Authors expresse wordes, thefe folowing. *Among whomsoeuer the truth of doctrine and Sacraments are houlden : thereby it is knowne the Church is there.* Him self sayeth *Apud quos hæc omnino sint salua: ex iis constare veram Ecclesiam. Amongst whom these are altogether sincere: of them to consist the true Church.* That which Valentia speaketh of the persons of whom the Church consisteth : your worship pleaseth to apply to the markes by which it is to be knowne, as though there weare no difference betwixt the members of the Church, & the externall badges & tokens whereby the said church is discerned

is difcerned. But peraduenture you will pretend for
your excufe, the alledging in the mergēt of your boke
thefe latin wordes, *ex iis conftare veram Ecclefiam*. But
the truth is this doth rather plead you guilty of groffe
ignorance in not knowing how to tranflate aright, or
as I rather think, of laboured and affected malice,
who hauing fene and perufed the place, would fo def-
peratly produce it againft the manifefte fence of the
wordes and the direct intention of the Author. And
though the word *conftare*, doth not onely fignify to
confift or *ftande*, but fom-tymes likewife to be manifeft
or knowne, yet in the place cyted neither the wordes
precedent nor fubfequent, nor the fcope or arift of the
Author will permitt it, yea they all conuince and conclude the contrary. But if itwere lawfull for me M.
Whyte in wordes *Amphibologicall* which haue a dou-
ble fence, without all refpect either to the fubiect or
matter treated, the intention of the fpeaker, or other
circumftance, to tranflate or apply the worde onely
for myne owne aduauntage: I would eafely defend a-
gainft your learnedft Doctor-fhip, fundry of the celeftiall fignes to be liuing and fenfible cicatures, and fo
much more to be efteemed then your felf: for I would
likewife, vpon the fame ground, defend your felf to
be no fubftance, but a mere accident: Into fuch groffe
abfurdities doth your beggerly herefie euer plunge
you.

Bellarmine egregiously corrupted againft the
Markes of the Church.

M. Whyte defiring to extenuate the worth, and to
obfcure the fplendor of thofe glorious markes which
the Catholick Church as fo many cleare rayes mofte
plentifully affordeth, produceth pag. 137. Cardinal
Bellarmine as faying. *They make it not euidently true*,
that is the Church, but euidently probable. Here M. D.
as it femes wanted lantorne and candle light : but moft
certainely he wanted either honefty, or knowledg, or
both : in beft confirmation whereof, I will onely fet
downe the wordes of Bellarmine him felfe *de notis eccl.*
lib. 4. *ca.* 3. *Eft autem initio obferuandum, Ecclefiam Ca-*
tholicam effe &c. *It is in the beginning to be obferued that*
the Catholick Church is a Soon which on euery fide powreth
out the cleareft beames of light, fo that by them fhe may moft
eafely be knowne. For fhe haith many Markes or teftimo-
nies, and fignes which difcerneth her from all falfe religions
of Pagares, Iewes, Heritykes. And they do not make it
euidently true that fhe is the true Church of God, but yet
they make it euidently 'credible: for that is faid euidently
true that is feene either in it felf or in it principles: that is
faid euidently credible which is not feene either in it felfe or
in it principles, yet (which)haith fo many, and fo graue
Teftimonies, as that euery wyfe man deferuedly ought to be-
leue it.

Here the minifter, all excufes fet apart, muft nedes
confeffe that he haith falfly corrupted the text of Bellarmine, changing this parcell *euidently credible*, into
euidently probable, betwene which two there is no leffe
difference, then betwixt him felf and an honeft man,
which is not fmall. For example, if but one hundreth
of learned and fincere writers, fhould confeffe that D.
Whyte

Whyte had corrupted then bookes in sundry places, this confession would make it *euidently credible* that D. Whyte were an impostor, a deceauer, a mercionary minister and the lyke : but if onely two or three should auouch it & as many of equall authority deny it, then it were but *euidently probable* : If the matter were brought to this issue, himself would plainely see the greateste difference betwixt these two. And I dare bouldly say that with lesser labour I will empanell an hundreth, who will all geue their verdictes against his foulest forgeries, then himself a coople to auoueare in his behalf.

But speake M. Whyte (once) in good sincerity, why did you translate it *euidently probable*? was it to make the Cardinall for his learning and sanctity most Illustrious, to speake as ignorantly as a protestant minister? Do not your so foule and frequent corrupting of his writinges, make it more then probable, yea euidently credible, that no other meanes is left you to euade the force of his Argumentes? Wel my wholesome aduyse is this, if you presume to reade Bellarmine, be lesse conuersant with *Bacchus*.

The 7. paragraph.

S. Thomas fouly corrupted concerning the popes authority.

M. Whyte is not ashamed to affirme that *we take all authority and sufficiency from the Scripture, & geue it to the Church, & finally the Churches authority to the Pope.* and thereupon insinuateth that we houlde that the Pope at his pleasure is able euen to stampe or create a new faith or Crede neuer afore heard of. To this end he alledgeth pag. 68. this sayiug out of S. *Thomas.* 2. 2æ. *quest* 1. *ar*. 10. *The making of a new Crede be-*

longeth to the Pope as all other thinges doe which belong to the whole Church, thus infinuating all Catholickes within this errour as houlding that the chang of the articles of our Crede, refteth vpon the change of the Popes mynde therein .

For the fuller difcouery of this diabolicall deprauation (for I can terme it no better) I will here fet downe at large the wordes of *S . Thomas*. Thus then he faith. *Ad folam authoritatem Summi Pontificis pertinet noua Editio Symboli &c* . *A new Edition of the Crede*, *belongeth to the Pope*, *as all other thinges doe which concerne the whole Church*. And then fome few lynes after foloweth (which belyke the Doctors hand would haue aked to haue writen downe . *Hæc noua Editio Symboli, non quidem aliam fidem continet, fed eandem magis expofitam. This new Edition of the Crede conteyneth not an other faith but the former more fully explicated*. Here our minifter haith practifed his profeffion of corrupting two wayes, firft in tranflating *noua Editio Symboli, The making of a new Crede*, whereas it fhould be *The new Edition of the Crede* thus caufing the newnes to confift in the newnes of our beleefe or Crede, and yet as you fee in S. Thomas the worde *new*, is ioyned onely with the Edition or explication of the Crede. Secondly in retayning from the Reader thofe other latter wordes which doe expreffe S. Thomas his meaning therein, to wit, that no new faith or Crede contrary to the firft is decreed thereby, but the former onely is more fully explicated, the reafon whereof he thus deliuereth euen in the fame paragraph. *In doctrina Chrifti & Apoftolorū &c*. *The truth of faith is fufficiently explicated in the doctrine of Chrift and his Apoftles: but becaufe wilfull men do peruert, to their owne deftruction, the doctrine of the Apoftles and Scriptures: therefore it was neceffary that there fhould be in proceffe of tyme, an explication of faith againft all enfuing all enfuing erroures.* Here you haue manifefted the true reafon of S. Thomas his former wordes : and confequently here is difcouered the vncharitable impudency of our minifter , to diuorce the faid wordes from their legitimate and maine fence: but it femeth that he profeffing him felf a publick aduerfary to the catholick Religion, thinketh it iuftifiable to impugne the fame by any deceitfull or indir et ftratagems whatfoeuer. *Dolus an virtus quis in hofte requirat . Virg .*

The 8 Paragraph.

Doctor Stapleton corrupted concerning the fame fubiect.

In lyke fort to fhew to his Reader what fuppofed tranfcendency of foueraignty and power the Catholickes geue to the Pope: he, pag. 68 . thus writeth. *Stapleton Præfat . princip . fidei doctrinal . faith . The foundation of our Religion is of neceffity placed vpon the authority of this mans teaching* (meaning of the Pope) *in which we heare god him felf fpeaking .* In all that Preface I affure thee good Reader, there is no fuch faying at al; and therefore it is merely forged by our calumnious minifter , thereby firft to fuggeft that we make the Pope the foundation of our faith which we afcribe to Chrift Iefus onely . Secondly that we beare the ignorant in hand that we accompt the Pope as an other God: the neareft wordes in that Preface that can beare any refemblance at all to thefe, I will here fet downe. *Quæ prima funt fidei noftræ elementa &c . Such pointes as are the firft elements or principles of our faith , and yet the baifes or foundation thereof as the true Catholick and Apoftolick Church of God, the neceffary and infallible power of the Church to teach and Iudg matters of*

E 4 *faith*

faith, the perfons in whom this power remayneth, the meanes which the faid perfons ought and are accuſtomed to vfe in iudging and teaching, the cheif heades or branches about which this power is exercyfed, as to determine fome certaine and authenticall Canon of Scripture, to geue the vndoubted and authenticall interpreta⸱ion thereof, and finally (befydes the decreeing of the Canon of the Scripture) to deliuer and commend the vnwriten Articles of faith : all thefe I fay, which are principia doctrinalia, doctrinall principles of our faith, and which do teach, confirme, and explaine, the fame, the heritikes of our vnfortunate tyme, haue moſt fowly denyed, contaminated, and depraued .

How many wheeles and deductions of inferences here neede we before we can draw out M. Whytes alledged fence, and yet he deliuereth it in a different letter with the vfhering wordes of, Stapleton faith, as though they were the very precife wordes of the faid Authour; or what is geuen more to the Pope then to the refte heare fpecifyed? Yet our minifter blufhed not to particularyze, what here is fpoken in refpect of the principles of faith in generall, onely to the pope. Againe, his fleight further appeareth in taking the word *foundation*, in an equiuocall and dooble fence, for he will needes accept it (to make the faying more odious) for that which is an effentiall and primatiue foundation of faith, (which is Chrift Iefus) whereas D. Stapleton here meaneth (according to th tytle of his booke) *Principia fidei doctrinalia*, onely *Doctrinall principles* or Secondary foundations, which as him felf faith *fidem docent, confirmant, explicant*, doe teach, confirme, and explaine our faith . Thus th further we dog him in his allegations, the more we fhall be affured that deprauing and ftrangely detorting the wrytinges of Catholick Doctors, and the Fathers, is (among the reft) thofe feble fupportes whereupon his

caufe

cauſe leaneth.

The 9 paragraph.

S. Ciprian ſtrangely handled againſt Ap-
peales to Rome.

It haith euer bene the courſe of former heritikes not
onely with contumelies to diſgrace the deſerued re-
nowne of the Popes and Church of Rome, but alſo
with their ſubtilty and corruption falſely to detracte
from theire iuſt authority and prerogatiues. In which
kynd our miniſter (to ſhew himſelf lawfully deſcended) in proofe of his diſlyke of Appeales from other
Biſhopes to the Biſhopes of Rome: produceth pag.
188 S. Ciprian in theſe wordes, *Nay Ciprian ſaith, The*
vnity of Biſhopes is broken, when men runne from theire
owne, to the Biſhope of Rome. which wordes (if they had
bene true) being much materiall, cauſed me diligently to peruſe the Epiſtle quoted; but indede agreable to
my expectation, I found none ſuch, and therefore truly deemed them to be framed in the fournace of M.
Whytes forgeries.

And though in the Epiſtle cyted, S. Ciprian reprehē-
deth certaine heritikes, who being iudicially cōuicted
in Africk, *ſayled to Rome with the marchandiſe of their lyes,*
endeuoring by their ſubtill and *cunning raſhnes, to break*
the concord of Biſhopes, yet was he ſo farr from diſpro-
uing of any lawfull Appeale to Rome, as that in the
ſame place he auoucheth Rome to be the Chaire of *Pe-*
ter, and principall Church from whence preiſtly vnity ary-
ſeth: yea he ſcorned the ſaid heritykes as not *knowinge*
the Romanes to be thoſe vnto whom vntruth could haue no
acceſſe: and withall further affirming *that the truth ſhould*
ſayle after them to Rome, which with proofe of the thing
certaine ſhould cōuince their lying tongues. All which doth
plainely make knowen S. Ciprianes true conceipt of

F   Romes

Romes superiority: and indeede doth strongly confirme our Catholick doctrine concerning Appeales.
For if those heritykes censured by the Bishopes of A-
frick to auoyde their present punishment appealed to
Rome : no doubt this argueth that Appeales to Rome
were in vse as then, and though the Appellantes were
heritykes, yet in that otherwise their Appeale had bene
plainely vaine, foolish, and fruitlesse: it manifestly
supposeth the foresaid Authority of admitting Appeales to reside in the Bishope of Rome. Further
though S. Ciprian reprehended them being lawfully
conuicted for their further Appealing and not submit-
ting them selues to their immediate Pastors : yet doth
he no-where so much as insinuate vpon iust occasions
the vnlawfulnes of Appeales, but euen in this very
place doth imply the contrary by his sending after the
foresaid heritikes to the Romane Church to enforme
her of the truth : which, if it had not bene in regard of
her foresaid Superiority or Primacy, had bene altogether neede-les, & peraduenture inconuenient.

And whereas M. Whyte a litle before cyteth these
wordes of S. Ciprian, *vnlesse peraduenture a few despe-
rate and gracelesse persons think the Authority of the Bishopes in Africk that iudged them to be lesse*: it is plaine
by the text that he maketh not this comparison with
the Bishop of Rome, but with those hereticall Bishopes
which were censured and condemned by the Bishopes
of Aftick. To conclude when M. Whyte sheweth me
in the Epistle cyted of S. Ciprian these wordes obiected, *the vnity of Bishopes is broken, when men runne from
their owne to the Bishope of Rome*: I will publikely de-
claime him the cuningest Optician, or rather Magi-
cian, that the whole ministery of England affordeth.

The 10 Paragraph.

The Rhemifts abufed concerning the Au-
thority of the Church.

Againe pag. 119. our fraudulent Doctor laboureth much to induce his credulous Readers to beleue, that we hold that the Church can at her pleafure make that Scripture which is not, and vnmake that which once is fcripture, thereupon faying, that *the papifts haue a principle among them, that the Scriptures receiue all their authority from the Church.* he feketh to proue it in the next lynes from a teftimony of the Rhemiftes gal. 6. thus alledging them. *The Scriptures are not knowne to be true, neither are Chriftians bound to receaue them, without the atteftation of the Church.* Here againe he curtayleth their fentence, concealing fuch their wordes as do lymite the Churches authority therein, and wherein they do acknowledg an infallible truth of the Scriptures before any approbation of the Church: therefore you fhall haue their wordes alledged at large. *The Scriptures (fay they) which are indeede of the Holy Ghofts indyting, being put into the Churches tryall, are found proued and teftifyed vnto the world to be fuch (and not made true, altered, or amended by the fame)* without which atteftation of the Church *(the holy Scriptures in them felues were alwayes true before) but not fo knowne to be to all Chriftians, nor they fo bound to take them.*

Here the Rhemiftes onely fay that the truth of the Scriptures can not be made knowne to vs without the atteftation of the Church: And that this is all which M. Whyte can collect from this teftimony which we willingly graunt. Yet where the Rhemiftes in this very place do vfe wordes of reuerence to the Scriprures

F 2   & embrace

& embrace their infallibility, as thefe, *The Scriptures are not made true, altered, or amended by the Church.* And againe, without the *atteſtation of the Church, the holy Scriptures in themſelues were always true;* As alſo wheare it is ſet downe by them in the mergent euen in that place. *The Church maketh not canonicall Scripture, but declareth that it is ſo.* Theſe I ſay, though parcels of the former ſentence or merginall explications thereof, the D. haith after his accuſtomed maner moſt calumniouſly ouerſkipped. Thus it will ſtill be found that the ſphere of this his learned Treatiſe (what glorious motion ſoeuer it ſemeth hitherto to haue in the ſight of his ignorant fauorites) turneth vpon the poles of ſhame full corruptions, & lying deceiptes.

The 11. Paragraph.

Cardinall Cuſanus corrupted concerning the ſame ſubiect.

Againe continuing his former proiect. pag. 51. he bringeth in the Cardinall Cuſanus ſaying Epiſt. 3, pa. 3. *When the Church changeth her Iudgment, God alſo changeth his.* This he vrgeth to make vs mantayne that God doth ſo ſubiect his iudgment to the church, that ſuppoſing (for it is a mere ſuppoſall) the church ſhould alter or change any eſſentiall or fundamentall poynte of faith whatſoeuer, by interpreting the Scripture otherwyſe then before it did (for M. Whyte ſetteth this ſentence downe without any reſtraint, & ſo conformably thereto ſtyleth the page, *The ſence of Scripture changed with the tyme*) that then god alſo doth chãg his mynde therein ſo warrantiug the truth of this new ſtamped article. But let vs ſee how the wordes do lye in Cuſanus, thus they are. *Sicut quondam coniugium præferebatur*

ferebatur Castitati &c. *As in former tymes* (meaninge in the firster ages of the world) *matrimony was preferred by the Church before Chastity: so was it preferred euen by God. But after the Iudgment of the Church being changed therein* (meaning after the world was fully peopled) *gods Iudgment is chauged also.* (*If therefore the Church doth Iudg any act to be of great merite in regard of the present circumstances, and in an other tyme after shall Iudg an other act to be of greater valew, &c. it is euident that the greatnes of the merite doth much depende vpon the Iudgment of the Church.* Thus what is here spoken onely of the diuersity of merit of one and the same action according to the different circumstances of tyme or place: M. Whyte will needes extend (besides the intention of the Author) to the chang of any dogmaticall point how great soeuer of Religion: and this he doth by nakedly setting downe one lyne which is the middest of the periode, but subtily according to his maner omitting both the wordes precedent (wherein the instance is geuen, and whereunto the sence of the former sentence is peculierly tyed) as also the wordes subseqüet contayning the reason thereof. But it semeth he haith vowed with him self neuer to alledg any one testimony ingeniously and plainely, seing his true quotations (if any such be) may, for their quantity, be engrauen within a ring, whereas his wilfull deprauations doe stretch beyond all reasonable dimension.

The 12 Paragraph.

The Canon Law corrupted concerning the Pope.

In nothing more doth M. Whyte manifest or continue his implacable hatred or his dexterity in falsification, then against the Church and Pope of Rome: a-

F 3 mongest

mongeſt many take this example folowing . pag . 433 .
I am affrayd (ſaih he) I haue bene to bold in medling with
theſe matters : for the Church of Rome haith a Law within
her ſelf , that it is (and then foloweth in a different letter as though they were the wordes of the Canon law)
ſacriledg to reaſon about the Popes doinges whoſe murders
are excuſed lyke Sampſons , and theftes lyke the Hebrues , &
Adultries lyke Iacobs . But here I muſt charg you with
much fowle demeanour : for firſt you affirme that the
wordes cyted are a Law of the Romane Church ,
whereas they are onely taken out of the gloſſe or comment , which is a thing much different , and of incom-
parable leſſe authority then the Law it ſelf . Secondly
whereas in the Law it is diſputed what cenſure is to be
geuen when the caſe is doubtfull whether the Pope
haith ſinned or noe , as by committing adultry or mur-
der : to which it is anſweared , that in that caſe it is to
be preſumed in the Popes behalf , yea (ſaith the gloſſer in this caſe) *ſacrilegii inſtar eſſe t diſputare de facto ſuo .*
Vel dic quod facta Papæ accuſantur vt homicidia Samſonis ,
& furta Hebræorum , & adulterium Iacob . It were lyke Sa-
criledg (in that doubtfull caſe) *to diſpute of his fact . Or*
ſay that the deedes of the Pope are accuſed as the murders of
Samſon , the thefis of the Hebrues , & the Adultery of Ia-
cob . What is here ſpoken in defence of the pope which
euery Chriſtian ought not to performe in defence of his
neighbour , to wit , in a caſe doubtfull , to think and
ſpeake the beſt ? Are not thoſe factes of Samſon , the
Hebrues , and Iacob , piouſly cenſured by the learnedſt
Doctors ? But with what front do you auouch ſo abſolutely and in generall , that according to the law of the
Romane Church it is *ſacriledg to reaſon about the Popes do*
inges , whereas the gloſſer ſaith onely *In dubiis &c .*
when the caſe is doubtfull of the Popes fact , *inſtar ſacri-*
legii &c . It were lyke Sacriledg to diſpute of his fact . Will
you of

you of doubtfull premiſſes inferre an abſolute concluſion? Would you take it kindly if in a caſe (admitting
it but doubtfull) whether a certaine miniſter had beene
drunke , ſhould abſolutely affirme that the *proteſtants
Church haith a Law within her ſelf, that it is Sacriledg to
reaſon about miniſters doinges , whoſe drunkeues is excuſed
as Noes &c .*

The 13. Paragraphl.

Bellarmine corrupted againſt the Popes Authority.

As the former deprauations were practiſed in ouer-
much aduauncing and extolling the Authority of the
Church and Pope : ſo here on the contrary part he falſly
alledgeth Bellarmine extenuating and leſning the ſaid
power : For thus entytling the page 167. *The papiſtes
them ſelues refuſe the Popes Iudgment* , he laboureth to
make good this aſſertion from the confeſſion of Bellarmine , who *de Rom . Pon . lib . 4 . ca . 7 .* ſpeaking
of S . Ciprian withſtanding Pope Stephen touchinge
rebaptiſation, writeth (as M . Whyte ſaith) that *after
the Popes definitiō, it was free for Ciprian to think otherwiſe:*
our miniſter intimating hereby to the *Reader*, that Bellarmine mantayneth , that it is lawfull to beleue contrary to that which is once defyned as a matter of faith
by the Pope . Here againe he beſtowes on his Reader a
broken ſentence leauing of in the middeſt thereby to
auoyde the ſetting downe of what is moſt materiall ,
for Bellarmines wordes are theſe . *Fuit enim poſt Pontificis definitionem. &c . It was lawfull after the definition of
the Pope to think otherwyſe as Auguſtine affirmeth beoauſe
the Pope , noluit rem ipſam de fide facere ſine generali concilio , would not make it as a matter of Faith without a generall Councell , but onely in the meane tyme willed the auncient cuſtome to be obſerued)* And then after , *Stephanus nō*

definiuit

definiuit rem illam tanquam de fide . P . Stephen did not de-
fyne the matter as a poynt of Faith , yet he commaunded ear-
neſtly that heritykes ſhould not be rebaptyſed .

See here now the integrity of our miniſter, who
purpoſly concealeth that part of the ſentence which is
expreſly contrary to that ſence in the which he alledgeth the former wordes thereof. For Bellarmine vn-
derſtandeth by the wordes *poſt definitionem,* after it was
commanded that rebaptiſation ſhould not be vſed, and
not after it was ſententially defined as an article of faith
(as M . Wayte ſemeth to force.) Now Catholickes do
graunt that it is lawfull to hould or beleue contrary to
the practiſe of what the Pope commandeth , ſo that
we doe according to his commandement , and as long
as the matter it ſelf is not definitiuely decreed by the
Pope for a dogmaticall poynt of our beleefe ; & thus
much thereof , from whence we may diſcerne the Miniſters inueterate hatred againſt the head of Gods
Church, who anſverably thereto ſpeaking of the words
of our Saviour *Paſce oues meas* , thus ſtyleth ſome of
his pages in his Lucian and ſcornfull phraze , *Feede my*
ſheepe is not poping . But howſoeuer to *feede* in this place
be to *pope* it : I am ſure moſt egregiouſly and impudently to corrupt Authors is to *Whyte it* .

Chapter. 4.

Wherein are diſcouered ſundry corruptions
concerning the ſacred Scriptures
and Traditions .

The 1. Paragraph.

Bellarmine corrupted in behalf of the Scripture pro-
uing it ſelf to be the word of God.

The next

THE next poynt we are to come to are such his corruptions wherein he pretendeth that the Catholickes doe acknowledge all sufficiency of Scripture both for the interpreting of it self without any needefull explication of the Church thereof, as also for it fulnesse in contayning expresly all thinges necessary to mans saluation, excluding thereby all Apostolicall Traditions whatsoeuer.

And first pag. 59. shewing that the Scripture is knowen to be the word of God without the attestation of the Church which as he houldeth may be deceatfull, he alleageth Bellarmine *de verb. dei li. 2. ca. 2.* thus confessing. (*other meanes may deceaue me*) but *nothing is more knowen, nothing more certayne then the Scriptures, that it were the greatest madnes in the world not to beleue them &c.* See how loth our minister is to cease to be him self, I meane to cease his notorious corrupting, for the wordes of Bellarmine are these. *Sacris Scripturis quæ Propheticis & Apostolicis literis continentur, nihil est notius, nihil certius, vt stultissimum esse necesse sit, qui illis fidem esse habendam neget. There is nothing more knowen, nothing more certaine, then the holy Scriptures which are contayned in the wrytinges of the Prophets & Apostles, in so much that it were a most foolishe thing for any man to deny them.*

Here first to make Bellarmine insinuate that he houldeth the authority of the Church in any thing to be doubtfull and vncertaine: our minister of his owne brayne haith added these wordes, *other meanes may deceaue me,* whereas there is not a sillable thereof in Bellarmine. Secondly this place, as we see, is produced by him against the authority of the Church, whereas indeede it is directed against the *Swinkfeldians,* who denying the Scriptures, relyed vpon their priuate illuminations, as hereafter shall appeare by displaying a

G   strange

ſtrang corruption, and wreſting of Bellarmines ſaying practiſed by M. Wnyte in pag. 17. at the letter
q. of which place of Bellarmine, this here alledged is
a parcell. Thus our miniſter extremely ſtrayneth euery
Authority that he ſetteth downe, till at the length it
burſt out into an open and inexcuſable corruption.

The 2 Paragraph.

Bellarmine corrupted in proofe that the Scriptures
are the onely rule of Faith.

Againe pag 17. to proue that all poyntes in controuerſy muſt definitiuely be determined by the writen
word alone without any reſpect to the Churches Authority in the explication thereof, he marcheth owte
once againe making Bellarmine his buckler, & thereupon alledgeth theſe wordes of his. *The rule of Faith*
muſt be certaine and knowen, for if it be not certaine, it is
no rule at all: If it be not knowen, it is no rule to vs, but
but nothing is more certaine, nothing better knowen then
the ſacred Scriptures contayned in the writinges of the Pro-
phets and Apoſtles: wherefore the ſacred Scripture is the
rule of Faith moſt certaine and moſt ſaife, and God haith
taught by corporall letters which we might ſee & read, what
he would haue vs beleue concerning him. Obſerue here the
refractory and incorrigible frowardnes of our miniſter, and how artificiall and exact he ſheweth him ſelf
in his art of corrupting: For Bellarmine in this Chapter (as is aboue touched) writeth againſt the *Swink-*
feldians, who denyed the Scripture to be the worde of
God, and reſted onely vpon their priuate and hidde reuelations, and anſwearably hereto the Tytle of this
Chapter is, *Libris quæ Canonici appellantur, verbum dei*
contınere

contineri, *That the word of God is contayned in thofe bookes which are called Canonicall*. Now the wordes at large are thus in Bellarmine. *Regula fidei, certa notaq̃, & c.* *The Rule of faith ought to be certaine and knowen, for if it be not knowen, it can be no Rule to vs, and if it be not certaine, it can be no Rule at all. But the reuelation of the priuate fpirit although in it felf it might be certayne, yet to vs it can no way be certaine, except haply it be warrãted with diuyne teftimonies, to wit true miracles.* And then fome fixe lynes after. *At facris Scripturis &c.* *But nothing is more knowen, nothing more certaine then the facred Scriptures which are contayred in the bookes of the Prophets & Apoftles.* And fome fourtie or fiftie lynes after. *Quare cum facra Scriptura Regula credendi &c. Wherefore feing the holy Scripture is a moft certaine and a moft fecure rule of beleefe: doubtleffe he can not be n yfe who negleĉtirg the fame committeth him felf to the iudgment of the priuate fpirit which is often deceiptfull but ener vncertayne.* And againe fome twenty lynes after. *Non igitur omnes vul-gó &c. Teerefore God teacheth not all men by internall infpirations, what he would haue the faithfull to beleue of him, or what they are to doe: but it is his pleafure to inftruĉt vs by corporall letters which we might fee and reade.*

Here now I referre this point to the moft earnefte proteftant in England (if he be Candid and ingenious) with what face M. Whyte could alledg Bellarmine in this place, to proue from him that the *Scripture onely is the Iudg & Rule of Faith* (for fo doth the minifter enty-tle that page) thereby to make Bellarmine to reiĉt all Authority of the Church in expofition thereof, & all Apoftolicall Traditions, where we fee vpon what different occafion from that he writeth in this Chapter againft the *Swinkfeldians*.

Now here let vs note the particuler fleightes vfed in this corruption. Firft M. Whyte you tye together

G 2   (without

without any &c. or other word, or note, fignifying
the contrary) feuerall fentences of Bellarmine for your
greater aduantage, as though one did immediatly folow the other, though they lye in Bellarmine diftinct
by interpofition of many lynes. Secondly you haue
concealed three feuerall parcels of different fentences
expreffing Bel. true mynde herein: and all thefe parcels are euen partes (and therefore the fowler fault)
of the fentences alledged by you. Your concealemēts
are thefe. *Porro priuati Spiritus reuelatio et fi in fe certa fit,
nobis tamen nota nullo modo poteft nifi fortè diuinis teftimo-
niis, id eft veris miraeulis, confirmetur.* And againe,
Sanus profeĉto non erit, qui ea neglecta (vz. the Scripture)
*fpiritus interni fæpe fallacis & femper incerti iudicio fe cō-
miferit.* And finally: *Non igitur omnes vulgó per inter-
num afflatum Deus docet;* All which your omiffions,
are impaled and marked in the faid englifh authority.
O how happy M. Whyte were you, if you neuer had
bene fcholler, fince the tyme will come that you fhall
fay with the Romane Emprour (after he had fubfcri-
bed to an vniuft caufe) *Vtinam literas nefcirem:* For
good thinges, as learning, are moft perniceous to him
who declyneth the true vfe of them as you doe. And
in this refpect you are to remember that the Arcke
which was a bleffing to the Ifraelites, was yet a curfe
and hurt to the *Philiftians* that abufed it.

The 3. Paragraph.

*Eckius fouly abufed concerning the Authority
of the Church and Traditions.*

As heretofore he laboured to ouerthrow the doctrine of traditions from the corrupted teftimonies of
Catholicks and auncient Fathers: fo heare he endeuoreth from

reth (from their lyke abufed teftimonies) to intimate
that we afcribe to them a greater perfection then we
doe. And to this end pag. 145. thereby the rather to
caft vpon vs an vnworthy afperfion of vnderualewing
the Scriptures, he bringeth in Eckius *in Enchirid. ca.*
1. faying. *The Scripture receaueth all the authority it
haith from the Church, and from Tradition.* The wordes
of this Author are thefe. *Scriptura non eft authentica
fine authoritate Ecclefia.* whereby we fee the wordes *and
from Tradition*, are falfly inferted by our deprauing minifter, making vs thereby to geue (which we doe not)
a greater prerogatiue to Tradition, then to Scripture.
And though perhaps he could light vpon thofe wordes
and from Tradition in fome other place or Chapter in
Ecckius though in a different fence (which hitherto I
can not find) yet it is no fmall difhonefiy in M. Whyte
thus vnkindly to match and ioyne together fuch difcep-
ting fentences without the parents confent. Againe
what a ftrange conftruction or tranflation is this?
*Scriptura non eft authentica fine authoritate Ecclefia.
The Scripture receaueth all the authority it haith from the
Churh, and from Tradition.* If this liberty be Iuftifiable,
what errour fo groffe may not eafely be iuftifyed a -
gainft all Scripture, thongh neuer fo plentifull, though
neuer fo manifeft.

The 4. Paragraph.

Canus corrupted concerning Traditions.

Againe perufing his former proiect, he (pag. 2.)
fortifyeth him felf with a wreft d authority of Canus,
whom *li. 3. ca. 3.* he bringeth in thus teaching. *There
is more ftrength to confute heritykes in Traditions, then in
the Scripture, yea all difputations with them, muft be determined*

termined by Traditions. Here againe the proteruity of our Doctor more and more discouereth it self: For thus Canus speaketh. *Non modo aduersum hareticos &c. Not onely against heritykes Tradition is of more force then Scripture, but also omnis (ferme) disputatio (almost) all disputation with them is to be reduced to Traditions receaued from our Aunceftors. (For seing both Catholickes & heritikes doe alledg Scripture for themselues, the difference betwene them is in the sence and interpretation thereof. Now which is the true and lawfull sence of it can not otherwise certainly be knowen, then by the traditiō of the Church)*

Here now our minifters fleight is three-fould; for firft Canus borroweth this saying from Tertulian of whom twenty lynes before this place Canus thus writeth. *Tertulianus monet vt aduersus hareticos, magis Traditionibus quam Scripturis differamus : Scriptura enim varios sensus trahuntur, Traditiones non item. Tertuliā connsfeleth vs that we hould dispute against heritikes rather with Tradition then with Scripture, since the Scriptures are drawen into seuerall constructions, whereas Traditions are not so.* Thus it appeareth that the opinion is Tertulians, and borrowed onely from him by Canus: yet M. Whyte thought it more conuenient to deliuer it, as proceding onely from Canus, so concealing Tertulian as vnwilling to haue it graced and countenanced with the Authority of so auncient a Doctor.

The second deceipt here, lyeth in not tranflating, but concealing the reafō of Canus his Iudgmēt therein though it be expreffed by Canus in the wordes immediatly folowing the place alledged, which fhew that the caufe why we are to dispute with heritykes with Traditions rather then with Scriptures, is not (as our minifter falfly pretendeth) our diftruft in the Scripture or want thereof to proue our Catholick Faith, but (as Canus faith) becaufe the true fence of it is cheifely to be taken be taken from Tradition warranted by the Church.

Thirdly and laftly he abuſeth his Reader in concealing the aduerbe *fermè*, in thoſe wordes aboue, *omnis fermè diſputatio, almoſt all diſputation*, whereas he tranſlateth *all diſputations*. Thus Canus by vſing the worde *fermè*, exempteth ſome point s from being decyded onely by traditions, whereas by our miniſters tranſlation, not any one is excepted. Thus haue we ſeene how our Doctor by his fowle colluſions haith laboured ſeuerall wayes, to depreſſe and obſcure the worthines of gods Catholick Church, as by making her become ſomtimes inuiſible, by falſly aſcribing to her and her head (in the catholickes name) an vſurping ſoueraignty, thereby to make her due Authority the more contemned, & to conclude by depryuing her of all Apoſtolicall Traditions and of all preheminency in explayning and expounding the Scriptures, whereas ſhe (eſpecially now in the tyme of the Goſpell) euer ſendeth from her ſelf moſt glorious beames and ſplendor of truth and perpetuitie, according to that of the princely pſalmiſt, *In ſole poſuit Tabernaculum ſuum*: for indeede ſhe is that Soon which (contrary to our inuiſibiliſtes) for theſe ſixteene hundreth yeres, did neuer once ſet vnder the horizon of an vniuerſall latency, that Soon which neuer expatiates beyond the tropickes of Gods Traditionary or writen word, that Soon which with it defyning and infallible authority in explicating the true ſenſe of Gods word, diſſipates and diſſolues all cloudes of errour exhaled through the weake influence of the reuealing ſpirit, finaly that Soon whoſe concentrous vniformity could yet neuer broke any *Phaniomena*, or apparances of innouation and nouelty, whereas all other ſectes profeſſing the name of Chriſtians, are (in regard of it) but as *Planetary and wandring ſtarrs*, producing many *Anomalous irregularities* of vncertainty, diſſen-

G 4

tion and

Chapiter. 5.

Concerning Faith & heresy.

The 1. Paragraph.

Bellarmine rorrupted against the necessity of true Faith.

BVT to returne to our Doctor, from Traditions we will descend to such other his deprauations, as concerne Faith in generall, as pag. 212. suggesting that we exact not (besides other vertues) any true or inward Faith to denominate or make one a perfect member of Gods Church, but onely an outward show hereof, he introduceth Bellarmine thus speaking. *de Eccl . mil . lib . 3 . ca . 2. Noe inward vertue is required to make one a part of the true Church, but ouely the externall profession of Faith.* And then M. Whyte ryoteth in great profusion of wordes, that vpon this grounde in the papistes Iudgment, all holines of lyfe and conuersation is superfluous and needelesse. But let vs recurre to Bellarmines wordes them selues. *Nos credimus in Ecclesia inueniri &c. (We doe beleue, that in the Church are found all vertues, as Faith, Hope, Charity, & the rest) yet, vt aliquis (aliquo modo) dici possit pars vera Ecclesia &c. That any one may be called (in some sort or manner) a part of that true Church whereof the Scripture speaketh: we doe not think any inward vertue to be requyred, but onely an externall profession of faith &c.* And in the folowing paragraph he saith, that those who (wanting all vertue) haue onely an externall profession of Faith &c: are as it were *de corpore,* but not *de anima Ecclesia, of the body, not of the soule of the Church,* & are
but *s*

but *ſicut capilli, aut mali humores in corpore humano*.
So wrongfully here we ſee is Bellarmine traduced by
our Doctor: Firſt in concealing the beginning of the
ſentence, wherein he acknowledgeth all theologicall
vertues euer to be found in Gods Church. Secondly
in ſuggeſting to the Reader, that Bellarmine requy-
reth no true inward vertues as neceſſary for a Chriſtian ſoule, but onely an externall faith; this is a falſe
and ſclanderous contumely, for *pulchra es & decora fi-
lia Hieruſalem. Can. 6.* And Bellarmine is ſo farre frō
teaching that ſuch doe take any benefite by this theire
outward profeſſion, that he ſaith (as we ſee) *they are
but onely of the body of the Church, & not of the ſoule* (to
which kynd of members internall vertues at leaſt are
neceſſary) and that they are to be reſembled to the leſſe
profitable and but excrementall partes of mans body,
as the hayres of the head, the nayles, and other ſuch
bad humors. Thirdly he wrongeth the Cardinall who
ſaith, that a man onely of outward profeſſion, is but
aliquo modo pars Eccleſiæ, meaning onely in a imperfect &
equiuocall manner of being, whereas our miniſter concealing the wordes *aliquo modo*, maketh Bellarmine to
aſcribe to ſuch a one, as perfect a being a member of
the Church, as to any other man endewed with all the
Theologicall vertues. But M. Whyte (as we haue
ſeene in others of his corruptions, ſo alſo in this) haith
a great facility, in paſſing ouer and concealing diuers
ſuch wordes, as *ſi, fermè, aliquo modo*, and the lyke,
in any Author that he alledgeth, though they migh-
tely alter the meaning of the ſentence. It may be perhaps he haith framed to him ſelf a new Accidence, &
houlding ſuch poore particles, but as imperfect partes
of ſpeach, he accomptes them as vnworthy to be tráf-
lated or ſet downe by his learned pen.

H　　　　　　　The

The 2. Paragraph.

Bellarmine corrupted against the knowledg of the mis-
teries of our Faith, & in preferring of ignorance.

Againe, to our more depressing of faith, & our supposed aduancing of ignorance: the Doctor telleth his
Reader how among vs the lay people are not bound to
know, what the matters of their faith be, but that *ig-*
norance is better: and thereupon in his mergent he fortifyeth him self with a sentence of Bellarmine *de Iust. l.*
1. ca. 7. in these wordes. *Fides melius per ignorantiā,*
quam per notitiam, definitur. Faith is better defyned by ig-
norance, then by knowledg. I think the minister euen for
feare of breach of his oath taken (as it should seme)
to the contrary, is loth to alledg any one sentence en-
tyrely, ingeniously, and truly. For mark here how vn-
truly he diuorceth Bellarmines wordes from his owne
drift and mynde. For the Cardinall entytuling that
Chapiter, *Fidem iustificantem non tam esse notitiam, quā*
assensum. Iustifying Faith, rather to be assent then know-
ledg, there proueth, that faith (euen according to the
Apostles definition thereof) can not be demōstrated,
and that the assent which we geue thereunto (saith he)
followeth not *rationem & euidentiam rei, a cleare euidēce*
of the poynt beleued, which is properly called *notitia*,
but it followeth *authoritatem proponentis, the authority*
of the proposer, and therfore it is more properly called *fi-*
des. And then some three lynes after he thus sayeth.
(*Igitur misteria fidei quæ rationem superant, credimus,*
non intelligimus, ac per hoc fides distinguitur contra scien-
tiam) & melius per ignorantiam quam per notitiam defini-
tur. Therefore we beleue the misteries of faith, which are a-
boue reason, we vnderstand them not, and in this respect,
Faith

(Faith is diſtinguiſhed againſt ſcience or knowledg) and is better defyned by ignorance then by euidency of knowledg .
Now here I doe demaund euen in ſincerity , whether theſe wordes (with any tecture or colour of poſſibility) can be wraſted to the ſupporting of a ſupine and an affected ignorance of the articles of our Faith ; as here our miniſter ſeeketh to ſtrayne them ? Wherefore I ſay that M . Whyte dealeth vnchriſtianlyke , and moſt irreligiouſly with Bellarmine herein . For firſt he inueſteth his wordes (which are ſpoken onely of the nature of faith) with a new conſtruction neuer dreamed of : and therefore you ſee the miniſter (beſides his paſſing ouer the ground and reaſon of his ſentence) purpoſly omitteth in his tranſlation , the beginning of the ſentence alledged , though it doth expound the wordes following , to wit , *Therefore we beleue the miſteries of Faith (which are aboue reaſon) we vnderſtand them not , and in this reſpect Faith is diſtinguiſhed againſt ſcience .*

Secondly he taketh aduauntage in tranſlating the word *notitia* , which though it ſignifyeth in large conſtruction knowledg in generall (in which ſence he forſaw the ignorant reader would take it) yet with the ſchoolemen it is reſtrayned , as Bellarmine here expreſly noteth , to that kynd of knowledg which is properly *Scientia* , which procedeth out of a demonſtrable euidency of the thing knowen , and conſequently it is incompatible with Faith .

For ſhame of your owne credit M . Whyte , and for the feare that you owe to God , forbeare to ſeduce any longer the ignorant by theſe deceauable meanes : and making your benefyte of theſe my trendly admonitions , which indeede procede from Chriſtian Charity , remember that *meliora ſunt vulnera diligentis , quā fraudulenti oſcula . prou .* 27 .

The 3 Paragraph.

Nauar corrupted concerning the sinne committed by the Laity in disputing of matters of Faith.

Now next let vs come to one or two deprauations consisting of the word heresy, where pag. 6. to intimate that we hould it no lesser offence then heresy, for a Lay man to argue of matters of Religion, as though the Church barred them in any sort whatsoeuer, not to speake thereof, he alledgeth Nauar, *Manual. ca. 11. nu. 26. It is heresy for a Lay man to dispute in a point of Faith.* Nauars wordes are these. *Quinto, qui disputat de fide cum sit Laicus, sciens Laicis esse prohibitum sub excommunicationis pœna, de illa disputare. Fiftly, who being a Lay man, disputeth of Faith, knowing that Lay men are forbidden vnder payne of excommunication to dispute thereof.* Here you see there is no mention of heresy, and indeede without reference to some other wordes, the sense is here imperfect; therefore the Reader is to vnderstand, that the Tytle of this Chapter in Nauar, is this. *Modi vsitatiores peccandi mortaliter, contra præceptum de recte colendo & honorando Deo &c. The seuerall more accustomed kindes of sinning mortally against the precept of worshiping and honoring God aright &c,* and so answearably to this tytle, he setteth downe dyuers wayes of sinninge mortally in that sort, keping the methode of *primo secundo &c.* and so comming to *quinto,* he sheweth in what manner a man sinneth therein: therefore the offence here committed is not heresy (as our minister falsly saith) but it is a mortall sinne, which yet is so to be vnderstoode, as when a Lay person pertinaceously without subiecting his Iudgment to the Church

Church, waucreth in diſputatiõ in any point of the Catholick faith: and thus much of M. Whytes ſynding the word hereſy, in Nauar. But I may well ſay he is a man of a very ſtrange, and (as I may terme it) imper ſect perfect eye-ſight, ſince he can not ſee wordes in teſtimonies which euery other man doth ſee: and yet ſeeth other wordes in them which no man els can ſee.

Chapter 6.

Concerning mariage of Preiſtes: Faſting: and Miracles.

The 1 Paragraph.

Sineſius impudently abuſed concerning his owne mariage.

The next corruption ſhall be touching mariage of Preiſtes, the lawfulnes whereof this our yoked miniſter is more willing to iuſtify, in that ſuch as profeſſe voluntary Chaſtity, are (according to the principles of his faith) accompted noe better then ſuperſtitious, & wilfull Eunuches. Now then for the warranting thereof page 343. he produceth a teſtimony from *Sineſius* Biſhop of *Ptolemais*, who in his Epiſtle to a frend called *Euopius*, thus writeth of him ſelf. *The ſacred hand of Theophilus haith geuen me a wyfe, and hereupon I teſtify to all men, that I will neither forſake her, nor yet priuily as an adulterer kepe her company, but I will pray to God to ſend me by her many & good children.* This Authority, as you ſee, maketh a ſpeceous ſhow, but examine it truly, & you ſhall confeſſe, that it is M. Whytes proper ſcene to acte the falſary, and corrupter, ſo notoriouſly haith he behaued him ſelf herein. For the better vnderſtanding therefore of this foule imposture, thou art to conceaue (good Reader) that this Epistle of *Sinesius* , out of which our M . taketh this Authority, is set downe at large by *Nicephorus Eccl . hist . lib .* 14 . *ca .* 55 . And that at the tyme when it was writen , *Sinesius* was but a Lay man , yet very eminent for diuers kyndes of good literature , and in reguard of such his partes , he was much solicited by many to vndertake rhe function of Preisthood : he a longe tyme yelded not to their perswasions, and did wryte this very Epistle to *Euopius* , (who was one that wished him to that course) to iustify hereby his resolution not to make him self Preist . And in this Epistle amonge other of his reasons, as his loue to humane studies , and his temporall pleasures diuerting him from that course , he alledgeth the wordes here set downe by M . Whyte , to wit , that in reguard he was a maried man , and intending to continue and liue in a wedlock state with his wyfe, he was not to enter into that sacred function . Thus doth *Sinesius* acknowledg euen in this Epistle (which by our minister is wrested to the mantaining of the contrary) that mariage (with a determination not to leaue the company of his wyfe) is a sufficient barre or let to Preisthood .

Now it hapned that some reasonable tyme after the wryting of his former Epistle, he was ouer-perswaded, and so assenting to his frendes importunity , was made Preist , and then after created Bishop of *Ptolemais* , & liued for all the tyme after , euer seperated from the company of his wyfe . Here then our ministers incredible deceipt (of which he is to him self most conscious) lyeth in applying the wordes spoken by *Sinesius* when he was a lay man , to him as he was after Preist and Bishop , and so by the wilfull confusion of these two seuerall tymes , doubted not but to bleare the weake iudgment of his ignorant reader . Good Reader, if thou ynderstandest derftandeft larin, I could wifh thee to fee the Epiftle of *Sinefius*, in the abouenoted place of Nicephorus, wherein thou fhalt fynd it moft euident, that at that tyme, *Sinefius* was not Preift, for euen there (befides many other paffages) he faith of him felf. *Ego fane qni meipfŭ noui, ineptiorem comperio, quam vt facerdotali dignitati gerendæ idoneus fim.* *I who am priuie to mine owne weakenes, doe fynde that I am not fit to vndertake the dignity of Preifthood.* In lyke fort euen at the end of this Epiftle, Nicephorus him felf thus concludeth. *Sinefius hæc fcribens, apertè facerdotalem dignitatem auerfatus eft &c.* *Sinefius wryting thefe thinges, was clearely vnwilling of the dignity of Preifthood:* So as it is moft vndoubted and perfpicuous, that at the wryting of this Epiftle (out of which M. Whyte did take the former wordes) he was not then Preift, much leffe Bifhop of *Ptolemais*, as our M. fubtily ftyleth him.

Now what do you fay to this M. Whyte, do you not think that this your perfidious dealing being once made knowen, will becom odious, not onely to Catholickes, but euen to all ingenious and welmeaninge proteftantes, though hitherto with extraordinary applaufe and allowance, they haue much admyred you? no doubt it will: and therefore feing you can not otherwife warrant (for your owne intereft) the mariage of the Cleargy, but onely by fuch difhoneft meanes : I hope that the fortune of Acteon, before your deathe, will happen vnto you, (feare not man, I preffe not the word in any difloyall fence) in being maligned, afflicted, and bayted, euen by your owne frendes and followers.

The 2. Paragraph.

Paphnutius abufed concerning the mariage of Preiftes.

For

For his further patronizing of Preiftes mariage, he,
pag. 343. vrgeth that often obtruded place of Sainct
Paule *Heb.* 13. *Mariage is honourable among all men.*
and at thefe wordes cyteth in the mergent Sozomen.
li. 1. ca. 22. as wryting that *Paphnutius* mantayned
the proteftantes conftruction of that place, fo as that
Preiftes might abfolutely at any tyme mary. In the difcouery of his deprauation here vfed, I will not much infift in difplaying his corruption of this text of Scripture, by adding the wordes, is, and, men, (the which
he borroweth from the englifh falfe tranflatió) for neither in the Geeke text can we fynd the verbe, is, of the
Indicatiue moode, neither the worde, men, that place
being thus according to the greeke, *mariage is honou-*
rable in all: which worde, *all,* may afwell haue reference
to all refpectes or endes of mariage, as to all men.
But I will cheifely relye, in fhewing how fmall reafon
he haith to alledg *Sozomen* or *Paphnutius* in this poynt,
and how litle their true meaning doth fort to our minifters drift: for M. Whyte vndertaketh in this place
to proue, that Preiftes may take wyues at any tyme,
(meaning afwell after their confecration as before) and
fo anfwearably in generall ftyle in the former page,
Preiftes mariage, and lykewife thus beginneth that very
Paragraph, wherein the former wordes of S. Paule are
alledged, *Fourthly touching the mariage of minifters,*
&c. Now if we looke into the former quotation of *So-*
zomene touching *Paphnutius,* we fhall fynde that he recordeth, how the Councell of Nyce, did onely tolle-
rate and permit the mariage of Preiftes, before theire
entrance into preifthood, but not after their confecration: which doth abfolutely croffe the fcope of M. W.
intention in this place. For firft this is the tytle of the
quoted Chapiter of *Sozomen. De Canonibus quos Con-*
cilium pofuit: & quod cum Canonem ftatuere voluerat, vt
quicunq̃

quicunq̃, ad sacerdotii dignitatem euecti essent, cum vxori-
bus, quas antequam sacris initiati erant, duxerant, non dor-
mirent: in medium proferens Paphnutius quidam Confessor
intercedebat. Of the Canons of the Councell (meaning of
Nyce) and that whereas the Councell determined to decree,
that euen those who were called to the dignity of preisthood,
should not liue with those their wyues, whom they had maried before they were ordeyned Preistes: one Paphnutius a
Confessour being amonge the Councell, began to plead the
contrary. But if the Councell thought it once conuenient to decree, that such Preistes as were maried before
theire entrance into Preisthood, should not liue together with their wyues in state of matrimony, then *a for-*
tiori, it did vtterly condemne the mariage of Preistes
after they be made Preistes. which is the contrary
whereunto is here cheifely defended by M. Whyte.
This poynt is further confirmed out of the wordes of
Sozomen, euen in the foresaid quoted Chapiter, for
there Sozomen doth thus wryte. *Veterem Ecclesiæ tra-*
ditionem esse, vt qui Calibes gradum sacerdotalem consecu-
ti fuissent, postea minimè vxores ducerent: qui autem post
nuptias, ad eum ordinem vocati essent, hii ab vxoribus quas
habebant minimè separarentur, & ista quidem licet Coniu-
giie:p̃rs, suasit Paphnutius. It is an ancient Tradition of
the Church, that such as be vnmaried when they enter the
dgree of preisthood, should not after take to them selues any
wyues: but those who being afore maried, and after are called to that order, should not be therefore seperated frõ theire
wyues, and this Paphnutius (though him self vnmaried)
perswaded the Councell vnto: and thus far Sozomen of
this poynt. Now I referre to the iudiceous reader how
worthily and sincerely M. Whyte haith quoted *Paph-*
nutius out of *Sozomen*, for interpreting of S. Paules
wordes in defence of Preistes mariage in generall, without any distinction of tymes, whereas indeede *Sozomen,*

I *Paphnutius*

Paphnutius, and the Councell of Nyce, did abfolutely
forbid mariage of the Cleargy after their ordination of
preifthood, directly oppofite againft the moft generall
practife of our englifh minifters, who for the moft part
firft feeke after a fteeple, and then a woman : and thus
with them, a fat benefyce, and a fifter in the Lord (for
herefy euer lyes groueling in fenfuality) are become in
our new euangelicall philofophy, the *termtnus ad quem*,
whereunto all other their motions; doe finally propend
and are directed.

The 3. Paragraph.

S. Auguftine corrupted againft fafting.

The Doctor (through his great auerfion which he
haith of fafting, and of forbidden meates for certaine
dayes (pag. 307. wryteth, that the auncient Monkes
made no diftinction of meates, & alledgeth in the margent for proofe thereof, S. Auguftine *de mor. Eccl.
li. 1. ca.* 33. Now you fhall fee how truly he auoucheth the Father herein ; for in that very Chapiter (not
to infift of his fpeaking of the Monkes fafting in thofe
wordes, *Ieiunia prorfus incredibilia, multos exercere di-
dici*. I haue learned that many Monkes did practtife euẽ
incredible faftes) he thus wryteth touching forbearãce
of the eating of flefh *multi non vefcuntur carnibus &c.
Many Monkes do not feede vpon flefh, though they are not
perfwaded fuperftitioufly, that flefh is an vncleane meate*. &
after againe. *Continent fe illi, qui poffunt (qui tamen funt
innumerabiles) & a carnibus, & a vino &c. Such Monks
as in body are hable (who yet are innumerable) do abftaine
from flefh, and from wyne*. Here it is euident what the
cuftome of the ancient Monkes was in thofe tymes, &
how different from the practife of the new gofpellers,
fince in

ſince infinite of them eating fiſh, neuer taſted of fleſh,
whereas to the contrary, I dare auouch in the behalf
of this my ſanctifyed miniſter, that euen out of conſcience, he forbeares to feede of ſuperſtitious fiſh. But indeede M. Whyte doth well to ſhew him ſelf ſo reſo-
lute an aduocate, as afore of venery in the mariage of
Preiſtes, ſo now of Epicuriſme, ſince he well knoweth that there is a ſecret reference, and mutuall depen-
dency, betwene theſe two moſt ſpirituall and ghoſtly
Characters of our late ſtamped goſpell: a poynte ſo
cleare, that euen the Poets do tell vs, that *Venus* was
euer much befrended by *Ceres* and *Bacchus*.

The 4. Paragraph.

Baronius notoriouſly corrupted, in proofe that heri-
tykes can worke true miracles.

To depryue the Catholick Church of her glory, of
moſt certaine and vndoubted miracles, wherewith
god haith ſeuerall tymes ſealed vp the truth of the faith
profeſſed by her Doctors: our miniſter laboureth to
proue from the confeſſion of Catholickes, that woor-
king of true miracles, are alſo common to heritikes, &
therefore no peculiar note of the true Church or Faith.

Now to this end, pag. 301. he alledgeth Baronius *Annal. An. 68. nu. 22.* touching the miracles of
Simon Magus. *Simon made Images to walk, & would lye*
in the fyre without hurt, & flye in the ayre, & make bread
of ſtones: he could open doares faſt ſhut, & vnlooſe boundes
of Iron &c. But doth our M. here leaue his accuſtomed
trade of corrupting think you? No, for he paireth the
teſtimony round aboute, for euen both immediatly before and immediatly after the Authority alledged, he
concealeth Baronius his owne wordes wherein he ac-

$\maltese$ now he 'geth, that these were no miracles, but impoftures, and sleightes onely : For thus he wryteth before. *Quæram autem hæc fuerint, cum reuerá non essent, tamen ab hominibus videri videbantur, referam &c.* (I will relate what prestigies or sleghtes these of Simons were, seeing indeede they were not true, yet semed to be in the sght of men) and the mentioneth those reckned by M. Whyte. And after Baro. haith nūbred the said supposed miracles, he thus instantly concludeth. *Hucusq, de Simonis imposturis, quibus hæc per imaginem ostendebat, & visum, cum nulla veritate consisterent.* Thus farr of the impostures of Simon, which appeared but in show and in the eye, seing indeede they were not truly performed. Now I appeale to the iudiceous Reader, with what candor and sincerity M. Whyte could produce part of the sentence of Baronius (omitting both the beginning and ending) to euict, that true and vndoubted miracles, are incident also to heritykes, and consequently are no competent marke of the true Faith or Church.

Chapiter 7.

Concerning the Sacramentes of the Euchaist and Pennance.

The 1. Paragraph

$\mathcal{B}$ armine corruped agaist Transubstantiation.

OVR Doctor pag. 24. haith a foule deprauation touching the doctrine of Transubstantiatió, alledging Bellarmine saying, *de Euch. lib 3. ca. 23* That it may iustly be doubted, whether the text be cleare enough to infer Transubstantiation, seing men sharpe & learned, such as Scotus was, haue thought the contrary. The

Reader

Reader shall see the whole periode of Bellarmine at
large, and so may discerne how strongly both he & Scotus impugne transubstantiatiõ, as they are here by our
M. traduced to doe. Thus then. *Scotus dicit non ex-*
tare &c. Scotus saith, that there is no place of Scripture so
expresse, which (sine Ecclesiæ declaratiõe) without the de-
claration or interpretation of the Church, can euidently force
transubstantiation. And this is not altogether improbable:
(for although the text of Scripture, which aboue we haue
alledged, seeme so cleare to vs, that it is able to conuince ho-
minem non proteruum, a man not obstinate) neuertheleße
whether it do so or no, it may it seth be doubted of, seing that
learned and sharp men (such as Scotus was) haue thought
the contrary. But Scotus addeth, that seing the Catholick
Church hath expounded the said text of Scripture in a gene-
rall Councell, therefore saith he, from the said Scripture so
declared by the Church, transubstantiation is manifestly
proued. Thus far Bellarmine. Now I doe aske, that
if we consider the whole cõtexture of this passage together, whether according to the mynds of Bellarmine
& Scotus, it maketh against transubstantiation or no?
I say it euen fortifyeth the Doctrine thereof: For Bellarmine first teacheth, that the text is euident enough
to conuince any man that is not froward or obstinate:
and Scotus (as we fynde here) grauntes, that transubstantiation is manifestly proued from the Scripture, being so already expounded by a generall Councell:
wherefore our ministers sleight resteth, in nakedly set-
tinge downe the former parcell of Bellarmine, and in
concealing the wordes afore, *sine declaratione Ecclesiæ*,
& againe, *hominem non proteruum*, to both which, the
sentence alledged hath a necessary reference: So as if
M. Whyte would haue deliuered Bellarmines true meaninge here, he must haue deliuered it in this sort: *It*
may be iustly doubted, whether the Text without the decla-

I 3 *ration*

ration of the Church, *be cleare enough to conuince an obsti-*
nate man in the poynt of transubstantiation, *seing men sharp*
& learned, *such as Scotus &c*. But this deportment had
bene ouer candid & sincere, and in no manner sort inge
to the calumnious proiect of our deprauing minister,
who by his perfidious dealinge throughout his whole
booke, semeth to haue made ship-wrack of all morall
honesty, reputation, religion, and shame. *pertere mo-*
res, *ius*, *decus*, *pietas*, *fides*: *& qui redire nescit*, *cum perit*
pudor. *Seneca*. *in Agam*.

The 2. Paragraph.

The Maister of sentences corrupted against confessi-
on to a Preist.

In this next place we will descend to the Sacrament
of Penance, prophaned by this our Doctors deprauations: and first to beare the reader in hand, that by the
acknowledgment of Catholickes, auricular Confession, and other partes of this Sacrament, are not necessary, he, pag. 254. produceth the M. of Sentences *li* 4.
d. 17. saying. *By contrition onely without Confession*, *or*
payment of outward punishment (or liberality of the pre-
late, *or paynes in purgatory) I may goe straight to heauen*.
The wordes of this Author are these. *Sanè dici potest*,
quod sine confessione oris, *& solutione pœnæ exterioris*, *pecca-*
ta delentur per contritionem & humilitatem. *Verily it may*
be said, *that sinnes are remitted by contrition & humility*,
without confession of the mouth, *or payment of exteriour pu-*
nishment. Where we fynde, first these wordes, *or libera-*
lity of the prelate, *or paynes in purgatory*, to be added by
M. Whyte, though set downe in a peculiar character,
& letter of the Author: but this our minister did, to
make the confession of this Author, more full & swel-
linge

ling : neuerthelesse to passe ouer this , I affirme that the sentence is fraudulently alledged, to take away auricu-ler confession . And therefore the reader ought to con-ceaue , that though all Catholickes teach, that perfect contrition is of force to blot owt a mans sinnes : yet they houlde , that this contrition can not be without confession, at least *in voto* , as the schoole-men speake , that is , that the party haith a desire to coufesse his sinnes to a preist , when opportunity shall serue . And that this is the very meaning of the Maister of the sen-tences in this place., appeareth , first out of his owne wordes , euen in the said paragraph or distinctiō where he saith . *Non est veré penitens , qui confessionis votum non habet : he is not truly penitent , who haith not a desire to con-fesse his sinnes.* Which poynt is also further made cleare by the tytle of the next paragraph sauinge one of this Author , which is this , *quod non sufficit soli Deo confiteri, si tempus adsit , si tamen homini possit . That it is not suffici-ent onely to confesse our sinne to God , if so we haue tyme or opportunity, to confesse to man .* Thus it appeareth what reason our Doctor had , to alledg the Authority of the Maister of the sentences , for the absolute abolishing of the Sacrament of Confession : whereas he meaneth that onely in tyme of necessity , and when opportunity is not to confesse them to man , then with a true contri-tion , the sinnes may be remitted without Confession . Such you see is the proceding of our minister through-out his booke , euer inuesting his doctrine and asserti-ons, with most foule and stained deprauations, wel dif-couering the spotted guiltines of his owne soule where fore for the tyme hereafter , I could wish M . Whyte (that so his mynde might be appareled answearably to his name) to follow the admonition of the Euangelist, *Get thee a whyte garment* (to wit , of repentance and fu-ture integrity) *that thou maist be clothed , and that thy*

The 3 Paragraph.

Bellarmine corrupted against Satisfaction.

Lastly touching the Sacrament of Penance, where-of Satisfaction is one part, to make the Catholick doctrine thereof become more vngratefull, he, pag. 249. produceth Bellarmine, *li. 1. de pur. ca. 14.* thus writing. *Christes satisfaction it self, taketh not away the punishment due vnto vs, but it removeth it so farr forth, as we haue grace from thence, to make our owne satisfaction of power.* For the better apprehending of Bellarmines true meaning in this place, the Reader is to conceaue that the Cardinall here handleth a schoole poynte which being no matter of Faith, but a poynt of indifferency, is seuerally defended by Catholick wryters. The poynt is this: that seing all the force of our satisfaction, is originally deryued, and receaueth it force: (as all Catholickes do graunt) from the passion and satisfaction of Christ: whether therefore this satisfaction of Christes and ours, may be teamed but one satisfaction or two satisfactions: Bellarmine houldeth that it is but one satisfaction, and that *formaliter*, ours, and thereupon wryteth in the alledged place. *Vnatantum est ibi dissatisfactio &c. There is here but one actuall satisfaction, and the same ours: neither by this is excluded Christe or his satisfaction: for by his satisfaction, we haue grace from whence we doe satisfy, & in this sense the satisfaction of Christ is said to be applyed to us,* non quod *immediaté ipsa eius satisfactio, tollat pænam temporalem nobis debitam, sed quod mediaté eam tollat, quatenus videlicet ab eo gratiam habemus, sine qua, nihil valeret nostra satisfactio:* Not that his satisfaction immediatly taketh a-

way

way the punishment due vnto vs: but that it taketh it away mediatly, in so much as from his satisfaction, we receaue Grace, without the which our satisfaction would be of noe force .

Here all men may see, that Bellarmine doth in noe sort detract from the passion or satisfaction of Christ, for he saith, that Christes satisfaction is not excluded by our satisfaction: that by his satisfaction, we haue grace to satisfy: that our satisfaction applyeth Christes satisfaction to vs: Finally, that without Christes satisfaction, ours can be of no force. But before I ende, I will be the Readers remembrancer of two or three sleightes vsed by you M. Whyte, in this one testimony. First in these wordes, *Not that Christes satisfaction (immediatly) taketh away the punishment due vnto vs ,* you conceale in your translation, the word, *immediatly*, and so makes vs to say, that Christes satisfaction doth not at all take away the punishment due vnto vs, which to affirme, is no lesse then a monstrous blasphemy . Secondly in those wordes, *sed quod mediaté eam tollat,* which you translate not in that naturall sense which the wordes import, but onely thus , *but that Christes satisfaction remoueth the punishment* : so by your feeble translation, making vs in an ignorant eare, to ascribe lesse to Christes satisfaction then we doe . Thirdly in that last parcell of the sentence, *sine qua nihil valeret nostra satisfactio . Without which grace of Christ , our satisf. were of noe force .* Which wordes as soundinge fully in our acknowledgment of the valew of Christes passion, you also haue fully translated in a more remisse phraze and tenour of speach, to wit, *from which grace , our satisfaction is made of power .* Thus well knowinge that (according to the rules of Rhetorick) different phrases bearing one and the same sence, doe make a different (and so more or lesse) impression in the hearers

K eares

eares. But you doe well, and in one fenfe we will not
much complaine of you, fince this perfideous deportment in your wrytinges (as neceffarily difcoueringe
that you are confcious and guilty of your owne bad
caufe) doth much aduantage your aduerfaries.

The 5. Paragraph.

S. *Thomas corrupted concerning the remiffion of*
veniall finnes.

Touching veniall finnes, pag. 246. and how they
are remitted, our minifter extremely corrupteth a faying in S. Thomas par. 3. q. 87 ar. 3. making him
thus, without any further illuftration of the poynte,
to fpeake, *Veniall finnes may be forgeuen by knocking of*
the breaft, going into the Church, receauing of holy water,
or the Bifhopes bleffing, or croffing our felf, or by any fuch
work of Charity, though we do not think actnally of them.
Tell me M. Wh. when muft we expect at your handes
one pertinent allegation without any deprauation or
impofture? I do think euen then (and not before)
when, as the poet wrytes.

> *Terra feret ftellas, cælum fcindetur aratro.* Ouid.l.
> *Vnda dabit flammas, & dabit ignis aquas.* 1 de tri.

For, according to your accuftomed vaine, you haue
moft fowly wronged S. Thomas, and fo your felf here
(by wilfully falfifying the doctrine of veniall finnes)
haith committed a mortall finne. For he in the place alledged fhowing how veniall finnes are remitted, either
by an act of deteftation of finne, or an act of reuerence
towardes god, thus concludeth. *Manifeftum eft gene-*
rali confeffione &c. It is manifeft, that veniall finnes are
remitted by a generall confeffion, knocking of the breaft, &
faying of our Lordes prayer (*quatenus cum deteftatione pec-*
cati fiunt

cati fiunt , as thefe actions are done with a deteſtation of
finne) as alfo by the Biſhopes bleſſing , by ſprincling of holy
water , and other fuch actions (quatenus cum dei reuerentia
exercentur , as they are performed with a reuerence towards
god.) Here you fee firft, how you haue moſt fraudulently difcarded thefe two parcels of the fentence , to wit,
quatēus cū deteſtatione pēti fiūt ; & quatenus cum dei reue -
rentia exercentur, as they are done with a deteſtatiō of finne,
& as they are performed with reuerence to god, which parcels do enlcuen and feafon the whole . For we do not
hould that thefe actions , except they be accompany-
ed either with a deteſtation of finne , or reuerence to -
wardes god , do remitt veniall finnes . But your intended calumny and deceipt here , was to make your credulous reader thinke , that the fuperſtitious papiſts (as
you tearme them in your rayling and calumnious language) do beleue that thefe externall actions of them
felues alone , are as it were certaine fpells or charmes
to extinguiſh and dryue away all veniall finnes whatfoeuer . Secondly touching the laſt part of the fentēce
as it is fet downe by you , vz , *or by any worke of Charity,*
though we doe not think actually of them, is not in this
third article , but afore in the firſt article of 87 . queſtion , and is only an obiection of S . Thomas , vrged
for forme fake , (according to his Methode) and then
afterwardes anfweared by himfelf .

K 2 Chapiter

Chapter 8.

Concerning the author of sinne, & reprobation.

The 1 Paragraph.

Bellarmine egregiously falsifyed, in proofe that god is the Author of sinne.

TO the iustifying that Catholicks are as far ingaged in defendinge that blasphemous and horrible doctrine, that god is the Author of sinne, as the proteſtantes are, pag. 271. he alledgeth Bellarmine *de amiſ. gra. l. 2. ca. 13.* thus wryting. *God by a figure commandeth sinne, and excyteth men vnto it, as a huntsman setteth a dog vpon a hare, by letting goe the slippe that held the dog. God therefore doth not onely permit the wicked to do many euils, neither doth he onely forsake the godly, that they may be constrayned to suffer the thinges done against them by the wicked, but he also ouerseeth their euill willes, and ruleth & gouerneth them, & boweth & bendeth them, by working inuisibly in them. And not onely inclyneth euill willes to one euill rather then to an other, by permitting them to be caried into one euill, & not permitting them to be caried into an other: but also positiuely he bendeth them, by inclyning to one euill, & turning them from an other, oc casionally & morally &c.*

Thus our miniſter alledgeth Bellarmine, and then triumphantly this concludeth. *Let our aduerſaries looke well into theſe ſpeaches, & they ſhall fynde that we ſay in effect nomore.* Your aduerſaries, M. Whyte, haue loked well into theſe ſpeaches, and they do fynde and ſay in effect, that you are a moſt faith-leſſe, diſhoneſt, and corrupt wryter, and indeede one of thoſe whom the ſpaniſh phraze calls *vnhombre deſalmado*, a fellow
without

without a foule, for if you either feared god, had a
true cóceate of any Religion, or thought that the foule
were immortall, to anfwear for what it performes in
this lyfe: you would neuer depraue this Author as you
do, making the Catholickes to be patrones of that
blafphemy which in their foules they damne to the pit
of hell. Wherefore good Reader, I am to intreate thy
patience, if I infift fomwhat longe in the full difco -
uering of this corruption. Well then Bellarmine in
the Chapiter alledged, fheweth how that God may be
faid feuerall wayes to inclyne a man to euill: And there
upon faith. *Primus modus effet, fi Deus per fe & proprié
&c. The firft way fhould be, if god by him felf and properly
eitherphyficé, phifically and naturally by mouing the will immediatly, or moraliter, to wit, by truly and properly commaunding the will, fhould impell it to euill: but this kind
is manifeftly falfe, impious, aud blafphemous againft God.
Therefore this kind as wicked being omitted, a fecond way
as that we may vnderftand god to be faid in the Scriptures,
to excyte and prouoke fome vnto euill, or to commaunde that
they work wickedly, and to vfe them as inftrumentes be -
caufe he permitteth them to do euill, although euery one
that permitteth any thing, can not be rightly faid to commaund it, that it may be done, neither to excite or prouoke
an other thereto. Notwithftanding god (without whofe
permiffion nothing can be done) when as he fuffereth any
thing to be done, to the obtayning of fome certayne ende of
his: may rightly be faid by a certaine figure, to commaund
that, and to incite one thereto: euen as vfually we fay, the
dog was fet vpon the hare by the hunter, when as he onely
loofed the flippe wherewith he was tyed.* And then fome
three paragraphes after, *deus non folum permittit &c.
god doth not onely permitte the wicked to doe much wicked-
neffe, neither doth onely leaue the godly that they may be
forced to fuffer wronges of the wicked, but ouerfeeth the euill*

K   3   *willes &*

willes, and doth gouerne and rule them, and bend them,
working in them inuisibly : So as though theire willes be e-
uill through their owne default, yet they are inclyned by di-
uine prouidence, rather to one euill then to an other (non
positiué, sed permissiué, not positiuely, but by permission .)
And then in an other paragraph after. *Deum non solùm*
inclinare &c. *god doth not onely inclyne wicked willes to*
one euill rather then to an other, by suffering them that they
shall be caried into one euill, and not suffering them that
they shall be caried into an other(as Hugo rightly teacheth)
but also by positiuely inclyning them to one euill, and auer-
ting them from an other (non quidem per se et physicé mo-
uendo voluntatem ad vnum et remouendo ab alio, quod li-
bertati arbitrii preiudicare videretur, not by him selfe and
physically or naturally in mouing the will to one euill and
remouing it from an other ; which may seme to be againste
the liberty of the will)sed occasionaliter, et moraliter, but
occasionally and morally, as S .. Thomas speaketh (to wit,
in sending some one good thought, from the which the wicked
man (though his owne fault) may take occasion, that it is
better to hurt this man, then that man, to yeld to this sinne
rather then to that sinne.

Thus farre doth Bellarmine literally wryte. Now
we will see what a mount of impostures and deceiptes
our minister haith heaped vp in producing of this one
Authority. First he omitteth altogether (without the
least intimation of it, or Bellarmines dislyke thereof)
the first kynde or manner how god may be said to impell man to sinne, to wit, properly and immediatly,
which Bellarmine calleth impious and blasphemous, &
yet M . Whyte endeuoreth throughout all the passage
here vrged, to charge him therewith. Secondly for the
more engaging of Bellarmine herein, he immediatly
applyeth that example of a hunter lettingr goe the slip,
to gods commaundinge & excyting men to sin, which

Bellarmine

Bellarmine onely by illation, applyeth thereto . Thirdly where Bellarmine faith that wicked men *by diuine
prouidence , are inclyned to one euill rather then to another,
non pofitiuê, fed permiſſiuê, not pofitiuely , but by permiſſiõ:*
the miniſter haith left out thefe wordes , *non pofitiuê ,
fed permiſſiuê* , though in them lyeth all the folution of
the doubt here controuerted . Fourthly when Bellarmine after faith , that *god inclynes alfo the will of the wicked to one euill rather then to another, pofitiuê, non quidem
per fe et phificê mouendo voluntatem ad vnum , et remouendo ab alio , quod libertati arbitru præiudicare videtur : fed
occafionaliter et moraliter , pofitiuely , yet not by him felfe
and phifically , mouing the will of the wicked to one finne , &
withdrawing it from an other , which may feeme to be a -
gainſt the freedome of the will , but occafionally & morally
&c* . Our miniſter fubtily taking hould of the word *pofitiuê* , doth leaue out all the reſt , wherein is expreſſed
how the word *pofitiuê,* is to be vnderſtoode , and ioy -
neth it immediatly with the wordes *occafionaliter, et moraliter.* Fiftly he purpofly forbeareth the example wher
in Bellarmine immediatly doth interprete the wordes
occafionaliter & moraliter , to wit , in fending a good
thought , but not an euill thought , as M . Whyte by
his wilfull omiſſion thereof , would feme to pretende .

And thus far of this teſtimony , where you fee I haue
as it were diſſected , all the perticular vaines & finewes
wherein lyeth the very lyfe and ſtrength of the miniſters fraude and colluſion herein : onely good Reader
I would wiſh thee for thy fuller fatiffaction , to vew
the place in Bellarmine him felf , and then geue vp thy
true iudgment , whether M . Whyte or I deale fincerely herein .

The 2. Paragraph.

S. Auguftine abufed concerning reprobation.

Our minifter to proue his blafphemous doctrine of reprobation or damnation pag. 9. doth fhrowd him felf vnder an abufed teftimony of S. Auguftine Epift. 107. ad Vital. med. whom he thus cyteth. *It is a ma-nifeft truth, that many can not be faued, not becaufe them felues will not, but becaufe god will not.* The wordes of S. Auguftine are thefe. *Multi falui non fiant, non quia ip fi, fed quia deus non vult, (quod fine vlla caligine manifef-tatur in paruulis. Many are not faued, not becaufe they will not, but becaufe god will not: Which without all obfcuri-ty is manifefted in infantes.* Thefe latter wordes, *which without all obfcurity is manifefted in infantes,* are fraudu-lently left out by the minifter, becaufe they expreffe S. Auguftines mynde herein: for S. Auguftine here one-ly fpeaketh of the damnation of infantes, who dye be-fore they receaue baptifme, which M. Whyte well knowing, thought good to omitt the latter Part of this fentence, and therefore this teftimony is wrong-fully ftretched to fuch as be of capacity and rype yeres. That this Place of S. Auguftine is onely intended of in fants not baptifed before their death, is alfo manifefted (befides the proofe taken from the former wordes) by that which this Father wryteth fome two or three lines afore this place, where he maketh the queftion con-cerning reprobation and perticulerly reftraineth this fpeach to infantes in thefe wordes, *Quomodo deus vult &c. How faleth it owt, that god would haue all men fa-ned, feeing that infantes who haue no will contrary or re-pugning to their faluation, do not pertake of gods will in this poynt*

*this poynt, in that diuers of them do dye without the grace ge-
uen in baptifme ?* Thus our Doctor after his vfuall manner abufeth this auncient father, by concealing a part
of the fentence alledged, wherein his mynde is manifeſted. Neither can M. Whyte falue the matter in anfwearing, that in an other place after vpon the like
occafion, he haith alledged this fentence without concealement : this I fay aduauntageth him nothing. For
though perhaps not in the other cytation, yet in this
it is cleare that his intention was to deceaue the reader :
but it is expected from the pen of a man of integrity,
to deale fincerely not in one onely, but in all the paffages of his wrytinges, fince a wryters cafe herein, may
feme, in fome fort, to beare a refemblance to an acte
morally vertuous, which is vitiated by any one bad
circumſtance, but perfected by the concurrency of all
due circumſtances.

Chapiter 9.

Concerning the honour to be geuen to
Sainctes and their Images.

The 1. Paragraph.

*S. Epiphanius corrupted in diſhonour of the bleſſed
Virgin Mary.*

W Hereas, according to Catholick doctrine,
different degrees of honour are to be exhibited to god and his bleſſed Angels and Sainctes : as to
the firſt Adoration, an 1 to the other in a far lower degree : not onely damned fpirites, but damnable heritykes (their painefull fchollers) as enuious emula-
tors of glorious Sainctes, do euer labour by many fub-
L tiltyes

tiltyes, to rob them quyte of all deferued veneration.
In which kynd M. Whyte willing to acte his part, euen
againft the B . Virgin the Mother of God, & modele
of all piety, for better fhadowing of his envy, pag.
344, he alledgeth *Epiphanius. c. her . l . 3 . her , 79.
c . Collyridianos .* faying . *The Virgin Mary was a virgin
and honorable , but not geuen for vs to worfhip , but her felf
worfhipped him that tooke flefh of her :* But for the clearer
reuealing of this illufion, it is to be obferued, that *Epiphanius* wryteth here purpofly againft certaine women
*who adoring a Chariot , or foure fquared feate , and couering the fame with linnen cloath , did at one folemne tyme
of the yeare , bring forth bread , and offer the fame vp in the
name of Mary ,* which he proueth at large to be vnlawfull, in that it was neuer permitted to women , *to offer
vp facrifice ,* as alfo in that facrfice is an honour onely
peculiar to god, yea he maketh an expreffe difference
betwene adoration and honour or woorfhip, attributing the firft onely to god, and the fecond with vs
Catholickes, to the bleffed Virgin, and Sainctes,
which is further manifeft euen by the wordes obiected
being truly tranflated, which are thefe . *Verily the body
of Mary was holy, but yet not God, Verily the Virgin was
a Virgin and honorable, but not geuen vnto vs for adoration , but her felf adored him, who was borne of her flefh .*
As alfo , *Let Mary be honoured, and the Father and Sone
and the holy Ghoft adored. Let no man adore Mary &c.
This miftery is due to God* And againe , *Though Mary
be moft excellent , and holy , and honourable , yet not for adoration :* And fundry other fuch lyke, all which do euidently conuince, that S . *Epiphanius* alloweth woorfhip , and honour to be geuen to the B . Virgin, but
not adoration, to wit with facrifice, which is an honour Peculiar onely to God.

The 2

The 2 . Paragraph

*S . Gregory notoriously corrupted against the woor-
shiping of Images .*

Speaking against Images pag . 152. he affirmeth
that the Church of Rome *forbade the woorship of them ,
as appeareth* (faith he) *by the Epistle of Gregory to Serenus,* which he noteth in the margent to be *Epist ,* 109.
li . 7 . It is this ministers euill hap , by most of his cita-
tations , to manifest to the world , his foly and falfhood. For who not distracted, would vrge that against
his aduersary which impugneth him felf , and that in
such a maner, as will eafely conuince him of fraude and
wilfull malice . For fiirft S . Gregory in the place cyted , reproueth Serenus for breaking & cafting downe
of Images which were fet vp in Churches , though the
said Serenus did the fame through zeale , by reafon of
fom: who committed Idolatry thereby , affiiming further , that therefore *Pictures are vfed in Churches , that
thofe which know not letters , at leaft should reade by feeing
in the wales , thofe thinges which they could not reade in
bookes .* And then he concludeth . *Thy brotherhood therefore ought to haue preferued the pictures , and to haue hindred the people from their adoration , that fo the ignorant
might haue from whence to gather knowledg of the hiftory ,
and the people not finne in adoration of the picture :*
Here S . Gregory alloweth the vfe of pictures in Churches , fhewing the commodity arrifinge thereby , and
withall reprehendeth Serenus , though through zeale ,
for breaking and cafting them downe : what may we
thinke then he would haue faid against Whyte and o-
ther his brethren , who through herefy and malice ,
prohibite all vfe or place thereof in Churches , if they

had bene

if they had bene then extant and made knowen vnto him. But though with Catholickes he allow the placing of them in Churches, yet M. Whyte will vrge, that he forbiddeth their woorship. The woorship which he forbiddeth according to his owne wordes is adoration, which word the Fathers frequently vse for that honour which is onely proper to God. And that S. Gregory ment no other, is manifest by an other Epistle writen to the said Serenus, *Ep. 9. l. 9.* vpon the self same occasion, where hauing repeated the forsaid vtility of pictures, and adding that not without *cause antiquity admitted Histories to be painted in the venerable places*, or Churches, *of Sainctes*, he directe the Serenus & in him all pastors how to instruct the people in theire lawfull vse, as *shewing them by testimonies of sacred scriptures, that nothing made with hand, ought to be adored, seing it is writen, Luc. 4. The Lord thy god thou shalt adore &c.* As also, *By sight of the thing done, or the history, let them conceaue the feruour of compunction, and let them be humbly prostrated in the adoration of the onely omnipotent holy Trinity.* By which it is most manifest, that the woorship here forbidden by S. Gregory to Images, is onely that adoration which is proper to god.

And that otherwise he thought Images duly to be worshipped, appeareth by his 7. booke and 5. Epistle, wheare wryting to Bishop Ianuarius concerning one Peter lately conuerted from Iudaisme to Christianity, who violently had taken a Sinagoug from the Iewes, and *placed therein the Image of the Mother of God and our Lord, and the venerable Crosse &c.* In redresse whereof he exhorte the the said Bishope, that *the Image and the Crosse taken away againe from thence, with that veneration (or reuerence) which is meete, to restore that which was violently taken away*, to wit the Sinagouge

nagouge. So that in fteed of impugning due worfhip to Images, thefe poyntes folowing may all heritikes learne of S. Gregory. Firft, that he proueth the vfe thereof from antiquity. Secondly, that he alloweth the placing thereof in Churches, and impugneth the breakers or pullers of them downe, though their ex-cufe or pretence, be feare of Idolatry in the People. Thirdly that the fame, in fteed of hurt, do much pro-fit the ignorant that can not reade: And laftly that in plaine tearmes he calleth the Croffe, *Crucem venerandam*, *Venerable*. And directeth, that both the Image of our B. Lady, and the Croffe, fhould be remoued, *cum ea qua dignum eft veneratione*, *with that worfhip which is meete*, or they deferue. So that I could wifh our needy minifter, to be better aduyfed hereafter in his citinge of S. Gregory againft Catholick religion.

The 5 Paragraph.

The Councell of Eliberis corrupted againft Images.

Here now I am come to the laft corruption, which I intende to difplay, the which I haue purpofly refer-ued, therewith to clofe vp the taift of my Reader: fo notorious it is for the Authors depraued, and fo preg nant and dextrous in the conueyance.

As touching the firft, wheras euery one of the for-mer deprauations (thofe of the Rhemiftes onely excep-ted) refteth in abufing the authority of fome one par-ticuler man, this ftryketh at a whole Councell confif-ting of many fcores of Fathers, fo happy a progreffe M. Whyte haith made in his profeffion of corrupting. Now for the conueyance, though it be not to be pa-ralleled with diuers of the former, *extenfiué* (as the fchoole-men fpeake) in multitude and ftoare of wordes

M   corrupted

corrupted, it lying onely in flye tranfpofition of one or two wordes, yet *intenfiué*, for the art thereof, it may be equalled with any.

This then it is. Our minifter there, pag 344. to ouerthrow the religious vfe of Images, produceth the 36. Canon of the Councell of Eliberis, to wit: *No picture is to be made in the Church, left that be adored which is paynted on wales.* The wordes of the Canon are thefe. *Placuit picturas in Ecclefia non debere, ne quod colitur & adoratur, in parietibus depingatur. It pleafed the Councell, that pictures fhould not be in the Church, lefte that which is worfhiped and adored, be painted on the wales.*

Be obferuant here Reader, and marke the difference which is made of the fame wordes, by a witty interchange of their place in their tranflation: & thou fhalt fee that my delicate minifter here euen tranfcends him felf. The Councell faith, *Images are not to be in the Church, left that be painted on the wales which is worfhipped.* M. Whyte tranflateth, *left that be worfhiped which is painted on the wales.* Thus the difference breefely refteth in this, *left that which is worfhiped be painted*, And *left that which is painted be worfhipped.* A fmall difference in fhew of wordes, but great in fence: For the wordes of the Councell acknowledging the worfhip of Images, maketh the worfhip due to them, to be the caufe why they are not to be painted on wales: But M. Whyte faith that they are not to be painted on wales becaufe they are not to be worfhiped, and fo maketh the Councell to fpeake lyke good proteftantes.

Now the reafon why the Councell would not haue the wales of Churches to be painted with Images, was in reguard of the due refpect they bare to them, & not as M. Whyte falfly fuggefteth: For being fo painted, they were fubiect to be defaced, either by the inuafió of the enemies in thofe tymes, or els by the rayne and
bad

bad wether: whereas Images drawne in Tables (of
which the former Councell maketh no reftraint) in that
they are portable and remoueable, do not lye open to
the fame daunger. Therefore the intention of the Coū-
cell herein, was the fame with the intention of that decree by the which it was ordained, that in reuerence
to the Crucifix, no Croſſe ſhould be made vpon the
plaine ground, becauſe it being ſo made, muſt needes
be often irreuerently betramped with the feete of mē.
Thus is M. Whyte in ſeking to diſproue the lawfull
vſe of an Image, become himſelf a perfect Image of deceate, fraude, and colluſion.

But here now I make an ende of his corruptions &
deprauations (haſting my ſelf to the ſecond Part of his
ſcene which is his lyes and falſhoods.) Onely I muſt
ſay, that in reguard of the impurity and conſcionleſſe
deportment of him in his whole Treatiſe: I can not
but commiſerate all ſuch poore credulous ſoules, as
do highly Preiudge of his booke, as being writen in
all ſincerity and plaineſſe, and free from the leaſt touch
or aſperſion of any wilfull deprauation.

And therefore I hould it moſt ſtrange, that M. *Pur-
chaſe* (a ſcholer and ingenious, though extremely maliuolent) ſhould in his owne booke, pag. 100. en-
tytle M. Whyte *Via Lactea*, alludinge perhaps both
to his name, and his ſuppoſed candor in wrytinge.

But ſince his miſtakinge is not iuſtifiable: I will allow to M. Whyte the fame tytle, though through a
differeut reaſon. For as the *Via Lactea* appeareth to a
vulgar ſight to be a part of heauen, and yet indeede is
not, being (if we follow the iudgment of the auncient Philoſophers) far lower then the heauens, as it is
neceſſarily euicted from the different parallayes and va-
riations thereof, taken from ſeuerall places: So is M.
Whyte reputed in the comon eye and cenſure of vn-

learned

learned proteſtantes, as a man which in all truth haith
much laboured in that heauenly courſe of dilating the
Goſpell and faith of Chriſt: whereas we ſynd that the
contrary is moſt true, as haith fully appeared from his
ſeuerall exorbitant deprauations of ſo many Catholick
Authors and others. Wherefore to be ſhort, I greatly feare that except hereafter there follow a feeling
remorſe of this foule and vnchriſtianlike dealing, the
wordes of S. Iohn the Euangeliſt, may be more truly
applyed to our Sir Iohn the miniſter, *Nomen habes, quo
viuis, mortuus es. Apoc.* 5.

The ende of the firſt part.

WHYTE

DYED BLACK.

THE SECOND PART.

Contayning fundry notorious vntruthes or
Lyes, proued to be fuch, euen by
the confeffion of the moft learned Proteftantes.

*And firſt is preuented a weake euaſion, which may
be vſed by M. Whyte againſt this
ſecond parte*

FROM Corruptions good Reader we are rext to
defcend to vntruthes, for lying indeede, is the fecond piller which fupporteth the whole weight &
frame of M. Whytes worke.

This paffage I here make diftinct from the former:
For although all the precedent deprauations of the firft
part do potentially include vntruthes and falfhoodes:
yet our Doctors proteruity therein doth cheifly reft,
either in corrupting other mens wordes, or in alledging them directly againft the knowne intention of the
Authors: whereas here, the reduplicatiue formality
(as I may terme it) of his hereticall deportment, con-
fifteth in plaine lying, to wit, in fetting downe and
inftifying certaine moft falfe affertions, and pofitions,

N   a courfe

a courfe little forting to one who ftyleth him felf a minifter of gods word, in that his facred word, is altogether incompatible with falfhood.

The ftoare of thefe his vntruthes is fo greate, as
that our Doctor affordeth vnto vs many fcoares of this
nature: yet becaufe he would make fhew to mantaine
diuers of them vnder fome pretext, either of much reading, or in wrafting the fence of fuch produced authorities, if I fhould fortify the contrary truth from their
particuler teftimonies, of Scripture, Fathers, Hifto-
ries &c. (being a kynd of proofe, in reguard of the often fuggefted doubtfulnes of the true fenfe directed by
many wheeles of inferences and deductions.

Therefore to the end that I may eu'n ch okingly,
and irreplyably conuince him of fuch notorious mif-
cariage: I laue thought good to fupercrogate with
him in difprouing his faid falfhoodes, I meare in reftrayning my felf precyfely to fuch his lyes, as the contrary thereto is acknowledged for true euen by his own
brethren: and thefe not men obfcure or vulgar, but
the moft eminent and learned proteftantes of Chriften-
dome, and fuch as haue euer bene accompted ftarres of
the greateft magnitude in their euangelicall Spheare:
Neither will I alledge fo many of them as I could, but
for the greater expedition, I will content my felf for
the moft part, with the teftimonies of two or three of
our learnedft aduerfaries.

Now here I would haue the iudiceons reader to obferue that M. Whyte can not reply in anfwear hereto,
that becaufe there are fome other proteftantes that do
mantaine the faid pofitions with him againft his former learned brethren, that therefore fuch his pofitions, are freed from all imputation of vntruth, and confequently

ſequently him ſelf of lying.

This his anſweare is moſt inſufficient: Firſt becauſe
ſome of his vntruthes do reſt, in affirming that not a-
ny one Father, or any one proteſtant, taught ſuch or
ſuch a poynt or doctrine: againſt which generall aſſertion (including all Fathers and prot ſtantes) if I can
produce but any one Father or proteſtant (as indeede
I can for the moſt part, produce many) it is enough to
conuince him of lying. Secondly in that all Maiſter
W. vntruthes, do make head againſt the Catholick
Faith, and ſtrengthen the proteſtantes religion (in
which reſpect they may be preſumed to be the more
wilfull) it cannot therefore with any ſhew of reaſon
be otherwiſe conceaued, that ſuch learned proteſtants
(for the moſt part mantaining againſt the Catholicks
the poynt or concluſion of faith, out of which ſuch aſſertions do ryſe, and therefore are not become parties
againſt M. Whyte therein) would euer defend againſt
the Doctor the contrary aſſertions, much weakning
their owne cauſe thereby, were it not that the euidency of the truth on the Catholick ſide, doth force
them thereunto. And therefore it followeth euen in
reaſon, that the voluntary acknowledgment of any
ſuch one learned proteſtant, ought to ouerbalance &
weigh downe euen ſcoares of others not confeſſing ſo
much: ſo true is the ſaying of Ireneus _li_. 4. _ca_. 14.
Illa eſt vera & ſine contradictione probatio, quæ etiam ab
aduerſariis ipſis, ſigna teſtificationis profert.

But to make this poynt more perſpicuous to the reader by example, our miniſter in one place (which
hereafter ſhall be alledged) anoucheth, that the doctrine of Tranſubſtantiation, was neuer heard of before the Councell of Lateran. (for here he ſpeaketh
not of the definition of that Article, but of the doc-

trine

trine onely) To conuince this as a moſt notorious vntruth , I produce not Catholick authorities (for they
would ſeme to the readers eye ouer partiall) but becauſe all perfect differences are made vpon vnequall
ſtandinges , I inſiſt in dyuers learned proteſtantes (o-
therwyſe our profeſſed enemies) who do not beleue
our Catholick doctrine herein as true : neuertheleſſe
do confeſſe , that ſuch & ſuch Fathers, liuing in the primitiue *Church* (and therefore many ag s before the
foreſaide Councell) did teach the ſaid doctrine of
Tranſubſtantiation . Now here I ſay M . Whyte is not
excuſed from lying , in that he is able to bring forth o-
ther particuler proteſtantes teaching with him the ſaid
innouation of Tranſubſtantiation euen at the ſame tyme
(and not before) in reguard of his former learned
brethren confeſſing the further antiquity thereof, to
the much diſabling of their owne cauſe .

   Now what can our Doctor obiect herein ? not their
ignorance , for they are the moſt accompliſhed proteſtantes for their literature , that euer liued : not their
partiality in the cauſe , for they here ſpeake againſt
them ſelues , and do conſpyre in the fundamentall and
primitiue point of faith therein , with M . Whyte him
ſelf: Onely therefore it is to be ſaid , that theſe proteſtantes thus confeſſing to their owne preiudice , are
more ingenious , vpright , and leſſe impudent in their
wrytinges , and M . Whyte and his compartners , are
of a cauterized and ſeared conſcience, not caring (e-
uen againſt their owne knowledg , by their ſhame-
les maintayning of lyes) to ſuppreſſe Gods truth and
Religion .

   Now this Baſis and groundwork being immouea-
able , and thus firmly laid: let vs proceede to theſe
his vntruthes .

The

*The first vntruth: that Proteſtantes embrace
that kinde of tryall which is by antiquity .*

1 Therefore firſt in his preface to the Reader ,
pag. penul. (thus you ſee the very front of his book
is no leſſe ſubiect to lying, then before , as I haue
ſhewed, it was to corrupting) our miniſter (ſtill for-
geating, that a great ſore in the body, is more tolle-
rable, then a moale in the face) there ſpeaking of the
Fathers of the primitiue tymes, and of their Iudgmēts
in matters of Faith, betwene the proteſtantes & vs,
thus writeth. *We are ſo well aſſured* (meaning of the re-
ſolution of the Fathers) *that we embrace that kind of tryall which is by antiquity, and dayly fynde our aduerſaries
to be gauled thereby .* A moſt vaſt vntruth, and acknowledged to be ſuch euen by the moſt iudiceous proteſtantes . For we fynde, that wheareas M. Iewell with
the lyke hipocriſy . did appeale to the auncient Fathers at *Paules Croſſe*, euen his owne brethren did re-
buke him greatly for thoſe his inconſiderate ſpeaches :
in ſo much that D . Humfrey (the half-arch of the Engliſh Church in his dayes) affirmeth, that to vſe his
owne wordes) *M . Iewell gaue the papiſts therein too* In vita Iuelli.
large a ſcope: that he was iniurious to him ſelfe: and af- printed at Lon
ter a manner ſpoyled him ſelf, and his Church . don. pag. 212.
  To the lyke ende D . Whitaker (but with extraor-
dinary ſcurrility) wryteth that, *The popiſh Religion, is* Cont. Dur.
but a patched couerlet of the Fathers errours ſowed toge- Lib. 6 . pag .
ther . From whence it followeth that D . *Whytaker* 423 .
would be loth inappealably to ſtand to their determi-
nations . Finally Luther him ſelf (the firſt mouer of our
new Goſpels Spheare) ſo farr diſclaymeth from the
Fathers Iudgmentes, as that he thus inſolently tradu- a Tom. 2.
ceth them . a *The Fathers of ſo many ages (* ſpeaking of Wittenberg.
  O   the

Erro 1551.
Lib. de seruo
arbitrio. pag.
434.
pimitiue tymes) *haue bene blynd and moft ignorant in
the Scriptures : they haue erred all their lyfe tyme, & vn-
leffe they were amended before their deathes, they were neither Sainctes nor perteyning to the Church.* Thus Luther.
Here now is euident the vntruth of M. Whyte appealing to the Fathers, fince we fynd that the moft learned members of his owne Church, do reiect them with
all contempt, charging them with flat papiftry, which
they would neuer haue done, if they could haue vfed
any other conuenient euafion.

Be affrayd M. Whyte of Gods iuft reuenge, for
this your mantayning of euill by euill (for thus you
here do, firft by impugning the true faith of Chrift: &
then for your better warranting thereof, in traducing
the auncient and holy Fathers, as enemies to the faid
Faith.

b Seneca,
in Agam.
And remember the fentence, b *Metum auget, qui
fcelere fcelus obruit.*

The fecond vntruth: Againft Traditions.

But to procede to other vntruthes, pag. 2. our
M. Whyte laboureth to proue, that the proteftantes
Church receaueth not neceffarily any one Tradition,
and anfwearably thereto in his firft Table before his
booke, he thus wryteth. *No part of our faith ftandeth
vpon Tradition.*

Now here his owne brethren will charge him with
falfhood. For feing M. Whyte muft and doth acknowledg, that to beleue, that fuch bookes (as the wrytinges of the *four Euangeliftes, the Actes of the Apoftles, the Epiftles of S. Paule &c.*) are the facred word
of god, is a mayne article of both his and our Faith:
The falfhood of his former Affertion is euidently e-
uicted

uicted from the wordes of learned proteſtantes, who teach, that not from our pryuate ſpirit, or ſcripture it ſelf, or conference thereof: but from the tradition and Authority of the Church, ſuch wrytinges are certainly knowne to be the vndoubted word of God, moſt contrary to M. Whyte, pag. 47. who ſaith, that *The Scripture proueth it ſelf to be the very word of god, & receaueth not authoritie from the Church* .

To this end we fynde D. *Whitakar* firſt reiecting the teſtimony of the pryuate ſpirit, to ſay thus. e *Non nego Traditionem eccleſiaſticam eſſe argumentum, quo argui et conuinci poſſit, qui libri Canonici ſunt, qui Canonici non ſunt* . *I do not deny, but that Eccleſiaſticall tradition is an Argument from the which it may be proued which are the Canonicall bookes, and which are not* .

e. Aduerſ. Stapl. pag. 298 .

In lyke ſort M. *Hooker* aſſenteth hereto ſaying, f *In thinges neceſſary, the very cheifeſt is to know, what bookes we are bound to eſteeme holy: which poynt is confeſſed impoſſible for the Scripture it ſelf to teach* . But what the Scripture teacheth not, is by our aduerſaries confeſſion, a mere Tradition. Hookers iudgment in this poynt, is iuſtifyed by Doctor g *Couell* .

f Eccl. Pol. lib. 3. pag. 146 .

g In his def. of Hookers 5. booke. pa. 31

Now if theſe eminent proteſtantes do aſcrybe onely to the Church, the Indgment of diſcerning which is Scripture, and which is not Scripture: then we know from the Authority and Tradition of the Church, & not from the Scripture it ſelf, which is the true & vndoubted word of God, and what bookes are but ſpurious and adulterated, and conſequently M. Whyte lyed moſt groſly in affirming that no part of their faith ſtandes vpon Tradition, thus ranging him ſelf amonge thoſe who (according to the Scripture) *mendaciorum funiculis conantur ſubuertere* . *By the meanes of lyes, endeuour to ouerthrow* .

Heſter. ca. 16.

O 2   *The*

The Third vntruth in proofe of the continuance of the protestantes faith in all ages .

Our minister labouring to enamell and bewtify his deformed faith with the speceous tytle of antiquity & succession, pag. 86. vseth thefe swelling speaches.

Against all papistes whatsoeuer we make it good, that the very faith we now professe, haith successiuely continued in all ages since Christ, & was neuer interrupted so much as one yere, month, or day, and to confesse the contrary were sufficient to prooue vs no part of the Church of god.

Wordes of brasse, but (if he be put to the proofe) no doubt leaden performance. To set downe the Iudgmentes of the learned protestantes touching the interruption of their faith for many seuerall ages since Christes tyme, were laboursom, and withall needeles, since to conuince this bould assertion of fashood, it is sufficient to insist in any one age or tyme. Therefore I will content my self with the authorities of two learned protestãts touchĩg the very time of Luthers first Apostacy and departing from our Church: they graunting that their faith before Luthers reuolt, was not to be found in any man liuing: which they neuer would haue done, if the euidency of the matter did not force them thereto, considering how much such a confession doth enaruate and weaken their cause.

First thẽ we finde euen Luther himself to acknowledg this poynt, who thus wryteth hereof. i *Ego principio causæ meæ &c. In the beginning of this my cause* (speaking of his change of religion) *I had this guift graunted me euen from heauen: that I alone should vndertake so great a matter, and I did conceaue that it should be made good onely by me, neither did I put any confidence in the*

i Epist. ad Arguitinenses.

truft

truß of others. Here we fee that he graunteth him felf
to haue bene alone in this his fuppofed reftauration
of the Gofpell. And hereupon it is, that Luther in
an other place thus vaunteth. k *Chriftum a nobis pri-* k Loc. com.
mo vulgatum audemus gloriari. We dare glory, that claff. 4. p.
Chrift was firft made knowne by vs. ſI.

In lyke fort *M. Iewell* (no meane Rabbi in our 1 In the Apo-
Englifh Sinagoge) faith, l. that *the truth was vnknowne* logy of the
at that tyme and vnheard of, when Martin Luther, and Church of En-
Vldrick Zuinglius, firft came vnto the knowledg and prea- glande. par.
ching of the Gofpell. 4. ca. 4.

The 4. *Vntruth.*

In proofe of the vnity of faith & doſtrine amongſt
proteſtantes.

Pag 138. For the more iuftifying of the proteftantes doſtrine, he thus faith of the booke entituled
The Harmony of confeſſions. The Harmony of confeſſi-
ons wherein the particuler Churches fet downe and name
the articles of their faith, if the Iefuite can ſhew to iarr
in Dogmaticall poyntes of faith: I am content you beleue
him in all the reſt. Here the reader haith a bould affertion, which as you fee the more eafely to winne a
credulous eare, is fteeped in mufke: but I feare M.
Doſtor the note *Diapafon*, which implieth an abfolute
and generall concord, and which is fo much commended by all the moſt fkilfull in that fcience, will here be
wanting. And therefore for the more exaſt difquifition of that poynt, we will refer our felues to that very booke called the *Harmony of confeſſions*, englifhed &
printed at Cambridg by *Thomas Thomaſ.* 1586. where
(for the greater expedition) I will touch but fome

few ftringes thereof onely, to heare how they found.

First then we fynde this harmony to teach, that *finnes are eftfons punifhed euen in this lyfe*, as *Dauids*, *Manaffes*, and *the punifhments may be mitigated by good woorkes*. pag. 229. See here how fully it acknowledgeth the abterfiue nature of penance and fatiffaction? *Againe, this obedience towardes the Law, is a kind of Iuftice* (marke you this difcord) *and deferueth rewarde*. pag. 266. *Like as the preaching of penance is generall, euen fo the promife of grace is generall &c. Here needeth no difputation of Predeftination, or fuch like, for the promife is generall*. pag. 268. & 269.

As touching priuate Confeffion &c. we affirme, that the ceremony of pryuate abfolution is to be retayned in the Church, and we do conftantly retayne it. pag. 231.

In lyke fort it faith, that *the Bifhops haue inrifdiction to forgeue finnes.* pag. 366.

Finally not to reft vpon euery perticuler ftop thereof, we thus fynde there, *We do not fpeake of the Church as if we fhould fpeake of Platoes Idea, but of fuch a Church as may be feene and heard &c. The eternall Father will haue his Sonne to be heard amonge all mankinde.* pag. 326. A note which muft needes found moft harfhe with our inuifibiliftes. Now I referr the matter to M. Whyte him felf, wheth r there be in thefe poyntes any concordance betwene the harmony of Confeffions, & the doctryne of our Erglifh proteftantes, of the *Hugonots* in France, and the *Caluenistes* in Germany : fo affured I was that a diligent eare would eafely obferue many iarring ftringes in the Ccefort.

The 5. Vntruth.

In proofe of the immutability of the prefent Erglifh
              Religion

Rehgion.

Page 138. He particulerly infifteth in his fuppofed conftancy of religion here in England, and thus
wryteth. *If the Iefuite can fhew the Church of England
fince papiftry was firft abolifhed, to haue altered one article of the prefent faith now profeffed, I am content &c.*

For the difproofe of this falfhood, we will conuince the fame by difcouering the manifould & weightieft alterations of our publick Englifh Lyturgy, fince
the firft entrance of proteftancy into England.

And firft it is euident that the Lyturgy of the Church
of England in King Edwardes tyme, (at which tyme
there was an euidcnt bringing in of proteftancy) pu-
blifhed by *Cranmer*, *Peter Martir*, & *Bucer*: and approued by the authority of the Parleament, kept almoft all the prayrs and ceremonies of the Maffe (the
reall prefence onely reiected) with croffing of both
their Sacramentes, and the accuftomed rites of Baptifme, as a formall confecration of the water of Baptifme with the figne of the Croffe, the vfing of Chrifme
and the annoynting of the child.

Againe, it retayned prayer for the dead, and the
offering of our prayers by the interceffion of Angels.

But when Quene Elizabeth came to reigne, the faid
Lyturgy was fo altered, as that it is needles to refte
long in the difcouery thereof: for it tooke away prayer for the dead, and prayer to Angels, befides moft
of the former Ceremonies vfed in *King* Edwards time.
In lyke fort in the Communion booke of K. Edward
we fynde confirmed, baptifme by lay perfons in tyme
of neceffity, and grace geuen in that Sacrament, the
Confirmation of children, and ftrength gei en thereby, the Preift bleffing the Bryde grome and the bryde
euen with the figne of the Croffe. The Preiftes ab-

O 4   folution

solution of the sick penitent by these wordes. *By the authority committed to me, I absolue thee of all thy sinnes.* The speciall confession of the sick penitent, and finally the annoynting of the sick. Of all which particulers, see the Communion booke of K. Edward printed in fol. by Edward whitchurch *cum priuilegio ad imprimendum solum.* An. 1549. All which (dyuers of them including poyntes of faith and doctrine) are now vtterly left out in the Communion booke published in Q. Elizabeths tyme: In so much as Parker an english protestāt, thus writeth thereof. m *The day starr was not risen so high in their dayes, when as yet Q. Elizabeth reformed the defects of K. Edwardes Communiō booke. Answearably hereto wryteth Cartwright saying.* n *The Church of England changed the booke of Common prayer twyce or thryce, after it had receaued the knowledg of the Gospell.* Thus *Cartwright* in his 2. Reply, par. 1. pa. 41. who in that very booke laboureth yet for a fourth change. And thus is M. Whyte not affrayd to suggest to the world euen in printe (fonde man that could not be idle enough in pryuate talke) such vnwarrantable vntruthes: which course of his, if it proceded from his owne inaduertency and ouersight as not hauing seene the Common prayer booke of K. Edward declaring the contrary, then were it more pardonable, but this I think him self, out of his pryde and shew of much reading, will not acknowledg, & therefore we may probably ascribe it to his mere wilfull forgery, who to defend his owne heterogeneous and mongerell faith (which mantayneth at different tymes different doctrines) dare aduenture to broach falshoodes though neuer so eminent. But let him remember that by so doing, he (with disauantage to his cause) vainly spendeth his labour, for *Qui nititur mendaciis.*

m Against Simbolizing. par. 2. ca. 5.

dacius hic pascit ventos. Who trusteth to lyes, feedeth the wyndes.

The 6. Vntruth.

In proofe of the Romane Churches mutability in matters of Faith.

Page 150, he confidently auerreth, that *The Church of Rome is varied from her self in matters of Faith, since she began to be the seate of Antichrist*: Thus charging our Church with great mutability of beleefe, as before he laboured to grace and adorne his owne Sinagouge with all speceous constancy in the same.

Now for the better ouerthrowing of this vntruth, it is necessary to recurr to those first supposed tymes of Antichristes being, perusing the doctrine then taught, to see if the Church of Rome haith made at this day any change thereof in any matters of Faith, for euen so far doth the minister stretch out his lye.

First then the most receaued opinion of the protestantes touching Antichrist his coming (for they are most various amonge them selues therein) is, that S. Gregory the great, was the first Antichrist. Now to obsetue what his Religion was, will be made euident by taking vew of the Religion which S. Augustine (being a Monke of the Church of Rome, and sent by this S. Gregory) did here plant in England.

For the tryall of which poynt, I will first produce D. Humfrey, who thus writeth hereof. n *In Ecclesiam verò &c. What did Gregory & Augustine bring into the Church? &c. A burden of Ceremonies &c. They brought in the Pall for the Archbishop in celebrating of Masse, and purgatory &c. They brought in the oblation of the healthfull Hoast, and prayer for the deade &c.*

n Iesuit. par. 2. rat. 5. p. 5. & 627.

Q   *Relickes*

Relickes &c. Transubstantiation &c. A new consecrati-
on of Churches &c. From all the which, what other thing
is gathered, then that Indulgences, Monachisme, the Pa-
pacy, and all the rest, confusion of the Popes superstition,
was then erected: all which thinges, Augustine the greate
Monk, and taught by Gregory a Monk, brought to vs
English men. Thus farr D . Humfrey.

In lyke sort the *Triumuiri* of *Magdeburg* (whose
censuring pennes haue controuled more ages, then e-
uer the Romanes *Triumuiri* gouerned Prouinces) I
meane the 3 Century wryters in the *Index*, or Alphabeticall Table of the 6. Century, after the first Edition thereof at the word *Gregory*, do relate the particuler doctrine of S . *Gregory*, as popish and erroneous :
For thus they here note with particuler references to
the places of S . *Gregories* writinges prouing the same
Eiusdem error &c . The same (Gregories) errour of good
workes , of Confession, of Wedlock, of the Inuocation of
Sainctes, of hell, of Iustification, of Free will, of purga-
tory , of Penance , of Satisfaction .

Now this former doctrine contayning the cheife
pointes wherein we differ from the sectaries of this
tyme, being acknowledged to be the Faith of Gregory, who is supposed to be the first Antichrist, &
most articulatly at this day beleued of all Romane Catholickes : I would aske M . Whyte with what forhead
he can auouch his former wordes, to wit, that the
Church of Rome is varied from her selfin matters of faith,
since she began to be the seate of Antichrist . But all this
ryseth from an inward repugning of the Min. against
our Church, in regard of the vnchangeable certainty
and constancy of faith professed by her : whereas the
want thereof in our aduersaries religion is most no -
torious, as appeareth not onely from their seuerall
confessions

confeſſions, one euer impugning an other; but alſo from their different tranſlations of their Bybles, ſtill made to ſort to the faith of their laſt Edition; ſo as in reſpect of their wonderfull mutability, and variance among them ſelues, whereby indeede they indignify and wrong the nature of true faith; we haue reaſon to demaund of any of the profeſſors, of what thinking he is, rather then of what faith.

The 7. *Vntruth*.

In proofe of the proteſtantes concord in matters of Religion.

Page. 139. To proue that proteſtantes haue true vnity, he ſheweth, that the diuiſions among them, are either *falſly layd to their charge through ignorance & fury of their enemies &c. or els they are not iars of the Church, but the defectes of ſome few therein, whereof the Church is not guilty, or laſtly, not diſſertions in thinges of faith, but ſtryfe about Ceremonies &c*. Thus doth the D. Apologize for his diſcording brethren.
Now to conuince this, the Reader ſhall heare what ſome of their owne brethren do acknowledge therein.
Firſt then Doctor *Willet*, rehearſing ſeuerall opinions of *Hooker* and D. *Couell*, of which *Willet* preſuming that they can not ſtand with true proteſtancy thus wryteth. n *From this fountaine haue ſprong forth theſe and ſuch other whirle-pointes, and bubles of new doctryne, as that Chriſt is not originally God. That Scriptures are not meanes concerning God, of all that profitably we know &c. That mannes will is apt naturally without Grace, to take any perticuler obiect whatſoeuer preſen-*

n Willet in his medit. vpon the. 122. pſ.

Q 2   *ted*

ted vnto it , and so consequently beleue, that mennes na-
turall workes , or to do that which nature telleth vs (with-
out grace) must needes be acceptable to God &c . Thus
haue some bene bould to teach and wryte, as some Scisma-
tikes (meaning the puritanes *) haue disturbed the peace*
of the Church , one way , in externall matters concerning
discipline : these haue troubled the Church an other way, in
opposing themselues by new quirkes and deuyces to the sound-
nes of doctrine amongst protestantes . But if the position here ment be against the soundnes of doctrine, then
can it not be restrained onely to ceremonies.

      Doctor Whitaker speaking of the contentions a -
mong the protestantes , saith . o *Nostra contentiones*

o
de Eccl. con.
Bellar. contr.
2 . q . 5 . pa.
327.

(si quæ sint) sunt pia , et modesta , et propter fidem &
religionem &c . Our contentions (if there be any) are pi-
ous , and modest , and for religion . From which wordes
it followeth , that they are not personall , or onely a-
bout ceremonies, as M . Whyte pretendeth .

      Now if we further take a vew of the intemperate

p Con. Loua.
Thes. 27 . to.
2 . Wittemb .
fol 503.

speaches geuen by Luther against the Zuinglians, it
may satisfy any one , that the differences were not in
small points of gouernment or ceremonies. Thus the
Luther speaketh. p *We censure in earnest the Zningli-*

q
To . 7 . Wit-
temb . fo .381
& 382.

ans , & all the Sacramentaries, for heritykes , and aliena-
ted from the Church of God, And in an other place .
q *Cursed be the Charity and concord of Sacramentaries*
for euer and euer, to all eternity . As also in the 3 . place.

r de Cæna do.
Tom. 2. Ger.
fol. 174 .

r *I hauing now one of my feete in the graue , will carry*
this testimony and glory to the tribunall of God, that I will
with all my heart condemne aud eschew Carolostadius, Zuin-
glius , Oecolampadius, and their schollers , nor will haue
with any of them familiarity , either by letters or writinges.
&c . And thus farr of this point . From all which may
be inferred, that dissentions among the protestantes
                         are not

are not merely perfonall, or but pointes adiaphorous,
indifferent, being as it were but peccant humors, and
not true or formed difeafes in their church, but they
do concerne moft profound doubtes of their religion,
fince otherwaies they would neuer anathematize, or
condemne one an other with fuch acerbity of wordes.
Which irreuocable contentions among the proteftāts,
(being moft preiudiceous to them felues) is aduanta-
geous to vs, for *bellum hæreticorum , eft pax Ecclefiæ .*
The warr of heritykes, is the peace of Gods Church,
none otherwife then the reciprocall ftryfe and reluc-
tation of the 4. humors, kepes the whole body in a pea-
ceable & healthfull ftate.

The 8 . Vntruth .

Againft the vnity of Catholickes in matters of Faith .

Page. 153. The Doctor feing his owne finagogue
torne in fonder with diuifions and contentions (howfoeuer he flubered the matter ouer before with his
faire pretence of concord) and well knowing how
preiudiciall the want of vnity is to the true Religion
of Chrift. f For *God is not a God of diffention , but of* f 1. Cor. 15.
peace ; doth maliceoufly endeuour, to caft the lyke afperfion vpon our Catholick Church in thefe wordes.
They which know Rome and papiftry , are fufficiently fatif-
fyed in this matter, to wit, that the papiftes liue not in
that vnity which is pretended . & thē p. 156. he telleth
of what kynd thefe difagreementes are faying. *The*
contentions of our aduerfaries touch the faith . And pag.
159, he concludeth in thefe wordes. *Thus are the pa-*
piftes denyded about the principall articles of their faith .

R   Vpon

Vpon which ſubieƈt, he then after with much earneſtnes, vainely and idly ſpendeth dyuers leaues, bringing therein euen *obtorto collo*, whatſoeuer he haith read or heard touching the leaſt diſagreemẽnt among the Catholickes, which labour of his, will ſerue no doubt, to a iudiceous eye, lyke to the ſpyders web, painfully wrought, but to no purpoſe.

Wherefore I will breeſly make plaine how free we are from all breach of faith euen by the acknowledgment of the proteſtantes them ſelues. Firſt then D. Whitaker wounding him ſelf and his cauſe by his confeſſion, ſaith. t *Neſtræ contentiones (ſi quæ ſint) ſunt pia, et modeſtæ, propter fidem, & propter religionem &c. Contentiones papiſtarum ſunt friuolæ & futiles, de figmentis et commentis ſui cerebri. Our contentions (if there be any) are godly and modeſt, touching faith and religion: wheras the contentions of the papiſtes, are but tryſlinge, concerning the fiƈtions of their owne brayne.* Thus graunting the diſſentions of the proteſtantes more nearly to concerne faith and religion, then the diſſentions among the Catholickes do.

Doƈtor Fulke ſaith of our vnity in this ſort. v *As for the conſent of the popiſh Church, it proueth nothing but that the deuill then had all thinges at his will and might ſleepe;* So acknowledging our vnity truly; but falſly and abſurdly aſcrybing it to the deuill who is the deſigned enemy to vnity.

To be ſhort *Duditius* a famous proteſtant and highly reſpeƈted by Beza, doth no leſſe acknowledg the vnity of our Catholick Church, for thus doth Beza u relate *Duditius* his woordes. *Etſi (inquis) multa eáq̃ horrenda propugnantur in Romana Eccleſia &c. Although many dreadfull thinges are defended in the Romane Church, which are buylded vpon a weake and rotten foundation, not*
withſtanding

t de Eccl.
cont. Bell.
contro. 2. q.
5. p 227.

v Againſte
Heſk. Sand.
&c. 295.

u Beza in Ep.
theol. ad Andræam Dudit.
Ep. 1. pa. 13

withstanding that Church is not deuyded with many dissentions: for it haith the plausible shew of reuerent Antiquity, ordinary snccession, and perpetuall consent &c.

Thus *Duditius* related by Beza, and not impugned herein by him.

Now here we are to note, that the testimonies of these and other protestantes (here omitted) acknowledging our vnity and consent, must necessarily be vnderstoode touching vnity in the misteries, and other fundamentall poyntes of our Religion, which is the thing onely that we are here to mantaine, since if vnity alone about pointes of indifferency, or of thinges not defyned should be ment by them, then in reguard of many such disputable questions yet among the schole men; the former iudgmentes of our aduersaries should be false and not iustifiable. And thus much for this poynt; from whence the Doctor may learne that among those which are true Catholickes, vnity of doctrine is most religiously obserued, since such not ouer partially resting in their owne natiue iudgmentes, to what way soeu'r they be inclyning, do most diligently follow, the supreme resolution & current of the Church: in part resembling herein the inferiour orbes which with greater speede, sedulity, and expedition, performe the reuolutions of the highest Spheare wherunto they are subiect: then they do accomplish their owne naturall & perticuler motions.

The 9. Vntruth.

Againstt the Popes Primacy.

Page 185. The Doctor wryteth in his digression thus. *The Primitiue Church did not acknowledg the Popes*

Primacy.

Primacy. Here I see that M : Whyte will euer be M. Whyte, I meane that he will euer be lyke to him self, first in coyning, and after mantayning most impudent vntruthes.

Now as touching the discouery of this his false position, since to go through all the centuries of the primitiue Church, would be needlesly laboursome : I think it good to restraine my self onely to the fourth century or age after Christ, an age wherein Constantine the first Christian Emprour liued, and which for that respect not vndeseruedly seemes to be most entertayned and approued by the graue iudgment of the Kinges Maiesty. w

w As appea-reth out of his Maiesties wordes touching the same, in the summe of the conference before his Maiesty. pag. 97

Now for the greater clearing of this poynt, it will be needefull to obserue, what authority the Popes did exercyse, by the acknowledgment of our learned aduersaries, since the authority and soueraignty ouer all other Churches, and Prelates, is that which doth, as it were, organize and perfect the Popes Primacy.

Now then answearable hereto *Cartwright* wryteth, that x *Iulius Bishop of Rome at the Councell of Antioch, ouerreached, in clayming the hearing of causes that did not appertaine vnto him.* Now this *Iulius* liued in the fourth age. Againe the said *Cartwright* saith of S. *Damasus* who was Pope in this age. y *that he spake in the dragons voyce, when he shameth not to wryte, that the Bishop of Romes sentence, Was aboue all other, to be attended for in a Synode.* So far was this sectaries censure different from the iudgment of S. Ierome, deliuered of the same Pope in these wordes z *Ego nullam primum nisi Christum sequens beatitudini tuæ, id est Cathedræ Petri communione consocior : super illam Petram Ecclesiam ædificatam scio, quicunǫ extra hanc domum Agnum commederit, prophanus est &c. quicunǫ tecum*

x Reply 2. part. 1 p. 501

y Reply part. 1. p. 502.

z Ep. 57. ad Damasum.

P

tecum non colligit , ſpargit ,

In lyke ſort touching appeales to Rome , (an eſſentiall poynt of Eccleſiaſticall Supremacy) we finde
that the Centuriſts a do acknowledg , that *Theodo-* a Cent . 5.
ret a Greeke Father , and one of this fourth age , being Col . 1013 .
depoſed by the Councell of *Epheſus* , *did accordingly
make his appeale to Pope Leo* , and thereupon was by
him *reſtored to his Biſhoprick* . And to conclude , the
Centuriſtes do no leſſe acknowledg , that *Chriſoſtom*
b did appeale to Innocentius , who decreed *Theophilus* b Cent . 5.
Chriſoſtomes enemy , to be depoſed & excommunica- Col . 663 .
ted .

Thus we fynd how diſſonant this our miniſters aſſertion touching the Primacy is , to the practiſe of
the Primitiue Church , euen in the iudgment of thoſe
who are deſigned enemies to the ſaid Primacy , as
might well be exemplifyed , throughout all the Cen -
turiſtes , and ages of thoſe tymes , ſeing all reuerent
antiquity , (no leſſe then the Catholickes of theſe
dayes) was fully perſwaded , that S . Peter and his
ſucceſſors , were euer to be accompted the viſible Ba -
ſeis , or foundations of gods Church : and all other
Biſhops but Column s : And as this foundation immediatly ſupportes theſe pillers , ſo theſe pillers the
reſt of this ſpirituall edifice and ſtructure .

The 10 . *Vntruth* .

*That Gregory the great , deteſted the Popes Pri-
macy .*

Page 193 . M . Whyte deſcendeth to the example
of S . Gregory the great , and firſt Pope of that name ,
in whoſe wryting he hopeth to fynd great ſttrength ,
R for the

for the impugning of the Popes foueraignty: and a-
mong other thinges the D. faith. *Gregory had no fuch
iurifdiction as now the Pope vfurpeth, but detefted it' not
only in Iohn of Conftantinople, but alfo in him felf. &c.*
Where now the Reader may be inftructed, that the
reafon why this Gregory is by fome fuppofed to dif-
auow the doctrine of the primacy, is in that he reiecteth in *Iohn of Conftantinople*, the title of vniuerfall
Bifhop as facrilegious, which his faying was groun-
ded onely in taking the name of vniuerfall Bifhop, to
exclude the true being of all other Bifhops, as it is

c de Eccl.
lib 2. ca. 10.

confeffed by *Andreas Brictius*. c

But now that S. Gregory did both claime and practife the Primacy, is acknowledged by our aduerfaries,

d Cent. 6.
Col. 425.

for the *Centuriftes* write d of him that he faid. *The
Romane Sea appoynteth her watch ouer the whole world,*
and that he taught that *the Apoftolick Sea, is the head
of all Churches : that Conftantinople it felf is fubiect to the
Apoftolick Sea .* Furthermore S. Gregory is charged

e Ibidem.

by the *Centuriftes*, e *that he chalenged to him felf power
to commaund Archbifhops : To ordaine or depofe Bifhops

f Col. 427.

at his pleafure : that f he tooke vpon him right to cyte
Archbifhops to declare their caufe before him when they
were accufed :* That actually Gregory did vndertake

g Col. 427

to excommunicate g fuch and fuch Bifhops : That *in

h Col. 428.

their Prouinces h he placed his Legates, to know and determine the caufes of fuch as appealed to Rome .*

Finally, to omitt many other poyntes recorded by

i Ibidem.

them, that *i he vfurped power of appointing Synodes in
their prouinces .*

Here now I referr this point to the indifferent Reader, whether he wil beleue M. Whyte denying to
the benefyte of his caufe, the Primacy of S. Gregory,
or the Centuriftes being diuers learned proteftantes,

all

all confessing the same, though to their owne preiudice.

The 11, *Vntruth.*

*In proofe that Catholickes are more viceous then
protestantes,*

Page 209. For the extenuating and lesning of the
sinfull liues of the protestants, the Doctor much ex-
tolleth their imputatiue, and supposed vertues, and as
much depresseth the liues of all Catholickes in generall, and thus he entitleth that leafe, *The protestants
people as holy as the papistes.* In lyke sort, from page
213. to 218. he spendeth him self in gathering together whatsoeuer Catholick writers haue spoken touching the liues of some loose liuers, thus scornfully
entytling the leaues, *The holines of the Church of Rome
deciphered:* most of which sayinges being found in ser-
mons, or exhortations, and in heate of amplification,
deliuered generally as the custome is, and this without any reference or comparison to the lyues of the
protestantes, can not iustly be extended to all Catholickes, nomore then the reprehensions of the Prophets
in the ould testament spoken without any restraint,
could be truly applyed to all the Iewes.
Wherefore for the further vpbrayding of this our ministers lye which is wouen vpon the threede of malice, and for the more punctuall conuincing him of
falshood, I will proue from the Protestantes owne confessions, that the lyues of Catholickes, are generally
more vertuous, then those of the protestantes (in
which kind of proofe, from the lyke acknowledgment of vs Catholickes in fauour of the protestantes,

the D. haith not brought so much as one lyne.

To this purpose then is not Luther forced thus to write, to the eternall shame of his owne religion? k _Before when we were seduced by the Pope, euery man did willingly follow good woorkes: and now euery man neither saith nor knoweth any thing, but how to get all to him self by exactions, pillage: theft, and vsury, &c._

In lyke sort he confesseth more saying thus. l _The world groweth daily worse, men are more reuengfull, contentious, licenceous, then euer they were before in the papacy._ And yet Luther. m _It is a wonderfull thing, & full of scandall, that from the tyme in which the pure doctrine of the Gospell was first recalled to light: the worlde should daily grow worse._ See here the acknowledged fruites of his owne Gospell. In lyke manner _Iacobus Andreas_ a very learned protestaut, thus confesseth of his owne religion. n _Mandat serió Deus in verbo suo, &c._ God earnestly commaundeth in his word, and exacteth of Christians, _seriam et Christianam disciplinam,_ a serious and Christian discipline: but these thinges are accompted by vs, _nouus papatus, nouúsq̃ Monachismus,_ a new papacy, and a new Monachisme: for thus they dispute. _Didicimus modò per solam fidem in Christum saluari &c._ We haue now learned to be saued in Christ onely by faith, &c. wherefore suffer vs to omitt all such workes of disciplyne, seing that by other meanes we may be saued by Christ. And that the whole world may not acknowledg these to be papistes nor to trust in their good workes: they do not exercyse any one of the said good workes, for in steed of fasting, they spend both day and night in drinking &c. their praying is turned into swearing &c.

So this learned protestant, who also termeth this kynd of lyfe the _Euangelicall instruction,_ thus making protestancy a good disposition to draw on all wickednesse.

k Dom. 26.
post Trin.

l In Postilla
super Euang.
Domin. 1.
Aduen.

m In sermon.
couiuialibus.
Ger. fol. 55.

n Conc. 4. in
c. 21. Luc.

neſſe: Where you ſee that the goſpellers (euen in this mans iudgment being a goſpeller him ſelf) are ſo geuen ouer to licenceouſnes of manners, as they may be ſaid to hold it onely a ſinne not to ſinne, and a vertue, to abandon all vertue; ſince they make their faith & Religion (contrary to which they be bound not to do) to be the foundation or ſanctuary of their prophane and heathniſh comportment.

But now ſeeing that by laying contraries together, the one often receaueth much force from the other in the apprehenſion of our iudgment; let vs a litle enter more perticulerly into the courſes of ſuch our miniſters as from whom we are to expect the greateſt ſatiſfaction in this poynte, that ſo in an euen libration of the matter, the Reader may reſt more fully ſatiſfyed, and M. Whyte more clearly and irrepliably conuinced of his former vntruth.

Forbearing therefore at this tyme all other teſtimonies, I will content my ſelf onely with the example of Zuinglius and other miniſters confederated with him in *Heluetia*, who preaching our new euangelicall doctrine to that common wealth: exhibited certaine petitions to the ſtate, the tenour whereof, is here euen literally taken from Zuinglius, and the other miniſters owne writinges, bearing this tytle. *Pietate & prudentia inſigni Heluetiorum Reipub. Huldericus Zuinglius, alitḡ, Euangelicæ doctrinæ miniſtri, gratiam & pacem a Deo.* Now we fynd in this former booke, that they thus firſt petitioned.   *Hoc vero ſummis præcibus contendimns &c. We earneſtly requeſt that the vſe of mariage be not denyed vnto vs, who feeling the infirmity of the fleſh, perceaue that the loue of chaſtity is not geuen to vs by god: For if We conſider the wordes of the Apoſtle, we ſhall fynd with him none other cauſe of mariage, (marke*

o Tom. 1. fol. 115

what a spirituall scholia these illuminated brethren do geue) *then to satiffy the lustfull desires of the flesh , which to burne in vs , we may not deny , seing that by meanes thereof , we are made infamous before the Congregations .*

Would any man beleue this , were it not that their own certaine wrytings are yet extant to vpbraide them withall? And in an other place they thus renew their petition. p *Non carnis libidine , for the loue , not of lust , but of chastity , lest that the soules committed to our charg by example of our sensuality , should be any longer offended.* Thus they euen confesse , that till this tyme , their former licence ous lyfe , had much scandalized their folowers , And further yet. q *Quaré cum carnis nostra infirmitatem nobis non semel (proh dolor) &c . Wherefore seing we haue made tryall , that the infirmity and weaknes of our flesh , haith bene (o the greife) the cause of our often falling &c .* The same Zuinglius with other 8 ministers , in their Epistle to the Bishop of Constance , subscrybed with their owne handes to the lyke purpose , thus wryteth. r *Hitherto we haue tryed , that the guift of chastity haith bene denyed vs .* And yet further , s *Arsimus (proh dolor) tantoperé , vt multa indecoré gesserimus . We haue burned (o the shame) so greatly , that many thinges we haue committed very vnsemely .*

And for the clausure of all , they thus salue the matter. s *Non vsq̃ , adeò inciuilibus moribus sumus &c .* To speake truly . *we are not otherwise of such vnciuill conuersation , that we should be euill spoken of among the people committed to our charge , for any wickednesse , Hoc vno excepto , this one point excepted .*

Here you haue the wordes of our holy and spiritualized sectmaisters , who you may well perceaue insisted further touching the same poynt , with the Heluetians

p lb . fo . 119

q Ibidem

r Zuinglius . Tom 1 . fol 121 .

s Ibid . fol . 122 .

s lb . fol . 123

uetians and the former Biſhop, in or the lyke dialect &
phraſe of expoſtulation.

Since according to the doctrine of our reuerend father
Luther, t *(which we are bound both to teach and prac-* t Lutheru⸗ in
tiſe) N*othing is more ſweete and louing vpon the earth,* Prouerb. 31.
then is the loue of a woman: Alas why ſhould we, who
haue of late reuealed the goſpell of Chriſt heretofore ſo
longe eclipſed, be recompenſed therefore with the want of
that moſt delightfull and naturall comfort of a woman, be-
ing forced to imitate the ſuperſtitious papiſt in embracing a
votary and barren lyfe. Or why ſhould the Heluetian ſtate
ſo ſeuerely exact at our handes, that we who onely preach
vncorruptedly the Chriſtian faith, ſhould onely be depryued
herein of our Chriſtian liberty. Heu quanta patimur.
Libidenous and goatiſh miniſters, whoſe very penn s
ſpumant venerem, and with whom euen to meditate of
a woman, is the center of your moſt ſerious thoughts:
well may you vſe your int.riections of *proh dolor, proh*
pudor. o greiſe, o ſhame, as the burden to your ſen-
ſuall and laſciuious wrytinges. For what can be a greater ſhame and greif vnto you (if you be ſenſible of either) then you who venditate your ſelues, for the re-
ſtorers of the goſpell ſo long hidden, to be (to the diſ-
edifying of your owne followers) thus wholly abſorpt
in ſuch luſtfull and fleſhly cogitations. But we par-
don you, for we know v *quod natum eſt ex carne ca-* v Io. ca. 3.
ro eſt: So great, each man ſees, is the diſparity betwene our euangelicall miniſters (who enioying the
primitias of the ſpirit, were in reaſon obliged to warrant it, with greater effects and frutes of vertue) and
the confeſſed better lyues, euen of ſeculer Catholicks.
And ſo lewdly and lowdly did M. Whyte lye in who
there is much Zuinglius) when he affirmed that the proteſtantes were as holy as the papiſtes. But I feare that
2 S through

through my earneftnes in difplaying of the minifters vanity, I haue bene ouer long in this poynt, therfore I will defcend to the next vntruth.

The 12. *Vntruth.*

Againft auriculer Confeffion.

Page 227. difcourfing of auriculer Confeffió, he faith, that *the Primitiue Church knew it not.*

For the difcouery of this falfhood, we fynd, that the Centuriftes do confeffe, w that in the *tymes of Ciprian and Tertulian, priuate Confeffion was vfed, euen of thoughtes, and leffer finnes* : And which is more, they acknowledge, x that it was *then Commaunded, and thought neceffary,* And D. *Whytaker* writeth y that *not onely Ciprian, but almoft all of the moft holy Fathers of that tyme, were in errour touching Confeffion, and Satiffaction.*

w Cen. 3. c. 6. Col. 27.

x Ibid.

y con. Camp. rat. 5. pag. 78.

Thus we fee how little bloud was in M. Whyte his cheekes, when he was not afhamed to fet downe this former bould affertion, touching the doctrine of Confeffion. But indeede it feemeth that our minifter accompteth it onely a fhame, to feele in him felf any touch of fhame, fo far is he of (in likelyhood) from all hope of future amendement, feeing on the contrary fyde, that faying (for the moft part) is true, z *Erubuit, falua res eft.*

z Terent. in Adelh.

The 13. *Vntruth.*

Againft Fafting.

Page. 224. Our delicate minifter as a profeffed e-nemy to all aufterity of lyfe, writeth thus againft faf-ting. *All antiquity can witnes, that in the primitiue Church, Fafting was held an indifferent thing, & euery man was left to his owne mind therein.* This falfhood is made difcouerable by thefe acknowledgmentes following.

And firft it is fo certaine that *Ærius* was condem-ned by *Epiphanius, hær.* 76. and by S. Anguftine, *hær.* 53. for taking away all fet dayes of fafting, as that D. Fulke thus wryteth of this point. a *I will not diffemble that which you think the greateft matter : Aerius taught that fafting dayes are not to be obferued.*

The fame condemnation of *Aerius* by the former Fa-thers, is acknowledged by doctor Whytaker, b By Pantaleon, c and Ofiander. d But if *Aerius* was condemned by the former auncient Fathers for an he-ritike, for denying certaine prefcribed tymes of faf-ting; it inauoydably followeth, that fafting was not houlden as a thing indifferent in the primitiue Church.

This lye will appeare more euident, if we inftance it in the faft of Lent, which faft was fo farr from be-ing accompted arbitrary, or a thing indifferent, in the primitiue Church, as that Cartwright reproueth S.-Ambrofe for faying. e *It is finne, not to faft in Lent.*

Thus you fee how familierly this minifters pen drops lye after lye, and fuch as the contrary affertion is man-tayned for true, euen by the moft eminent protef-tantes.

The 14. *Vntruth.*

In proofe that Montanus the herityke, was the firft that brought in the lawes of Fafting.

T   Page

a In his anfwer to a counter-fait Catholick p. 45.

b Con. Dur. lib. 9. p. 830

c In Chrono-graphia. p. 28.

d Epitom. Cent. 4. pag. 434.

e Cartwright in Whitgiftes defence.

Page 224. Our Doctor in further difgrace of fafting thus writeth . *Montanus a condemned herityke, was the firft that euer brought in the lawes of Fafting, from whom the Papiftes haue borowed them .* The wilfull mifapplication of which, is fo forced and racked, that no inferiour a proteftant then Hooker him felf, confeffeth ingenioufly in thefe wordes, that *e the Montaniftes were condemned for bringing in fundry vnacoftomed dayes of fafting, continued their faftes a great deale longer, & made them more rigorous &c .* Whereupon Tertulian mantayning Montanus, wrote a booke of the new faft . But what is this to vs Catholickes, for we fee that the errour of Montanus confifted formally, not in abfolutly bringing in of fafting, but in varying from the former practifed faftes of the whole Church.

e Eccl. Pol. lib. 5. Sect. 72. p 29 .

Anfwearably hereunto the proteftant wryter of *Quærimonia Ecclefiæ,* reiecteth the former idle affertion in thefe wordes. *Eufebium (inquunt) Montanum primas de ieiuniis tuliffe leges &c . They fay that Eufebius did vndoubtedly teach, that Montanus firft brougt in the lawes of fafting, but they are fowly deceaued in this as in fome other pointes: for Montanus abrogating the fafts of the Church, brought in a new kind of fafting.*

pag 110 .

Thus we fee by the former affertions, that M . Whyte like a good felow, and one that meanes to enioy his Chriftian liberty, can not well relifh the vnfauery doctrine of fafting, as in fome pages hereafter we fhall fynd that in lyke fort he reiecteth all voluntary chaftity : which two pointes (as before I noted) do entertaine the one the other : for who knoweth not that Epicurifme is the oyle which norifheth the flame of luft .

The 15 *Vntruth.*

In proofe that they make not god the author of finne.

Page 263. M. Whyte being defireous that his religion fhould decline all contumelious reproach, and
ftaine, touching the author of finne, thus wryteth.
The doctrine of the proteftantes, doth not make God the
author of finne, nor inferreth any abfolute neceffity, con-
ftrayning vs that we can not do otherwife then we doe.

That the indifferent Reader may the better difcouer
whether thefe his wordes be falfe or true, I will only fet downe the fentences of the cheifeft proteftants,
and withall will deliuer the iudgmentes of other proteftantes, againft the former defending of the faid fentences.

Zuinglius faith, that g *God moueth the theefe to*
kill. And that *the theefe killeth god procuring him.* And
that *the theefe is inforced to finne.* Thus in the heritykes iudgment, God (who in euery leafe of his facred
woord denounceth his comminations againft finners)
doth incyte, procure, and force man to finne.

Beza in lyke fort teacheth, that h *God exciteth*
the wicked will of one theefe to kill an other, guideth his
hand, and weapons, iuftly enforcing the will of the theefe.
Fynally Caluin writeth, that i *In finning, the deuill is*
not author, but rather an inftrument thereof: thus refer-
ring the author of finne, to God him felf.

Now that thefe fayinges of the former proteftants
do, if not actually, immediatly, and primarioufly,
yet at leaft potentially, and neceffarily, include in thē
felues, that god is the author of finne: is gtaunted by
other more modeft proteftant wryters, who do altogether condemne the forefaid doctrine of Caluin, Zuin
glius, and Beza.

Thus is the faid doctrine condemned by Caftalio
who wrote a fpeciall treatife hereof againft Caluin.
By Hooker, in his *Ecclefiaft. Pollicy lib* 5. *pag.* 104.

sidenotes: g Tom. 1. de prouid. dei. fol. 366. h In his difplay of popifh prac tifes. i Lib. 2. Inft. ca. 4.

By D . Couell in his defence of M . Hooker pag 62.
Yea in further conuincing of M . Whytes former vntruth , we fynd that *Iacobus Andreas* a Proteſtant *in E-
pitom* . *Coloq* . *Montiſbelgar* . *pag* . 47 . thus plainely
writeth . *Deus eſt Author peccati ſecundum Bezam* .

Here now I referr the matter to the iudiceous Reader , whether he will beleue M . Whytes former aſſertion as true , politikly onely deliuered by him to
ſalue the honour of his Church , or the plaine contrary meaning of Caluin , Zuinglius , and Beza , ſet downe
in their owne ſayinges , & ſo acknowledged by others
of their owne Religion : where we fynd that the proteſtant , doth charge & condemne the proteſtant , for
teaching that *God is the author of ſinne* . But as in the
former vntruthes , ſo particulerly in this , we ſee how
Antipodes-lyke , & oppoſitly , our Doctor treadeth to
the feete of his owne brethren .

The 16 . *Vntruth* .

In proofe that S . Bernard was no papiſt .

Page . 298 . He is not affrayd to publiſh by his pen ,
that *Bernard was a papiſt in none of the principall poyntes
of their religion* . And then he addeth . *He ſtoode againſt
the pryde of the Pope* . *&c* . Good Reader , here is no
lying : for whoſoeuer will but obſerue what is confeſſed by the proteſtantes , muſt acknowledg that impudency it ſelf would be aſhamed to haue mantained ſuch
a groundleſſe vntruth .

k Vpon the
Cataloge .

For firſt it is graunted by *Symond de Voyon* a proteſtant , k that he was Abbot of *Clareiuaux* . And *Oſiander* ſaith of Bernard l that *Centum et quadraginta
Monaſteriorum author fuiſſe creditur* . He was thought

l in Epitom.
cent . 12 .
pag . 309 .

to be

to be the Author of a hundreth & 40 Monasteries.

In lyke fort S. Bernard was fo great a Patron of the Popes Primacy, that the Centuriftes wryte of him *m Coluit deum Maozim &c. Bernard did worfhipp e-uen to the laft end of his lyfe, the god Maozim, he was à moft eager defender of the feate of Antichrift.* A point fo cleare, that he is charged by D. Fulke, n and D. Whytaker o for defending the Popes Ecclefiafticall Authority, and yet if we beleeue M. Whyte *he ftoode againft the pryde of the Pope*, fo euident you fee is this made by the free acknowledgment of the proteftantes, whofe cenfures are paffed vpon S. Bernardes Religion and faith in generall. And therefore we may well inferr, that if they had thought S. Bernard to haue bene but in part a catholick (or as the terme is a papift) and in other poyntes a proteftant, they would haue bene glad to haue chalenged him to themfelues in the fuppofed pointes of his proteftancy.

Thus M. Whyte we ftill obferue, that the Reader is euer entertaynd by you with nought but falfhoods, but no meruell, for it is your owne pofition, p *that a man can not hope to learne truth in the fchoole of lyes.*

m Cen. 12.

10.

n Againft the Rhem. Teft. in Luc. 22. fol. 133.

o lib. cont. Dur .pag. 154.

p In M. W. his booke. pag. 1.

The 17. *Vntruth.*

Againft the miracles wrought by S. *Bernard &* S. *Francis.*

Page 299 Talking of the miracles of the former S. Bernard, of S. Francis, and others: he thus concludeth. *What is reported cf Bernard, and Francis &c. are lyes and deuyfes.* This is fpoken to difhonour the Romane Faith, diuers of whofe profeffóurs through Gods omnipotency, and for the manifeftation, and

ftrength

ſtrengthning of his truth, haue in all tymes bene a-
ble to exhibite diuers great miracles, the remēbrance
of which prerogatiue reſting onely in our Church, is
moſt diſpleaſing to our miniſter, in whoſe nyce noſe-
thrilles, nothing well ſauoreth, that taſteth of the
praiſe of our Catholick Religion.

But now let vs ſee, whether the miracles recor-
d'd of the former Sainctes, be lyes or no, as the D.
fondly ſuggeſteth. One moſt remarkable miracle
of S. Bernard, is recorded by *Godfridus* in the lyfe
of S. Bernard. It was wrought in proofe of certaine
Catholick Articles denied in thoſe dayes by the heritykes *Apoſtolici* or *Henriciani*, as at this inſtant they
are denyed by the proteſtantes. The miracle was done
in the Country of *Tolouſa* in France, and conſiſted in
S. Bernardes bleſſing of certaine loaues of bread, of
which loaues (for proofe of the truth of our Catholick
doctrine then preached by S. Bernard) whoſoeuer, being in any ſort diſeaſed of body, ſhould eate, ſhould
be healed of their ſicknes: whereupon infinite people
eating of the ſame, were cured moſt miraculouſly of all
kind of diſeaſes. This miracle was ſo illuſtrious and
markable, that *Oſiander*, one of the Century writers,
q doth not ſay it is a lye and forged, as M. Whyte
doth, but graunting the thing as true, doth aſcribe
it to the power and working of the deuill, as the wicked Iewes did the miracles of our bleſſed Sauiour, vnto *Belzabub*.

In lyke ſort *Mathew Paris* in his hiſtory which is
printed by the proteſtantes at *Tigur*. 1589. whoſe
booke is by the ſaid proteſtantes highly commended
in their Preface annexed thereunto, and who him ſelf
is reckoned for his defence of certaine poyntes of proteſtancy, in the number of proteſtantes by *Illiricus*. r

This

q Epitom.
Cent. 12.
l.b. ca. 6.
pag. 310.

r In his Cata-
logue of the
witneſſes of
truth.

This man now moſt ſeriouſly recordeth, that before S. Francis death, there appeared certain wcundes in his handes and feete, and his ſyde, freſhly bleeding, ſuch as were ſeene in our Sauiour when he ſuffered on the Croſſe. The reaſon of which appearance was (as S. Francis ſaid) to ſhew that he did truly preach the miſtery of the Croſſe: and that in further demonſtration of the ſame, he tould them before, that preſently after death, the former woundes ſhould be healed & coherent lyke to the reſt of his fleſh: the which accordingly did fall forth. And thus much but of theſe for breuity ſake inſtanced in theſe two Sainctes, from whence we may confidently affirme, that it is a lye to ſay with M. Whyte, that theſe Sainctes Mirakles are but lyes.

The 18. *Vntruth.*

In proofe of the proteſtantes Churckes euer viſibility.

Page 335. and 336. In defence of the continuance of his owne Church, he thus ſaith. *The learned among vs confeſſe and proue againſt all that contradict it, that euer ſince Chriſtes tyme without interruption, there haith bene a company of men viſibly profeſſing the ſame faith that we do, though the Church of Rome degenerating into the ſeate of Antichriſt, perſecuted them, and ſo many tymes draue them owt of the ſight of the world, that to it they were not viſible.* Thus he.

But before we conuince this, I would demaunde where our miniſters head peece was, when he thus wrote, ſince theſe few lyres do inuolue an irreconciliable contradiction: *A company of men viſibly profeſſing &c. yet to the world not viſible.* O ſtrang & neuer before heard of *Inuiſible-uiſible*: aſwell he might

mantaine

mantaine whyte, remayning whyte, to be black, or the moone in her greatest eclipse, to shyne, as the Church euer to be visible, and yet latent : and latent to whó? to the world: still good, as if it were to be seene only by some who are out of the world.

But now to the falshood, the lyke whereof he ventilated before, and haith accordingly bene before refelled. Yet because for the honour of his Church he insisteth much in the visibility and want of all interruption of his faith, to repell such an idle suggestion, with the testimonies and acknowledgmentes of seuerall learned protestantes.

m vpon the Renelat. prop. 37. pag. 68.

And first Napper wryteth m that *betwene the yere of Christ 300, and 1316. the Antichristian and Papisticall reigne began, reigning vniuersally, and without any debateable contradiction 1260 yeares, gods true Church most certainly abyding latent and inuisible.*

n In Ep. de abrogandis in vniuersum omnibus statut. Ecclesiast.

Sebastianus Francus a famous protestant in lyke sort faith. n *For certaine through the worke of Antichrist, the externall Church, together with the faith and Sacramentes, vanished away presently after the Apostles departure: and that for these thousand four hundreth yeres, the Church haith bene no where externall and visible.*

Now during all these ages, when was M. W. company of men visibly professing the same faith that he doth? Finally D. Fulke (though not acknowledging so great an inuisibility yet) wryteth, o that *in the tyme of Boniface the third, which was Anno 607. the Church was inuisible, and fled into wildernesse, there to remaine a long season.*

o In his answ. to a counterf. Catholick. pag. 16.

To these testimonies we may adde the former heretofore alledged, touching their Churches not being vpon the first reuolt of Luther. From all which it is ineuitably concluded against this our Architect of

lyes,

tyes, that the proteſtants imaginary Church, conſiſ-
ting of aery ſuppoſales of certaine inuiſibiliſtes : had
no ſubſiſting or being in the world for theſe laſte
thouſand yeres at the leaſt, before the Apoſtacy of
that vnfortunate & wicked Monke.

The 19 *Vntruth*.

In defence of Preiſtes mariage.

Page 343. The Doctor much Apologizing & defending the mariage of the Cleargy, affirmeth that
*the Church of Rome houldeth contrary herein, to that
which was taught in the Primitiue Church.*

Now for the triall of this falſhood, let vs concurr
to that which is confeſſed by our learned aduerſaries
concerning the ſame. Firſt then Cartwright confeſ-
ſeth o of the firſt Councell of *Nyce*, which was celebrated in the 3. Century or age afrer Chriſt, that it
taught, *that vnto thoſe which were choſen into the miniſtery, it was not lawfall to take a wyfe afterwardes, only being maried before entrance into the miniſtery, it was
lawfull for them to vſe the benefyte of the precedent mariage.* In lyke ſort M. Iewell, in the defence of the A-
pology, page 195. after the editió of Anno 1571.
ſpeaking of preiſtes mariages, thus acknowledgeth.
*Here I grant M. Harding is lyke to find ſome good ad-
uantage as hauing vndubtedly a great number of holy Fathers on his ſide.* Laſtly *Chemnitius* graunteth, that this
doctryne that preiſtes cannot mary, is taught by *O-
rigen, Ierome, Ambroſe, Innocentius, Ciritius, & E-
piphanius.*

Now here I referr to the iudgment of any indifferent reader, whether we are to beleue theſe former

learned

o In his 2.
Reply part. 1.
p. 485.

Exam. part. 3
p. 50.

learned proteſtantes ingeniouſly confeſſing the prae-
tiſe of this our Catholick doctrine in the primitiue
Church, to the preiudice and endangering of theire
owne cauſe: or M. Whyte denying the ſame for the
better tecture and pretext of his owne ſociable lyſe,
and his miniſteriall copulation.

The 20 *Vntruth.*

Againſt Images.

page 344. Inueighing much againſt the religious
vſe of Images, among other thinges he ſaith (according to the tytle of that his digreſſion) that *touching*
Images, the Church of Rome houldeth contrary to that
formerly was houlden. And after alledgeth, that *the*
auncient Chriſtians of the Primitiue Church, had no Ima-
ges. But the contrary hereto is moſt true. For firſt
we finde that the Centuriſtes do wryte, 4 that *Lac-*
tantius (who lyued in the fourth Century or age) affirmeth *many ſuperſtitious thinges concerning the efficacy*
of Chriſtes Image. Doctor Fulke affirmeth, a that
Paulinus a very auncient Author, *cauſed Images to be*
painted on Church wales. In lyke ſort touching the ſigne
of the Croſſe, of which there is the ſame reaſon and
ground, the Centuriſtes teach b that *Ambroſius*
multa commemorat ſuperſtitioſe de cruce inuenta. The ſaid
Centuriſtes alſo affirme c of the third age after Chriſt
that *Crucis Imaginem* &c. *Tertulian is thorght to af-*
firme, that Chriſtians had the Image of the Croſſe in the
places of their publike meetinges, as alſo priuatly in their
owne houſes. So farr did M. W. erre from the truth
in affirming, that touching Images, *The Church of*
Rome houldeth contrary to that which was formerly houl-
den

4 Cent. ca.
10. 108.

a Againſt
Heſkins. &c.
p. 672. 675.

b Cent. 4.
col. 302.

c Cent. 3.
Col. 121.

den. But I fee if it be proofe erough for M. Whyte onely to condemne: the Church of Rome muft not be innocent.

The 21. *Vntruth.*

Againft Tranfubftantiation.

Page 246. The D. thus writeth. *Laftly I name Tranfubftantiation &c. wherein it is plaine, that they* (meaning the Catholickes *) haue altered the Faith of the auncient Fathers.*

Here for the tryall hereof, we are to appeale to the fayinges and confeffions of his owne fyde, where we fhall fynd that M. Whytes credit and eftimation, is particulerly in this (as in the former)moft daungerouf-ly wounded, euen by the handes of his owne bree-thren. For we fynd it confeffed by the Centuriftes, d. that *Chrifoftomus tranfubftantiationem vid. tur con-firmare. Chrifoftom is thought to confirme tranfubftan-tiation.* In lyke fort by the Iudgment of other pro-teftantes e *Theophilactus, & Damacenus, plane in-clinant ad tranfubftantiationem. Theophilact & D. maf-cen, do euidently inclyne to Tranfubftantiation.*

Anfwearable hereto *Oecolampadius* f doth charge *Damafcen* with the faid doctrine. Finally D. Hum-frey writeth, g that Gregory the great brought in *Tranfubftantiation. In Ecclfiam verò (* faith he fpeaking of our conuerfion *) quid inuexerunt Gregorius et Au-guftinus? Intulerunt &c. Tranfubftantiationem.*

Now I would demaund of our minifter with what countenance he can auerre, that *in the doctrine of Tra-fubftantiation, we haue altered the faith of the auncient fa-thers,* if he obferue what is taught to the contrary

V 2 by

d Cent 4.
Col. 496.

e Vifinus in his commonefacti-o cuiufdam Theologi. pag. 211.

f lib Epift. Oecclamp. & Zuing. lib. 3.

g Humfr. Iefuit. part. 2. rat. 5.

by his owne brethren, who not beleuing the doctrine it felf, yet do confesse the great antiquity thereof.

May we thinke that M. W. was ignorant of thefe Fathers myndes therein? If fo, then are his followers much deceaued, in oueualuing his good partes and literature, and withall the obfcurity of his owne iudgment touching the faid fathers in this poynt, haith thus farr preuailed, that it haith miniftred fitt opportunity to the Reader, to take notice, how cleare, perfpicuous, & fhyning, our Catholick faith of Tranfubftantiation was, euen in thofe primitiue tynes: So the Opacity and darknes of the earth, is occafionally the caufe of the dayes light.

The 22. *Vntruth.*

Againft the conuerfion of England by S. Auguf. tine the Monke.

Page 354. and 355. to depriue S. Auguftine the Monke, of the honour and reuerence due vnto him by vs Englifh for our conuerfion, the M. thus wryteth. *Touching the conuerfion of England by Auguftine the Monk (in which our aduerfaries make fo much a doe) I anfweare two thinges, fift that fuppofing he did conuert it, it was not to the prefent Romane faith &c. Secondly I fay, he conuerfed not our Country at all, excepting the planting of fome tryfling Ceremonies.*

Here you fee that the firft poynt of this paffage, to wit touching Auguftines conuerfion and his faith, is Hipotheticall, and deliuered with fom hefitation and doubting: the other recalling the firft, *Categoricall,* abfolute, and peremptory. Now in my reprouall of this his falfhood, I will vnyte together, the two
                                                                                former

former difioynted parcels, and directly proue from
our aduerfaries penaes, that S. Auguftine did conuert our Country to the prefent Catholick Romane
faith: in the euicting whereof, I will content my felf
with the confeffions of the Centuriftes, and of D.
Humfrey: For if we perufe the hiftory of thofe Cen-
forions *Magdeburgians*, who reproue and controule
at their pleafure, all the Fathers of all ages : we fhall
fynd that thefe Centuriftes acknowledging S. Auguftines conuerfion of vs in their Alphabeticall Table of
the 6. Century at the wotd Gregory, do fet downe
certaine erroures (in their iudgmentes) of S. Gregory in thefe wordes following. *Eiufdem error de bo-*
nis operibus, *de Confeffione*, *de Coniugio*, *de Ecclefia*, *de*
Sanctorum inuocatione, *de Inferno*, *de Iuftificatione*, *de Li-*
bero arbitrio, *de Purgatorio*, *de Pænitentia*, *de Satiffacti-*
one. And further in the faid Century they charge him
with *Celebration of Maffe*. Col. 369 . *with claime &*
practife of fupreme Iurifdiction ouer all Churches. col.
425. 426. &c. *with Relickes and fprinkling of holy wa-*
ter. col. 364. *with Pilgrimage*. col. 384. *with Mona-*
chifme col. 343 . Finally (to omit many other pointes)
with Chrifme & oyle col. 367 .

Now this being the confeffed Faith of S. Gregory,
I think no reafonable mã will deny, but that S. Auguftine who was fent by him to conuert our Country, was of the fame Faith with S. Gregory.

In lyke fort D. Humfrey is moft full in this point,
who thus writeth. *In Ecclefiam verò quid inuexerunt* Iefuit. part.
Gregorius & Auguftinus? &c. *What brought Gregory &* 2. rat. 5.
Auguftine into the Church? They brought in the Arch-
bifhops veftment for the folemnè celebration of Maffe,
they brought in Purgatory, and oblation of the healthfull
hoaft, and Praiers for the dead &c. they brought in Re-
W   *lickes*

lickes. Tranſubſtantiation &c. New conſecration of Churckes &c. From all which pointes, what other concluſion is
gathered, then that Indulgences, Monachiſme, the Papacy, and all the other chaos and heape of ſuperſtition was
erected thereby, And thus farr of this teſtimony though
heretofore vpon other occaſion alledged.

Now here it being confeſſed both by the Centuriſtes, and by this learned Doctor, that S. Auguſtine
did not onely conuert vs, but alſo did teach vs all the
former doctrines: I would be reſolued of M. whyte,
by what extenuation or figure in Rethorick, he can
ſtyle our inſtruction in the ſaid maine articles of Catholick Religion, *the planting of certaine tryſling Cere-*
monies · But I ſee he is moſt willing for his owne behalf to alleuiate and leſſen the weight and conſequence
of our former conuerſion.

The 23. *Vntruth.*

Concerning the Conuerſion of Countries.

i Eſa. 60.
62. & 49. ſſ.
2. & 102.

     Page 357. Touching the conuerſion of other hea-
then Countries to the Faith of Chriſt, fore-tould ſo
long ſince by the Prophets i of God to be accompliſhed onely in the true Church of Chriſt: the D.
as being emulous of the Romane Catholick Church
her honour therein: flatly affirmeth of certaine Countries, by him mentioned, that they were conuerted by
that Church which was of his owne faith and profeſſion, and not by the Church of vs Catholickes, for
thus he writeth. *Allowing all theſe Covntries to haue*
bene conuerted by ſuch as were members of the Church of
Rome, yet this was a thouſand yeres agoe, when that Church
was the ſame that ours is, and ſo the conuerſions weare
              wrought

wrought by perfons adhering to th protestantes faith.

This point is difcoucred to be falfe, firft by refuting the reafon deliuered by the Doctor, why the faid Countries fhould be conuerted by the profcffois of the proteftantcs faith. Secondly by the teftimonies of the faid proteftantes flatly confcffing, that their Church as yet ncuer conuerted any Country to Chriftianity.

As concerning the firft poynt, I fay, that the Church of Rome more then a thoufand yeres agoe, haith feaced (fuppofing that before it was) to be proteftant, and therefore her felf profcffing the contrary faith, as then could not coruert the faid Countries to proteftancy.

That the Church of Rome acknowledged not in thefe tymes the proteftantes religion, is moft abundantly confeffed by the proteftantes them felues, who do frequently teach that the true Church of God (& confequently in their fuppofales, their owne Church) haith bene latent and inuifible more then thefe lafte thoufand yeres, during all which tyme, the Antichriftian and popifh Religion (as they terme it) haith poffeffed all Chriftian Countries whatfoeuer.

The proteftantes abundant confeffions, haue bene already made fo euident in this point, incidently in the difcouery of fome of M. W. vntruthes, as that I prefume an iteration of the fame, would be ouer faftidious aud wearifom to the Reader, and therefore I will paffe on to the other point, confifting in the confeffions of the proteftantes, that their Church neuer yet conuerted any one Country to Chriftianity.

And firft for confirmation hereof, we fvnde that *Sebaftian Caftalio* (a learned Calueniſt, ana highly praifep by D, Humfray) k writing of the accomplifhment of the prophefies of conuerting of kingdomes, faith thus. *Equidem aut hæc futura fatendum eft &c.*

k De rar. in-
terpr. li. 1.
q. 62.

W   2   *Truly*

In his Preface of the great latin Byble dedicated to King Edward the 6.

Truly we must confesse, that these thinges shall be performed hereafter, or haue bene heretofore, or God is to be accused of lying. If any man answer that they haue bene performed, I will demaund when? If he say, in the Apostles time, I will aske, how it falleth out, that neither then the knowledg of God was altogether perfect, and after in so short a time vanished away, which was promised to be eternall, and more abowndant then the floods of the sea.

And then there somwhat after, the said protestant thus acknowledgeth. *The more I do examine the Scriptures, the lesse I obserue the same performed, howsoeuer the said Prophets be vnderstoode.*

To conclude this point, the prophecies deliuered by Esay and others the Prophets, for the spreading of Gods Church, are so farr from being yet acomplished in the protestantes Church, that diuers protestantes haue not onely acknowledged so much, but by reason of the not performance thereof, haue in the end become most wicked Apostataes : mantaining that if the faith and Religion preached by Christ and his Apostles had bene true, and his Church, that Church which was figured out by the auncient Prophets : that then should the said Prophesies, touching the enlargment of the Church, and the conuersion of nations, haue had their successiue euent, and infallible performance in the said Church, which they affirme hitherto haith not bene effected.

Answearably hereunto we find, that the want of the performance of the said prophesies in the protestantes Church, wrought so forcibly with *Dauid George* a Hollader, 1 & once professor of the protestants faith & religion in *Basill* (to omitt the lyke examples of diuers others) that in the end he taught most fearfull & horrible blasphemy, affirming Christ to haue bene a seducer

1 See the History of Dauid Georg printed at Antwerpe, 1563. & first published by the Diuynes of Basill.

eer: his cheifeſt reaſon being, in that the true Religion
(our Catholick Religion being by him ſuppoſed to be
falſe, and therefore the conuerſions of Countries made
to it, not admitted to be intended by the Prophets)
according to the predictions, ſhould haue ſpred and
diſſeminated it ſelf before this tyme, through the moſt
Nations & Countries of the world, which poynt (ſaith
he) hitherto is not accompliſhed.

Here now the iudiceous Reader may collect, both
from what haith bene acknowledged aboue, as alſo
from the preſent confeſſion of the former Apoſtata (being accompanied with ſuch a dreadfull euent) how vn-
true the D. wordes were, when he affirmed diuers
Countries ſome thouſand yeres ſince, to haue bene
conuerted from paganiſme, vnto Chriſtianity by that
Church which in doctrine and faith conſpired with the
proteſtantes Church.

Thus you ſee M. W. that not I, but ſuch as in o-
ther poyntes of Nouelſme, do interleague with you,
geue you the lye therein: and thus is falſhood truly
controuled, euen by the Patrones of falſhood.

The 24. *Vntruth.*

Againſt the Popes authority in calling of Councells.

Page 375. He (in charging the Pope with innouation of his iuriſdiction) thus ſaith.

The beginning of the Popes Supremacy ouer Councells,
was of late, ſince the Councells of Conſtance and Baſill,
decreed within this hundreth yeres in the Councell of Late-
ran, by a few Italian Biſhops, wheras in the aunciēt Church
it was otherwiſe. In this poynt, for the more compendiouſnes thereof, I will inſiſt onely in the fourth

　　　　　　　　X　　　　　　　　　and

and fifth Century after Chrift, both being within the
circuite of the primitiue Church.

First then we fynd, that D: Whitaker confeffeth
m an Ecclefiafticall Canon to be in the fourth Century, that *Noe Councell fhould be celebrated, without the
Bifhop of Rome*. He alfo further acknowledgeth,   **n**
that *Pope Iulius made challenge therby* (meaning by the
benefite of the faid Canon) *to affemble a Councell*.

And where Bellarmine infifting in the prefident of
Iulius and other Bifhops vrging this Canon, *Danæus*
a learned proteftant, thus onely replyeth. **o**   *Nullius
eft momenti &c . The example is of noe force , fince it is proued from the Teftimony of the Bifhop of Rome who is a party in his owne caufe* . Thus confeffing the poynt it felf
(outfaced by the minifter) but denying onely the lawfulnes thereof.

Now in the fyfth age we fynde , that the *Magdeburgians* do thus plainely Cenfure the Popes of that
tyme. **p**   *Generalia Concilia &c . The Bifhops of Rome
haue challenged to themfelues , power of celebrating Councells , as appeareth out of the* 93 *. Epiftle , &* 7 *. chapter of
Leo* . And yet further the faid Centuriftes do fay   **q**
*Ac Synodos &c . They haue reiected fuch Councells as vn-
lawfull , which were not called together by their Authority*.

And thus farr of this poynt : where you fee , that our
minifter faying , that no Bifhop of Rome challenged
authority of affembling of Councells , or being aboue
them , but within this hundreth yeares laft , is con-
tradicted by the former learned proteftantes , who
confeffe that the Bifhop of Rome practifed it , eleuen
or twelue hundreth ages. I pray you whether of thefe
is more likly to lye?

m de Concil.
9. 2. p. 42.

n Ibid. p. 4.

o Refp. ad
Bel. par. 1.
p. 595.

p Cent. 5.
Col. 781.

q Ibidem

The

The 25. *Vntruth: Againſt merite of woorkes.*

Page 378. For the more diſauthoriſing of the doctrine of merit of workes : our miniſter thus outlaſheth. *The doctrine touching the merit of workes, was begon lately by the ſchoolemen.*

For the triall of this poynt, ſome of the Fathers of the primitiue Church confeſſed euen by the proteſtants to teach this our Catholick Faith, ſhall becom the wittneſſes bewene the D. and me.

Firſt then the *Magdeburgians* do thus write of one Father. r *Chriſoſtome hardleth impurely the doctrine of Iuſtification, and attributeth merite to workes.*

Luther ſ calleth *Ierome, Ambroſe,* and *Auguſtine, Iuſticiarios Iuſtice-workers of the ould Papacy.*

Finally D. Humfrey s aſcendeth euen to *Ireneus, Clemens,* and others pronouncing of them, that *they haue in their writinges, the merite of workes.*

And thus farr of this poynt. Wherefore our miniſters ouerſight was moſt groſſe, in diuulging ſuch a notorious vntruth, contrary to the expreſſe Iudgment of his owne moſt learned brethren.

r Cent. 5. Col. 1178.

ſ In Galat. c. 4.

s Ieſuit. part. 2. p. 530.

The 26. *Vntruth.*

Againſt the Sacrifice of the Maſſe.

Page 378. The miniſter endeuoring calumniouſly to diſhonour the moſt healthfull and incruent Sacrifice of the Maſſe, writeth, that *the Maſſe began not all at once, but by degrees.*

Now here to inſtruct the Doctors ignorance, or at leaſt to detect his malice : I am to lay downe the Iudg-mente of the Catholick Church, teaching what is maintayned to be essentiall to the Sacrifice of th Masse, and what but accidentall. The true nature then and essence of this Sacrifice, we hould to consist, in the oblation of the most sacred body and blood of Christ and consummation thereof: what praiers or ceremonies do either precede or follow the wordes of the institution, are no essentiall part of the Masse, & if they were all omitted in the celebration thereof, yet were the Sacrifice of it true and perfect. And therefore we willingly confesse without any preiudice to our cause, that most of the said prayers or Ceremonies, were added by seuerall Popes, at different tymes: yet from our acknowledgment thereof, it in no sort followeth, that the Masse came in by degrees, since we all teach, that they are neither the Masse, nor any essentiall parte of it.

Now wheareas the minister by subtilty, and by falsly suggesting to the Reader, that the Masse came in at seuerall tymes, would haue it to be vnderstoode for our greater disaduauntage, of the essence and nature of the Masse it self: I will lay downe the Iudgment of the Primitiue Church herein, vnanimously teaching, (euen by the confession of the most iudiceous protestantes) the true and vnbloudy Sacrifice, & oblation of Christes body and bloud, to be performed in the celebration of the Eucharist: so shall the Reader be instructed in the antiqnity of that which is essentially the masse: and withall (in reguard of the ministers calumnious dealing herein) he shall haue iust reason to say, t *Astonishment and meruelous thinges are done in the land: the prophets prophesied a lye.*

‡ Ierem. 5.

And here for greater compendiousnes, I will forbeare to set downe the Protestantes confessions of
particuler

particuler Fathers teaching the doctrine of the Maſſe,
and will reſtraine my ſelf onely to ſuch their ſayinges,
whereof ſome do belong to the primitiue Church in
generall, and others to the firſt age or Century thereof.

And firſt we fiind Caluin to wryte of them in generall u *Veteres excuſandi non ſunt &c* : *The auncient*
Fathers are not to be excuſed, ſeing it is euident that they
turned from the true and genuine Inſtitution of Chriſt .
For whereas the lordes ſupper is celebrated to this end , that
we ſhould communicate with the Sacrifice of Chriſt , the
Fathers not being contente therewith , haue added thereun-
to an oblation . And to the lyke purpoſe he ſaith in his
Inſtitutions. x *Veteres quoq̃, illos video &c I do ſee*
that thoſe Auntient Fathers , did detort the memory there-
of (meaning of the *Euchariſt*) *otherwiſe then was agree-*
ing to the Inſtitution of Chriſt : *for their Lordes Supper ,*
doth make ſhew and repreſentation of I can not tell what
reiterated and renewed Sacrifice . *They haue more neare-*
ly imitated the Iudaicall manner of Sacrificing , then ei-
ther Chriſt did ordaine , or the nature of the Goſpell did
ſuffer . Thus Caluin.
Add hereunto for the greater Antiquity of the doctrine of the Sacrifice of the Miſſe , that the proteſtantes
them ſelues do confeſſe the faith thereof to be vniuerſall , euen in the firſt age or Century after Chriſt.
For we ſynde , that *Hoſpmian* a famous proteſtant doth
thus write. y *Iam tum primo &c* . *Euen in the firſt*
age the Apoſtles being yet liuing , the deuill did deceaue men
more about this Sacrament , then about Baptiſme , & did
withdraw men from the firſt forme thereof .

In lyke ſort *Sebaſtianus Francus* an other learned proteſtant , thus plainely writeth. a *Statim poſt Apoſto-*
los &c . *Preſently after the Apoſtles , all thinges were tur-*
ned

Y

u lib. de ve-
ra Eccleſiæ re-
form. extant.
in Tract. The
ol. Caluin.
p. 389 .

x Inſt. l. 4.
ca. 18. Sect.
11.

y In his Sa-
cram. l. 1.
Ca. 6 . p. 20

a Epiſt. de a-
brog. in vni-
uerſum omni-
bus ſtat. Eccl.

ned vpfide downe , cana domini in facrificium tranfforma-
ta &c . The Lordes fupper is turned into a Sacrifice .

b In his Trea
tife entituled,
The relickes of
Rome . p . 344

To conclude , M . Bacon a great proteftant here in
England , thus confeffeth . b *The Maffe was concea-*
ned , begoten , and borne , anone after the Apoftles tymes , if
all be true that Hiftoriographers do write .

Thus much of the antiquity of the Maffe : which
poynt thus acknowledged , who feeth not that the teftimonies of the former proteftantes , do vtterly ouerthrow the fuppofed truth of the D . Wordes , affirming
that the *Maffe came in by degrees* , and intimating to
the credulous Reader , that it was brought in by litle
& litle in thefe latter ages . But M . Whyte , if in the
defending of your former vntruthes , you can not blufh
for fhame ; yet here grow pale through feare , for your
finne is not ordinary , feeing your mendaceous affertion doth obtrude an innouation vpon no leffer Article , then the immolation and offering vp of the moft
facred body and bloud of our Sauiour and Redeemer ,
to his heauenly Father for the expiation of our finnes ,
firft inftituted (out of the bowels of his mercy) euen
by Chrift : fo as him felf being the Preift , did the facrifice him felf . 2 *Quid gratius offerri* (faith one Fa .
aut daripoteft , quam caro facrificii noftri , corpus effectu
facerdotis noftri .

2 Aug . li . 4 .
de Trin . ca .
14 .

The 27 . *Vntruth .*

Concerning wafer Cakes .

Page 289 . the Doctor inueighing further againft
the Maffe , that wafer-cakes were firft brought into the
Sacrament , in the eleuenth age or Century after Chrift ,
and anfwearably thereunto he haith made a reference
to this

to this place in his Alphabeticall Table, at the latter
end of his booke at the word *wafer*, thus setting down,
wafers, when brought in . Sect. 5 . *num.* 31 .

Now that this proceedeth from the same sprayne,
to wit, *a spiritu mendacii*, from whence all his former
assertions had their origine, is proued in that it is con-
fessed by D. Bilson, c　that in the dayes of *Epipha-*
nius, it was rownd in figure. Cartwright though he will
needes find a begining thereof after the Apostles,
yet thus writeth of the bread of the Sacrament. d
It was a wafer-cake brought in by Pope Alexander : which
Pope euen by the testimony of *Osiander,* e　liued fif-
teene hundreth yeres since : And yet contrary to all
these authorities, we mightily wrong our minister if
we will not beleue him affirming that wafers were
brought in, about a thousand yeares after Christ.

c In his true
defence. part.
4 . p . 566.

d Whyteg.
def. p . 593 .

e Cent. 2.
p . 10.

The 28. *Vntruth.*

Against the adoration of the B *. Sacrament.*

Page 399 . The minister persisting in his serpentyne
and venemous disposition against the most B . Sacrament touching the Adoration thereof, this lyingly
forgeth . *The Adoration of the Sacrament, is a late in-*
uention ; folowing vpon the conceit of the Reall presence,
and prescribed 1220 *yeres after Christ, by Honorius the*
third. &c,

That Adoration followeth vpon the beleefe of the
reall presence, it is graunted, but that it is a late in-
uention begon in the tyme of *Honorius,* is false.
Thus the Doctor for the better countenancing of this
lye, doth calumniously couple with it a truth, that the
one might be shrouded vnder the winges of the other .

Now that there was no innouation touching the Adoration of the Sacrament at that tyme, is euinced from two reasons. First because no Historiographer doth geue the least intimation of any such institution as then but newly brought into the Church: onely Honorius decreed, that the preist should more diligently admonish the people thereof, in reguarde of some former negligence crept in concerning the same: And this is all which can be truly collected from the Decree of the said Honorius.

Secondly the former poynt is proued, from the abundant testimonies of our aduersaries, charging the tymes precedent to Honorius, with the said doctrine of Adoration. For first we reade, that *Auerroes* a heathen Philosopher (who liued aboue 80. yeres before the prescribed time of Honorius his former supposed innouation) did perticulerly deride the Christians of his dayes, for the Adoring of the Sacrament.

This is acknowledged by D. Fulke, f and D. Suliffe. g　　But to ascend to higher times, the Centuristes speaking of the prayers of S. Ambrose, h in his booke entituled, *Orat. præparat. ad Missam.* do thus write. *Continent adorationem panis in Sacramento.* Those prayers do conteyne the Adoration of the bread in the sacrament. *Chemnitius* produceth diuers sentences of *Augustine, Ambrose, and Nazianzen,* which sentences in *Chemnitius* his Iudgment, do affirme the Adoration of the Sacrament. k

Now all these authorities, do demonstratiuely conuince, that the Adoration of the Sacrament, was not introduced in the Church, as an innouation in the time of Honorius. From all which it is manifest, that as in any other poynt of Catholick Religion, so also in this of Adoration, we altogether do conspire and agree

f Against Heskins. &c. p. 235.

g In his Suruey of popery. p. 295.

h Cent. 4. Col. 43.

k Exam. part. 2. p. 92.

gree with the venerable Fathers of Gods Church.
And therefore as Ariftotle and other aunctent Philo-
fophers did teach, that this our inferiour world, was
ioyned to the Superiour and Celeftiall world, that by
the helpe of this coniunction, we might more perfectly participate of the influences and vertues of thofe
heauenly bodies : So we may fay, that thefe our latter
tymes through a continuall and vninterrupted current
of beleeuing God, and practifing the fame poyntes
of Faith with the Auncient Doctors, are indiffolubly
and nearely tyed to thofe primitiue dayes, fo as nothing is found in thofe reuerent dayes inftituted ci-
ther by Chrift or his Apoftles, which by this meanes
is not fecurely deryued to the Catholick Church of
thefe moderne tymes.

The 29. *Vntruth.*

Againft the Succeffion of Catholick Paftors.

Page 412. After the D. haith Trafonically boaf-
ted of the fucceffion of the proteftantes in his owne
Church, he procedeth further, affirming that Succeffion of the paftors and Bifhops in the Church of Rome,
haith bene interrupted : And anfwearably hereto, in
the Table in the end of his booke, at the worde *Succeffion*, with reference to this place, he thus faith.
The Romane Church haith no true outward Succeffion.
Where you fee by his owne wordes, that the queftion here intended by this minifter, is not of fucceffion
of doctrine (by which fleight and euafion, diuers of
our aduerfaries vfe to decline the teftimonies of the
auncient Fathers alledged by vs for ftrengthning the
argument drawne from Succeffion) but onely of ex-

Y 3 ternall

ternall fucceffion of Bifhops and Paftors, which the
minifter falfly challenging heretofore to his owne
church, doth now as falfly take away from ours.
How maliceous a lye this is, fhall appeare from the
mouthes of his owne brethren.

And firft we finde that the Centuriftes do very diligently and elaboratly fet downe, the fucceffion particulerly of the Bifhops of Rome in the 10. Chapiter of euery Century: And this Methode, they pre-
cifely obferue in all ages of the Church euen from S.
Peter, to their owne tyme, entituling the faid Chapiter, *de Epifcopis & Doctoribus.*

Doctor Fulke doth in like manner ingenioufly acknowledg the fame in thefe wordes. *You can name the
notable perfons in all ages, in their gouernment and miniftery, and efpecially the Succeffion of the Popes, you can
rehearfe in order vpon your fingers.* Thus writeth he in
his anfwear to *A counterfait Catholick,* p. 27. And
the lyke doth he write in his Reioynder to *Briftoes reply* p. 343.

Thus do our aduerfaries acknowledg in our behalfe
touching Succeffion, which Caluin flatly denyeth to
be found in his owne Church, who plainely teacheth
l that *with them, the true fucceffion of ordination, was
broke of:* fo daungeroufly wounding him felf with that
fentence of S. Auguftine. m *In Ecclefiæ gremio me
iuftiffimè tenet ab ipfa fede Petri &c. vfqʒ ad prefentem
Epifcopatum: fucceffio Sacerdotum.*

To conclude, the vninterrupted defcent and current of Succeffion in the Catholick Church, is infallibly euicted from our aduerfaries acknowledgment,
of the continuall vifiblenes thereof, fince the one doth
reciprically imply the other. For if our Church was
euer vifible, and the doctrine thereof neuer fuffered
any

l Inftitut.
li. 4. ca. 3.
Sect. 4.

m tom. 7.
cont. Epift.
Manich. c. 4.

any difparition or vanifhing away: then were the Bifhops and Paftors in lyke fort euer vifible, fince without Paftors to minifter the word and Sacraments,
and to gouerne the flock: the Church like a maift-
leffe fhippe, can not for any tyme fubfift or bee.

And thus far of this point. Wherein our minifter
by denying Succeffion to be in our Church, and falfly afcribing it to his owne new congregation, doth
thus in aduancing the one aboue the other, make innouation, to take the wall of true Antiquity, & herefy
of true Religion.

The 30 *Vntruth.*

In defence of Martyn Luthers lyfe and manners.

From page 425. to 433. The D. becometh Lu
thers Encomiaft, and much laboureth to free his life,
and death, from all obloquy, and infamy, often affirming, that what foeuer touching his lyfe may feeme
worthy of reprehenfion, is onely forged by his aduerfaries, meaning the Catholickes: and therefore in his
table in the end of his booke, at the word *Luther*, he
thus faith. *Luthers lyfe iuftifyed, againft the maliceous reportes of the papifts.*

Now to conuince this fhameleffe vntruth, I will
(forbearing herein the credible reportes of Catholickes) alledg onely the confeffion of Luther him felf
deliuered in his owne wordes, or els the teftimonies
of learned proteftantes; fo fhall we fee that our minifter here perfectly acted his part, in bouldly mantayning againft fuch euident teftimonies, that what
may feeme to detract from Luthers honefty, and integrity, are but the fictions of his enemies.

And here for greater compendiousnes, I will insiste
onely in two pointes, first in displaying in part his
Sensuality: Secondly his *Pryde.*

a Sermo de
Matrimonio.

And first touching his sayinges of lust and incontinency, he thus admonisheth. a *Si non vult vxor,*
aut non possit, veniat ancilla. If the wyfe will not or can
not, let the maid come. Againe he thus writeth. b

b Tom. 5.
wittem. ser.
de Matrim.
fol. 119.

As it is not in my power that I should be no man: so it is
not in my power that I should be without a woman. And
there after. *It is not in our power either that it should*
be stayed or omitted, but it is as necessary, as that I should
be a man, and more necessary then to eat, drink, purge,

c De colloq.
mens. fol. 526

make cleane the nose &c. And yet more fully he speaketh of his owne incontinency in these wordes. c

d To. 1. Ep.
fol. 334. Ep.
ad Philippū.

I am almost mad through the rage of lust and desire of wo-
men. As also he thus further confesseth. d *I am bur-*
ned with the great flame of my vntamed flesh: I who ought
to be feruent in spirit, am feruent in the flesh, in lust,
slouth, &c. Eight dayes are now past, wherein I neither
write, pray, nor study, being uexed partly with temptation
of the flesh, partly with other trooble.

This point is so euident, that *Benedict Morgenstern*
a protestant writer saith of the Caluenistes, when they
intend at any tyme to geue assent or prouocation to
nature: *Non verentur inter se di ere, hodie Luther inicè*
viuemus. They were not afraid to say among themselues,

e Tract. de
Eccl. p. 221.

to day we will liue after the manner of Luther. e Thus
vsing the name of Luther, the more fully to expresse
the libidenous lyfe and custome of Luther.

Now to all these confessions of his owne & other
protestantes, it can not be replyed that him seif did
write thus when he was a papist, aud before his reuolt:
for of his lyfe during his stay in the papacy, you shall
heare his owne report, that f *he honoured the Pope*
                                                     of mere

of mere conscience, kept chastity, pouerty, and obedience, and whatsoeuer (saith he) I did, I did it with a single heart, of good zeale, and for the glory of god, fearing greauously the last day, and desireous to be saued from the bothom of my heart. Thus he confesseth of the integrity of his mind and intention, during the tyme of his continuing a catholick. And thus much of his inclination to lust and wantonnes.

f Vpon the Epistle to the Galathians in engl. in ca. 1. fol. 35.

Now touching Luthers pryde (forbearing his owne sayinges deliuered most insolently, in contempt of the auncient Fathers, and of King Henry the eight) I will content my self with the testimonies onely of protestants, who particulerly inueighed against him for his pryde. Zuinglius, in reguard of his insupportable pryde, thus saith of him. g *En vt totum &c. Behould how Sathan laboureth wholly to possesse this man.* And OEcolampadius admonisheth Luther, h *to beware, lest being puffed vp by arogancy and pryde, he be seduced by Sathan.* Answearably hereto *Conradus Regius* a learned and famous protestant, thus writeth of him. i *Deus propter peccatum superbiæ &c.* God, by reason of the sinne of pryde wherewith Luther was puffed vp (as many of his owne writinges do witnes) haith taken away his true spirit from him, as he did from the Prophets 3. Reg. 22. and in place thereof, haith geuen him a proud, angry, and lying spirit.

g To 2. Ref. ad confes. Luth. fol. 478

h In resp. ad confes. Luth.

i In libro German. con. Io. Hof. de cæna Domini.

To conclude, omitting diuers other learned protestantes testimonies, the Diuines of *Tigur* being Caluenistes, thus censure Luthers booke writen against the Sacramentaries, and Zuinglians, that it was k *Liber plenus demoniis, plenus impudicis dicteriis: scatet iracundia et furore.* And thus we synd in what height of spirit, and elation of mind, he did write against his owne brethren, and how for the same he was rebuked by them. Z Now

k In confes. Germanicè im pressa, Tiguri. An. 1544. in 8. fol. 3.

Now hauing difplaid in part Luthers deportment, and this, either from his owne mouth, or from the confeffions of his owne brethren: I refer two thinges to the Readers confideration, one, whether our D. did auer an vutruth or no, in iuftifiing, that whatfoeuer could be produced againft Luthers life & conuerfation, was malignantly forged onely by vs his enemies.

The fecond (and that much more importing) whether it ftandeth with probability of reafon, or the accuftomed courfe of Gods proceding (who euer electeth meanes futable and proportionable to their ēdes) to make choice, for the reftoring and replanting the truth of his Gofpell and Religion (fuppofing it was then decayed) of a man whofe courfe of lyfe, writings, and doctrine, do euen breath onely pryde, contumacy, fenfuality, *Sardanapalifme*, and luxury.

Here now M. Whyte I haue thought good in the enumeration of your lyes, to end with Luther, as originally from him, you firft did fuck your lyinge doctrine. Onely I will conclude with this, that fince you are entred with our vulgar multitude (who cheifly reft vpon the outward graine and appearance of thinges) into the number and catologue of our new Euangelicall Prophets: I would wifh fuch your folowers, to entertaine an impartiall vew and confideration of this and other your forgeries and fleightes, which if they do, doubtleffe they fhall in the ende fynde and acknowledg, that you are guided therein euen by that ghoftly enemy of mannes foule, who

I 3. Reg. 22. once faid: 1 *Egrediar, & ero fpiritus mendax in ore omnium Prophetarum eius. I will go forth, and will be a lying fpirit in the mouth of all his Prophets.*

WHYTE

DYED BLACK

THE THIRD PART.

Contayning diuers impertinences or abſurd Illations, or reaſoninges, drawne from Maiſter
Whyte his alledged Authorities.

The 1. Paragraph.

Wer ein are diſcouered ſtrange Illations or argu-
inges, in proofe that the Scriptures are
the ſole rule of Faith, &
againſt Tra-
ditions.

Hᴀuing in the two precedent partes ſet downe
many corruptions and lyes practiſed by M.
Whyte: it now followeth according to my former intended Methode, that I alſo diſplay diuers of his impertinent and abſurde inferences and argumentes (for
theſe three pointes, to wit, corrupting, lying, & idly
or abſurdly diſputing, are the three ſeuerall threedes
whereof the whole worke of his Treatiſe is wouen.
In all which (though different in them ſelues) he ſtill
retayneth one and the ſame intention of deceipt, like
the loade-ſtone, which though often changeth his
place, yet neuer changeth it center.

Now touchinge thoſe his impertinences and looſe
illations, the Reader is to conceaue, that they conſiſt

2 Z   in his

in his alledging of such testimonies **both of Scrip-**
tures, Fathers, and Catholick writers, as being truly set downe, do not neuerthelesse impugne that point
of our Catholick doctrine, against which they were
by him so vrged. Which course of writing, whether
it may be ascrybed to our Doctors ignorance & want
of learning, or rather (which is more probable) to his
malice against the Catholick Faith, and desire to deceaue the simple and vnlearned, or lastly to the beg-
gery of his cause, being deuoide of better arguments,
I leaue to him self to decide. But howsoeuer it is,
here I am to aduertise the Reader, that in perusing
of such authorities produced by M. Whyte, he would
euer recurr to the true state of the question, and particulerly that he would apply the said sentences, to
that verie point or touch wherein the life of the question consisteth, and then he shall find how rouingly,
& wandringly they are directed, still glauncing by,
vpon some ignorant or wilfull mistaking or other, neuer reaching the mark intended. And so he may apply the wordes of Tertulian, though in a different
sense, to the loose writinges of M. Whyte and such
others *Quemcunq; conceperint ventum argumentationis
scopii isti, quocunq; se acumine impegerint, vna iam line-
a ista:* to wit the lyne drawne from our vnderstanding
to the mayne point in controuersy.

Tertull. ad-
uers. Gnost.

And here M. Whyte can not say, in excuse of him self,
that such testimonies of this nature are produced by
him onely to proue so much and no more, as the wordes
in their litterall and a knowledged sense, do immediatly import: Which euasion is insufficient for two
respects.

First because the proofe of that which litterally &
plainely they signify, is not in controuersy betwene
the

the proteſtantes and vs, and therefore the iuſtifiing of ſo much being not denied by any learned Catholick, is needeleſly vndertaken.

Secondly in that M. Whyte doth moſt labouriouſly, painefully, and purpoſly, alledg the ſaid teſtimonies, to conuince, and impugne, ſome one Catholick poynt or other, taught by vs, and denyed by the proteſtantes, and this his drift and ſcope is manifeſted, either by his anſwearable entituling of the leaues wherein ſuch authorities are found, or els by his owne wordes precedent or ſubſequent to the ſaid ſentences.

But to detayne the Reader no longer from theſe his allegations: The firſt point of this kynde which preſenteth it ſelf, is as touching the Rule of Faith, & reiecting of all Apoſtolicall Traditions: For pag. 13. we thus read, digreſ. 3. *Wherein by the Scriptures, Fathers, Reaſons, and papiſtes owne confeſſions, it is ſhewed, that the Scripture is the rule of Faith:* As likewiſe he entituleth that leafe and ſome others following, in this manner. *The Scripture onely, is tho iudg & rule of Faith.* And ſo anſwearably hereto, pag. 17. bearing the former tytle, he thus ſaith. *Shall the Libertynes be recalled from their blind reuelations, to their writen text: and ſhall not the papiſtes be reuoked from their vncertaine Traditions to the ſame rule?*

But that we may the better behould how valiantly our miniſter impugneth all Traditions, by erectinge the Scripture as ſole rule of Faith: we are here to call vnto mind what the Catholick Church teacheth in this poynt.

It then teacheth, that the word of God is to limit and confine our Faith, and that nothing is to be accompted as matter of faith, which reccaueth not it

proofe

proofe from thence. Hereupon it teacheth further, that this word is either writen, which is commonly called the Scripture, or els deliuered by Chrift & his Church, and this comprehendeth Traditions. Both thefe we beleue to be of infallible authority, fince the true and inward reafon why the word of God is the word of God, is not becaufe it is writen, rather then deliuered by fpeach, (for this is merely extrinficall to the point) but becaufe the faid word proceded from them, who were infallibly and immediatly directed therein by the affiftance of the holy Ghoft.

This fuppofed, let vs fee how M. Whyte proueth that the writen word is onely the rule of Faith, and confeque̅tly that there are no Traditions of the Church which may alfo in part be a rule thereof,

First then our Doctor vrgeth to this end feuerall places of Scripture, as (among others) that of Salomon. a *The fcripture will make a man vnderſtand righteoufnes, and iudgment, and equity, & euery good path*. Againe that of Efay. b *We muſt repaire to the Law, to the teſtimony: if any fpeake not according to that word, there is no light in him*. Alfo out of Malachy. c *Remember the Law of Moyſes my feruant, which I commaunded him in Horeb for all Ifraell, with the ſtatutes & Iudgmentes*. In lyke fort he alledgeth, that Abraham anfwearing the rich glutton, faid, that d *his brethren had Moyſes and the Prophets*.

a prou. 2. 1.

b Efa. 8.

c Malach. 4.

d Luc. 16.

Now that the Reader may fee, how well thefe texts are to the point controuerted, I will fet fome of them downe in forme of Argument, and fo apply them to M. Whytes purpofe. As firſt thus. Salomon faid of the Scriptures of the old Teſtament. *The Scripture will make a man vnderſtand righteoufnes, and Iudgment, and equity, and euery good path: Ergo now in the tyme of Chriſtianity*

*Chriſtianity, there are no Traditions, but the Scripture
of the old Teſtament, is the onely rule of Faith.* Againe,
*Remember the Law of Moyſes my ſeruant, which ι com-
maunded him in Horeb, for all Iſraell, with the ſtatutes &
iudgments; Therefore no Traditions.* Laſtly. *The brethren of the rich glutton had Moyſes and the Prophets:
Therefore no pointes of Chriſtian Faith, are to be proued frō
any Traditions of the Church.* Strangly, wildly, & moſt
exorbitantly concluded: for what reference haue theſe
textes with the rule of Faith, the which is not ſo much
as glaunced at in any one of them? or graunting that
they had, why ſhould the old Teſtament, be a paterne
for the Faith profeſſed in the new Teſtament, ſince all
Chriſtians do graunt, that the time of Grace, is enri-
ched with many priuiledges and immunities, whereof
the old Law was altogether depriued?

After theſe and ſuch like textes of Scripture, he deſcendeth, to proue the foreſaid point, from the teſtimonies of the auncient Fathers: as, to omitt diuers others,
he alledgeth Tertulian ſaying. e *The Scripture is the* e cont. Her-
rule of Faith, which we graunt, fot we teach that it is mog.
Regula partialis fidei, a Rule of our faith in part, yet
hence it followeth not (which is the point here onely
to be proued) that it is *Regula totalis,* an entyre & ſole
rule of Faith, without the help of any Traditions, and
as large in extent as our faith is.

Alſo S. Auguſtine thus wryting f *This controuerſy de-* f De nupt.&
pending betwene vs, requyres a Iudg, let Chriſt therefore concup. ad
iudg, and let the Apoſtle Paule iudg with him, becauſe Valer. l. 2.
Chriſt alſo ſpeaketh in his Apoſtle. As if Chriſt & his ca. 33.
Apoſtles could not aſwell ſpeake in Traditions, as in
writinges, or becauſe graunting that that particuler
controuerſie there ment by S. Auguſtine, was proued
from the wrytinges of S. Paule: therefore all other

Articles of Christian Religion, should thence also receaue their sole proofe. Againe Gregory Nyssen tear-
ming the Scripture, g *a strait and inflexible Rule*, as
in that the Scripture is inflexible and inchangeable for
those pointes which it proueth, therefore it alone and
no Apostolicall traditions, is to proue any article of
our Faith. Lastly he introduceth S. Austine againe
saying. *Whatsoeuer thing it be that a man learnes out of the
Scripture, if it be hurtfull, there it is condemned, if it be
profitable, there it is found.* Which place particulerly
concerning conuersation of life, as vertue and vyce,
of both which, the Scripture most fully discourseth,
how it may condemne Apostolicall traditions, which
may deliuer supernaturall and high misteries of Christian faith, I leaue to the censure of any iudiceous man.

This done, he next falleth to the sentences of more
late Catholick writers, as first of S. Thomas *Aquinas*
saying. k *The doctrine of the Apostles and Prophets, is
Canonicall, because it is the Rule of our vnderstanding,*
But what do these wordes force, onely in the behalfe
of Scripture, and against Apostolicall Traditions, since
indeede they do not peculierly concerne the Scripture,
but (as the wordes litterally import) that the doctrine
of the Apostles and Prophets in generall, whether it
be written or vnwritten, is Canonicall. Againe he
vrgeth S. Thomas the second tyme l *Our Faith resteth and stayeth it self, vpon the reuelation geuen to the A-
postles and Prophets, which write the Canonicall bookes,
and not vpon reuelation (if any such haue bene made) to a-
ny other Doctors.* But who denies that the prophets &
Apostles did write the canonicall bookes? Or who
teacheth that our Faith ought to rest vpon the reuelation of any other Doctors then the Prophets & the
Apostles? Or shew any reason (which is the cheif point
in this

g Orat. de iis
qui adeunt
Hietos.

De doct. chrif.
li. 2. ca. 42.

k Lect. 1. in
1. Tim. 6.

l 1.q. Art. 8

In this ſentence to be ſhewed) why the reuelations of the Prophets, and eſpecially the Apoſtl:s, may not aſwell comprehend traditions, as the writen word.

In like ſort he bringeth in Gerſon ſaying. *The Scripture is the Rule of our faith, which being well vnder-ſtoode, noe authority of men is to be admitted againſt it.* As I haue ſaid before, we do teach that the Scripture is the Rule of Faith, but not the ſole Rule, which M. Whyte ought to proue. Againe we willingly acknowledg, that no authority of man is to ſtand againſt the Scripture : but what doth this impeach Apoſtolicall tra ditions, which are nomore the bare authority of man, then the Scripture it ſelf, both equally proceding frō God, by the aſſiſtance of the holy Ghoſt ?

in margin: m de com. ſub vtr. ſ.cc.

Finally he comes in with Periſius, wryting that *The Authority of no Sainct, is of infallible truth : for S. Auguſtine geues that honour onely to the ſacred Scriptures.*

in margin: m de ration?. Con. l. 2. ca. 19.

But here the queſtion is not touching the tradition of any other Sainctes, then onely of our Sauiour & his Apoſtles, and the whole Church : yet we ſee Pereſius here ſpeaking of Sainctes, muſt needes meane only of Particuler Sainctes, or holy men ſince the tymes of the Apoſtles, ſeing otherwiſe he ſhould teach (which were moſt wicked) that the authority of the Apoſtles and the Euangeliſtes, are not of infallible truth.

Beſides S. Auguſtine in that place reſtrayneth, without any reference at all to Traditions, his meaning onely to the writinges of priuate Doctors, in reſpect of the ſacred Scripture : and in this reguard (ſtill ſpeaking of bookes written) we all graunt that the Scripture is of an infallible truth.

Such vnprofitable and waſt teſtimonies M. Whyte is accuſtomed to heape together in his booke, the which, that they ſhall not ſo eaſely be eſpied, he ſubtilly

A

tilly (for the moſt part) mingleth them with other Au-
thoricies more pertinent, at leaſt in outward forme &
ſhew of wordes: lyke a good Captaine, who rangeth
his worſt & weakeſt ſouldiers, in the middeſt & throng
of the more experienced, ſo making thoſe former to
ſerue onely to encreaſe (in the enemies eye) the number, though not their force.

The 2. Paragraph.

Wherein are diſcuſſed certaine Arguments drawne
from Scriptures and Fathers, in proofe that the
ſacred Scriptures, & the true ſenſe there
of, are made ſufficiently known vn-
to vs without any approbation
or explication of the
Church.

The next ſubieƈt of his looſe kind of Inferences,
wherein I will inſiſt, partly conſpireth with the former, and is touching the abſolute and ſupreme ſoueraignty of the Scriptures in determining of controuer-
ſies, without any needefull explicatiō of gods Church,
this aſſertion being indeede a head *Theoreme* or principle with the ſectaries of this age. For page 43.
M. Whyte thus writeth, Digreſſio. 11. prouing,
that *The Scripture it ſelf, haith that outward authority*
whereupon our faith is built, and not the Church.

Now here for the better vindicating and freeing vs
from all contumelious calumnies touching our ſuppoſed contempt of the Scriptures, as alſo for the more
manifeſt diſcouery of M. Whytes weake arguing herein: the Reader is to take notice, that the Catholicks
do aſcribe all due reuerence, eſtimation, and reſpeƈt
to the

to the Scripture whatſoeuer, acknowledging it to be gods embaſſadour, which vnfouldeth vnto man vpon earth, the ſacred will and pleaſure of our heauenly King: as alſo that it is the ſpirituall Tenure by the which we make claime to our eternall and celeſtiall enheritance. In like ſort they willingly confeſſe, that Scripture is Scripture, and the word of God, before it receaue any approbation from the Church: as alſo that this or that is the true ſenſe of any particuler text of the Scripture, before the Church do confirme the ſame. Notwithſtanding, ſeing the true ſenſe of the Scripture, is as it were the very Soule which informeth the body of the letter, and that the Scripture is to be vnderſtoode by the Reader, with that ſpirit with the which it was written, to wit, with the ſpirit of the holy Ghoſt: Therefore we do hold, that (ſo far as concerneth our taking of notice, that this or that is the Scripture or Gods word, or that this is the true ſenſe of ſuch a paſſage thereof, intended by the holy Ghoſt) we are to recurre to the authority of the Church, which we beleue to be directed and guided therein by the ſame holy Ghoſt, according as the Scripture it ſelf in ſeuerall places 1 aſſureth vs.

But now let vs come to the proues and teſtimonies produced by M. Whyte, to conuince, that the Scripture, ſo far forth as we are to take acknowledgment thereof (for this onely is here the point of the doubt as I ſhewed aboue) needeth not (for warranting to vs that it is the word of God, or for explicating the true ſenſe thereof) any Anthority or approbation of the Church. And firſt he bringeth to this end diuers texts 2 of Scripture contayning the worth and dignity of it ſelf, as when it is tearmed an 2 *Immortall ſeede. The* 3 *demonſtration of the Spirit & power.* that it is 4

i 1. Tim. 3.
Mat. 18.

2 1. Pet. 1.

3 1. Cor. 2.

4 Heb. 4.

A 2 *linely*

5 Luc. 24.

6 Io. 6.

7 2. Pet. 1.

8 1. Io. 5.

9 Ibid.

10 Io 5.

Liuely & powerfull: that 5 *it maketh our heartes to burne within vs.* that 6 *It geueth a greater testimony to Christ, then Iohn Baptist could geue.* that 7 *A voice from heauen is not so sure as it.* that 8 *It is the spirit which beareth witnes to the truth thereof.* that 9 *if we receaue the witnes of men, the witnes of God is greater,* Lastly he alledgeth those wordes of Christ. 10 *They which will not beleue Moyses wrytinges, will not beleue him.*

Now let vs see how towardly our Minister can conclude from these textes, against our former doctrine. *The scripture is an immortall seede, and it is liuely and powerfull:* Therefore it ought to receaue no authority touching the manifesting of it true sense to vs, from Gods Church which is guided with the holy Ghost. Againe. *It is the demonstration of the Spirit and power, and it maketh our harts to burne within vs:* Therefore it ought to receaue no authority &c. *If we receaue the witnes of men, the witnes of god is greater, and he that beleueth not Moyses writings, will not beleue Christ:* Therefore the Scripture ought to receaue no authority &c: What inferences are these? Or who would think, that a learned minister of gods word, the *via lactea,* r a Doctor made onely for desert, before his due ordinary tyme: Finally that M. Whyte (since this very name is supposed to comprehend woorth enough) should thus exorbitantly, and extrauagantly inferre and conclude, contrary to all precepts of art & Logicall rules?

r For so is M. Wh. cyted by Purchase in his late booke.

But to passe on, the more in his iudgment to depresse the Authority of the Church, he bringeth in D. Stapleton, though most impertinently alledged, saying. 12 *The Authority of the Church, is but a thing created, distinct from the first verity,* which position we willingly admitt, who acknowledg the Church to be a thing

12 Lib. 8. de princip. fid. doct. cap. 20.

a thing different from god who is the firſt truth though guided by his Spirit. Againe he produceth to the like effect S. Ambroſe, who thus writeth. 13 *Let God* ¹³ l. 3. Ep. 51. *him ſelf teach me the miſteries of heauen, not man who knoweth not him ſelf: Whom may I beleue in the thinges of god, better then god him ſelf?* which ſentence alſo we embrace, yet do affirme that god teacheth vs more ſecurely by the authority of the Church directed by his aſſiſtance (and conſequently not by the authority of man) then by the mediation of each mannes priuate and vncertaine ſpirit.

Alſo *Saluianus* is brought by him ſaying. 14 *All* ¹⁴ l. 3. de Prouid. *that men ſay needes reaſons and witneſſes, but Gods word is witnes to it ſelf, becauſe it followeth neceſſarily, that whatſoeuer the incorrupt truth ſpeaketh, muſt needes be an incorrupt witnes of it ſelf:* As if what the Church, aſſiſted by the holy Ghoſt, ſaid, were the ſaying onely of man, or as if the queſtion were here, whether Gods word be Gods word before it be defined by the Church (which no man denyeth) and not whether the members of the Church (which indeede is the point here iſſuable) is to accept of Gods word as his word, by the Authority of his ſaid Church.

In like ſort pag. 53. to the former ſcope he produceth S. Auguſtine thus writing to the *Manaches.* 15 ¹⁵ Contra *You ſee this is your ende: our, to take away from vs the Au-* Fauſt. l. 32. *thorityes of the Scriptures, and that euery ones mind mioht* ca. 19. *be his Author what to allow, and what to diſalow in euery text, and ſo he is not for his faith made ſubiect to the Scripture, but maketh the Scripture ſubiect to him ſelf &c.* Which wordes how they can touch the Catholickes, I ſee not, ſeing they ſeeke not to take away the Authority of the Scriptures, which they willingly reuerence, neither teach they, that euery ones mind ought

to be an authour what to allow, or what to difalow
in the expofition of any text, for they rely herein vpon
the iudgment of Gods vniuerfall Church, the former
being indeede rather peculiar to the fectaries of this
age, in reguard of their priuate interpreting fpirit.
And prefently after, he alfo cyteth S. Auguftine againe
in the former booke. *Why doft thou not rather fubmitt
thy felf to Euangelicall Authority, fo fteedfaft, fo ftable,
fo renowned, and by certaine fucceffion commended from
the Apoftles to our tymes: that thou maift beleue, that
thou maift behould, that thou maift learne, all thofe thinges
which hinder thee from doing it through thine owne vaine &
peruerfe opinion.* How can thefe wordes be tentred &
ftrained to vs Catholickes? Or how can it be tearmed
a mannes owne vaine and peruerfe opinion by receauing Euangelicall Authority as it is manifefted to vs,
not by our owne imaginations, but by the cenfure of
the Church of God, which is ftyled by the Apoftle,
Columna & firmamentum veritatis.

  Thus we fee how wandringly M. Whyte difcour-
feth, matching and coopling together through his malice and ignorance in arguing, adulterate aud baftard
conclufions, with legitimate premiffes. And after the
like manner euen in the firft leafe here alledged, though
fomwhat before thefe laft teftimonies, he vrgeth certaine textes of Scripture intended of Chrift, as **15**
The Scriptures are written that we may beleue in him. A-
gaine. **16** *He that beleueth in him, haith a witnes in
him felfe.* Thirdly **17** *We are all built vpon the foundation of the Apoftles & Prophets, Chrift him felf being the
head corner ftone, in whom all the building is coopled together by the fpirit.*

  Now to what end he muftereth all thefe fentences
of Scripture god him felf knoweth: for neither do they
derogate

15 Io. 20.
16 1. Io. 5.
17 Ephef. 2.

derogate any thing frō the Churches Authority, ſince indeede they do not concerne it, neither do they aſcribe any more to Chriſt, then all Catholickes doe acknowledg and beleue· But it ſemeth M. Whyte thought it good pollicy thus to lead forth in triumph, whole ſquadrons of textes, and other humaine teſtimonies, that ſo they might ſeeme powerfull and terrible (how weake ſoeuer otherwiſe through his miſapplications they were) againſt the Churches Authority, the eye of the vnlearned. But to end this Paragraph, here the Reader may ſee, in how many impertinent allegatiōs M. Whyte haith inſiſted, euen within the reading of two leaues together, and all implicitly directed to charg the Catholickes with their diſualuing the Scriptures, through their acknowledging the Churches lawfull authority, as if to contemne the church of God, were an argumᵉnt with him, the more to admire the word of god. Thus he ſemeth to pertake (though in a different example) with a certaine man recorded by *Sulpitius*, 18 with whom euery one ſtudious of vertue or abſtinence, was ſuſpected with the hereſy of the Priſcilianiſtes.

18 Sulpitius Seuerus Epiſt. Hiſt. Eccl. ſo writeth of Ithacius.

The 3. Paragraph.

Wherein are examined ſome of M. Whytes proofes againſt the Churches viſibility.

An other paſſage whereupon our miniſter ſpendeth his frothy and immateriall proofes, is touching the inuiſiblenes of the Church: firſt bearing the Reader in hand that by inuiſibility he meaneth not an vtter extinction or diſparition of the true Church, and ſaith: yet after in effect he recalleth the ſame and thus writeth

teth

teth. pag. 87. *When we say the Church is inuisible, we*
meane that all the externall gouernment thereof, may come
to decay, in that the locall and personall succession of pastors
may be interrupted, the discipline hindred, the preachers
scattered, and all the outward exercise and gouernment of
religion suspended, whereby it shall come to passe, that in all
the world you can not see any one particuler Church profes-
sing the true faith whereunto you may saifly ioyne your self,
by reason persecution and heresyes, shall haue ouerflowed
all Churches, as Noes flood did the world &c. Thus you
see how liberally and fully he here deliuereth (though
in the beginning of that Chapter he speaketh more
mincingly thereof.) Now if the discipline may be hindred, the preachers scattered &c. then shall not the
word be preached, nor the Sacramentes ministred,
which are (at least by our aduersarie sprinciples) in-
feperable markes of the true Church, and consequently, they being taken away, the Church for the tyme,
must be vtterly extinct.

This being the true meaning of M. Whyte, he vndertaketh to proue that the Catholickes do generally teach, the like inuisibility of Gods Church, and
therefore he thus fyleth those leaues, *The papistes say*
the Church is inuisible, which iuuisibility to be taught
by the Catholickes, that he may proue, he haileth in
all sayinges of any one Catholick Doctor or other,
which shew only that the Church of God, is more cö-
fpicuous at one time then another, which we all graüt,
yet from thence it can not be enforced, that therefore
by the Catholick doctrine, it may be somtimes so latent, as that it can not be knowne where it is.

But to fortify this his false assertion, he alledgeth
Pererius in these wordes. 3 *In the tyme of Antiehrist*
there shall be no Sacrament in publick places, neither shall

3 In Daniel.
pag. 714.

                                                         any

*any publick honour be geuen it , but priuatly and priuily ſhall
it be kept and honoured .* In the ſame manner he vrgeth
Ouandus, 4 that the maſſe in the time of Antichriſt
ſhall be celebrated but in very few places , ſo that it
ſhall ſeeme to be ceaſed . Now (to omitt that if the
maſſe ſhall be celebrated in few places , then muſt it be
in ſome places , & if in ſome places , then is the Church
viſible euen in thoſe places) what illation is this?

4 Breuiloq.
in 4. ſent.
d 18. p. 602.

*The Euchariſt or the maſſe , ſhall not be publikly honou-
red or celebrated in Antichriſts tyme , but onely in priuate
or in ſecret : therefore then the Church ſhall be inuiſible and
vnknowne .* The ſilynes of which argument is controuled euen by the wofull experience of our owne country
at this preſent , where the world ſeeth that the Maſſe
and other Catholick *Sacramentes ,* are exercyſed onely in priuate howſes , and not in publick Churches ; &
yet who will from hence conclude , that the Catholick
Church here in England , is latent and inuiſible , ſince
the immoueable conſtancy and perſeuerance of Engliſh
Catholickes , haith made them knowne and remarkable
to all the partes of Chriſtendome .

He next alledgeth diuers Catholickes , ioyntly teaching , 5 that in the tyme of Antichriſt , *The Sacrifice of the Euchariſt ſhall be taken away ,* which point being graunted , yet proueth not that the true faith of
Chriſt ſhall ſo fall away , that none can then be named
who ſhall profeſſe the ſame . For ſeing that the celebrating of the Euchariſt , is an externall worſhippe of
god , which though it be ſuſpended for the time , yet
it is not neceſſarily accompanied with an inuiſibility of
the Church , and a vaniſhing away of the true Faith
of Chriſt , euen in reguard of the perſons who ſhould
performe the ſame . For this point is likewiſe made manifeſt by the impriſoed Preiſtes here in England , whoſe

5 Boſius de
ſig. Eccl. l.
24. ca. 9.
Dom. a Soto
2. d. 46. q.
1. art. 1.

B   publick

publick exercife of their Religion, though it be prohibited and reftrained, yet are they well knowne to the ftate, by profeffing them felues in thefe times of preffures (through a true heroicall and fpirituall fortitude) members of the Catholick Church.

Next to the former teftimonies, he marfhalleth *Gregory de Valentia* thus writing. 6 *When we fay, the Church is alwaies confpicuous, this muft not be taken, as if we thought it might at euery feafon be difcerned alike eafily. For we know that it is fom-times toffed with the waues of erroures, fchifmes, and perfecutions, that to fuch as are vnfkilfull, and do not difcreetly euough weygh the circumftances of tymes and thinges, it fhall be very hard to be knowne &c. Therefore we deny not, but that it will be harder to difcerne the Church at fome tymes, then at other fome: yet this we auouch, that it alwaies migt be difcerned, by fuch as could wifly efteme thinges.* Thus this Catholick Author with whom D. Stapleton is alledged 7 by M. Whyte, to confpire herein. Now what doth this teftimony make againft vs, fince it cheifly proueth, that the fplendour of Gods Church, is more radiant and fhyning, at one tyme, then at an other (which we willingly graunt) but it is impertinently vrged to proue that it fhould be abfolutly eclipfed, (the point that ought to be euicted) nay it clearly conuinceth the contrary. For firft the former wordes fay that the *Church is alwaies confpicuous.* Secondly, that the Church is alwaies difcerned by thofe who wyfely efteeme of thinges, therefore to fuch it is, alwaies vifible: And thus doth M. Whytes owne teftimony, recoyle with great force vpon him felf.

After our Doctor haith ended with Catholick moderne wryters, he beginneth to proue the inuifibility of the Church, from the authority of the auncient Fathers

6 Anal.fid.
l. 6. ca. 4.

7 Relect.
contr. 1. q.
3. p. 30.

thers, and among others (whom for breuity I pretermit) he alledgeth S. Chriſoſtome, and vſhereth his
authority with this preface. *And that Chriſoſtome*
thought, the Church might be ſomtimes inuiſible, appea-
reth by the 49. homily vpon Mathew where he ſaith.
Since the tyme that hereſy haith inuaded the Church: it
can no way be knowne which is the true Church of Chriſt,
but by the Scriptures onely, in this confuſion, it can no
wayes els be knowne. From which wordes, I do collect
a continuall viſiblenes of the Church: for if the Scriptures be euer able to make the Church knowne, then
by them it is euer made viſible, and conſequently,
(ſince the ſcriptures haue euer hitherto bene preſerued,
and through Gods good prouidence no doubt ſhall
be euen to the end of the world) the Church haith
bene, and ſhall be at all times made knowne and viſible through the meanes of the Scripture. And thus
diſputing onely *ad hominem*, do I turne the point of
M. Whytes reaſon vpon him ſelf.

And this may ſuffice touching M. Whytes weake
prouing of the latency of Chriſtes Church: where the
Reader may behould a longe teame (as it were) of his
lame, feeble, and impotent authorities, one ſtill following an other, taken from the writinges of Catholick Doctors and the Fathers, whereof ſome do neither
fortify, nor hurt his cauſe, and others do proue euen
contrary to that, for which he alledgeth them. In reguard of which his dull, groſſe, and abſurd kind of
reaſoning and arguing, if it be true in Philoſophy,
that the vnderſtanding doth work better, or worſe,
as the ſpirits are more or leſſe pure, and that the ſpirits are become more or leſſe pure, according to the
quality of the nutriment that the body taketh: I muſt
then conclude, that when M. Whyte penned this his

Treatiſe

Treatiſe particulerly for his deare Country men of Lancaſhyre (as himſelfſaith) it ſemeth he then remayning there, did vſe to feede much on his Lancaſhire diſh, the *Gooſe*.

The 4. Paragraph.

Wherein are diſcuſſed certaine proofes of M. W. *in behalf of the proteſtantes markes of the Church*.

M. Whyte, in page 104. and ſome few leaues after, diſcourſing of the notes of the Church, vndertaketh to proue, that *The true doctrine of faith, and lawfull vſe of the Sacramentes, are the proper and infallible*
7 Io. 10.   *markes, wherby it muſt be iudged which is the true Church*.

8 Mat. 18. In proofe hereof, he produceth diuers paſſages of Scripture, where our Sauionr ſaid, 7 *My ſheepe here my voice*. And againe. 8 *Where two or three are gathered together in my name: there am I in the middeſt of them*. In lyke ſort thoſe wordes of S. Mathew.
9 Mat. 7. 9 *You ſhall know the falſe prophets by their frutes*. And
10 Gal. 6. finally that ſaying of S. Paule, 10 *As many as walk according to this rule* (meaning according to the rule of a true Faith) *peace vpon them, and mercy, and vpon the Iſraell of God*. Againe thoſe wordes of the Apoſtle
11 Ephe. 2. touching the Church. 11 that *It is the howſhold of God, built vpon the foundation of the Apoſtles and Prophets*. As alſo where it is ſaid, that the Scripture *is a*
m 2. Pet. 1. m *ſhyning light*.

Now what Alcumiſt in the world can abſtract out of any of theſe textes, that ſenſe or meaning which ſhall prooue, that true doctrine is a ſufficient mark to vs, wherby we may infallibly diſcerne, which is the
true

true Church of God? He may as eaſely draw fyre out
of water, or earth out of ayre, betwene which, there
are no ſymbolizing qualities. For let vs ſee how probably we can inferre, what is intended out of the ſaid
Scriptures: as thus. *Chriſt ſaith, My ſheepe here my voice :
Therefore true doctrine is to vs a ſigne of the true Church .
Againe, Where two or three are gathered together in my
name, there am I in the middeſt of them : Therfore we are to
learne the true Church from the true doctrine* . Strangely
inferred : for how ſhall we know (euer abſtracting the
Authority of the Church) who are Chriſtes ſheepe ?
or who are they which are gathered together in his
name? If it be replyed, they are thoſe who haue true
doctrine : then I demaund, how can we be aſſured who
haue true doctrine? If it be anſweared, they haue true
doctrine, who heare the word truly preached, & enioy
a perfect miniſtration of the Sacraments : then I aſke,
how ſhall I be acertained, that ſuch do heare the word
truly preached, and enioy a perfect miniſtration of the
Sacramentes? But here my anſwear is at a ſtand, and
flieth for ſanctuary, to his Apocalypticall and reuealing ſpirit. Thus it is cleare in what circles & mazes
M. Whyte, or any other walketh, through the vaine
ſuggeſtions and imaginations, of a light, vaperous, &
giddy braine.

The like connexion with the former concluſion,
haue the other places of Scripture aboue cyted : The
which after he haith ſet downe, then page 107. he
deſcendeth to the Authorities of Fathers, and Catholick Authors, labouring (though moſt weakly) to
hayle from their wordes, his former Illation. To this
end he bringeth in S. Epiphanius ſaying of an heri-
tike 12 *This man is found altogether different from the* 12 li. 2. hær.
holy Scriptures &c . If then he be diſſenting from them, he ca. 48.

is altogether an alyen from the holy Catholick Church.

Here we graunt, that in the true nature of faith, who diſſenteth from the Scriptures, diſſenteth from the Church, but yet this proueth not, that the doctrine of faith, or adminiſtration of the Sacramentes, may ſerue to vs, as markes, to demonſtrate out the Church. Againe he produceth M. Raynouldes affirming that 13 *The true Church, and the true faith, are ſo knitt together, that the one inferreth and concludeth the other, for from the true Church, is concluded the true faith, and from the true faith, the true Church.* All this is true, yet it followeth not from hence, that *faith is more knowne to vs then the Church,* and couſeqnently that it ought to ſerue to vs, as a cleare and euident mark, to point out aſwell to the vnlearned, as learned, which is the true Church.

Adde hereto, that theſe wordes euen in M. Whytes ſenſe, aſmuch impugne him as vs: for if they imply faith to be a marke of the Church: they alſo reciprocally imply the Church to be a marke of the true Faith.

Finally, to omitte many other teſtimonies of Catholickes produced to the lyke end (whoſe particuler anſweares do ryſe from the circumſtances of the places, and therefore here omitted) he labouring to ſhew, that Faith is knowne before the Church, and conſequently that it is a note thereof: bringeth in *Picus Mirandula* thus ſpeaking of the Scriptures. 14 *They do not moue, they do not perſwade, but they enforce vs, they dryue vs forward, they violently conſtraine vs. Thou readeſt wordes rudely and homely, but ſuch as are quick, liuely, flaming, ſhyning, pearcing to the bottome of the ſpirit, and by their admirable power, tranſforming the whole man.*

Now who can inferr out of theſe wordes, that the Scripture is knowne to vs before the Church, ſeeing indeede the priority of the one or the other, is not ſo

14 Refert.
Poſſen.

much as intimated here at all? And what praiſes are here aſcribed to the Scriptures, may truly belonge vnto them after we are aſſured of their being, and ex-poſitions by the warrant of Gods Church.

Thus we fynde, that the further we enter into our miniſters booke, the greater ouercharge of boote-leſſe and vnneceſſary teſtimonies, do euer preſent them ſelues to vs, manifeſting vnto the iudiceous and obſer-uant Reader, that this worke (though the firſt borne of his braine) is abortiue, imperfect, and weake, from all which ſtoare of impertinent proofes thus vaunting-ly by him alledged, demonſtratiuely (forſooth) to confirme, what he ſtill pretendeth to prooue : We may euict one irrefragable demonſtration *ex poſteriori*, to wit, that M. Whyte is abſolutly ignorant in the doc-trine of demonſtrations,

The 5. Paragraph.

Wherein are examined ſtrange kindes of arguinges,
againſt the authority of the Church.

M. Whyte labouring to depreſſe the Churches au-uhority, and euer more and more venting out his ve-nome and poyſen againſt her, in the ſome of that good ſpirit wherein he ſpeaketh, vndertaketh pag. 126. & ſome others following, to proue, that the teaching of the Church is to be examined (for ſo he entituleth thoſe leaues) As alſo he ſaith, *It is neceſſary for euery particuler man, to examine and iudge of the thinges the Church teacheth him*; thus geuing the raynes to euery priuate and ignorant fellow, vnder the tecture & pre-text of gods ſecret illuminations, to iudg his owne iudg, and ſo to call in queſtion, the reputation & ho-

nour

nour of her from whose chaſt loynes euen him ſelf is (at leaſt originally) deſcended. But that we may better ſee how little conducing his teſtimonies alledged are to the purpoſe: let vs firſt ſet downe what the Catholickes do freely graunt & teach in this point.

They ioyntly teach, that the bound of ſubiecting ones ſelf to the Churches Authority, is properly incumbent vpon Chriſtians, who are made members of the Church by baptiſme, and conſequently do owe their obedience thereunto, and not vpon infidels or Iewes, who are not obliged to embrace Chriſtian Religion, except they ſee it confirmed by miracles, or ſome other enforcing reaſons of credibility: Neuertheleſſe, though an heritike do ſinne, in doubting of the Churches Authority, yet ſuppoſing that his doubt and ſinne, he doth not euill to examine the doctrine of the Church, according to the Scriptures, if ſo be he procedeth herein, onely with a deſyre of ſynding the truth.

Now let vs ſee what Authorities M. Whyte alledgeth to proue his former poſitions. Firſt he vrgeth thoſe wordes of the Apoſtle, **a** *Try all thinges, & hould that which is good.* As alſo thoſe of our Sau. **b** *If any man will do the will of God, he ſhall know of the doctrine, whether it be of God, or whether I ſpeake of my ſelf.* And againe that of S. Iohn. **c** *Derely beloued beleue not euery ſpirit, but try the ſpirits whether they be of God.* In like ſort thoſe wordes of Chriſt. **d** *Beware of falſe prophets, by their frutes you ſhall know them.* And finally (beſides the example of the men of Berææa ſearching the Scriptures, **e**) he vrgeth that where the Apoſtle counſeleth the Hebrewes, that **f** *Through longe cuſtome, they ſhould haue their wittes exerciſed both to diſcerne good and euill.* But for greater perſpicuity

a 1 Theſ. 5.
b Io. 7.
c 1. Io. 4.
d Mat. 7.
e Act. 17.
f Hebr. 5.

cuity, let vs fhape one or two of thefe textes, to the
true point here of the queftion. Thus then. *Try all
thinges, and hould what is good: therefore euery priuate
man may vndertake to cenfure the whole Church of God.*
Which wordes indeede do not preffe the doubt, feeing both thofe wordes, and that place of S. Iohn, c.
4. are directed properly to fuch onely, to whom it belongeth to trye and examine, both doctrine, and fpi-
rits, to wit, not to euery particuler member of the
Church, but onely to the Bifhops and Paftors thereof,
who are a *Speculatores domus Ifrael.* Againe if by Ezech. 33.
this text euery priuate man, may trye, reiect, or allow,
all thinges at his pleafure: then may he reiect or allow (as him felf thinketh good) the holy Scriptures:
for in the former wordes of the Apoftle there is no limitation at all. But to procede to an other text.
*Beware of falfe prophets, by their frutes you fhall knowe
them: therefore euery priuate man is to examine the doctrine
of all the Prophets and Paftors of the Church affembled together in a lawfull generall Councell.* Againe the men
of Berea (who were no Chriftians) were allowed to
trye the doctrine of S. Paule: therefore euery Chriftian (who by force of his fecond birth or regenerati-
on, is made a member and fonne of the Church) may
examine, controule, and reiect, the publick faith of
the faid Church.

Doctor-lyke inferred, as if there were no difparity
herein, betwene him who is not a Chriftian (& confequently acknowledgeth not any fubmiffion or reuerence to gods Church) and an other who is a Chriftian, and therefore in his baptifme doth implicitly re-
figne him felf, and his Iudgment, to the Authority
of the Church.

With the lyke want of connection or true referēce,
M. W.

M. Whyte preffeth to the fame purpofe, the teftimonies of certaine auncient Fathers, whofe drift in fuch
their writinges, was to wifh men to examine by the
Scriptures, the doctrine of priuate and particuler men,
left, as the Apoftle faith, *Circumferantur omni vento
doctrinæ.* b all which he will needes extend, to the
difcuffing of the doctrine of the whole Church. And
thus particulerly he alledgeth that faying of S. Chry-
foftome. c *Seeing we take the Scriptures which are fo
true and plaine, it will be an eafy matter for you to iudge.
And tell me, haft thou any wit or iudgment? For it is not
a mannes part, barely to receaue whatfoeuer he heareth.
Say not, I am no fcholler, and can be no Iudg, I can condemne no opinion, for this is but a fhift &c.* The fcope
onely of which place, is (as is faid) to refute the doctrine of euery new fectary euen from the Scriptures,
a courfe which we willingly admit and allow.

Thus you fee how our minifter is not afhamed to
peruert and detort, the graue Authotitie of this auncient Father.

But here the Reader is to vnderftand, that M. W.
his cheif proiect in this firft part of his booke, is to de-
preffe with all contempt & fcorne, the venerable authority of the Church. For the more facilitating
whereof, he mafketh this his intent, vnder the fhadow
of afcribing all reuerence and honour to the Scriptures,
both for their fufficiency, as contayning exprefly all
thinges neceffary to faluation, as alfo for their abfolute Soueraignty and Prerogatiue, indetermininge
inappealeably, all controuerfies of faith and religion
whatfoeuer. The which courfe is not embraced by him
(or any other fectary) fo much for any peculier honour they beare to the Scriptures: But that by this
fleight and euafion, they may declyne the waight and

force

b Eph. 4.

c Chrifoft.
in Act. ho.
33.

force of all proofes & authorities, deduced either frō
the vnanimous confent of Fathers, from Oecumeni-
call and generall Councels, or vnintermitted practife of
the Church: And fo all doubtes of Faith, being for
their proofes reduced onely to the written word, their
owne priuate fpirit onely, muft finally decree, how
the faid word is to be vnderftoode, either for the impugning or defending, of any fuch pointes controuerted.

The 6. Paragraph

Wherein are examined fundry argumentes framed by
M. W. againft the vnity of Catho-
lickes, in matters of Re-
ligion.

Not many leafes after, M. Whyte, as well knowing the force of vnity in Faith, fince it is true, that
God 1 *Non eft diffenfionis Deus, fed pacis,* goeth a- 1 Cor. 14.
bout to fhew, that the Catholickes enioy not any vnity and concord in their doctrine, and therefore he thus
ftileth thofe leafes. *The papiftes haue no vnity in doctrine.*
And page. 156. he further faith. *The papiftes agree in*
nothing wherein they diffent from vs. If either M. W.
or any other can proue fo much, I muft graunt that he
greatly aduauntageth his caufe, feeing thofe wordes 2 Ifay. 19.
of the Prophet 2 *Concurrere faciam Aegiptios contra*
Aegiptios, are tipically vnderftoode of the inteftine
warres and diffentions mantained by the profeffors of
falfe doctrine. This his vaunt he beginneth to exem-
plify in diuers particulers, in the proofe whereof, the
iudiceous Reader fhall fynde, that this our imparti-
ment minifter (for fo he may well be tearmed, fince he

altogether infifteth in fuch vnneceffary and immateriall ftuffe) endeuoreth moft calumnioufly to bleare the
iudgmentes of the ignorant, they not being able at the
firft fight, to perceaue the very tuch of any doubt or
queftion betwene the proteftants and vs. Many autho
rities of Catholickes he produceth to this ende, the
fenfe and meaning of which, he moft ftrangely peruer-
teth from the true intention of the writer, which receaue their full fatiffaction, from the circumftances of
the place.

But now here I am (according to my former prefcribed methode) to difplay the weaknes of fuch teftimonies, which being acknowledged in their true &
natiue fenfe and conftruction, do nothing at all contradict the Catholick doctrine againft which they are
vrged, and confequently do not conuince any wante
of vnity in doctrine amonge the Catholickes. Firft the
he alledgeth againft prayer in an vnknowne tongue,

3 Chrift. In-   *Cotarenus.   3   The prayers which men vnderftand not,*
ftruct. p. 212 *want the frute which they fhould reape if they vnderftoode*
them: for they might both fpecially intend their myndes to
god, for the obtayning euen in fpeciall of that, which with
their mouthes they beg: and alfo through their pyous fenfe
of their praier then vttered, they fhould be more edefyed.
They want therefore this frute. Thus farre Contarenus.

Now here M. W. is to know, that Contarenus
doth not here abfolutely condemne prayer in a ftrange
tongue (which is the lyfe of this controuerfy betwene
the proteftantes and vs, fince they fay it is merely vnlawfull, and we hould it lawfull) but onely feemes to
preferre praier in a vulgar and knowne tongue before
it, which in regaurd onely of the particuler frute a-
boue fpecifyed, is in the iudgment of moft (if not all
Catholickes) more profitable then the other, though
the

the other haue certaine peculier helpes and aduanta-
ges to it ſelf: But what is this to the lawfulnes or vnlawfulnes of praying in a ſtrange tongue? or what kind
of logick is this: *Prayer for ſome particuler reaſons, is
better in a vulgar tongue then in a ſtrang tongue: therefore it is abſolutely vnlawfull in a ſtrange tongue?* In lyke
ſort, touching latin ſeruice, he bringeth in *S.* Thomas of Aquine, & Caietaine, affirming that it were
better for the *edification of the Church, if ſuch Prayer   4 In 1. Cor.
were in a vulgar tongue.* 4 What Catholick deny-   14.
eth this, if he haue onely reſpect to the edification &
inſtruction of the hearers, and of nothing els?. But
ſeing the publick Liturgies and prayers of the Church,
are principally directed to other endes, then to the inſtruction of the ſtanders by, what doth this teſtimony force againſt the contrary practiſe of the Church
therein?

Againe for the euacuating of the force and opera-
tion of confeſſion of ſinnes, he bringeth in Caietane   5 3. Tho. q.
teaching that 5 *A man by contrition without any con*   8. art. 4.
feſſion, is made cleane, & a formall member of the Church,
which indeede is the generall doctrine of all Catholickes: and therefore the receaued poſition with them
in the ſchooles is, that *Attrition* (being a greeuing
for our ſinnes in a lower degree) *with Confeſſion, is
anſwearable to Contrition, without actuall Confeſſion.*
Yet here is to be noted, that true Contrition (which
is a repenting for our ſinnes in the higheſt degree, onely for the loue of God) can not be without Confeſſion, at leaſt *in voto,* and deſire, ſeing he can not be
truly and perfectly penitent, who neglecteth the ordinary meanes (if opportunity ſerue for the obtay
ning of them) appointed by God for the expiation of
ſinne. Now who ſeeth not the independency of this
inference

inference, *Sinne is remitted by Contrition without Con-*
feffion : therefore Corfeffion is abfolutely to be taken away.
Moft demonftratiuely concluded, as if euery man had
true and perfect Contrition, or hauing it, were infallibly affured thereof: and yet this is M. Whytes
tryfling kinde of arguing .

In like fort touching Iuftification by workes, which
(according to our Catholick doctrine) are to be done
in ftate of grace, and not by force of nature, and de-
riue their worth, not from the worker, but both from
the promife of God, as alfo from the paffion of our
Sauiour, (in the blood wherof they receaue a new
tincture) the Doctor idly introduceth ·S. Thomas A-
quinas thus teaching . *6 No workes , either Ceremo-*
niall, or Morall, are the caufe why any man is iuft before
God &c . And in an other place the fame S . Thomas,
7 The Apoftle fheweth Iuftification to be wrought by faith
onely : there is in the woork of the Law , no hope of iuftifica-
tion , but by faith onely . As if the queftion were, whether Ceremoniall , Iudaicall, and Legall workes, did
iuftify (which all Catholickes deny) and not workes
now in the new Teftament, as is aboue explaned.

Finally as vnwilling to be ouer labourfome & pain-
full, in fetting dowe more of M . Whytes trifling &
childifh ftuffe of this nature, feeing in this fenfe, that
faying houldeth . *Abfurdum eft res futiles, nimis ferio*
redarguere : I will therefore (forbearing diuers others)
conclude with the teftimony which againft the merit
of workes he vrgeth out of C. Bellarmine (a place before alledged, being a wilfull corruption, in concealing the wordes immediatly following explayning the
fenfe, but here vrged as a mere impertinency, though
taking the wordes in that very fenfe wherin M. W.
pretendeth) his wordes are thefe . *8 In regarde of*
the

6　In Galat .
3 . Lect. 4.

7 In Rom . 3.
Lect. 4.

8 de Iuftif.
l. 5 . ca. 7 .

the vncertainty of our owne righteoufnes, and becaufe of
the daunger of vaine-glory: *The faifeft way is to put our
confidence in the fole mercy of God* . Now wherein doth
he impugne the Catholick doctrine of merit, who teacheth (for the greater humbling of our felues, and by
reafon of our manifould finnes committed againft god,
and of our vncertainty of knowing whether the wotks
done by vs, be performed in fuch fort, as they are
truly pleafing to God) that we fhould for greater fe-
curity, afcribe nothing to our felues, but onely like
the Centurion, fhould flie to the boundleffe and infi -
nite mercy of his diuine Maiefty. Wherefore M . W .
can not difpute thus from the Cardinals wordes. *In
reguard of the vncertainty of our owne righteoufnes, and
becaufe of the daunger of vaine glory, the faifeft way is to
put our fole confidence in the fole mercy of God: Therfore
workes in generall do not merite, or therefore workes done
in true humility, and proceding from one that is righteous,
donot merite* . For the doubt here which Bellarmine in-
timateth, refteth not in the doctrine of merite, but in
the vncertainty of our doing of them, to wit, whe -
ther th y are performed by vs in that ftate, and with
all thofe due circumftances, as are requifite for them
that they may merite. But it feemeth that M . W .
can not fall vpon any obfcure fentences of Catholicks,
but inftantly he ftriueth to turne them as if they were
the fayinges of his owne brethren, like the fyre which
coueteth to conuert euery thing it toucheth into it
felf.

This done M . Whyte page 159. defcendeth to
fhew the different opinions of Catholickes touching
fome pointes of the reall prefence, as firft whether
(after the bread and wyne being changed by the words
of Confecration into the body and bloud of Chtift)

the accidences do remaine without a fubiect, or that
they haue their inherence in the quantity, or that the
body of Chrift fuftaineth them, or the lyke.

Secondly, how the accidents remaining after confecration, haue power *to* nourifh, to wit, whether the
thing nourifhed therewith, procede from the quantity, or that the fubftance of bread and wyne retur-
neth againe, and fo it caufeth the nutrition, or that
the accidences by Gods power, are changed into the
thing nourifhed, or fome fuch lyke manner.

Thus our minifter goeth on difcourᵢng very fober-
ly, how it appeareth from thefe and the like examples, that the *papiftes agree not in their doctrine*; and
further thus faith. *You may fee by thefe few examples,
how the papiftes are deuided about the principall articles of
their faith &c.* But here the iudiceous Reader may
fee, that touching the firft fort of Catholick teftimonies aboue explayned, we finde no difference of iudgment at all, betwene the Catholickes by him alledged, and other Catholickes. And as concerning their
feuerall opinions about thofe fecondary queftions of
the bleffed Sacrament, they are onely pointes of indifferency, and do not at all imply any difunion in
matter of faith. For touching the B. Sacrament, th t
which is principally an Article of our faith is, whether bread and wyne, be really, and truly changed by
the wordes of confecration, into the Body and bloud
of Chrift, the which all Catholickes whatfoeuer do
iointly and conftantly beleue. And as concerning
thofe other doubtes refulting out of the former confeffed Article, and vrged here by M. Whyte, they are
onely indifferences, and philofophicall queftions-dif-
puted in the fchooles, and by feuerall men, feuerally
mantained, without any breach of faith. But here I
fhould make bould (on the contrary part) to put M.

M. Whyte in mynd touching the diuifion in doctrine
among the proteftantes (a point heretofore touched in
this Treatife) that they are fuch, euen by the acknowledgment of them felues, as do wound the foundnes of
Chriftian faith : I think the difplaying thereof would
be litle pleafing vnto him, or gratefull to his caufe.
But for this prefent I will forbeare, and will onely
adde hereto (for the greater difaduantage of our aduerfaries, that when a Catholick obftinatly, and per-
tinaceoufly, mantaineth any herefy (for fuch accompted by the Church) he, *ipfo facto*, deuideth him felf
from the Church, and fo feaceth to be a member there
of, as feuerall tymes we graunt it hapneth : But the
cafe is otherwife among the proteftants . For albe-
it each of them doth defend his feuerall opinions in
the weightieft pointes of faith : yet they neuertheleffe
accompt one an other, as members of one and the fame
Church, as we fee by experience it faleth out, not only betwene the Lutherans and the Calueniftes, but alfo betwene our Englifh proteftantes, and the puritanes, who (notwithftanding the great difparity of
faith and doctrine amonge them) do in their owne o-
pinions, make vp one and the fame proteftants Church :
and do ftill repute each other, as faithfull brethren of
the faid Church, and zealous profeffoures of the gofpell .

Here now I will clofe vp this third and laft part of
this fmall Treatife, wherein I truft I haue difcouered
M . Whytes difioynted and loofe kynd of writing, all
which his reafoninges and authorities (feruing onely
as a taift to the Reader, what more he may expect in
this kind, if the minifters whole booke fhould be iudicially perufed) are taken out (deuiding his booke
into three partes) onely of the firft part, and fewer

D then

then twenty leafes of the said part, affordeth them all.
Many oth'r scores there are, which are scattered here
and there, by one or two, as incidentally he taketh
occasion to write, but all such I haue omitted, and
purposly made choice of such passages, within the former small compasse of his booke, as do minister seuerall and diuers testimonies of this nature, of one and
the same subiect. It were ouer laboursome to examine
his whole book in this sort, since indede it is throughout euen loaded with an ouercharg of the like boote-
lesse testimonies, he still filling vp many blankes and
spaces thereof, with such idle impertinecies, the
which perhaps to a vulgar sight, may seeme to crosse
our Catholick doctrine, yet indeede the transparency
of them is such, as they cause not so much as any re-
flection in the eye and vnderstanding of the iudiceons,
but in reguard of their emptines and want of force,
they may be resembled (to speake in S. Peters wordes
2. *Pet.* 2.) to *wells without water, and cloudes carried
about with tempestes.*

WOrthy and iudiceous *Academians*, here now I am to géue a full ftop vnto my pen, fince I hope (according to my vndertaken tafke) I haue difcouered fuch ftoare of impoftures in this my aduerfaries booke, as that they may in reafon be fufficient to difopinion you of his fuppofed worth and eftimation. He is I graunt your fonne, in refpect whereof I know you can not but with a motherly and compaffionate eye, behould his blemifhes, and inwardly lament to fee your Whyte thus foyled. Notwithftanding it refteth on your part (euen for the faluing of your owne honoures) to withdraw hereafter your fauoures from fo vndeferuing a branch; fince pittie it is, that learning, ingenuity, and integrity (whereunto your felues deferuedly pretend) fhould become a fanctuary to collufion, falfhood, and impurity.

And now feeing here I haue vntwifted the cheife threedes whereupon the whole loome of his Treatife is wouen : I doubt not but out of your owne cleareeyd Iudgmentes, you will immediatly looke vpon the fame, as it is in it felf fraughted with fuch vnworthy ftuffe, and not as it haith receaued light and grace from the weake opinion of the ignorant, and feduced multitude : which I rather expect peculiarly at your handes, fince your felnes know, that in a true vew of any thing, *refracted beames* neuer afford a perfecte fight. And thus to your owne cenfure and chaftifment I remitt M. Whyte, whom not without iufte caufe, I may well range in the Catalogue of thofe, of whom God by his Prophet faith *Non mifi eos, & ipfi prophetabant in nomine meo mendaciter. Ier. 27.*

And next to come to thee (good reader) here thou

feeft what fcarres do remaine vpon the face of this our minifters reputation, him felf firft playing the corrupter, then a lyer, and then a tryfling writer. But feeing thou art now partly inftructed of the minifters foule deportment herein, I appeale euen to thine owne confcience, whether thou art inwardly perfwaded, that he haith any honefty, any faith, any Religion, finally, any feare of God, who is not affraid thus fhamelefly, prophanely, and heathnifhly, to handle the higheft mifteries of Chriftianity. And if thou feeft reafon to be induced fo to thinke, what ftupor and dulnes of vnderftanding, yea what madnes then is it in thy felf, to aduenture thy foules euerlafting faluation, or damnation vpon the bare affiance and credit of fo perfideous and corrupt a writer. Therefore let this mans want of fincerity and true dealing, awaken thy iudgment in the difquifition of gods infallible truth. Make triall by thine owne particuler fearch, whether thefe deceiptes, wherewith I charge the Doctor, be true or no: and if thou findeft that he ftandes guilty thereof, then retyre back, and inftantly caft of both him and his doctrine, affuring thy felf, that the caufe which he iuftificth is wrong, in that God (who

pfal. 100 ones faid d *Ambulans in via immaculata, hic mihi miniftrabat)* will not fuffer his facred will to be reuealed by fuch impoftors and deceiuers, Let not the already conceaued opinion of his learning, ouer-fway thy Iudgment, but rather fay with thy felf, that faith muft needes be erroneous, which can not fufficiently be mantained by learning, except withall it be mantained with lying, feeirg truth nedeth not the fupport of falfhood. Be affured that though for the tyme M. W. or any other of our aduerfaries, feeme to make good their caufe by their much writing, whereby in a vul

gare-

gare eye, they vent out good ftoare of litterature and
reading, yet after fuch their workes are diligently
perufed and anfweared, by laying open their falfhoodes, corruptions, and fuch other cullufions : the
Catholick caufe (as experience haith taught) is greatly aduauntaged thereby, themfelues by this meanes
running into greater difeftimation and contempt euen
of their owne followers : Such is the fweetnes of gods
prouidence, that the *Ifraelites* of the Catholick Church
are euer in the ende deliuered from the handes of the
Egiptians, and fee their enemies drowned in the *red
fea* of fhame and confufion   e *Non commouebitur in*   e pf. 121,
æternum qui habitat in Ierufalem.

But now laftly M. Whyte to come more nearly to
your felf, with whom I muft in a word or two take
leaue : Tell me euen betwene god and your owne
confcience (if as yet you retaine any touch of confcience) did you not write this your booke with a
fearefull trembling hande, in remembring, that as god
(according to his Iuftice) doth euer punifh all kinde
of finnes : fo particulerly he poureth out his vyols of
wrath and indignation in greater aboundance, vpon
thofe who feduce the ignorant by fuch deceauable
meanes : How many poore foules fhall ryfe againft you
at the moft dreadfull day, who fhall continew in e-
ternall torments, for being mifled by this your moft
poyfenous, corrupt, and lying writinges : Are not
your owne perfonall finnes fufficient to draw on your
perdition, but you muft be loaded with the euerlafting ouerthrow of diuers others foules to further the
fame : If feuere punifhmentes be to be inflicted vpon
them, who will expugne or deface, any one publick
record of ciuill and temporall matters : what confufion then are they to vndergoe, who not once, not

twice, but many fcoares of tymes, haue wickedly cor-
raded, corrupted, and belyed (of which your felfe is
found moft guilty) the auncient monumentes of the
primitiue Fathers, and the writinges of other moft
learned Doctors, wherein (next to the holy Scriptures) is contained the fpirituall tenure of our Chriftian faith, and by the producing whereof, we make
good our tytle, to the rich inheritance of mannes
faluation. Reflect vpon your owne cafe (you, euen
you) who remaines in f *the gaull of bi.ternes, & in*
the bond of iniquity. Your ftate yet is remediable, fince
fo longe as you haue tyme of repentance, fo longe
g *your ficknes is not vnto death.* Wherefore make vfe
of that fhort remnant, and fuffer not earthly confide
rations of preferment, ambition, and the like, any
longer to interpofe them felues, betwene your fight
and the truth. I fhall be glad (as the light appeared to Adam to bewray his finne and fhame) if
this my difcouery, may be of force to difpell that fpirituall darkneffe of your malice againft the Catholick
Church, fo repentingly acknowledging your inex-
cufable faultines in your former worke. Be not agre-
ued at thefe my fharpe admonitions (fince the more
feuere, the more medicinable) but remember that the
fight of Toby was reftored, by the bitter gaule of the
fifhe. I can not but bewaile your incorrigiblenes, if
this my councell, proceding onely from Charity, fhall
be fo farre from winning you to a better courfe, that
(as in fome natures it hapneth) it may be found to
raife your malice hereafter againft Gods Church, to
a higher ftrayne, like vnto fome medicines, which (as
the Phifitions fay) if they do not purge the humour
intended: them felues doe turne into the faid hu-
niour.

                                                    But

But to conclude , M . Whyte (howfoeuer you entertaine my wordes) fare well , *feare hell* , *feare dam-*
nation , and do not thus precipitately and defperat -
ly runne vpon the dinte of gods moſt dreadfull comminations & threates , him ſelf thundring ,   h *Erit-* h Ezech. 13.
manus mea ſuper Prophetas &c . *My handes ſhall be vpõ*
the Prophets that ſee vaine thinges , and diuine a lye : in the
Councell of my people they ſhall not be , & in the Scripture
of the houſe of Iſraell , they ſhall not be written , neither
ſhall they enter into the Lande of Iſraell : And you ſhall
know that I am the Lord God , for that they haue decea-
ued my people ſaying , Peace , & there is no peace .

Laus **Deo** , & B . Virgini Mariæ .

D 4

THOMAS PRESTON and
THOMAS GREEN
Appellatio
1620

APPELLATIO

QVA

REVERENDI PA-
TRES, *THOMAS PRESTONVS,*
& *THOMAS GREENÆVS*

Añgli Benedictini, ac Sacræ Theologiæ Professores, ab Ill.ᵐⁱˢ Dominis Cardinalibus ad Indicem deputatis ad Romanum, Summumq;
Pontificem immediatè pro-
vocarunt.

(*Cardinalibus*)   (*Pontificem*)
Nemo poteſt me (illis) donare, (Cæſarem) appello.
Aᴄᴛ. 25.

AVGVSTÆ,
Apud Bᴀᴘᴛɪsᴛᴀᴍ Fᴀʙʀᴠᴍ.
1 6 2 0.
Permiſſu Superiorum.

AD LECTOREM.

Cias (*Lector benevole*) nos iftis rationib⁹ motos infrafcriptam hanc noftram *Appellationem* typis, quamprimùm commodè potuimus, excudendam curaffe. *Primò*, vt citiùs, & fecuriùs perveniat ad notitiam *Suæ Sanctitatis*, quam perfonaliter adire, cùm in cuftodia detenti fimus, non poffumus, neque *Procuratorem* ad *Curiam Romanam* mittendi nobis facultas competit, cum ad victum, & veftitum vix nobifmetipfis, & multò minus *Procuratori* neceffaria habeamus; atque infuper tanta eft *Card. Bellarmini*, eiufque fequacium

in *Curiâ Romanâ* potentia, vt vix quif-
quam Catholicus, vir prudens, & eruditus inveniri pofsit, qui noftræ caufæ patrocinium in ea *Curia* fufcipere, & *Card.*
Bellarmino fefe opponere, illique in faciem
refiftere audeat: nemo autem ad impoffibile tenetur. *Secundò*, quia non alia via
commoda, & fecura, quàm per fcripta publica, ob rationes iam dictas, hanc *Appella-*
tionem profequi, & *Suæ Sanctitati*, ad quam
appellamus, rationes, & merita noftræ
caufæ proponere, eaque, quæ contra nos
obijcientur, refellere valemus. *Tertiò*,
vt fratribus noftris Catholicis, quantum
in nobis eft, fatisfaciamus, qui audientes,
nos etiam ab *Ill^{mis} Dominis Cardinalibus* ad
Indicem deputatis ad *Summum* Pontificem
immediatè appellaffe, neque opprefsiones
noftras, & rationes, ob quas ab illis ad
Suam Sanctitatem provocamus, perfentien-
tes, fortè fcandalum inde accipiant, no-
bifque calumniam ea de caufa imponant.
Quartò, vt *Sanctitas Sua*, poftquam per-
fpexerit, nos, innocentiæ noftræ confifos,
intolerandas

intolerandas oppreſsiones, calumnias, & gravamina, quæ per ſummam iniuriam patimur, toti mundo propalaſſe, cauſam noſtram, abſque vlla perſonarum acceptione, quàm diligentiſſimè examinet, atque (vt toti mundo, qualiter cauſam noſtram terminare velit, nunc expectanti ſatiſfaciat) pro munere, quo fungitur, Paſtorali, vel nos quamprimùm liberet à calumnijs, & oppreſſionibus, quas iniuſtè patimur, atque declaret nos innocentes eſſe, minimè verò *hæreticos, Pſeudo-Catholicos, Eccleſiæ Catholicæ-Romanæ non filios, ſed hoſtes etiam iuratos, Sediq́ Apoſtolicæ rebelles*, provt à *Card. Bellarmino*, non ſolùm priuatim apud *Suam Sanctitatem*, ſed ſcriptis etiam publicis, totique mundo cognitis, iniquè, & per calumniam traducimur; Vel, ſi *Sanctitas Sua* nos de crimine aliquo, (cuius adhuc conſcij non ſumus) poſtquam, de eo ſpeciatim, iuxta iuris naturalis ordinem, accuſati, admoniti, citati, & auditi nos defendere non poterimus, condemnare velit, vt crimen illud,

illud, tum nobis, tum toti mundo inno-
tefcat, ob quod condemnari mereamur.
Londini, è Carcere Clinkenfi, die vndecimo
Decembris 1620.

Veftri in CHRISTO fratres,
& fervi

Thomas Preftonus.
Thomas Greenæus.

THOMÆ PRESTONI,
&
THOMÆ GREENÆI
BENEDICTINORVM ANGLORVM,
ad *Romanum, Summumq̃ Pontificem*
immediatè Appellatio.

1. Niverſis Chriſti fidelibus præſentes literas inſpecturis D. *Thomas*
(alias *Rolandus*) *Preſtonus*, Presbyter, Ordinis S. *Benedicti*, Congregationis *Caſinenſis* Religioſus, ac
Sacræ Theologiæ Profeſſor, &
Frater *Thomas Greenæus*, Presbyter, Ordinis S. *Bene-*
dicti, Congregationis *Hiſpanicæ* Religioſus, ac Sacræ
Theologiæ Profeſſor, Salutè in Domino. Notũ faci-
mus, quòd Nos, *Londini*, in Carcere *Clinkenſi* exiſtentes,
modo & forma contentis in quodam codicillo ma-
nuſcripto, cuius tenor inferiùs deſcribitur, & inſeritur,
ad *Sanctiſſimum Dominum* noſtrum *Papam* immediatè
provocavimus, & appellavimus, ac provocamus &
appel-

appellamus.   * Cuius quidem codicilli manuſcriptⁱ tenor ſequitur, & eſt talis.

2.   *In Dei nomine, Amen.* Præmiſſis expreſſè Prote-ſtationibus, quòd contra *Vnam, Sanctam, Catholicam,* & *Apoſtolicam Eccleſiam,* quam totius Orbis magiſtram, & obtinere principatum credimus, Sanctæque *Sedis Apoſtolicæ* authoritatem, ac *Sanctiſſimi Domini* noſtri *Papæ* bene conſulti, aut *Illuſtriſſimorum Dominorum Cardinalium,* qui ab ipſo *Domino Papa* Iudices conſtituti ſunt, bene etiam conſultorum poteſtatem, nihil dicere intendimus, ſi quid ex lubrico linguæ forſan malè dictum ſit, parati emendare. Sed, quoniam tum ipſemet *Dominus Papa,* quamvis à Deo poteſtatem immediatè habeat, tum multò magis ipſimet *Domini Cardinales,* quamvis à *Papa* Iudices conſtituti ſint, & ab eo poteſtatem delegatam accipiant, non inde tamen impeccabiles efficiuntur, aut poteſtatem iniquum iudicium iudicandi acceperunt: Idcirco, ſi prædicti *Domini Cardinales* aliquid, quod iniuſtum eſt, decreverint, virosq; innocentes, ex prava informatione, malove conſilio, ſuis mandatis, ac decretis iniquè oppreſſerint, illis parendum non eſt, immo illis reſiſti iure poteſt. Quòd ſi, præ ingenti eorum potentia, illis reſiſti commodè non poſſit, omniaq; ferme reſiſtendi remedia ſublata ſint, vnum tamen iure naturali proditum eſt (quod nullorum potentiâ tolli poteſt) ad *Superiorem,* in

quibus *Superior* eſt, *Appellationis* remedium, cùm ſit *quædam defenſio,* ᵃ & *præſidium innocentiæ,* quæ iure diuino, naturali, & humano cuique competit, quamque nemo, ᵇ quantumvis potentiſſimus, auferre poteſt.

                                            Ad

Ad huius ergo *Appellationis* remedium, quo oppreſſi ſublevantur, confugientes Nos, D. *Thomas* (alias *Rolandus*) *Preſtonus*, Presbyter, Ordinis *S. Benedicti*, Congregationis *Caſſinenſis* Religioſus, ac Sacræ Theologię Profeſſor, & Frater *Thomas Greenæus*, Presbyter, Ordinis *S. Benedicti*, Congregationis *Hiſpanicæ* Religioſus, ac Sacræ Theologiæ Profeſſor, nomine noſtro, & *Rogeri Widdringtoni* Catholici Angli, cæterorumq; eius doctrinæ [e] adhærentium, & adhærere volentium, à duobus decretis *Illuſtriſſimorum Dominorum Cardinalium* ad *Indicem* deputatorum, nempe anno Domini 1614. die 16. *Martij* contra *Apologiam pro Iure Principum*, & *Diſputationem Theologicam de Iuramento fidelitatis, eorumq; Authorem*, atque etiam die 12. *Novembris* 1616. contra eiuſdem *Rogeri Widdringtoni* ad S. D. *Paulum V. Pontificem Max. humillimam Supplicationem* editis, tanquam manifeſtè iniuſtis, & ab ipſiſmet *Illuſtriſſimis Dominis Cardinalibus* ad *Indicem* deputatis, tanquam parum æquis, ſuſpectis, & malè informatis Iudicibus, & à quacunque ſententia, ſiue definitiva, ſive interlocutoria, aut alio quovis nomine nuncupetur, ab ipſis intuitu prædictæ *Widdringtoni* doctrinæ, aut vllo ad illam reſpectu habito, vel iam lata & denunciata, vel deinceps ferenda & denuncianda, & à quavis alia authoritate etiam *Illuſtriſſimis Dominis Cardinalibus*, aut *Nuncijs Apoſtolicis*, alijsve quibuſcunque delegata, vel deleganda ad *Sanctiſſimum Dominum* noſtrum *Papam*, qui ſupremus totius Eccleſiæ, omniumq; noſtrûm, etiam *Illuſtriſſimorum Cardinalium*, Paſtor, Pater, & in ſpiritualibus Superior eſt, immediatè appellavimus, & provocavimus, & per præſentes ad eum imme-

[e] *Diximus* [doctrinæ Widdringtoni] *non quaſi ipſe iſtius doctrinæ primus inventor fuerit, quandoquidem, vt ex libris eius conſtat, eam Sancti Patres, antiqui Theologi, ac Iuriſconſulti, & moderni etiam Doctores Catholici, vnà cum Regno & Statu* Franciæ *propugnaverint, & propugnent: ſed quoniam* Widdrington' *iſtius antiquæ doctrinæ præcipuus hiſce temporibus propugnator eſt, eam idcirco (ſequuti in hoc ipſam Adverſariorũ phraſin)* Widdringtoni *doctrinam vocitamus.*

diatè appellamus,& provocamus,ob rationes,& gravamina, quæ ex narratione initij & progressus huius controversiæ perspicuè innotescent.

3. Notum inprimis est, *Rogerum Widdringtonum* Catholicum Anglum, multis iam abhinc annis, ad impia *Coniurationis pulverariæ* principia refellenda, *duos* præ cæteris libros, adversùs *Card. Bellarminum* potissimùm conscriptos, in lucem edidisse: *Primum,* anno Domini 1611. impressum, in quo ex *Card. Bellarmini* principijs probare contendit, non esse *rem certam,* & *de fide* (vti *Card. Bellarminus* prætendebat) quòd penes *Romanam Pontificem* sit potestas *Principes supremos* (qui, iuxta vnanimem *Sanctorum Patrum* [d] doctrinam, solo Deo in rebus temporalibus minores sunt) deponendi, suisq; Dominijs temporalibus privandi: Ob quam causam liber ille, *Apologia Card. Bellarmini pro Iure Principum adversùs suas ipsius rationes* &c. à *Widdringtono* nuncupatur, non quòd ipsemet *Card. Bellarminus* illam *Apologiam* composuerit, vti personatus *Schulckenius* calumniatur, cùm ipse *Widdringtonus* seipsum, & non *Card. Bellarminum* illius *Apologiæ* Authorem esse expressè affirmaverit, sed quoniam *Widdringtonus Apologiam* illâ ex principijs *Bellarmini* confecit, idcirco *Apologiam* Card. *Bellarmini,* seu ex principijs *Bellarmini* confectam, meritò nuncupavit. *Alterum,* anno Domini 1613. impressum, cui titulus est, *Disputatio Theologica de Iuramento fidelitatis Sanctissimo Patri Paulo Papæ V. dedicata,* in quo libro *Widdringtonus* per modum supplicis libelli, & ad *Suam Sanctitatem* plenius informandam, rationes proponit, ob quas Catholici Angli sibi firmiter persuadent,illud fidelitatis Iuramentum (ex occasione

[d] *Hos Patres citat Widdringtonus in detect. calum. §. 17. nu. 14.*

cafione *Coniurationis pulverariæ* , & ad diſtinguendos
ſubditos fideles, præſertim *Catholicos-Romanos* à perfidis
proditoribus, quiq; pulveris tormentarij *Coniuratorum*
(qui omnes *Catholici-Romani* erant) diſciplinæ adhæreſcunt, in generalibus Regni Comitijs lege publica
ſtabilitum, & per *Brevia Apoſtolica*, ex falſis præſertim
Card. Bellarmini, eiuſq; ſequacium informationibus
prohibitum, tanquam *multa continens, quæ fidei & ſaluti*
apertè adverſantur) poſſe ab illis, non obſtantibus prædictis *Brevibus*, licitè , & tutâ conſcientiâ præſtari.
Atq; omnia argumenta, quæ in contrarium obijci
ſolent, idem *Widdringtonus* clariſſimè diſſolvit, & ſpeciatim ad *Brevia Apoſtolica* Iuramentum prohibentia
copioſè reſpondet, & perſpicuè commonſtrat, ea in
duabus falſis ſuppoſitionibus fundata eſſe ; quarum
una eſt, quòd poteſtas Excommunicandi, Cenſuras
Eccleſiaſticas infligendi, ligandi & ſolvendi, & conſequenter ſpiritualis *Papæ* Primatus, in Iuramento a-
pertè abnegetur, quod apertiſſimè falſum eſſe *Wid-*
dringtonus contra *Card.* Bellarminum (qui ſcriptis publicis ᵉ illam falſitatem Catholicis obtrudere conatus
eſt) ex publica, & expreſſa *Regis* noſtri *Sereniſsimi* declaratione manifeſtè convincit: *Altera*, quòd poteſtas *Papalis* Principes in temporalibus *ſupremos* deponendi ſit res de *fide certa*, neq; vlla de ea apud eruditos Catholicos controverſia exiſtat, quod etiam non
minùs falſum eſſe, iam vniverſo orbi Chriſtiano ex
publicis Catholicorum ſcriptis, factis, & decretis, præſertim *Parliamenti Pariſienſis* , evidentiſſimè conſtat:
Vnde idem *Widdringtonus* ex notiſſimis Theologiæ
principijs euidenter concludit, poſſe Anglos Catho-

ᵉ *in ſuo* Torto
pag. 9. & in A-
pologia *cap.* 15.
in principio.

licos

licos tutâ conſcientiâ, & abſque vlla inobedientiæ, * aut irreverentiæ contra *Sedem Apoſtolicam* nota, prædictis *Brevibus*, in eiuſmodi falſis ſuppoſitionibus fundatis, * reſiſtere, & repugnare.

4. *Secundò*, dum prædicta *Diſputatio Theologica* ſub prælo eſſet, prodijt in lucem *Card. Bellarmini* ſub *Adolphi Schulckenij* nomine perſonati *Apologia* contra eundem *Widdringtonum* Coloniæ anno 1613 excuſa, quæ Romæ primùm, quoad libri ſubſtantiam impreſſa, ſed ab eodem *Card. Bellarmino*, ob rationes ſibi meliùs notas, nec tamen alijs planè incognitas, ſtatim ſuppreſſa erat; in quo libro perſonatus ille *Schulckenius*, extra omnis modeſtiæ, & charitatis Chriſtianæ limites, tam horrenda crimina *Widdringtono* imponit, illumq; tam inverecundè calumniatur, vt eum, quantumvis Eccleſiæ *Catholicæ Romanæ* ſe filium eſſe ſyncerè profiteatur, ipſo tamen *Luthero*, *Calvino*, aut alio quovis perditiſſimo, & in reprobum ſenſum dato homuncione deteriorem faciat, illumque, præter manifeſtæ hæreſeωs crimen, quod illi falſiſſimè obijcit, etiam impijſſimis *Chriſti Domini*, *Apoſtolorum*, *omniumq́*; *Chriſti Martyrum perſequutoribus*, & *Eccleſiæ Romanæ*, *Sediſq́*; *Apoſtolicæ hoſtibus iuratis* æquiparare non perhorreſcat.

5. Ecquis vir Catholicus, famæ ſuæ, & honoris non omnino prodigus, quique præſertim pro fide Catholica Romana palam agnoſcenda graues ærumnas, quibus alioquin non afficeretur, quotidie ſuſtinet, tam falſas, & horrendas calumnias æquo animo ferre poſſet, aut contra tam egregium calumniatorem, quantæcunque dignitatis fuerit, cœlum & terrá invo-

* *Quando enim Prælat⁹ aliquid præcipit, vnde periculum Religioni, aut Reip. aut tertiæ perſonæ timetur, & ſubdit⁹ dubitat, an Prælatus iuſtè præcipiat, nihil facit contra obedientiã ſubditus, ſi exigat à Prælato rationẽ præcepti, proponens humiliter* (vti Wriddrington⁹ Suæ Sanctitati ſæpiùs propoſuit) *rationes dubitandi. ita* Dom. Sotus *in lib.* de detegendo ſecreto *membr.* 3. *q.* 2. *in Reſponſ. ad* 1.

* *Quòd etiam obligatio præcepti declaratiui neceſſariò dependeat à ratione fundamentali, ſeu præcedenti præcepto, quod ſupponit & declarat., docet* Suarez *lib.* 3. de Legib⁹ *cap.* 14. *&* Leſſius *in* Suo Singletono *de diſcuſſione* decreti *magni* Concilij Lateran. *pag.* 45.

invocandi, & tam ab hominibus, quàm à Deo iustitiam postulandi finem vnquam faceret?

6. *Tertiò*, hac *Adolphi Schulckenij* seu potiùs *Card.*
Bellarmini Apologia in lucem edita, & Theologica *Ro-*
geri Widdringtoni de Iuramento fidelitatis Disputatione
(in qua quasdam prædicti *Schulckenij* calumnias,
quantùm brevitas Admonitionis ad Lectorem permitteret, nam ipsa Disputatio tunc sub prælo erat, perspicuè detexit) iam evulgatâ, & Romam delatâ, pub-
licatum est paucis post mensibus, nimirum mense
Martio anni sequentis, Sacræ Congregationis Illustrissimorum S. R. E. Cardinalium ad Indicem deputatorum (in qua Congregatione ipsemet *Card.*
Bellarminus, præcipuus *Widdringtoni* Adversarius, vel
primus, vel vnus ex primis erat, & proinde in ea causa
nec Iudex, nec Testis de iure esse poterat) Decretum
solemne, & Romæ in Typographia Apostolica impressum, in quo prædicti duo *Rogeri Widdringtoni* libri *penitus damnantur, & prohibentur*, & illorum Authori iniungitur, vt *quamprimùm se purget*, alioquin
Censuris, & alijs pænis Ecclesiasticis omnino coercendus,
nullo tamen prorsus crimine indicato, ob quod libri
illi *damnantur, & prohibentur*, uel à quo *illorum Author*
se *purgare* debet; quasi uerò posset aliquis ab illo
crimine se purgare, cuius nullum planè scrupulum,
aut notitiam habet.

7. Quin etiam Illustrissimus Nuncius Apostolicus tunc Bruxellis manens literis suis ad Reverendū
Dominum *Georgium Birkettum* Archipresbyterum datis 26 Novembris 1613 affirmavit, *se per* S. Romanæ
vniversalis Inquisitionis Congregationis *literas de*
mandato

mandato Suæ Sanctitatis *edoctum esse,* quòd Sanctitas
Sua *neque acceptare vellet dedicationem illius Disputationis*
(quæ tamen humillima tantùm ad *Suam Sanctitatem*
Supplicatio erat, vt Angli Catholici in fide Catholica,
atque in ijs rebus, quas *Sanctitas Sua* in Iuramento
fidei & saluti apertè aduersari suis *Brevibus* declarauerat, à Sua Beatitudine, vtpote supremo Ecclesiæ
Catholicæ Pastore, instruerentur) neque etiam *Au-*
thorem illius *Disputationis aut Catholicum esse, aut Ecclesiæ*
filium existimaret, cùm tamen *Author* ille & *Catholicum,*
& *Ecclesiæ Catholicæ Romanæ filium* se esse in ea *Disputa-*
tione profiteatur, & omnia sua scripta, atque seipsum
sacrosanctæ Ecclesiæ Catholicæ Romanæ iudicio
quàm humillimè subijciat. Talia certè piissimus, &
sanctissimus Pater, & Pastor de filijs & ovibus suis,
nisi ex sinistra Aduersariorum, & præsertim *Card. Bel-*
larmini, qui in Sacra illa Congregatione vnus ex primis erat, informatione, nequaquam iudicaret.

8. *Quartò,* statim atque Decretum istud Sacræ
Congregationis ad Authoris notitiam pervenit, ipse
intra paucissimos dies, nempe mense Iunio eiusdem
anni sese purgavit, humillima ad *Suam Sanctitatem*
Supplicatione transmissa, in qua plurimùm conqueritur, tam de prædictis *Illustrissimi Domini Nuncij lite-*
ris ad *Archipresbyterum* missis, quàm de iniusto illo, insolito, & planè inaudito *Illustrissimorum Cardinalium*
Decreto, & contra consuetudinem omnium totius
Orbis Tribunalium, quæ nemini præcipiunt, vt se
purget, alioquin pænis grauissimis castigandus, nisi
ipsum crimen indicent, à quo se purgare debeat:
Atque *Suam Sanctitatem* obnixè rogat, vt *Decretum*
illud

illud vel revocandum, & famâ *Widdringtoni*, eiufque
doctrinæ adhærentium inde grauiter, & iniuftè læfam reftituendam curet, vel aliquod faltem crimen,
ob quod libri Authoris damnati & prohibiti fint,
& à quo fefe purgare debeat, illi fignificare dignaretur, hac etiam proteftatione ab Authore adhibita, vt
quæ melius explicanda funt, explicare, quæ corrigenda, corri-
gere, quæ retractanda, retractare, & quæ purganda, purgare
quamprimùm velit; & *poftremò* feipfum, & quæcunq;
fcripfit, iudicio, & Cenfuræ Catholicæ Ecclefiæ Romanæ humillimè fubmittit.

9. *Quintò,* Purgatione hac facta, *Widdringtonus,*
cæterique Catholici eius doctrinæ adhærentes (quorum hîc in *Anglia* magnus eft numerus, [f] quicquid
Adverfarij *Suæ Sanctitati,* & *Illuftrifsimis Cardinalibus,*
plurimùm illis abutentes, in contrarium falfiffimè
fuggerant) fpem magnam conceperunt, *Decretum* illud
Sacræ Congregationis Illuftriffimorũ Cardinalium,
vel omnino revocandum, vel aliquo modo tempe-
randum, & mitius declarandum, vel faltem aliquam
propofitionem in prædictis *Widdringtoni* libris contentam, quæ fidei, aut bonis moribus adverfetur, illorum Authori intimandam, vt eam, iuxta quod pol-
licitus erat, retractare, & fi opus effet, abiurare poffet;
Vel certè *Suam Sanctitatem,* pro paterno illo amore,
quo omnes Ecclefiæ filios (eos præfertim, qui in omnibus Ecclefiæ Catholicæ Romanæ iudicio fe fubmittunt, & pro fide eius palam agnofcenda varias
calamitates fuftinent, à quibus alioquin fe liberare
poffent) profequi tenetur, ita grauiffimam hanc, &
fcandalofam *controverfiam* compofituram, ficut *con-*
tro-

[f] *Id etiam con-*
firmatur tefti-
monio P. Lean-
dri infrà num.
18.

troverſiam illam inter Patres *Dominicanos,* & *Ieſuitas* de *auxilijs gratiæ,* non minùs paternè, quàm ſapienter compoſuit; Vt ſcilicet Anglis Catholicis, qui *Card. Bellarmini* doctrinæ adhæreſcunt, strictè præciperet, ne *Widdringtonum,* cæteroſq; Catholicos doctrinæ illius adhærentes, quos *Sanctitas Sua* in *Francia* tolerat, & ad Sacramenta Eccleſiaſtica admittendos, permittit, hîc in *Anglia* tanquam *hæreticos, Pſeudo-Catholicos, Eccleſiæ Romanæ, Sediq́ Apoſtolicæ rebelles,* alteriuſve criminis ob eam doctrinam propugnandam reos, iniquè calumnientur, donec *Eccleſia,* quæ *columna,* & *firmamentum veritatis eſt,* hanc litem dirimeret: Vt ita tandem *Widdringtono,* eiuſque doctrinæ adhærentibus de hac controverſia, ad innocentiam ſuam defendendam, vlteriùs conſcribendi omnis occaſio adimeretur. Quamdiu enim tanquam *Pſeudo-Catholici, Sediq́ Apoſto-*

lica, quam toto corde venerantur, *rebelles,* aut *aliàs criminoſi,* pro veritate & innocentia tuenda, à fratrib' ſuis Catholicis, eiuſdéq; fidei Catholicæ domeſticis, (niſi alia ſit fides Catholica in *Anglia,* quàm ſit, & teſte *Petro Pithæo* [b], quem *Poſſeuinus virũ valde eruditũ, & antiquitatis ſedulũ perquiſitorẽ* appellat, ſemper fuerit in *Francia*) per iniuriam traducantur, de hac cõtroverſia cõſcribendi nunquam profectò finem facient, neque ab innocentia ſua vijs licitis propugnanda vllis minis, terroribus, Cenſuris, aut alijs pænis Eccleſiaſticis, quæ non niſi ob culpam infligi poſſunt, dimovebuntur, quin potiùs ad plures alias difficultates, innocentiæ ſuæ defendendæ gratia, clariùs, quàm adhuc fuerint, dilucidandas, eiuſmodi violentijs incitabuntur.

b *Nam in Codice ſuo libertatum Eccleſiæ Gallicanæ authoritate Senatus Pariſienſis in lucem edito anno 1594. ait, Franciam hoc ſemper pro certo tenuiſſe, quòd Papa non poſſit Regem Franciæ Regno ſuo privare, & quòd ſubditi obedientiâ pro temporalibus debitâ Regi præſtare teneantur, neque in ea per Papam diſpenſari aut abſolvi poſſint.*

10. *Sextò*, cùm *Widdringtonus* nihil planè emolumenti, aut intolerandæ fuæ oppreffionis levamenti, ex ea *Purgatione* fibi, cæterifque Anglis Catholicis eius doctrinæ adhærentibus, provenire pérfenferat, quin potiùs fuos Adverfarios, *Card. Bellarmini*, eiufque fequacium potentiæ confifos, vehementiùs in eos debacchari, magifque deinceps, quàm vnquam antea, maledictis infectari, eofque fama, honore, amicis, mediifque ad victum neceffariis (quantum in illis effet) penitus fpoliare conatos effe, aliam *Supplicationem* ad *Suam Sanctitatem* anno Domini 1616 tranfmittendam paravit, atque vt omnibus nóta fieret, imprimendam quoque curavit; in qua rurfus vehementer conqueritur de iniufta fua oppreffione (tam per præfatum Sacræ Congregationis Decretum, quàm per prædictas Illuftriffimi Domini Nuncii literas, & per alias *Card. Bellarmini*, eiufque fequacium calumnias illi facta) Atque *Suam Sanctitatem* fuppliciter rogat, *primò*, vt vel vnicam Iuramenti Claufulam, quæ fidei aut faluti repugnans fit, vti in fuis Brevibus, ex finiftra *Card. Bellarmini*, eiufve fequacium informatione, declaraverat, Catholicis Anglis patefacere dignaretur, vt ita & fuis confcientiis, & *Regiæ Maieftati, Suæq; Sanctitati*, quantum in ipfis effet, fatisfacere poffent : *Secundò*, vt prædictum Sacræ Congregationis Decretum, ex prava quorundam, præfertim *Card. Bellarmini*, fuggeftione latum, vel revocaret, vel vnicam faltem propofitionem in libris illius contentam, quæ fidei aut bonis moribus adverfetur, illi indicaret, vt ab ea fe purgare quamprimùm poffet. Et *demùm*, vt famæ, exiftimationi, & innocentiæ fuæ tam graviter, & per

C iniuriam

iniuriam læſę quamprimùm conſuleret; neque ſe,
ſuæque doctrinæ adhærentes, per effrænata maledicorum ora, tanquam *hæreticos, à fide Apoſtatas, Pſeudo-*
Catholicos, & *Eccleſiæ Romanæ, Sediſ_q Apoſtolicæ* non *fi-*
lios, ſed *hoſtes* vlteriùs, ob hanc doctrinam propugnandam, traduci impune permitteret.

11. Atque, vt *Sanctitas Sua* clarè perſpiceret, ſe
à *Card. Bellarmino,* eiuſue ſequacibus malè informatam eſſe, & *Widdringtonum,* eiuſque doctrinæ adhærentes ab ipſis iniuſtiſſimè oppreſſos, idem *Widdringtonus*
poſt finem prædictæ Supplicationis, in alio libello
ſupplici quaſdam nefandiſſimas calumnias, à *Card.*
Bellarmino, ſub *Adolphi Schulckenij* nomine perſonato,
illi falſiſſimè impoſitas clariſſimè detexit, eundemq;
de manifeſta calumnia in iudicium vocavit, & à
Sua Sanctitate iuſtitiam contra eum poſtulavit.

12. Sed o rem miram, & nimiùm ſtupendam!
Cùm enim iam *Widdringtonus,* poſt tam claram ſui
Purgationem, poſtque tam *horrendas calumnias,* quas
Card. Bellarminus illi per ſummam iniuriam impo-
ſuit, tam apertè detectas, perſuaſiſſimum haberet, fieri iam non poſſe, quin vel *Sanctitas Sua,* vel Illuſtriſſimi Cardinales ad particularia deſcenderent, & vel
vnicam ſaltem propoſitionem in ſuis libris contentam, quæ fidei, aut bonis moribus adverſetur, illi
notam facerent, vti toties à *Sua Sanctitate* ſuppliciter
poſtulaverat, aut ſaltem *Card. Bellarminus,* vel ſuo, vel
Schulckenij nomine, ab illis calumnijs ſe purgare, aut
Widdringtono, pro tanta iniuria illi illata, vtcunque ſatisfacere vellet, Ecce, Ecce (proh ſtupor) eadem ipſa
Sacra Illuſtriſſimorum Cardinalium Congregatio
hanc

hanc etiam Supplicationem verbis tantùm generalibus, (nulla prorſus propoſitione in ea contenta,quæ
fidei, aut bonis moribus repugnet, indicata) poſt tot
humillimas Supplicationes *Suæ Sanctitati* factas, vt
ad aliquod particulare deſcenderet, non ſolùm con-
demnavit, verùm etiam eam in medio librorum,
quos *Proteſtantes* ſcripſerunt, collocavit, ac ſi Supplicatio illa ab aliquo Proteſtante, & non ab vllo Eccleſiæ Catholicæ Romanæ filio compoſita eſſet, aut aliquid fidei Catholicæ Romanæ, vel bonis moribus
apertè contrarium in ea contineretur. Et nihilominùs de libro illo poſt finem Supplicationis addi-
to, in quo calumniæ *Card. Bellarmini* apertiſſimè deteguntur, & ipſe in iudicium de *aperta calumnia* à *Widdringtono* adducitur, Sacra illa Congregatio ne verbū
quidem facit : Neque etiam ipſemet *Card. Bellarminus*, vel ſuo, vel *Schulckenij* nomine, aut alius quiſpiam pro ipſis, poſt totos quatuor annos iam comple-
tos, ad prædictas calumnias hucvſque reſpondit:
quod ſanè evidens indicium eſt, ſe ab illis criminationibus purgare ſe nullatenus poſſe. Neque tamen
adhuc *Card. Bellarmini* fautores (quæ ſanè maior eorū
culpa eſt) à *Widdringtono*, cæteriſque Catholicis eius
doctrinæ adhærentibus iniuſtè divexandis deſiſtunt,
ſed in ſuis ſolitis contra eos clamoribus, & irreligioſis
calumniationibus etiam nunc (O tempora, O mores!)
perſeverant.

12. Mitto nunc, plures alios libros ad hanc con-
troverſiam accuratiùs explicandam à *Widdringtono*,
eiuſque doctrinæ adhærentibus, à tempore *Diſputationis Theologicæ* ab ipſo editæ, conſcriptos ; nempe;

C 2 vnum

vnum contra *Franciſcum Suarez*, alterum contra *Leo-*
nardum Leſsium ſub *Guilielmi Singletoni* nomine perſonatum, de Diſcuſſione *Decreti* magni *Concilij Lateranenſis*,
duos item contra *Thomam Fitzherbertum* Anglum Ie-
ſuitam, in quibus præcipua omnia argumenta à perſonato *Schulckenio* ad poteſtatem Papalem Principes
deponendi comprobandam allata clarè, & perſpicuè
diluuntur, & nunc vltimò *Strenam Catholicam* contra
Matthæum Kellinſonum Anglum, Sacræ Theologiæ
Doctorem, & Collegij *Dûacenſis* Clericorum Secularium Anglorum *Præſidem,* ſub nomine I. E. Theologiæ ſtudioſo perſonatum, & contra falſam eius ac
peſtiferam *Iuramenti fidelitatis* Explicationem, præcipuè compoſitam : Et nihilominùs nemo adhuc vel
vni ex prædictis *quinque* libris vllam omnino Re-
ſponſionem dedit : Sed omnes conticuerunt, &
Widdringtonum, eiuſque doctrinæ adhærentes, in aperta
acie, quaſi profugi, & de victoria deſperantes, reli-
querunt; quod profectò ſignum eſt, ſe vi argumentorum *Widdringtoni* doctrinam expugnare non poſſe,
& proinde eam, illique adhærentes, minis, terroribus,
Cenſuris, atque pœnis Eccleſiaſticis conculcare quàm
maximè ſtudent. Quin etiam quidam ex noſtro ipſomet Ordine *Benedictino* Frater, ſed parum fraternè,
nos duos præ cæteris *Thomam Preſtonum,* & *Thomam*
Greenæum plurimùm perſequitur, atque non ſolùm,
vt pœnis Eccleſiaſticis (non tamen ob crimen aliquod, quod ipſe, tametſi alioquin doctiſſimus, verè
crimen eſſe nobis, aut mundo monſtrare poterit) ca-
ſtigemur, verùm etiam vt illi ipſi nos caſtigandi poteſtas à *Sede Apoſtolica* concedatur, ſummo labore

&

& diligentia enititur, vti ex fequenti narratione perfpicuum fiet.

13. *Anno integro* abhinc elapfo contigit, vt ego
Frater *Thomas Greenæus* in Epifcopatu *Dunelmenfi* cap-
tus, & ad *Epifcopum Dunelmenfem* perductus, ab eo in
eadem Civitate *Dunelmenfi* Carceri mancipatus eſſem:
Vbi ab eo circa *Iuramentum* fidelitatis, *Coniurationem
pulverariam,* & illius principia fæpiſſimè examinatus,
quid de illis fenferim, fyncerè, provt confcientia mea
tunc mihi dictabat, fignificavi. Tandem, poſt duos
fermè menfer, ab eodem Epifcopo *Londinum* perductus, & in *Palatio* eius per aliquot hebdomadas, antequam huic Carceri *Clinkenfi* traditus eſſem, deten-
tus, & ab eo fæpiùs non tantùm rogatus, fed iuſſus,
vt fidelitatem meam, *Suæ Maieſtati* iure divino & naturali debitam, apertè declararem, per *Recognitionem*
manu mea propria fcriptam, ex prioribus meis Exa-
minationibus collectam , & quaſi in vnum corpus
redactam, quæque in *Strena Catholica* iam typis excufa
extat, opinionem meam de nefandiſſima illa *Coniura-
tione pulveraria,* atque de Iuramento fidelitatis ingenuè declaravi, affirmans inter cætera, *nibil in eo Iuramento contineri, vti mihi in privato meo judicio videtur,
quod iuxta Gloſſam, & Expoſitionem* Rogeri Widdringtoni *ab Anglis Catholicis* Maieſtatis Suæ *fubditis licitè
fufcipi non poſsit, quantumvis aliqui, tum eruditi, tum Religioſi contrarium teneant.*

14. Atque hinc prima & præcipua totius mei
gravaminis occaſio nata eſt. Hanc enim meam
Recognitionem duo præ cæteris ex Congregatione noſtra *Hiſpanica* viri primarij indigniſſimè ferentes,
nempe

nempe Reverendus Pater, Frater *Leander Iones* de
S. *Martino*, novæ Congregationis *Anglicanæ* Benedictinorum *Præſes*, & miſſionis *Hiſpanicæ* eiuſdem Ordinis *Vicarius generalis*, ac Sacræ Theologiæ Doctor,
& Reverendus Pater, Frater *Rudeſindus Barlo*, Sacræ
etiam Theologiæ Doctor, & *Duacenſis* Benedictinorū
Anglorum Collegij Prior, mihi per literas, partim
minis, partim blanditijs, ſed nullo planè argumento
(præter humanos reſpectus, & in Curia Romana fa-
vores aut vituperia) perſuadere conati ſunt, vt prædictam *Recognitionem* retractarem, & doctrinæ *Rogeri
Widdringtoni*, (quem præfatus Pater *Leander Authorem*
à *Sede Apoſtolica iamdudum proſcriptum, & damnatum* falſiſſimè, & per ſummam iniuriam appellare non eſt
veritus, cùm aliqui tantùm *Authoris* libri, ſed non
Author ipſe ab *Illuſtriſsimis Cardinalibus* ex *mandato*, vt
ipſi aiunt, *Suæ Sanctitatis*, damnati & prohibiti ſint)
penitus renunciarem.

15. Atque, vt maiorem mihi terrorem præfatus
Pater *Rudeſindus* incutiat, *inprimis* me certiorem
facit de *Epiſtola* quadam (cuius exemplar prædicti
P. *Rudeſindi* manu conſcriptum apud me habeo)
Illuſtriſſimi Domini *Nuncij Apoſtolici*, *Lucij* Archi-
epiſcopi *Salernitani*, qui *Bruxellis* manet, ad Reveren-
dum Patrem Fratrem *Leandrum* miſſa, & data 9 Martij
1620. in qua *Epiſtola* Illuſtriſſimus Dominus *Nuncius
Apoſtolicus* inter cætera affirmat, *ex relatióne gravium,
ac fide digniſsimorum* (ſunt enim ipſiſſima Domini
Nuncij verba) *nuper ſibi innotuiſſe, eſſe in Anglia Religioſos nonnullos* Benedictinos, *qui ſecretò favent* Widdringtono *ex eodem Ordine, & non ſolùm cum ſcandalo ſuæ opi-*
nioni

nioni de Iuramento fidelitatis, *sed ipsi* Iuramento, *non verentes commendare, & plaudere libro à dicto* Widdringtono *nuper conscripto adversùs librum Patris* Lessij *Societatis Iesu, sub nomine Doctoris* Singletoni, *in quo libro* Iuramentum *confutatur. Ne desit igitur Paternitas tua sedulò investigare, qui sint prædicti* Benedictini *plaudentes prædicto* Widdringtono, *ac ijs repertis expedire iudicarem, ut ij quamprimùm ex* Anglia *revocarentur, ac interim omni authoritate privarentur.*

16. *Deinde,* idem Pater *Radesindus* verbis expressis asserit, *Superiores meos apud se firmiter statuisse, ad me Ecclesiasticis Censuris compellendum, ut vel ab illa opinione defendenda abstineam, vel, si de ea tractare velim, ut illam impugnem, vel quod antea dixerim, aut scripserim retractem; alioquin me ab Altari, & cæteris omnibus, quæ ad functionem meam pertinent, suspendere, illis institutum esse:* Atque insuper addit, *Nuncium Apostolicum nunquam cessaturum, donec talia mandata ex Hispania obtineat. Et interim idem* Nuncius Apostolicus *Venerandum Patrem nostrum* Præsidentem, *&* Hispanicæ *Congregationis* Vicarium *generalem urget* (ait Pater iste) *ut me, quantum possit, coercere velit. Absque dubio hoc fiet, & fieri potest* (ait Pater *Rudesindus,* magis authoritativè, meo quidem iudicio, & tanquam *Prior* ad Novitios suos in Capitulo loquens, quàm eruditè, & inter Theologos, tanquam *Doctor,* ex Cathedra docens) *cùm exequutio meæ functionis possit esse actus obedientiæ, quam Superiores mei* (ait ille) *pro libito suo permittere, vel prohibere possunt:* Quasi verò, vel ego absolutam obedientiam in omnibus, & non ad regulam S. Benedicti, iuxta Constitutiones Congregationis nostræ Hispanicæ à Sede Apostolica

appro-

approbatas, duntaxat reſtriƈtam, & limitatam pro-
miſerim, vel quòd Superiores mei, aut alius quicunque, aut per modum præcepti, aut alio quovis modo,
me pœnis, præſertim Eccleſiaſticis, ad libitum, &
abſque omni culpa à me commiſſa, caſtigandi poteſtatem habeant.

17. Et poſtea adiungit, idque mihi tanquam ſe-
cretum, *ſcilicet,* pandere prætendit, *me hoc pro certo intelligere debere, Superiores meos firmiter ſibi propoſuiſſe, quòd
erga Eccleſiæ cauſam magis zelantes ſe præbere velint, quàm
Superiores illius, qui* Widdringtonus *putatur, ſeſe præbue-
rint.* Quaſi verò, *Eccleſiæ cauſa* ab opinionibus, quæ
apud eruditos Catholicos in controverſia verſantur,
dependeat, aut ex ijs ſtet, vel cadat; vel illi Theologi,
qui tot Summorū Pontificum opiniones, & praxim
circa diſpenſationes in voto ſolenni caſtitatis, & matrimonio rato; non conſummato, reijciunt, & direƈtū
Summi Pontificis in temporalibus dominium impugnant, tanquam parum *zelantes erga Eccleſiæ cauſam*
traducendi eſſent. Sed vtinam viri Religioſi, his
præſertim calamitoſis temporibus, ſub fucato *Eccleſiæ,*
& *Dei cauſæ* promovendæ prætextu, *cauſam propriam,*
non agerent, atque ad viros innocentes, Societatis ſuæ
vijs indebitis, & in fratrum ſuorum, eiuſdemque fidei,
& Ordinis domeſticorum iniuſtam depreſſionem,
nimiùm exaltandæ gratia, opprimendos, & iniquè
perſequendos, haudquaquam adniterentur.

18. *Poſtremò* (vt alia nunc taceam) addit *Pater*
iſte, (quòd ſanè Doƈtore Theologo prorſus indignū
eſt) *opinionem probabilem ſufficiens meis Superioribus fundamentum eſſe, vt ita contra me procedere poſſint, neque omnes*
totius

toti' orbis Widdringtonos *istud tollere posse.*Si enim Doctor iste notissima Theologiæ principia syncerè, & absq; vllo humani respectus intuitu, expendisset, profectò hæc *quatuor* ignorare non poterat. *Primum:* non posse quenquam puniri pœnis, præsertim Ecclesiasticis, nisi propter culpam. *Secundum:* nullam esse culpam, opinionem non omnino certam, sed duntaxat probabilem reijcere, in favorem tertiæ personæ, quæ in possessione sui iuris & dominij existit; & proinde opinione probabile sufficiens Superioribus meis fundamentu non esse, vt me, nullius criminis reum, pœna aliqua afficere possint; & hoc tam manifestum est, vt non opus sit *Widdringtono*, aut cuivis alteri Theologo in eo comprobando multùm desudare. *Tertium: Potestatem non omnino certam, sed duntaxat probabilem, non posse esse sufficiens fundamentum, quo immediatè aliquis puniatur, aut aliquo iure suo & dominio in re obtento spolietur, sed talis potestas certissimè debet competere* [h]. *Quartum:* me non absolutam, & omnimodam obedientiam in omnibus, sed solùm secundùm regulam *S. Benedicti,* eo modo, quo per statuta & constitutiones *Congregationis* nostræ licitas, & à *Sede Apostolica* approbatas, quando professionem emisi, observata est, Superioribus meis promisisse: nam alioquin possent Superiores mei me ad Statuta *Camaldulensium,* aut *Cistertiensium* reformatorum, qui omnes sub regula *S. Benedicti* militant, observanda volentem nolentem obligare, quandoquidé si ratiocinatio P. *Rudesindi* solida esset, observatio eiusmodi constitutionum potest esse actus *obedientiæ,* quam Superiores mei pro libito suo, *scilicet,* præcipere possunt, cùm tamen neque votum, neque

[h] *ita etiam docet verbis expressis* Lessius *in suo Singletono part.2. num. 38.*

D pro-

promissionem aliquam vltra intentionem illius qui
vovet, aut promittit, obligare, cuivis Theologiæ
perito nimis manifestum sit. Atque hæc sunt
quædam ex præcipuis, quæ in præfatis istorum
Patrum literis ad me scriptis contenta observanda
duxi.

19. Veruntamen prædictis omnibus, & singulis
eorum literis tam Illustrissimi Domini *Nuncij Apostoli-
lici,* quàm Reverendorum Patrum *Leandri,* & *Rude-
fundi,* ego etiam per literas respondi, affirmans inter
cætera, nullum planè crimen esse nobis Catholicis in
Anglia doctrinam verè probabilem, seu *opinionem* (ita
enim *Patres* isti eam in suis literis semper appellant)
quam plurimi Catholici eruditi approbant, in favoré
Regis nostri Serenissimi, qui dominia sua legitimè
possidet, & ad fidelitatem nostram illi iure divino,
ac naturali debitam recognoscendam, approbare, cùm

Card. Peron en
Harangue au
triers Estat.
pag 98.

præsertim doctrina contraria à plurimis Catholicis in
Francia, quos ipsemet *Dominus Papa,* teste *Card. Peroue,*
tolerat, non solùm improbetur, verùm etiam, vti
falsa, scandalosa, seditiosa, & *supremæ Regü in temporalibus
potestati apertè detrahens,* & *Coronis, ac Capitibus suis periculum afferens,* sub pœna *læsæ Majestatis* pluribus *Arrestis*

i Arresta in
fine Strenæ Ca-
tholicæ ponun-
tur.

[i] *expressè* condemnetur. Atque insuper in ijs literis
syncerè protestatus sum, me paratissimum esse, ad
omne illud, quod à me malè scriptum, aut dictum
fuerit, retractandum, dummodo ipsi quidquam prorsus, quod malè scripserim, aut dixerim, mihi notum
facere dignarentur. Et proinde eos obnixè rogavi,
vt ad particularia descenderent, mihique particulatim
significarent vel vnicam propositionem in mea *Declarat ione*

claratione contentam, quæ fanæ doctrinæ, aut bonis
moribus adverfetur.

20. Sed cùm Patres ifti nihil fe apud me profi-
cere perfpicerent, fed in caffum laborare, nifi ad particularia defcenderent, (quod illi, caufæ fuæ procul
dubio diffifi, non adhuc præftiterunt) prædictus Pater Frater *Leander* aliam viam, clandeftinis fuis, & iniuriofis machinationibus, & Iurifdictioni fuæ in alios
etiam illi non fubditos extendendæ, magis commo-
dam, non ad me tantummodò, fed etiam ad D. *Tho-*
mam Preflonum, quantumvis eius Iurifdictioni minimè fubiectum, caftigandum, & ad omnes omnino
Caffinenfes Benedictinos, in *Anglia* commorantes, fuæ
Iurifdictioni, & caftigationi, volentes nolentes, fub-
ijciendos excogitavit. Atque idcirco aliquot ab hinc
menfibus Epiftolam fatis prolixam, datam fexto Iulij
1620, ad præfatum Illuftriffimum Dominum *Nun-*
cium Apoftolicum, qui *Bruxellis* manet, confcripfit, in
qua, vt *Illuftriffimæ Dominationis Suæ* indignationem
etiam in D. *Thomam Preflonum* concitaret, totam mei
calamitofi lapfus (vt verbis illius nunc vtar) caufam in
eum conijcit, *meq́ ab eo dulcibus alloquijs, fermonibus, ac*
beneficijs feductum effe, intrepidè affirmat, quod tamen
falfiffimum effe ego ingenuè, & fyncerè coram Deo
profiteor.

21. Et in eadem Epiftola idem Pater, *Frater Le-*
ander, fed parum fraternè, non *Rogerum Widdringtonum,*
fed me *Thomam Preflonum* librorum à *Widdringtono* e-
ditorum Authorem effe verbis difertis affirmare non
veretur. Et, vt toti noftræ *Congregationi Caffinenfi* maiorem invidiam conflaret, me monachorum *Caffinen-*

ſium, qui in *Anglia* commorantur, *Superiorem* appellare
non erubeſcit, non levem inde notam *Superioribus*,
& R.ᵐᵒ *Præſidi* Congregationis noſtræ *Caſinenſis*
invrere ſtudens, quòd ipſi me de libris *Widdringtoni*
conſcribendis, aut ſaltem de doctrina eius propugnanda notoriè ſuſpectum (ſi doctrinam illam propugnare verè *nota*, ſeu *noxa*, & *culpa* eſſet) locum *Supe-*
rioris hîc in *Anglia* tenere hucvſque permitterent :
Cùm tamen notiſſimum ſit (idque Reverendus Pater D. *Anſelmus* Anglus, tunc *Romæ* exiſtens, & *Superior*
noſter hîc in *Anglia* manens , cæterique *Caſinenſes*
illi ſubiecti teſtari poſſunt) me pluribus abhinc annis
omnem, quam habui in *Caſinenſes* authoritatem, vltro
reſignaſſe.

22. Atque, vt omnes Patres *Caſinenſes* Sedi Apoſtolicæ magis ſuſpectos, & exoſos reddat, inſuper addit, *aliquos in Italia ipſa Congregationis ipſius* Caſſinenſis
monachos (iſtudq; quod dicit ſe ſcire aſſerit) *opinionem*
Widdringtoni *laudare, & mirari.* Atque *in Anglia Caſſi-*
nenſes omnes Iuramento favere.

23. Sed neque his contentus prædictus Pater
Leander vlteriùs progreditur, &, ſub ſpecioſo eos *Be-*
nedictinos, qui *Widdringtoni* doctrinæ adhæreſcunt, caſtigandi prætextu, omnes omnino, tam *Caſinenſis*,
quàm alterius cuiuſcunque Congregationis *Benedi-*
ctinos, præſentes vel futuros, quamdiu hîc in *Anglia*
manent, volentes nolentes, ſuæ Iuriſdictioni, & Correctioni ſubijcere quamplurimùm ſtudet(cùm tamen
Pater iſte, dum in minoribus eſſet, & Reverendi Patris *Auguſtini Bradſhaw* , Hiſpanicæ Congregationis
Religioſi Iuriſdictioni ſubiectus, in Congregationem
noſtram

noſtram *Caſsinenſem*, literis ſuis ad me ſcriptis, admitti
obnixè poſtularet) Sed *honores*, vt in proverbio eſt,
mores mutant. Ea propter Illuſtriſſimum Dominum
Nuncium in prædicta Epiſtola ſua inſtanter rogat, vt
à Sede Apoſtolica hoc Privilegium impetrare velit,
quòd omnes omnino *Benedictini*, cuiuſcunque tan-
dem *Congregationis* fuerint, ſuæ *Iuriſdictioni*, & *Correctioni*,
atque novæ *Congregationis* Anglicanæ *ſtatutis, ac legibus*,
quamdiu in Anglia manent, volentes nolentes, ſubij-
ciantur : quinetiam non parum conqueritur, quòd
Sanctitas Sua iſtud Privilegium, cùm anno præterito
Patres iſti id à *Sua Sanctitate* obnixè poſtularent, illis
denegaverit.

24. Atque vt, ſub ſpecioſo ſingularis ſuæ erga
Sedem Apoſtolicam devotionis, & *Widdringtoni* fautores caſtigandi prætextu, Dominationem ſuam Il-
luſtriſſimam ad hoc Privilegium pro illis impetrandū
faciliùs induceret, non ſemel, ſed iterum inculcat *Iuramentum* illud, cuius mentio in *Strena Catholica* habetur,
quo omnes, qui in nova *Congregatione Anglicana* pro-
feſſionem emiſſuri ſunt, obſtringuntur, ad *opiniones*
Widdringtoni *ex animo ſemper abrenunciandas, damnandas,
illiſq́; Anathema dicendum.* Et, vt nos omnes *Caſsinenſes*
Illuſtriſſimo Domino Nuncio magis odioſos reddat,
illi ſuggerere non dubitat, quòd, *vbi* Caſſinenſes *Sta-
tutum de Iuramento illo præſtando conſpexère, penitus ſe ab
eorum vnione ſubduxerunt, & adhuc ſubducunt* ; atque
etiam, *quòd non defuerit vnus ex* Caſſinenſibus, *qui prædicto Patri* Leandro *in faciem dixerit, inter reliquas cauſas
cur ſe ſubducant, illam eſſe præcipuam, quòd illas opiniones te-
merè* (vt dicebat Caſſinenſis ille) *condemnaſſent.*

25. Verun-

25. Veruntamen falsum omnino est, idcirco *Caßinenses* se ab eorum vnione subduxisse, eò quod Decretum de Iuramento illo præstando condiderint; cùm *Caßinenses,* ante omne prorsus Decretum de Iuramento illo præstando ab illis editum, sese ab eorum vnione subduxerint, & proinde *Caßinenses* nullo modo induci potuerunt, vt ad vlla planè Decreta condenda cum illis *Lutetiæ Parisiorum* convenirent. Sed idcirco *Caßinenses* se ab eorum vnione subduxerunt, quoniam non aliam vnionem Hispanicæ Congregationis *Benedictini* moliebantur, quàm vt omnes, tam *Cassinensis,* quàm *Anglicanæ* Congregationis Religiosi *Hispanicæ* subijcerentur; quod iam suis astutijs, quod ad Congregationem Anglicanam attinet, ad effectum k perduxerunt; neque tamen adhuc contenti, tam *Cassinenses,* quàm cuiuscunque alterius, tum *Gallicanæ,* tum *Lotharingicæ* Congregationis Anglos Benedictinos, sibi & Congregationi Hispanicæ (sub specie Benedictinos, qui *Widdringtoni* doctrinæ favent, si qui sint vel fuerint, castigandi,) subijcere etiamnum student.

26. Alia etiam præfatus Pater *Leander* in sua Epistola suggerit Suæ Dominationi Illustrissimæ, vel à veritate, vel à charitate & iustitia prorsus aliena (atque in tota hac sua cantilena opinio *Widdringtoni* versus intercalaris semper est) Veluti (vt alia nunc taceam) primò, in eo quòd asserit, *Cassinenses* Benedictinos *egisse* apud Summum Pontificem, *& semel obtinuisse, vt omnes Anglos etiam Congregationis* Hispanicæ *Benedictinos in vnã* Congregationem Anglicanam *ab ipsis Cassinensibus præsertim regendam coalescerent, & Congregationem* Hispanicam *sibi*

k *Aliqui tamen ex Congregationis Hispanicæ Benedictini sibi persuadent, novæ istius Congregationis Anglicanæ Superiores Hispanis fucum facere, hocq; illis institutum esse, vt, postquam, Hispanorû ope, & protectione freti, amplissima privilegia, ad quæ aspirant, à Sede Apostolica impetraverint, neque eorû patrocinio, aut protectione amplius indiguerint, hoc qualecunq; subiectionis, sive realis, sive verbalis tantùm sit, Congregationis Anglicanæ ad Hispanicam iugum omnino excutiant.*

fibi fubijcere tentaffe, eo fine, vt opinioni Widdringtoni *plu-*
res P atronos conciliárent: Quod tamen omnino falfum
eft, id que ex ipfomet Summi Pontificis Decreto, cuius
Pater ifte mentionem facit, manifeftè conftat. Neque
enim Patres Caffinenfes converfionem Congregationis Hifpanicæ in Caffinenfem, aut fubiectionem Hifpanicæ ad Caffinenfem vnquam meditati funt, fed
folummodo omnium trium Congregationum, *Caffi-*
nenfis, Hifpanicæ, & *Anglicanæ* vnionem inter fe (Procu-
ratore generali Congregationis Hifpanicæ, qui tunc
Romę agebat, & Patribus Congregationis Anglicanę
affentientibus) procurare conati funt: ita vt Anglicana Benedictinorum (qui omnes primùm Caffinenfes erant, & Patribus Caffinenfibus fubiecti) Congregatio nuper erecta tam à Congregatione Hifpani-
ca, quàm Caffinenfi in primordio fuæ fundationis
dependeret, tali tamen cautione adhibita, vt Superiores horum omnium Benedictinorum Anglorum ex
Congregationis *Caffinenfis, Hifpanicæ,* & *Anglicanæ* Religiofis alternatim quolibet triennio eligerentur.

27. *Deinde,* in eo quod Pater ifte Frater *Leander,*
parum quidem fraternè, omnes Caffinenfes Anglos
penitus extinguere & extirpare conetur. Et proinde
prædictum Illuftriffimum Dominum Nuncium A-
poftolicum obnixè rogat, vt R. P. D. *Hubertum Rolle,*
Præfidem Congregationis Lotharingicæ Benedictinorum, *grauiter monere velit, ne vllatenus pro Caffinenfibus*
(qui tamen quondá tum Congregationis Anglicanę,
tum Hifpanicæ Patres & Fundatores fuerunt) *aut pro*
vllis alijs Nouitios Anglos Benedictinos *educare præfume-*
ret, nifi eos tantùm, qui parati funt cum effectu parere Congregationi

gregationi Anglicanæ Benedictinæ, *cui præeſt hoc tempore* Pater Leander *de* S. Martino, *ex decreto* Suæ Sanctitatis, *à fratribus ſuis electus, propter rationes* Illuſtriſſimæ Dominationi Suæ *bene notas,* & Suæ Sanctitati *gratas.* Et *ſimiles literas ab* Illuſtriſsimo Nuncio Galliarum in eundem finem *ſe obtenturum confidit,* ait iſte Pater *Leander,* ſub ſpecioſo hoc prætextu, quod *ſi permittatur* Caſſinenſibus *Anglos Benedictinos multiplicare, totidē erunt Iuramenti vetiti propugnatores* (ſunt enim ipſamet Patris Leandri verba) *ſimulac in Angliam pervenerint.* Et quid hoc aliud eſt, quàm factionibus & oppreſſionibus doctrinam illam, quam ipſemet Papa in Francia tolerat, in ſummam Principum ſupremorum iniuriam, hîc in Anglia conculcare, quam rationibus & argumentis ſe vnquam infringere poſſe planè diffidunt? Sed de tota hac Patris *Leandri Epiſtola,* alibi forſan ad innocentiam noſtram, quam ipſe parum religioſè ac fraternè malis artibus opprimere ſtudet, defendendá, copioſior erit ſermo.

28. Atque interim, quàm parum iuſtam nos fratres ſuos, eiuſdemque *fidei Catholicæ,* atque eiuſdem *Ordinis Benedictini* domeſticos, ob doctrinam *Widdringtoni* propugnandam, tam acerbè perſequendi cauſam habuerit *Pater* iſte, facilè perſpicere poteſt (cùm vir eruditus ſit, & Sacræ Theologiæ Doctor) ſi ſeriò, & abſque vllo humani reſpectus, Pontificij præſertim favoris, intuitu, ſecum conſideret, doctrinam *Widdringtoni* (quam nec ipſe Pater *Leander,* nec P. *Rudeſindus* hæreſim, errorem, aut doctrinam non ſanam dicere auſi ſunt, ſed duntaxat opinionem in literis ſuis ſemper appellant) ipſummet Dominum Papam in

Francia

Francia tolerare, non solùm sicut fœneratores, meretrices, aut alij publici peccatores tolerantur, sed eos
etiam, qui illam propugnant, ad Sacramenta Ecclesiastica admittendos permittere ; eamque à Senatu
Parisiensi pluribus Arrestis confirmatam esse, & contrariam Card. *Bellarmini, Francisci Suarez,* & similium,
vti *falsam, & seditiosam,* sub pœna *læsæ Maiestatis,* condemnatam ; nec *debere hanc controversiam* (teste Card.
Perono) [1] *impedire revnionem eorum, qui Ecclesiæ reconciliari*   [1] *in sua Repli-*
desiderarent ; atque insuper, *Widdringtonum,* pluribus li-   *ca. cap. 91. pag.*
bris ab eo iam editis, quibus nulla adhuc Responsio   *633.*
facta est, perspicuè commonstrasse, doctrinam suam
vi argumentorum expugnari non posse : Et præterea si Pater iste *Leander* rite expendat, quid ipsemet in
Epistola sua Illustrissimo Domino Nuncio suggerere
non dubitet ; nempe, doctrinam *Widdringtoni,* non solùm ab *aliquibus Cassinensibus in Italia,* verùm etiam hîc
in Anglia ab omnibus *Cassinensibus,* & à pluribus *Cle-*
ricis Secularibus expresse, atque ab ipsismet *Patribus Ie-*
suitis saltem tacitè approbatam esse. Ait enim in illa
Epistola, *non paucos ex Clericis Secularibus, eosq́ etiam non*
contemptibiles, Iuramentum propugnare, & tanquam legitimũ
defendere, ac suadere. Et de Patribus Iesuitis ita scribit,
seipsos quidem ab illo Iuramento immunes se servasse. Cæterùm
certissimum est mihi, ex fide digna relatione (sunt ipsiusmet
Patris Leandri verba) *multos, magnosq́ viros Laicos ipsis*
addictissimos (quorum nempe consilio conscientias suas submi-
serunt dicti Laici) *non solùm Iuramentum illud approbasse, sed*
etiam de facto præstitisse. Neque tamen propterea (quantum
ego intelligere potui) à communione Sacramentorum prohiberi.
Et quid hoc est aliud, quàm Patré *Leandrũ* existimare,

E   Iura-

Iuramentum illud à doctiſſimis Ieſuitis tectè & tacitè
approbatam eſſe? Atque idcirco Pater iſte (cùm ſacræ
Theologiæ peritus ſit) ignorare non poteſt, doctrinâ
Widdringtoni verè probabilem eſſe, vtpote à plurimis
eruditis Catholicis, qui rem totam diligenter exami-
narunt, approbatam, quamque proinde, iuxta notiſſi-
ma Theologiæ principia, quilibet Catholicus abſque
omni prorſus culpa pœnæq; reatu, licitè & tutâ conſcientiâ propugnare poterit.

29. Ex quibus omnib' diligenter conſideratis perſpicuum eſt *primò*, quanto ſtudio & induſtria elabo-
ret præfatus Pater *Leander*, vt nos fratres ſuos *Thomam*
Preſtonum, & *Thomam Greenæum*, nullius planè criminis
reos, caſtigandi facultatem, & exorbitantia Privilegia,
in maximam quamplurium *Sui Ordinis* Fratrum iniuriam, à Sede Apoſtolica malis artibus & falſis ſuggeſtionibus emendicet.

30. *Secundò*, quàm proclivis ſit præfatus Illuſtriſſimus Dominus Nuncius Apoſtolicus, non bene
conſultus, ad Benedictinos Anglos, & ſubinde alios
omnes Catholicos, qui doctrinæ *Widdringtoni* favent,
pœnis Eccleſiaſticis caſtigandos, ſub prætextu criminis, quod neque Dominatio Sua Illuſtriſſima, nec
alius quiſpiam, quantumvis doctiſſimus, verè crimen
eſſe, vel adhuc probarunt, vel vnquam comprobare
poterunt: Sicut etiam prædictus Illuſtriſſimus Dominus Nuncius Apoſtolicus non bene conſultus e-
rat, quando in præfata ſua Epiſtola ad Patrem *Leandrū*
aſſeruit, *Patrem* Leſſium *Societatis Ieſu in libro ſuo ſub no-*
mine Doctoris Singletoni *Iuramentum confutaſſe* [m], cùm
tamen in illo libro ne verbum quidem de Iuramento
illo habeatur.

• ſuprà nu. 15.

31. *Ter-*

31. *Tertiò*, quàm propensa fuerit *Sacra* Illustrissimorum Cardinalium *Congregatio*, ex prava *Card.Bellarmini*, eiusque sequacium informatione, non solùm ad duos illos *Widdringtoni* libros modo planè insolito damnandos, & prohibendos, atque ad Authori iniungendum, *vt se quamprimùm purget*, alioquin *Censuris & alijs pœnis Ecclesiasticis omnino coercendus*, nullo tamen crimine vel speciatim, vel generatim indicato, ob quod libri eius damnati, & prohibiti sint, vel à quo ipse se purgare debeat, verùm etiam quod magis mirandum est, ad damnandam & prohibendam, verbis tantùm generalibus, illam ipsam Supplicationem, in qua idem *Widdringtonus Suam Sanctitatem* humillimè rogat, vt, pro debito sui officij Pastoralis, illi notam faceret vel vnicam propositionem particularem in libris suis contentam, vel sanæ doctrinæ, vel bonis moribus adversantem, ob quam libri illi *ex mandato Suæ Sanctitatis* (vti in Decreto dicitur) damnati & prohibiti sint, & à qua *Author* ipsorum se purgare debeat : cùm tamen vix credibile sit, *Suam Sanctitatem*, tot tantisque negotijs publicis, atque domesticis præpeditam, libros illos aut perlegisse, aut saltem diligenter examinasse; & proinde nec Illustrissimis Dominis Cardinalibus circa prædictos libros quidquam mandasse, quàm quod *mandandum* ipsimet Domini Cardinales *Suæ Sanctitati*, ex prava informatione, suggesserint.

32. Quapropter, prædictis omnibus, & singulis rationibus, gravaminibus, & oppressionibus maturè, ac diligenter perpensis, Atque etiam, ne præfata Illustrissimorum Dominorum Cardinalium ad *Indicem* deputatorum *Sacra Congregatio*, (in qua *Card.Bellarminus*

præci-

præcipuus *Widdringtoni* Adverſarius, vel primus, vel
vnus ex primis eſt) ex falſis prædicti Patris *Leandri* informationibus, aut importunis præfati Illuſtriſſimi
Domini Nuncij Apoſtolici perſuaſionibus, vel ſini-
ſtris *Card Bellarmini*, eiuſve ſequacium ſuggeſtionibus,
facilem hinc anſam arripiat nos de nullo adhuc crimine ſpeciatim accuſatos, neque iuridicè admonitos,
citatos, auditos vel defenſos, contra omnem rationem,
& iuſtitiam condemnandi, eo modo, quo contra libros à *Widdringtono* editos ſententiam tulit, nullo par-
ticulari crimine indicato, ob quod libri illi damnati,
& prohibiti ſint, & à quo eorum *Author* (iuxta *Admo-
nitionem* in ipſo *Decreto* contentam) ſeſe purgare debeat: Idcirco Nos D. *Thomas* (alias *Rolandus*) *Preſtonus*, Presbyter, Ordinis *S. Benedicti* Congregationis
Caſſinenſis Religioſus, ac Sacræ Theologiæ Profeſſor,
& Frater *Thomas Greenæus*, Presbyter, Ordinis *S. Benedicti* Congregationis *Hiſpanicæ* Religioſus, ac Sacræ
Theologiæ Profeſſor, ſentientes, tam noſmetipſos
quàm *Rogerum Widdringtonum* Catholicum Anglum,
cæteroſque eius doctrinæ adhærentes, & adhærere volentes, quàm maximè gravatos, læſoſque, & oppreſſos
eſſe, & prædicta *duo Illuſtriſſimorum Cardinalium* ad *Indicem* deputatorum *Decreta*, anno Domini 1614 die 16
Martij contra *Apologiam pro Iure Principum*, & *Diſputationem Theologicam de Iuramento fidelitatis* à *Rogero Widdringtono* editas, & anno Domini 1616 die 12 Novembris, contra humillimam *eiuſdem* Widdringtoni *Supplicationem ad* S. D. Paulum *V. Pont. Max. Romæ* pub-
licata, præcipuam noſtri gravaminis, læſionis, & op-
preſſionis cauſam eſſe, atque inſuper præſentientes,

nos

nos inprimis, & fubinde cæteros omnes, qui doctrinæ *Widdringtoni* favent, nifi finiftris Adverfarioru informationibus, dolofis machinationibus, & iniquis
conatibus confeftim occurramus, contra omnem ratione & iuftitiam magis gravandos & opprimendos
fore, à prædictis *duobus Decretis*, tanquam manifeftè
iniuftis, & ab ipfifmet *Illuftrifsimis Dominis Cardinalibus*
ad *Indicem* deputatis, tanquam parum æquis, fufpectis,
& malè informatis Iudicibus, & à quacunque fententia, five definitiva, five interlocutoria, aut alio quovis nomine nuncupetur, ab ipfis intuitu prædictæ
Widdringtoni doctrinæ, aut vllo ad eam refpectu habito, vel iam lata & denunciata, vel deinceps ferenda &
denuncianda, & à quavis alia authoritate, ipfis etiam
Illuftrifsimis Dominis Cardinalibus, aut *Nuncijs Apoftolicis*,
alijfve quibufcunque delegata, vel deleganda, ad
Sanctifsimum Dominum noftrum *Papam* (qui fupremus
totius Ecclefiæ, omniumque noftrum, etiam *Illuftrifsi-*
morum Cardinalium, Pater, Paftor, & in fpiritualibus Superior eft) nomine noftro, & *Rogeri Widdringtoni* Catholici Angli, cæterorumque eius doctrinæ adhærentium, & adhærere volentium, immediatè provocavimus & appellavimus, provt in his fcriptis ad eum
immediatè appellamus & provocamus inftanter, in-
ftantiùs, & inftantiffimè, atque etiam *Illuftrifsimum*
Cardinalem Bellarminum de atrociffimis illis calumnijs,
quas *Widdringtonus* in libello fupplici, anno Domini
1616 impreffo, *Suæ Sanctitati* perfpicuè detexit, quæq;
etiam maximã noftri gravaminis, & oppreffionis caufam præbuerunt, in iudicium vocamus, & iuftitiam
contra eum obnixè poftulamus; *Suam Sanctitatem* humillimè

millimè deprecantes, & per tremendum illum *Iudicē,* ante cuius Tribunal nos omnes, nescimus quàm citò, comparituri sumus, & exactissimā nostræ qualiscunq; villicationis rationē reddituri, suppliciter obtestantes, vt non velit causam nostram, nisi ordine iuris saltem naturalis seruato, iudicare, aut pro doctrina illa propugnanda, quam *Sanctitas Sua* in *Francia* tolerat,

n *supra nu.* 19.
● *supra nu.* 28.

p Arresta ponuntur in fine Strenæ Catholicæ.

ⁿ quæque *impedire non debet* ° *reunionē eorū, qui Ecclesiæ reconciliari desiderarent,* quæq; etiam à *Senatu Parisiensi* pluribꝰ *Arrestis* ᴾ approbata est, & contraria *Card. Bellarmini, Francisci Suarez,* & similium, tanquam *falsa & seditiosa,* sub pœna *læsæ Maiestatis,* proscripta, nos condemnare, aut pœna aliqua, quæ necessariò culpam supponit, cuius nos conscij non sumus, vel sententia vlla, quæ, si iusta non sit, in foro conscientiæ non obligat, nisi de crimine aliquo speciatim, & iuridicè accusatos, admonitos, citatos, auditos, defensos, & conuictos afficere vel innodare: Atque etiam, si post accuratam causæ nostræ discussionem, *Sanctitas Sua* perspexerit, se à *Card. Bellarmino,* eiusve sequacibus, delusam, & malè informatam esse, eosque incertas suas opiniones, collectiones, Scripturarum, & Conciliorū expositiones, in re tam graui, qualis est debita nostra fidelitas *Deo* & *Cæsari* exhibenda, pro certissimis fidei Catholicæ dogmatibus, & pro indubitato Scripturarū & Conciliorum sensu, *Suæ Beatitudini,* totiq; mundo obtrudere voluisse, vt saltem eo modo, quo controuersiam illam, inter *Patres Dominicanos,* & *Iesuitas* de *auxilijs gratiæ* religiosè, ac sapienter cōposuit ac sedauit, hanc etiam scandalosam controuersiam de potestate *Papæ* supra *Reges* in temporalibus, pacificè & quietè,

(alioquin

(alioquin fanè minis, terroribus, ac violentijs nunquâ terminandâ) componere, ac fedare, noftræq; tandem famæ à *Card Bellarmino,* eiufque fequacibus, graviffimè, & per fummam iniuriam, *ea de caufa,* læfæ, provt fuæ prudentiæ, charitati, & iuftitiæ magis expedire videbitur, confulere quamprimùm velit.

33. Atque infuper proteftamur hanc *Appellationem* profequi per viam nullitatis, abvfus, iniquitatis, vel iniuftitiæ, & aliâs, provt melius poterimus, optione nobis refervata, eo modo, quo perfonæ in cuftodia detentæ, & ad victum & veftitum vix fibi neceffaria, & multo minùs *Procuratorem* ad *Curiam Romanam* mittendi facultatem habentes (nemo autem ad impoffibile tenetur) nempe per fcripta publica, typifque excudenda, quæ *Suæ Sanctitati,* totique Orbi rationes & merita noftræ caufæ æquè manifefta facient, ac fi perfonaliter, vel per *Procuratorê* (fi talis inveniri poffet, qui in *Curia Romana* noftræ caufæ patrocinium fufcipere, & *Card. Bellarmino,* eiufque fequacibus in faciem refiftere non pertimefceret) hanc *Appellationem* profequeremur: Adijcientes etiam in teftimonium invocatum, addendi, diminuendi, mutandi, corrigendi, & in melius reformandi, omnique alio iuris beneficio, nobis, & *Rogero Widdringtono,* eiufque doctrinæ adhærentibus, & adhærere volentibus femper falvo. Datû, & actum *Londini* in *Carcere Clinkenfi* die 7. *Decembris* 1620.

Signatum

Thomas Preftonus }
Thomas Greenæus } qui fupra.

Et

Et quoniam *Sanctissimum Dominū* nostrum *Papam,* ad quem immediatè appellamus, adire non poterimus, cùm in custodia detenti simus, neque persona aliqua authentica, & in dignitate Ecclesiastica constituta nobis præstò adest, cui hanc nostram *Appellationē* intimare, infinuare, ac notificare valemus, & ab ea cum instantia & reverentia debita Apostolos petere ac requirere, eam coram *idoneis Testibus,* probis & honestis Catholicis, nobifcum in custodia detentis, & ad testificandum, nos hanc nostram *Appellationem* illis notificasse rogatis, quorum nomina subscripta funt, publicandam curavimus, die nono *Decembris* 1620.

Eodem die nono *Decembris* publicatam esse hanc nostram *Appellationem* eo modo quo diximus, *Testes* funt

Robertus Charnock Sacræ Theologię Baccalaure'.
Rodulphus Stansford.
Richardus White.
Christopherus Thulis.
Ioannes Barker.
Ioannes White.

Thomas Leke.
Edmundus Canon.
Ioannes Tomson.
Ioannes Brian.
Ioannes Farmer.
Guilielmus Davis.

THOMAS PRESTON and THOMAS GREEN

Supplicatio
1621

REVERENDORVM
PATRVM D. THOMAE
PRESTONI *Congregationis Cassinensis,*

&

FR. THOMAE GREENAEI *Congregationis
Hispanicae Ordinis* S.Benedicti *Reli-
giosorum, & Sacrae Theologiae
Professorum,*

Ad Sanctissimum ac Beatissimum Patrem
Gregorium Decimum quintum, Pontificem
Maximum, *Sanctamq, Sedem Apostolicam,*
Humillima Supplicatio.

IEREM. 5.

*Causam viduae non iudicaverunt, causam pupilli non direxerunt, & iudicium
pauperum non iudicaverunt : Nunquid super his non visitabo, dicit Dominus? aut super gentem huiscemodi non vlciscetur anima mea?*

AVGVSTAE,
Apud BAPTISTAM FABRVM.
1 6 2 1.
Permissu Superiorum.

SANCTISSIMO AC

Beatissimo Patri

GREGORIO DECIMO QVINTO,

PONTIFICI MAXIMO,

D. Thomas Prestonus Congregationis Cassinensis, & Fr. *Thomas Greenæus* Congregationis Hispanicæ Ordinis S. *Benedicti Presbyteri Religiosi, fœlicitatem sempiternam exoptant.*

I. Aud ignotum esse *Vestræ Sanctitati* arbitramur (*Pater Beatissime*) cùm res tam publica & pervulgata sit, Nos D. *Thomam Prestonum*, & Fr. *Thomam Greenæum* Anglos Benedictinos, & Sacræ Theologiæ Professores, nomine nostro, & *Rogeri Widdringtoni* Catholici Angli, cæterorumque eius doctrinæ adhærentium, & adhærere volentium, ob intoleranda quædam grauamina nobis multifariè, multisque modis tum illata, tum in futurum verisimiliter inferenda, quinque circiter ab hinc mensibus, nempe die nono *Decembris* anni iam proximè elapsi, à duobus potissimùm Decretis Illustrissimorum S. R. E. Cardinalium

ad Indicem deputatorum aduersùs tres prædicti *Wid-*
dringtoni libros ex ſiniſtra informatione editis, tanquam manifeſtè iniuſtis, & ex praua quorundam,
præſertim Illuſtriſſimi *Cardinalis Bellarmini,* ſuggeſti-
one latis, necnon ab Illuſtriſſimis Dominis *Cardinali-*
bus ad Indicem deputatis, tanquam parum æquis, ſuſpectis & malè informatis Iudicibus, & à quacunque
ſententia, ſiue definitiua, ſiue interlocutoria, aut alio
quouis nomine nuncupetur, ab ipſis, aut alijs quibuſcunque etiam *Nuncijs Apoſtolicis* intuitu præfatæ *Wid-*
dringtoni doctrinæ, aut vllo ad eam reſpectu habito,
vel iam lata & denunciata, vel deinceps ferenda & denuncianda, & à quauis alia authoritate etiam Illuſtriſſimis Dominis *Cardinalibus,* aut *Nuncijs Apoſtolicis,*
alijſue quibuſcunque delegata vel deleganda, ad *San-*
ctiſſimũ Dominũ noſtrũ *Papam* immediatè appellaſſe
& prouocaſſe, cauſamque noſtram ad *Sedẽ Apoſtolicã,*
ab ea pro ſingulari eius prudentia, charitate, ac iuſtitia, cognoſcendam, iudicandam, atque terminandam
detuliſſe, ipſumque Illuſtriſſimũ Cardinalem *Bellar-*
minum de atrociſſimis illis calumnijs, quas *Widdringto-*
nus in libello ſupplici, anno Domini 1616. impreſſo,
Suæ Sanctitati perſpicuè detexit, quæque præcipuam
noſtrorum grauaminum, & oppreſſionum cauſam
præbuerunt, in iudicium vocaſſe, & iuſtitiam contra
eum obnixè poſtulaſſe. Hancque noſtram Appellationem, prouocationem & poſtulationem, vt in totius mundi conſpectum prodiret, neque Aduerſario-
rum conatibus in latebris, vel paucorum manibus
abſcondita deliteſceret, typis publicis excudendam,
atque evulgandam, innocentiæ & cauſæ noſtræ æquitati confiſos, quamprimùm curaſſe.

2. Et

2. Et quantumuis firmiter nobis perfuadeamus, prædictam noftram *Appellationem, prouocationem,* & *poftulationem* ex morte *Prædecefforis* veftri, cuius tempore facta eft, nullam vim fuam aut robur amififfe, fed, non obftante illius obitu, integram, firmam, ac ftabilem in vigore fuo hucufque permanere, quandoquidem non fpeciatim & nominatim ad *Paulum Quintum* Pontificem Maximum (fcientes, quòd *vita noftra fit vapor ad modicum parens, & tanquam vmbra fint dies hominis fuper terram*) fed verbis tantum generalibus ad *Sanctiffimum Dominum* noftrum *Papam*, quicunque ille fit vel fuerit, feu generatim ad *Sedem Apoftolicam* de induftria appellauimus & prouocauimus ; Ad maiorem tamen cautelam, atque vt omnis cauillandi, & contra dictam *Appellationem* excipiendi occafio adimatur, eam denuo renouandam, inftaurandam, & confirmandam tutius effe iudicamus, ficut per præfentes eam de integro renouamus, inftauramus, & confirmamus, & iterum tum ad *Veftram Beatitudinem* nominatim, tum ad *Sedem Apoftolicam* generatim, ob caufam iam dictã, immediatè appellamus & prouocamus, atque præfatam noftram *Appellationem, prouocationem,* & *poftulationem* (quam cum hoc noftro fupplici libello typis etiam publicis, ob caufam fuprà memoratam, excufo, ad Illuftriffimum Dominum *Nuncium Veftrum Apoftolicum Parifijs* manentem, vt ad *Veftram Beatitudinem* quamprimùm tranfmittantur direximus) per præfentes, Deo auxiliante, renouare, confirmare, & ex parte profequi nobis eft inftitutum.

3. Quapropter *Veftram Beatitudinem*, communem omnium noftrûm, etiam Illuftriffimorum S. R. E. *Cardinalium* in fpiritualibus Patrem, Paftorem ac Iudi-

Iac. 4.
Iob. 8.

A 3   cem

cem ſupremum, ſummis precibus ſuppliciter obteſtamur (quæque totius noſtræ *Appellationis, prouocationis,
poſtulationis,* eiuſdemque *proſequutionis* ſumma & ſub-
ſtantia eſt) vt, abſque vlla perſonarum acceptione,
quod iuſtum eſt iudicare, vique oppreſſos de manu
calumniantium eruere, & ſcandaloſæ huic controuerſiæ de poteſtate Papali Principes ſupremos deponendi tanquam de fide Catholica ab omnibus neceſſariò
credenda (quæ tantorum in Eccleſia præſertim Anglicana tumultuum cauſa extitit) finem, quantum
fieri poteſt, tranquillum iam tandem imponere non
grauetur; atque vt vel *Breuia* Prædeceſſoris Veſtri Iuramentum fidelitatis prohibentia, & *Decreta* Illuſtriſſimorum *Cardinalium* ad Indicem deputatorum libros
Widdringtoni verbis tantùm generalibus proſcribentia,
cùm eorum vtraque in falſis informationibus, & ſuppoſitionibus fundata ſint (vti *Widdringtonus* clariſſimè
commonſtrauit, [a] & infra *Veſtræ* etiam *Sanctitati* ſatis
perſpicuum fiet) reſcindere ac abrogare, noſque omnino innocentes, nullique crimini eo nomine obnoxios, quin potius *Cardinalem Bellarminum,* cæteroſque
illius ſequaces, qui tam falſa & execranda crimina
Widdringtono impoſuerunt, falſamque fidem Catholicam in re tam magni ponderis procudere non formi-
darunt, calumniarum, impoſturæ, & criminis falſi
reos eſſe palàm declarare, vel vnicam ſaltem propoſitionem ſiue in præfato *Iuramento,* ſiue in *Widdringtoni*
libris contentam, quæ fidei aut bonis moribus repugnet, nobis notum facere, quò eam confeſtim retractare, abiurare, aut ab ea nos purgare valeamus, quamprimùm velit. Quàm autem rectæ rationi, charitati,
iuſtitiæ, & æquitati conſona, neque filijs à Patre,

ouibus

ouibus à Paſtore, & ſubditis iniuſtiſſimè oppreſſis
deneganda ſit à Iudice,& Chriſti Domini Vicario humillima hæc noſtra *Supplicatio*, apud *Veſtram* potiſſimùm *Beatitudinem*, cæteroſque omnes non planè iniquos rerum æſtimatores iudicium eſto.

4. Catholici enim ſumus (*Pater Beatiſſime*) & Eccleſiæ *Catholicæ Romanæ*, pro qua palàm agnoſcenda
grauia incommoda aſſiduè ſuſtinemus, filij deuotiſſimi, eiuſque iudicio & cenſuræ nos in omnibus humillimè ſubmittimus, illamque fidem *Catholicam Romanam*, prout verbis expreſſis à *Pio Papa Quarto* in fine
Concilij Tridentini edita habetur, ſyncerè profitemur:
Quaſcunque hæreſes, errores, & doctrinas non ſanas
ab *Eccleſia* damnatas, reiectas, & anathematizatas,nos
etiam toto corde vniuersìm damnamus, reijcimus,&
anathematizamus ; & ſi aliqua particularis propoſi-
tio vel in libris *Widdringtoni,* vel in alijs quibuſcunque
contenta, quæ fidei, ſaluti, bonis moribus, aut ſanæ
doctrinæ repugnans ſit, nobis ſpeciatim innoteſce-
ret, ad eam quoque ſpeciatim damnandam, reijcien-
dam, atque anathematizandam, quando id à nobis
poſtulabitur, nos paratiſſimos eſſe, ſyncerè & coram
Deo proteſtamur. Et hoc proculdubio nos ab omni
hæreſeως & erroris labe, quantumuis aliquid ſanæ
doctrinæ contrarium, quod adhuc nos latet,*Widdringtono* per ignorantiam excidiſſet, excuſare ac penitus liberare abundantiſſimè ſufficiet.

5. Sed non propterea *Veſtræ Sanctitatis* prudentiam
exiſtimare velimus, *Nos* vllam planè in mentibus noſtris dubitationem, diffidentiam, aut ſcrupulum de
cauſæ noſtræ iuſtitia concipere, quin immo innocentiæ noſtræ confiſi, certiſſimè nobis perſuademus,

Veſtram

Veſtram etiam *Beatitudinem,* ſi verum controuerſiæ ſtatum, quem Aduerſarij, quantum in ipſis eſt, diſſimulare indies ſtudent, ſeriò expendere voluerit, clariſſimè perſpecturam, neque *Widdringtonum,* neque alios eius doctrinæ adhærentes, qui non auri & argenti, ſed *Fidei Catholicæ,* quæ quouis auro & argento longè pretioſior eſt, falſarios detexerunt, eorumque artificia, fraudes, & impoſturas, palam fecerunt, vlla prorſus pœna, ſed præmio potius eo nomine dignos eſſe, atq; *Aduerſarios,* qui in maximam *Principum* ſupremorum, qui *Eccleſiæ* Sanctæ *Nutritij* & *Protectores* à Deo conſtituti ſunt, iniuriam, falſa fidei dogmata, cum grauiſſimo *Eccleſiæ Romanæ, Sediſque Apoſtolicæ* opprobrio & ſcandalo, procudere, cæteriſque Chriſti fidelibus per vim obtrudere, eoſque, qui tam pernicioſis ſuis nouitatibus non applaudunt, ſed aduerſantur, à communione Eccleſiaſtica tanquam Ethnicos & Publicanos excludere non verentur, de crimine *falſi, calumniæ, Schiſmatis,* & *læſæ Maieſtatis,* tam in *Eccleſiaſticam* quàm in *Ciuilem* Rempublicam reos, iure merito accuſandos, condemnandos, & grauiſſimè caſtigandos eſſe.

6. Si enim Dei veraciſſimi verbo & teſtimonio quidquam prorſus detrahere, vllumve verum fidei Catholicæ articulum abnegare ſcelus grauiſſimum eſſe nimis manifeſtum ſit, profectò Dei verbo aliquid ſuperaddere, falſumque fidei Catholicæ ac diuinæ dogma confingere, crimen etiam eſſe permagnum nemo inficiari poterit; cùm diuini teſtimonij veritas, & fidei Catholicæ puritas non integra & inuiolata ab illis conſeruetur, qui vel veros fidei Catholicæ articulos reijciunt, vel falſos cudunt, qui vel negant Deum ea reuelaſſe quæ reuelauit, vel pro certiſſimo aſſerunt,

Deum

Deum ea reuelaſſe, quæ reuera non reuelauit: Hinc enim fidei Catholicę pura veritas perniciofis falſitatibus, & corruptelis deprauatur; illinc Deus ipſe, qui eſt prima, & infallibilis veritas mendacij arguitur, quod apertè hæreticũ eſſe oẽs norunt. Non igitur Sedi Apoſtolicæ, aut cuiuis verè Catholico gratum eſſe debet, quòd falſa fidei Catholicæ dogmata à quoquam, quantæcunque alioquin dignitatis fuerit, vel procudantur, vel propugnentur, quantumuis prima facie in honorem *Summi Pontificis*, aut ipſiuſmet etiam *Beatiſsimæ Christi Matris* honorem tendere videantur. *Honor* enim *Pontificis* (vti de *Beatiſsima Virgine* dixit S.*Bernardus* illi alioquin deuotiſſimus) *iudicium*, ſeu diſcretionem *diligit*; Sedes Apoſtolica *falſo non eget honore, veris cumulata honorum titulis, infulis dignitatum*: Neque profectò expedit, aut licet vlli verè Catholico maiorem authoritatem *Summo Pontifici* tanquam illi abſque vlla prorſus dubitatione à *Christo Domino* datam, tribuere, quàm certò & abſque vlla prorſus dubitatione conſtet illi à *Christo Domino* conceſſam. Et qui *Summi Pontificis* authoritatem, præſertim in *Regiæ poteſtatis* derogationem, plus nimio extollunt, Sedis Apoſtolicæ *authoritatem labefactant, non fouent, euertunt, non firmant. Nam quid tandem aduerſus hæreticos*, ait doctiſſimus *Melchior Canus*, *diſputando ille proficiet, quem viderint non iudicio, ſed affectu patrocinium authoritatis Pontificiæ ſuſcipere, nec id agere, vt diſputationis ſuæ vi lucem, ac veritatem eliciat, ſed vt ſe ad alterius ſenſum, voluntatemq́ conuertat. Non eget* Petrus *mendacio noſtro, noſtra adulatione non eget.*

S. Bernard. in epiſt. 174. ad Canonicos Lugdun.

Canus lib. 5. de locis cap. 5. prope finem.

7. Notum eſt (*Beatiſsime Pater*) vniuerſis Theologiæ, & Iuris Canonici peritis, magnam eſſe inter eruditos Catholicos controuerſiam (vt alias ſimiles,

B veluti

veluti de dominio *Summi Pontificis* directè in tempo-
ralib', de poteſtate eius in ſolemni caſtitatis voto diſpenſandi, & res fidei abſque Concilio generali infallibiliter definiendi nunc mittamus) an *Sedes Apoſtolica*
in matrimonio rato non conſummato diſpenſandi,
ſeu à vinculo inter coniuges inde contracto abſoluendi poteſtatem habeat : Et profectò ſi aliqui Theologi, aut Iuriſconſulti authoritatis Pontificiæ promo-
uendæ percupidi iam exurgerent, & nouam de hac
re fidem Catholicam procuderent, affirmantes, eſſe
rem de fide certam, & ab omnibus neceſſariò credendam, quòd talis poteſtas *Sedi Apoſtolicæ* competat,
atque ad nouam hanc fidem confirmandam ſimilia
argumenta, quibus Card.*Bellarminus*,eiuſque ſequaces
ad nouam eorum fidem de poteſtate *Papali Principes*
deponendi,eorumque ſubditos à temporali fidelitate
abſoluendi, ſtabiliendam vtuntur, nempe, illa Chriſti
Domini verba,*Quodcunque ſolueris* &c.tot Summorum
Pontificum facta ſeu praxas pluribus eorum *Bullis*
confirmatas, & eiuſmodi argumenta producerent,
atque contrariam Catholicorum ſententiam, non
tam *ſententiam,* quàm *hæreſim* eſſe palàm prædicare,
eoſque Catholicos qui nouæ eorum fidei non applaudunt,ſed obſiſtunt, tanquam hæreticos, Pſeudo-
Catholicos, Eccleſiæ Romanæ, Sediſque Apoſtolicæ
hoſtes traducere, necnon à Sacramentorum perceptione, & communione Eccleſiaſtica tanquam indignos excludere non pertimeſcerent, nullatenus ſanè
dubitamus, quin ipſemet *Card. Bellarminus* eiuſmodi
nouæ fidei non ſtatim acquieſceret, ſed tales Theologos aut Iuriſconſultos, quantumcunque alioquin do-
ctiſſimos, & ſingulari *Sedis Apoſtolicæ,* & Pontificiæ
poteſtatis

poteſtatis exaltandæ zelo, ſed certè non ſecundum ſcientiam, ardentiſſimos, *temeritatis, ſcandali, calumniæ, Schiſmatis,* & *impoſturæ* ſeu *criminis falſi* reos, grauique ſupplicio dignos iudicaret. Quòd ſi Illuſtriſſimus *Bel-larminus ,* eiuſque aſſeclæ iſtiuſmodi exempla velint ſeriò & ſyncerè ſibiipſis applicare, veramque *Schiſma-tis* naturam diligenter expendere, quæ non ſolùm diſ-iunctionem à capite, ſed à corpore etiam, membriſque Eccleſiæ diſunionem ſignificat, quæque proinde in veri atque indubitati *Summi Pontificis* perſona (vt communiter Theologi ᵍ tradunt) reperiri poteſt, fa-cilè proculdubio animaduertent, quantorum crimi-num ſi non Authores præcipui, ſaltem participes & rei ſint, eo quòd falſam fidem Catholicam, *Sanctiſ̃g Patribus* incognitam, & proinde non verè *Catholicam,* id eſt, *ſemper, vbiḡ,* & *ab omnibus* ʰ *traditam,* de poteſtate Papali Principes deponendi, de qua magna ſemper fuit, & nunc etiam eſt inter eruditos Catholicos con-trouerſia, procudere & propugnare, cæteroſque Ca-tholicos qui illis refragantur, tanquam hæreticos, Pſeudo-Catholicos, Eccleſiæ Romanæ, Sediſque Apoſtolicæ hoſtes inſectari, &, ac ſi Ethnici ac Publi-cani eſſent, à communione Eccleſiaſtica ſecludere non vereantur.

8. Nam verus ſcandaloſæ huius controuerſiæ in-ter Card. *Bellarminum* eiuſque ſequaces, atque *Widdring-tonum* eiuſque doctrinæ adherentes, de poteſtate Papali Principes deponendi ſtatus eiuſmodi eſt (*Pater Bea-tiſſime*) vt neque *Widdringtono,* neque nobis, qui eius doctrinam hac in re amplexamur, inſtitutum ſit de *abſoluta* hac enunciatione, an Papa iure diuino Prin-cipes deponendi poteſtatem habeat necne, cùm Card.

g Turrecremata lib.4.Sum.de Ec-cleſ. p. 1. c. 11. Caiet. 2ª 2æ. q. 39. ar. 1. Bannes ibid. Valentia tom. 3. diſp.3. q. 15.punct.1. & aliſ. h Vincentius Lyrin. aduerſus prophanas hære-ſium nouitates.

Bellarmino eiuſque ſequacibus in præſenti contendere, ſed ſolùm de hac *modali*, an ſit doctrina de fide adeo certa talem poteſtatem illi à Chriſto Domino conceſſam eſſe, vt ab vniuerſis fidelibus neceſſariò & ſub pœna æternæ damnationis credenda ſit, neque vlla de ea inter eruditos Catholicos controuerſia exiſtat.

9.   Niſi igitur Card.*Bellarminus*, & quidam alij recentiores, præſertim Suæ Societatis Ieſu, Theologi eius veſtigijs inhærentes, in magnum Eccleſiæ Romanæ ſcandalum, in ſummam poteſtatis Regiæ derogationem, in maximam virorum Catholicorum, & de Eccleſia Romana benemerentium contumeliam, in non leue perpetuæ inter Regnum & Sacerdotium diſcordiæ periculum, atque in ingens Catholicorum noſtræ nationis Anglicanæ præiudicium, falſum hac in re fidei Catholicæ dogma ſtabilire (ſicut iampridem in materia de auxilijs gratiæ ſed fruſtra conati ſunt) priuatum ſuum ſpiritum pro indubitata fidei Catholicæ regula reliquis omnibus per vim obtrudere, eoſque Catholicos qui contrà ſentiunt, tanquam hæreticos, Pſeudo-Catholicos, & Eccleſiaſtica communione indignos traducere non formidaſſent, non habuiſſent profectò nos in hac controuerſia illis tam vehementer aduerſantes. Veruntamen cùm prædicti Theologi ſub ſpecie zeli, atque veritatis, & Pontificiæ poteſtatis euehendæ prætextu, falſam Sanctiſque Patribus ignotam fidem Catholicá, eamque, vti diximus, tam *Sedi Apoſtolicæ*, quàm *Regiæ Maieſtati*, cæteriſque quamplurimis Catholicis adeo pernicioſam fingere & firmare, atque *Romano Pontifice* turpiter abutentes eum in eundem errorem pertrahere, ſuamque fidem falſam vijs indebitis, maliſque
                                                                          artibus

ãrtibus ſtabilire non vereantur, non ægrè ferant, quòd
alij Theologi, tametſi illis Theologiæ peritia inferiores, etiam amore veritatis, & *fidei Catholicæ, Sediſque*
Apoſtolicæ, ac *ſupremæ* Regum *poteſtatis* zelo permoti,
illis palam & in oculis omnium contradicere, eorumque falſam, & peſſimè fundatam fidem Catholicam
reijcere, & vniuerſa, quibus ad eam roborandam
ytuntur, artificia patefacere non pertimeſcant.

10. Quis enim ſyncerè Catholicus, atque erga Eccleſiam Chriſti, & Regna mundi, ſpiritualem Pontificum, ac temporalem Regum poteſtatem bene affectus
æquo animo ferre poteſt, quòd pauci quidam Theologi recentiores, quantacunque alioquin eruditione,
dignitate aut potentia præ cæteris præpolleant, aude-
ant tam intrepidè cum tanto Eccleſiæ Catholicæ Romanæ ſcandalo, & maxima Principum Chriſtianorũ
iniuria, grauiſſimoque ſubditorũ fidelium præiudicio,
hoc præſertim ſæculo infœlici, in quo vera & antiqua
fidei Catholicæ Romanæ dogmata ab Eccleſiæ Romanæ Aduerſarijs non ſolùm in quæſtionè vocantur,
ſed acerrimè etiam impugnantur, nouũ, & antiquis
Patribus incognitum fidei Catholicæ articulum, in
rebus præſertim ad temporalem fidelitatem ſpectan-
tibus, confingere, atque in eiſdem priuatas ſuas opiniones pro certiſſima fidei regula cæteris contrà ſenti-
entibus per vim obtrudere, & pro doctrina incerta,
atque apud Catholicos controuerſa, & *quam ipſemet*
Dominus Papa, (ait *Cardinalis Peronus*) *ob pacis Eccleſiaſticæ*
bonum in Francia tolerat, quæque *impedire non debet reẅni-*
onem eorum, qui Eccleſiæ reconciliari deſiderant, Eccleſiæ
vnionem hîc in Anglia diſrumpere, Catholicos Anglos, qui falſæ ſuæ fidei obſiſtunt, ad communionem

Card. Peron en
Haraugne au
tiers Eſtat. pag.
98. & in magna
Replica cap. 91.
pag. 633.

Eccleſi-

Ecclefiaſticam non admittere, fed, ac fi Ethnici aut Publicani eſſent, à Sacramentis percipiendis excludere, atque ita perniciofiſſimum *Schiſma* non folùm accendere & fouere, verùm etiam ipfummet *Summum Pontificem*, communem Ecclefiæ Patrem, Paſtorem, & cui præ cæteris cura follicitè *feruandi in Ecclefiæ corpore vnitatem ſpiritus in vinculo pacis* à *Chriſto* Domino concredita eſt, vt fub illius vmbra peſtiferas fuas, fcandalofas, feditiofas, & *Principum Coronis* iniuriofas, eorumque *Capitibus* periculofas nouitates plaufibiliùs pallient, illifque maiorem authoritatem apud vulgus præfertim imperitum concilient, ad partes fuas falfis informationibus pertrahere, illique, vt fcandalofi & perniciofi huius *Schiſmatis*, & acerbiſſimorum grauaminum, quæ filij eius deuotiſſimi iniuſtè patiuntur, non focius duntaxat & confors, fed vt eius authoritate, *Breuibus*, & *Decretis* præcipuus Author fit, falfis fuis & iniquis fuggeſtionibus perfuadere non perhorrefcant? Cùm tamen potiùs ipfimet ob tam prauas fuas, peruerfas & peſſimè fundatas machinationes, atque tam *Ecclefiæ Chriſti*, quàm *Regnis* mundi, tam *fidei Catholicæ* puritati, quàm *supremæ* Regum *poteſtati* iniuriofas adinuentiones, de *fcandalo, temeritate, calumnia, Schiſmate, impoſtura*, & de *crimine falfi*, atque *Maieſtatis*, tam in *Ecclefiam*, quàm in *Regnum* læfæ (nam ficut cufor falfæ monetæ, proditor in Regnum, ita cufor falfæ fidei Catholicæ in Ecclefiam proditor eſt) tum apud *Sedem Apoſtolicam*, tum apud *Principes Chriſtianos*, accufari, condemnari, & poenis condignis caſtigari iure optimo mereantur.

11. Sed antequam præcipuas noſtrorum grauaminum caufas magis particulatim aperiamus, vnam

Ephef. 4.

inprimis quæſtiunculam *Veſtræ Beatitudini* ab ea pro ſingulari veſtra prudentia ſeriò diſcutiendam commendare non a re alienum arbitramur, An ſcilicet *Sedes Apoſtolica*, aut alius quiſpiam tutò, prudenter, & abſque falſæ informationis periculo, *Patrum Ieſuitarũ*, quantumuis alioquin doctiſſimorum, dictis, ſcriptis, aut ſuggeſtionibus, in maximum tertiæ perſonæ, quæ contra ipſos ſentit præiudicium, ea non plenè audita, fidem indubiam adhibere queat, in cauſis præſertim ſeu queſtionibus, in quibus ipſimet partes ſunt, quæque in fauorem *Summi Pontificis* tendere videntur, (in quibus ſanè quæſtionibus proponendis & pertractandis, ex humana fragilitate, cui ſicut cæteri homines ſubiecti ſunt, vel ſtudio placendi, vel diſplicendi formidine, alteriuſve proprij ſui commodi aut incommodi intuitu, à veritate tum ſyncerè examinanda, tum ingenuè agnoſcenda facilè abduci poſſunt) quandoquidem nuperis experimentis iam ſatis exploratum ſit, quàm turpiter quidam ex iſtis Patribus errauerint, non ſolùm in cauſa Sacerdotum Anglorum, qui ab illis, eorumque fautoribus plurimùm oppreſſi, & tanquam *Schiſmatici, inobedientes, Sedi Apoſtolicæ rebelles, ſuiſq; facultatibus priuati* per maledicorum ora hîc in Anglia traducti ad *Sedem Apoſtolicam* appellârunt; à quibus tamen omnibus & ſingulis criminib' *Clemens Octauus* fœliciſſimæ memoriæ Pontifex literis ſuis, per modum *Breuis* ad Magiſtrum *Georgium Blackuellum* tunc Archipresbyterum miſſis, cum non leui ipſius *D. Archipresbyteri* & *Patrum Ieſuitarum* qui ipſi à conſilijs erant, & præcipui tantorum contentionum, & calumniationum Authores putabantur, dedecore, eos planè liberos et immunes eſſe declarauit: Verùm

etiam

etiam in eo quòd nouam fidé Catholicam in materia
de *auxilijs gratiæ*, quæ poteſtati Pontificis nec fauet,
nec præiudicat, procudere tentauerint, et *Patres Domi-*
nicanos, qui neque doctrina, nec pietate, neque erga
Sedem Apoſtolicam zelo illis inferiores ſunt, fæda *Luthe-*
raniſmi, & *Caluiniſmi* nota aſpergere non erubuerint :
Sicut etiam nunc *Widdringtono*, eiuſque doctrinæ adhærentibus, non ſolùm *Lutheraniſmi*, *Caluiniſmi*, temeritatis, ſcandali, & inobedientiæ notas inuerere, verùm
etiam (ad eum planè modum, quo cum *Sacerdotibus*
Appellantibus procceſſerunt, & quod ſane intolerandum
eſt) eos, ac ſi Ethnici, Publicani, aut palam criminoſi
eſſent, à Sacramentis excludere, & ſi Sacerdotes ſint,
ſuis etiam facultatibus priuatos eſſe vociferari non
extimeſcant.

12. Atque hoc ipſum eſt (*Beatiſſime Pater*) quod
planè inſolens, intolerandum, & maxima reprehen-
ſione & caſtigatione dignum arbitramur, & de quo
apud *Veſtram Beatitudinem* iam dolentiſſimè conqueri-
mur, quòd ſcilicet *Patres* iſti incertas ſuas, & noſtro
iudicio malè fundatas opiniones, tanquam certiſſi-
mam fidei regulam nobis obtrudere ſtudeant, cæteroſque qui illis reſiſtunt, tanquam hæreticos, Pſeudo-
Catholicos, aut alias criminoſos, & proinde Eccleſiaſtica communione indignos traducere, atque ita Eccleſiæ vnitatem diſrumpere, & contra charitatis &
iuſtitiæ leges, Schiſma grauiſſimum, & capitales in
Eccleſia diſcordias potiùs quàm eorum placita, quæ
mordic' tenent, impugnari permittent, concitare non
vereantur. Nam opinentur *Patres* iſti, eorumque ſequaces, quantum velint, doctrinam ſuam, quam ſiue
in hac, ſiue in illa materia tenent, eſſe veram, certam,

Catholicam,

Catholicam, de fide tenendam, & contrariam Catholicorum falfam, erroneam, non tam *fententiam* quàm
hærefim, atque vel *Lutheranifmum*, vel *Caluinifmum* fapere,
nihil morabimur, neque ea de re cum illis tumultuosè
& proteruè difceptabimus, aut eorum confcientias de
crimine aliquo, ob quod à Sacramentis Ecclefiæ percipiendis arcendi fint, propterea accufabimus, fed eos
in fua fententia perfiftere ob pacis Ecclefiafticæ bonum æquo animo fuftinebimus, dummodo intra
opinionis cancellos fefe contineant, neque iuftitiæ
aut charitatis Chriftianæ fines excedant, aliofque Catholicos, qui contrà opinantur, tanquam criminofos,
& propterea Sacramentorum perceptione indignos
non traducant, fed quemlibet in fuo fenfu abundare
liberè permittant, ficut in quæftione *de auxilijs gratiæ*
fefe intra opinionis terminos continuerunt, neque
alios qui contrà opinati funt, à Sacramentorum perceptione tanquam fceleratos aut indignos excludere
præfumpferunt. Veruntamen adeo fibimetipfis fapere, vt cæteros omnes, qui cum illis non fapiunt, de-
fipere arbitrentur, & priuatum fuum fpiritum, incer-
tafque fuas opiniones, tanquam certiffimam fidei
regulam reliquis omnibus Catholicis eruditis, qui
contrà opinantur, per vim obtrudere, eofque, qui
cum illis in eadem fententia non confpirant, tanquam Pfeudo-Catholicos, Ethnicos, aut Publicanos
à Sacramentis excludere, & tanquam infames, fceleratos, cauteriatam confcientiam habentes, Ecclefiæ Romanæ hoftes, & in reprobum fenfum datos palam,
aut in occulto calumniari, hoc fanè intolerandum,
fcandalofum, fchifmaticum, & præterquam quòd in-
fignem arrogantiam, obftinationem, fuperbiam, &

C nimiam

nimiam priuati sui spiritus confidentiam sapiat, à fidei Catholicæ, & charitatis Christianæ regula planè alienum, atque hîc in Anglia, calamitoso Catholicorū statu perpenso, nefarium, crudele, tyrannicū esse, nos cum omni reuerentia & submissione debita loquentes arbitramur, & quivis mediocriter doctus, quique vel *Sacræ Theologiæ*, vel *Iuris Canonici* principia primoribus labris degustauit, clarissimè perspicere potest.

13. Sed non propterea *Vestram Beatitudinem*, aut alium quemuis imaginari velimus, nobis esse animum omnes in vniuersum *Patres Iesuitas*, (absit enim hoc à nobis) reprehendere, & tanquam reos, nostrisq; tam iniquis oppressionibus consentientes increpare, vllamve vel leuissimam *Reuerendo* admodùm Patri *Mutio Vitellesco, Generali* eorum *Præposito*, reprehensionis notam inurere, quem virum valde pium, prudentem, doctum, syncerum, pacisque Ecclesiasticæ & charitatis fraternæ inter omnes conseruandæ studiosum semper reputauimus : Neque enim quisquam (quod scimus) ex eius Societate Theologus à tempore quo ipse illius administrationem suscepit, doctrinam hanc de potestate Papali Principes abdicandi, tanquam de fide Catholica ab omnibus necessariò credendam, & contrariam tanquam hæreticam, erroneam, aut temerariam condemnandam scriptis publicis proprio suo nomine propugnare ausus est; quinimmo *Martinus Becanus*, qui antea *nihil esse apud Catholicos certius* affirmare non est veritus, [n] eam nunc tantùm esse *difficultatem certitudini* oppositam verbis disertis asserit, [o] quod sanè singulari præsertim prædicti Patris *Mutij Vitellesci* prudentiæ, charitati, doctrinæ, & synceritati tribuendum esse censemus.

[n] *in Controuersia Anglicana cap. 2. q. 3.*
[o] *in Tractatu de fide, cap. 15. q. 4.*

14. Et

14. Et tametsi quidam ex Patribus *Iesuitis* hîc in Anglia, & nonnulli alij tam Religiosi,quàm Seculares Presbyteri, eorum affectatores (quorum præcipuos, breuî, nisi ab iniquis suis calumniationibus quamprimùm desistant, apud *Vestram Beatitudinem* nominatim accusabimus) eò audaciæ & temeritatis perniciosæ processerint, vt *Widdringtonum,* cæterosque eius doctrinæ adhærentes, tanquam à fide Apostatas, Sedi Apostolicæ rebelles, Ecclesiastica communione indignos,&,si Presbyteri sint, omni Iurisdictione Sacerdotali priuatos, eo quòd *declaratiua* Vestri Predecessoris *Breuia* in falsis informationibus & suppositionibus, quæque in Francia tanquam seditiosæ sub pœna læsæ Maiestatis condemnatæ· sunt, præcipuè fundata, cum tanto ipsorum, *Regisq,* nostri *Serenissimi* præiudicio non admittenda esse arbitrentur, maledictis infectari,atque ita corporis Ecclesiæ Anglicanę vnitatem dissoluere non solùm non pertimescant, (quantumvis *Widdringtonus* pluribus *Supplicationibus* publicè excusis quamplurimas rationes, quibus adhuc satisfactum non est, *Summo Pontifici* humiliter proposuerit, ob quas Angli Catholici prædicta *Breuia* iniusta esse, & in falsis suppositionibus fundata, nec proinde ab illis recipienda existiment, seque in omnibus *Ecclesiæ Catholicæ Romanæ* iudicio syncerè submiserit) verùm etiam quod magis mirandum, & maximè dolendum est, palam affirmare & prædicare non reformident,minùs graue,& magis tolerandum crimen esse, templa *Protestantium* adire, & cum illis in sacris ritibus communicare, quàm Iuramentum fidelitatis ad coniurationis puluerariæ proditores, eosque Catholicos, qui eorum principijs adhærent, detegendos

C 2   ac

ac reprimendos de induſtria excogitatum ſuſcipere;
quæ eorum doctrina, quàm ſcandaloſa ſit *Eccleſiæ Ro-*
manæ, & *Principibus Chriſtianis*,qui præſertim fidem *Ca-*
tholicam Romanam non amplectuntur,periculoſa,vtpo-
te eos Catholicos qui Iuramento fauent, ad templa
Proteſtantium adeunda, & fidem *Catholicā Romanā* exte-
rius abnegandā alliciens, eoſque, qui illud illicitū eſſe,
ac multa continere quæ fidei & ſaluti repugnant, ſibi
firmiter perſuadent,ad Regicidia, nouaſque Coniura-
tiones puluerarias ſub ſpecie zeli excogitandas, &
quando opportunitas aderit,etiam exequutioni man-
dandas invitans,*Veſtræ Beatitudinis* prudentię,charitati,
ac iuſtitiæ diſcutiendum relinquimus. Attamen certiſſimè nobis perſuademus, prædictū Patrem *Mutium*
Vitelleſcum huiuſmodi pernicioſis dogmatibus,& tam
eruditioni ſolidæ, quàm prudentiæ, & charitati Chriſtianæ diſſentaneis, quæ fratres eius hîc in Anglia, &
quidam alij vel eorum emiſſarij,vel eorum potentiam
& calumnias formidantes,cum maximo ſcandalo di-
ſeminant, & in plebis imperitæ ac præcipitis aures in-
ſuſurrant, nullatenus aſſentiri, ſed eorum omnino in-
ſcium eſſe, & quamprimùm iſtorum notitia ad aures
eius peruenerit, eum,pro eximia eius prudentia,chari-
tate, & doctrina remedium opportunum confeſtim
adhibiturum, neque fratres ſuos hîc in Anglia tam
pernicioſa dogmata in vulgus ſpargere deinceps per-
miſſurum.

15. Iam vt potiſſimas grauaminum, quibus nos,
cæterique Catholici doctrinæ *Widdringtoni* adhærentes a *Patribus* præſertim *Ieſuitis*, eorumque aſſeclis iniuſtè opprimimur, cauſas paucis perſtringamus, *Duæ*
ſunt (*Beatiſſime Pater*) controuerſiæ principales his
noſtris

noſtris temporib' ab eruditis Catholicis hinc illincqʒ
agitatæ, quæque ſcandaloſis hiſce contentionibus &
calumniationibus initium dederunt, & non exiguam
etiam eiſdem nunc acceſſionem faciunt. *Vna* eſt de
poteſtate Papali Principes ſupremos deponendi, atqʒ;
de rebus omnibus temporalibus, & conſequenter de
Coronis & Capitibus Regum in ordine ad bonum
ſpirituale diſponendi, An ſcilicet ſit res de fide certa, &
ſub hæreſεως, alteriuſve criminis mortiferi pœna ab
omnibus fidelibus neceſſariò credenda, quòd Chri-
ſtus Dominus talem deponendi & diſponendi poteſtatem Summo Pontifici conceſſerit. *Altera* controuerſia, quæ ex priori maxima ex parte, vt infra mon-
ſtrabitur, dependet, eſt de prædicto fidelitatis Iuramento, An ſcilicet aliquid in ſe contineat necne, quod
fidei aut ſaluti ſi non apertè & expreſsè, ſaltem tacitè
& per neceſſariam conſequentiam, aduerſetur.

16. Quod ad *primam* controuerſiam attinet, ſatis
conſtat, *Illuſtriſſimum Cardinalem Bellarminum* nouæ &
ſcandaloſæ huius doctrinæ de poteſtate Papali Principes deponendi tanquam *fide Catholica* ab omnibus
certiſſimè credenda, & de contraria tanquam *hæretica*
condemnanda, præcipuum præ cæteris Authorem,
fautorem & propugnatorem extitiſſe. Nam tametſi
in *prima* eius Controuerſiarum editione anno Domini 1586. *Ingolſtadij* impreſſa cuivis Catholico abſqʒ;
vlla hæreſεως nota, vt quid de hac poteſtate ſentire
vellet, integrum relinquere videatur, in *ſecunda* tamen
earum editione anno 1603. *Venetijs* excuſa intrepidè
aſſerit, ᵉ *non tam ſententiam, quàm hæreſim eſſe, quæ docet,*   e *Lib: 5. de Rom.*
Pontificem vt Pontificem, & ex iure diuino nedum poſſe Prin-   *Pont. c. 1.*
cipes Seculares Regnis & Principatu priuare, etiamſi illi priuari

alioqui *mereantur*, cùm tamen in priori editione voca-
bulum illud [*hæreſis*] pænitus prætermiſerit, idque
meritò, cùm doctrina illa neque in vllo *Concilio* generali, aut etiam Prouinciali, & quod magis mirum, &
notandum eſt, neque in vlla Summorum Pontificum
Bulla,Breui,aut *Decreto* condemnata fuerit,neque inter
errores *Caluini, Lutheri, Marſilij Patauini*, aut alterius
cuiuſcunque ante *Bellarmini* tempora à Scriptoribus,
qui hæreticos eorumque errores annotarunt, veluti
Caſtro,Patreolo,Sandero, neque etiam ab ipſomet Cardinali *Bellarmino* in ſua Chronologia , vbi præcipuos
Marſilij,Lutheri,& *Caluini* errores recenſet,annumeretur.
Quam eius *nouam fidem* tum ipſemet poſtea in tractatu
ſuo contra *Barclaium*, & in ſuo *Schulckenio* contra *Widdringtonum*, tum nonnulli primarij ex eius Societate
nu. 31 · Ieſu Theologi (quos [f] infrà referemus) eius veſtigia
ſequuti,confirmare, ſed fruſtra conantur.

17. Sed contra fidem hanc nouam, ſcandaloſam,
ſupremis Principibus iniurioſam, eorumque Capitibus periculoſam, & antiquis Patribus incognitam, ac
proinde non *verè Catholicam*, vtpote non ſemper, vbi-
que, & ab omnibus traditam, ſed abſque ſufficienti
fundamento, & præter fidei Catholicæ regulam im-
prudenter admodum,ac intempeſtiuè, hoc præſertim
ſeculo turbulento, à quibuſdam recentioribus Theologis adinuentam, & contra præcipuos etiam nouæ
huius fidei Authores & defenſores, fortiter & fœli-
ciſſimè decertarunt celeberrimus *Pariſienſis Senatus*
Edictis & Arreſtis, quorum aliqua ad finem *Strenæ
Catholicæ* videre licet,& argumentis ac ſcriptis publicis
Guglielmus, ac *Ioannes Barclaius*, ſed præ cæteris *Rogerus
Widdringtonus* Anglus Catholicus, qui vniuerſa argumenta

menta a *Card. Bellarmino, Francifco Suarez*, cæterifque
Societatis Iefu Theologis ad nouam hanc fuam fidem Catholicam corroborandam allata adeo perfpicuè profligauit, vt ipfi quantumuis alioquin doctiffimi iam nouæ fuæ fidei propugnandæ quafi per-
tæfi terga vertere, ipfumque poft tot certamina in
aperta acie tanquam victorem relinquere, pugnamq;
redintegrare, & prædictam fuam fidem argumentis
& fcriptis publicis vlterius confirmare, ne deinceps
magis infirma, & planè nulla, vti reuera eft, omnibus
appareat, pertimefcere videantur.

18. Et quamuis non expediat in hac breui & com-
pendiaria noftrorum grauaminum expoftulatione,
vniuerfa argumenta & refponfa, quæ à *Widdringtono*
ad nouam, falfamque hanc fidem Catholicam euertendam allata funt, in medium proferre, vt tamen
Sanctitas Veftra ex paucis quæ referemus, perfpicuè
pro fingulari veftra prudentia colligere poffit, magnâ
fuiffe femper de hac poteftate Principes abdicandi inter Catholicos controuerfiam, & doctrinam à plurimis hucvfque approbatam, & confequenter *verè*
probabilem, quòd *Chriftus* Dominus talem poteftatem
Summo Pontifici non concefferit, quædam tantùm te-
ftimonia ex probatiffimis Authoribus, qui vel noftris
temporibus, vel vix centum abhinc annis floruerunt,
producemus, quæ apertiffimè confirmant, doctrinam
illam, quæ talem poteftatem *Summo Pontifici* negat, effe
apud Catholicos ad hæc vfque tempora controuer-
fam, & contrariam à nonnullis tanquá feditiofam, &
Principũ Coronis & Capitib' periculofam fub pœna
læfæ Maieftatis condemnatam, à *plerifq*, Doctoribus
Catholicis approbatá, & ex confequenti iuxta definitionem

tionem *probabilis*, quam *Ariſtoteles*, cæterique omnes
Philoſophi, & Theologi admittunt, eſſe *verè probabilem*, et proinde doctrinam contrariam non eſſe de fide
certam, aut ab omnibus Chriſti fidelibus ſub pœna
hæreſis, aut æternæ damnationis neceſſariò credendâ.

19. *Primum* teſtimonium eſt *Ioannis Trithemij* Ab-
batis Spanehemenſis Ordinis *S. Benedicti*, (*vir vndique
doctiſſimus*, vti etiam eius ſcripta teſtantur, à *Paulo Lan-
gio* nuncupatus) qui in Chronico Monaſterij *Hirſau-
gienſis*, [g] factum *Gregorij* Papæ VII. *Henricum* Imperatorem deponentis recenſens, ita ſcribit: *De hac re
certant Scholaſtici, & adhuc ſub Iudice lis eſt, vtrùm Papa
Imperatorem poſſit deponere; quam quæſtionem cùm ad nos
non pertineat, indiſcuſſam relinquamus.* Quam autem in-
ſcitè, et corruptè Card. *Bellarminus* in ſuo *Schulckenio*
pag. 127. vocabulũ illud [*Scholaſtici*] exponat, nempe
pro Hiſtoricis, vt *Sigeberto*, Grammaticis, vt *Laurentio
Vallâ*, Poetis, vt *Dante*, cùm tamen tres iſti præclari
etiam Theologi fuerint, *Widdringtonus* [h] manifeſtè
commonſtrat.

20. *Secundum* teſtimonium eſt *Iacobi Almaini* [i] Pariſienſis Theologi, et inter Doctores Claſſicos à *Ioanne
Azorio* [k] Ieſuita relati, qui in opuſculo, vbi propriam
ſuâ ſententiam refert, et non *Occami*, alteriuſve Theologi ſcripta exponit, ita ait: *De ratione poteſtatis Laicæ
eſt poſſe pœnam ciuilem infligere, vt ſunt mors, exilium, bonorum priuatio &c. ſed nullam talem pœnam ex inſtitutione diuina infligere poteſt poteſtas Eccleſiaſtica, immo nec incarce-
rare, vt pleriſq́; Doctoribus placet, ſed ad ſolam pœnam ſpiritualem extenditur, vtputa Excommunicationem, reliquæ
autem pœnæ quibus vtitur, ex iure poſitiuo*, id eſt, vt loquitur
[l] *Gerſon, ex conceſſione Principum, ſunt.* Quid clarius
contra

g *ad annum*
1106.

*Notentur illa
verba* [& adhuc,
id eſt, hucuſque,
hoc tempore, ſub
Iudice lis eſt.]

h *in Confutat.
Th. Fitzberberti
part. 1. cap. 1.*
i *in Tract. de
dominio nat. ciu.
& eccleſ. in pro-
bat. ſecundæ con-
cluſionis.*
k *Tom. 1. Inſtit.
moral. lib. 2. cap.*
14.

l *De poteſt. Ec-
cleſ. conſider. 4.*

contra nouam hanc fidem Catholicam de poteftate
Papali feu Ecclefiaftica Principes deponendi, eofve
fuis Regnis, Dominijs, aut bonis temporalibus priuandi dici poffet?

21. *Tertium* teftimonium eft *Petri Pithæi,* quem *An-*
tonius Poffeuinus ᵐ celebris Iefuita *virum valde eruditum,*
& antiquitatis fedulum perquifitorem appellat, qui diferté
afferit, ⁿ *Franciam femper hanc maximam vti certam tenuiffe,*
quòd Papa Regem Franciæ regno priuare non pofsit, & non
obftantibus quibufcunque monitionibus, Excommunicationi-
bus, vel Interdictis, quæ à Papa ferri poffunt, Subditi tamen
obedientiam pro temporalibus debitam Regi præftare teneantur,
neq; in ea per Papam difpenfari, aut abfolui queant. Illam autem Doctoris *Schulckenij* ᵒ ad hoc teftimonium Repli-
cationem, nempe, *neq; fe librum illum* Pithæi *vnquam vi-*
diffe, neq; Poffeuinum *vllam illius mentionem feciffe,* mife-
rum profectò, ne dicamus, puerile, effugium effe quis
non videt? cùm *Widdringtonus* & librum illùm vidiffe
teftetur, & quo in loco, quo anno, qua authoritate,
nempe *Parifijs* anno Domini 1594. authoritate *Sena-*
tus in lucem prodierit, recenfeat, eiufque verba fideliter referat, iftamque *Schulckenij* refponfionem in *Con-*
futatione Replicationis *Thomæ Fitzherberti* ᵖ copiofiùs
refellat. Atque hoc ipfum, quod *Pithæus* afferit, plura
Parliamenti Parifienfis Arrefta, libros Card. *Bellarmini,*
Francifci Suarez, & aliorum fub pœna *lefæ Maieftatis*
profcribentia, & eandem *Pithæi* maximam fuiffe *fem-*
per in Francia fuftentatam, & cum Corona congenitam affir-
mantia, perfpicuè confirmant.

22. *Quartum* teftimonium eft *Ioannis Azorij* celeberrimi Societatis Iefu Theologi, qui verbis etiam ex-
preffis afferit, *magnam fuiffe femper inter Imperatores,*

Regefq;

ᵐ *In verbo Pe-*
trus Pithæus.

ⁿ *In Codice li-*
bertatum Eccle-
fiæ Gallicane.

ᵒ *Pag.* 124.

ᵖ *Part.1. cap.6.*

Azor. tom.2. In-
ftitut. moral. lib.
11. *cap.5. q.8.*

Regeſque ex vna parte, & ex altera inter Romanos Pon-
tifices controuerſiam, an in certis cauſis ſit ius & poteſtas
Summo Pontifici priuandi Reges Regno ſuo. Quinetiam
alter eruditus Societatis Ieſu Theológus, nempe *Ioan-*
nes Hartus Anglus in *Epiſtola* ſua ad *Lectorem indiffe-*
rentem de concertatione literaria inter ipſum, & *Ioannem*
Rainaldum Proteſtantem Theologum in *Turri Londi-*
nenſi habita ita ſcribit: *Quod attinet ad illud, quod* D. Rai-
nald' *quodā in loco aſſerit, me illi dixiſſe, quòd iuxta meam*
ſententiam Papa Principes deponere non poßit, verum eſt,
me illi hoc dixiſſe. Et reuera exiſtimo, quòd tametſi pote-
ſtas ſpiritualis nobilitate & dignitate ſpirituali antecellat,
vtraque tamen à Deo ſit, neque vna ab altera dependeat.
Vnde tanquam concluſionem certam colligo, quòd opinio eo-
rum, qui tenent, Papam eſſe temporalem ſupra Reges &
Principes Dominum, irrationabilis, & omnino improbabilis
ſit. Non enim ſui muneris eſt contra eos ciuiliter proce-
dere, multò minùs eos deponere, aut regna ſua alijs donare;
hoc nulla ex parte ad eius Iuriſdictionem ſpectat. Habet
quidem meâ ſententiâ Eccleſiæ Paternitatem, non mundi
Principatum, ipſomet Chriſto Domino *talem titulum, ſeu*
ius, nec ſibi aſſumente, neque S. Petro, *vel cuiquam ex diſci-*
pulis tribuente. Atque hoc tantum & non alium Principa-
tum in eo defendere mihi inſtitutum erat.

23. *Quintum* denique teſtimonium eſt Illuſtriſsimi
Cardinalis Peroni, viri vndique doctiſsimi, qui expreſsè
¶ *En Harangue*
au tiers Eſtat.
pag. 98. aſſerit, tum ⁹ *ipſummet Dominum Papam ob pacis Eccle-*
ſiaſticæ bonum tolerare eos Gallofrancos (non eo modo,
quo meretrices, fœneratores, & palam criminoſi nonnunquam tolerantur, ſed ad Eccleſiaſtica Sacramenta
percipienda admittendos permittere) *qui doctrinam*
ſibi in hac parte, de poteſtate ſcilicet Papali Principes
deponendi,

deponendi,*repugnantem tuentur* ; tum^r *disputationem hanc,* *r In Replicâ cap. 91. pag. 633.*
feu controuerfiam, *de poteſtate Summi Pontificis indirectè*
in temporalibus non debere revnionem eorum qui Ecclefiæ re-
conciliari defiderant, impedire, & proinde neque iuſtam
& legitimam eos, qui in Ecclefia fùnt, ab Ecclefiaſtica
communione excludendi caufam præbere poſſe. Plurima alia tum Theologorum, tum Iurifprudentium
teſtimonia, quæ hoc loco recenfere nimis longum
eſſet, ad nouam hanc fidèm Catholicam euertendam
à *Widdringtono*^ſ producuntur, fed inter cætera vnanimis *ſ In Apologia nu. 4. & in Con-fut. Tho. Fitz-herb. part. 1.*
antiquorum Patrum confenfus quàm maximè ex-
pendendus eſt, qui verbis difertis aſſerunt, ^t *Principes* *t Quindecim ex his antiquis Pa-tribus citantur à Widdringtono in detectione 17. ca-lumniæ Adolphi Schulckenij.*
ſupremos *eſſe à Deo fecundos, folo Deo,* fcilicet quoad
temporalia, *minores,* & *ſi peccauerint,* à Deo folo, pœnis
videlicet temporalibus, *caſtigandos* ; atque illa Chriſti
Domini verba, *Tibi dabo claues, Quodcunq ligaueris, &*
folueris &c. de clauibus regni cœleſtis, non terreni, atque de vinculis, ligationibus, & folutionibus ſpiritualibus, vtputa peccatorum, & non de temporalibus
intelligenda eſſe, quod etiam Ecclefiæ primitiuæ, &
veterum Sanctorum Patrum, ac Pontificum praxis
euidenter confirmat.

24. Atque ex hac manifeſtiſſima *veritate,* non eſſe
fcilicet de fide certum, fed apud Catholicos contro-
uerfum, et proinde ad fummum quoad *fpeculationem*
probabile, quòd Summus Pontifex Principes fupremos deponendi, et ex Chriſti inſtitutione pœnas temporales infligendi (non dicimus imponendi aut præ-
cipiendi, hanc enim *Widdringtonus* Summo Pontifici
non negat) poteſtatem habeat, alia *veritas (Pater Bea-*
tiſſime) non minùs certa et manifeſta ad *praxim* perti-
nens, etiam iuxta Aduerfariorum doctrinam, euiden-

D 2   tiſſimè

tiſſimè deducitur ; non poſſe ſcilicet Summum Pontificem, ſtante hac controuerſia, abſque *aperta iniuſtitia* Principes ſeculares per ſuam ſententiam deponere, neque licitum eſſe ſubditis abſque *læſæ Maieſtatis crimine* eiuſmodi depoſitionum ſententijs obedire, quandoquidem poteſtas, quæ non omnino certa, ſed probabilis, non poteſt eſſe legitimum & ſufficiens fundamentum, quo immediatè aliquis puniatur, aut aliquo ſuo iure, dominio, vel Regno, quod poſſidet, ſpolietur. Nam vt expreſsè aſſerit *Leonardus Leſſius* inſignis Societatis Ieſu Theologus, *Poteſt quidem poteſtas, quæ non omnino certa, ſed probabilis, eſſe fundamentum alicuius diſpenſationis in aliquo impedimento, vel conceſſionis in Sacramentis adminiſtrandis, quia inde nihil incommodi, cùm agatur de fauore & beneficio, & nemo cogatur, nemo iure propinquo, ſeu in re obtento ſpolietur. Non tamen poteſt eſſe fundamentum, quo immediatè aliquis puniatur, & iure ſuo ac dominio priuetur, & generales canones pænales ſtatuantur &c. Sed talis poteſtas certiſsimè, non dubiè debet competere. Nullus enim Iudex poteſt irrogare pœnas adeo graues, aut condere decreta, quibus irrogentur, niſi conſtet illi talem poteſtatem conceſſam. Si enim illud vllo modo eſſet dubium, poſſet reus excipere, & ei non parere. Hinc neque delegatis creditur in alicuius præiudicium, niſi authentico inſtrumento oſtendant ſuam poteſtatem, ita vt nulla amplùs relinquatur iuſta dubitandi ratio.*

    25. Atque hoc veriſſimum *Leſsij* pronunciatum, tum communi Theologorum, quorum aliqui in *Strena Catholica* [u] citantur, ſententiæ, tum manifeſto rationis naturalis lumini, tum notiſſimis illis *Iuris* vtriuſque regulis, *In pari cauſa potior eſt conditio poſsidentis*, & *Cùm ſunt partium iura obſcura fauendū eſt reo potiùs quàm actori*, quàm maximè conſonum eſt, tum alius etiam

Leſſius in ſuo Singletono de Diſcuſſione decreti magni Concilij Lateranenſis pag. 71, 72.

[*] *In Præludio quinto. nu. 12.*

Widdringtoni Aduerſarius,*Matthæus Kellinſonus* Anglus,
Sacræ Theologiæ Doctor, & *Collegij Anglicani* Clericorum Secularium Duaci *Præſes,*ſub nomine I. E. Theologiæ ſtudioſi perſonatus,idipſum verbis etiam diſer-
tis confirmat ˣ. Ex prædictis autem duobus veriſſimis
pronunciatis manifeſtè concluditur, *primò,* poteſtatem,quæ non omnino certa eſt,ſed duntaxat probabilis, non eſſe veram, realem, propriam, ſufficientem,&
legitimam deponendi, aut puniendi poteſtatem ; &
proinde nullam verâ,realem, propriam, ſufficientem,
& legitimam Principes ſupremos deponendi,aut pœnas temporales infligendi poteſtatem Summo Pontifici, quâ Pontifex eſt, & ex lege Chriſti competere,
ſed tantùm imaginariam, impropriam, inſufficientê,
illegitimam, & ex conſequenti quamdiu incerta &
probabilis tantùm eſt, quod ad praxim attinet, planè
nullam, vtpote, vt rectè infert idem Doctor *Kellinſo-*
nus, nunquam à Papa *abſ̃q̃ aperta iniuſtitia,* & proinde
neque à ſubditis abſque *aperta perduellione* executioni
mandandam : *Secundò,*falſis ſuppoſitionibus,& fundamentis nixos eſſe tam Illuſtriſſimos Cardinales ad
Indicem deputatos, ſi libros *Widdringtoni* ea de cauſa
ſuis Decretis damnauerint, & damnandos eſſe decla-
rauerint,propterea quòd noua hæc & falſa Cardinalis
Bellarmini, eiuſque ſequacium fides Catholica de poteſtate Papali Principes ſupremos deponendi ab omnibus Chriſti fidelibus neceſſariò credenda in illis impugnetur, quàm *Veſtræ Sanctitatis* Prædeceſſorem *Pau-*
lum V. Pontificem Maximum, ſi Iuramentum fidelitatis, tanquam multa continens, quæ fidei & ſaluti
apertè aduerſantur, ea de cauſa illicitum eſſe ſuis *Bre-*
uibus declarauerit, propterea quòd omnis poteſtas

ˣ *In Tractatu*
de Eccle.& Reg.
poteſt. cap. 11.
pag. 235.

D 3 Summi

Summi Pontificis ſcilicet vera, realis, propria, ſufficiens,& legitima, Regem noſtrum Sereniſſimum, aut
alios quoſcunque Principes ſupremos , & Summo
Pontifici in temporalibus non ſubiectos, deponendi,
eorumve ſubditos à temporali fidelitate abſoluendi
in eo Iuramento abnegetur. Atque hæc pauca in
præſenti de *prima controuerſia* principali inſinuaſſe
ſufficiat.

26. Quod ad *alteram controuerſiam* principalem de
nouo fidelitatis Iuramento ſpectat, notum inprimis
eſt (*Beatiſſime Pater*) vti *Widdringtonus* in detectione
duodecimæ calumniæ *D. Schulckenij* copioſiùs mon-
ſtrauit, *P. Henricum Garnettum,* tunc Ieſuitarum in Anglia commorantium Prouincialem, (vt alios Ieſuitas
nunc taceamus) deteſtandæ illius, & planè diabolicæ
Coniurationis Puluerariæ notitiam ſaltem in genere extra
Confeſſionem Sacramentalem habuiſſe, illique generatim conſcium fuiſſe, idque ipſum eundem *P. Garnettum* in ipſo mortis articulo, coram infinita hominum multitudine & ingenuè confeſſum eſſe, & ve-
niam à *Regia Maieſtate* precatum, *quòd in Regem peccauerit, & conſcius illud reticuerit, & præuertere neglexerit,*
quicquid *Patres Ieſuitæ,* vel *Sedi Apoſtolicæ,* vel Illuſtriſſimis Dominis *Cardinalibus,* vel alijs quibuſcunque in
contrarium ſuggerere, immo & ſcriptis publicis per-
vulgare, non dubitauerint. Quod propterea *Veſtræ
Beatitudini* inpræſentiarum inſinuare voluimus, partim vt prudentia veſtra pleniùs perſpiciat, quantula
fides Patrum Ieſuitarum, eorumque fautorum informationibus, in tertiæ perſonæ, præſertim non plenè
auditæ, præiudicium, adhibenda ſit, quandoquidem
& ſuos, quantumcunque criminoſi noſcantur, ſeque
peccaſſe,

peccaſſe, & propterea *mortis ſententiam in eos iuſtiſſimè pronunciatam eſſe* fateantur, non ſolùm innocentes, ſed & Martyres prædicare, & in Martyrum Calendario etiam typis excuſo collocare non verentur; alioſque ſibi aduerſantes, quantumcunque ſe Catholicos, nulliuſque criminis reos palam profiteantur, ſeque in omnibus *Eccleſiæ Catholicæ Romanæ* iudicio humiliter ſubmittant, & rationes factorum & aſſertionum ſuarum ſupremo animarum Paſtori (eum, vt pro munere ſuo Paſtorali illis ſatisfacere dignetur, obſecrantes,) modeſtè ac reuerenter proponant, nihilominùs tanquam *hæreticos, Pſeudo-Catholicos, Schiſmaticos, Sedi Apoſtolicæ rebelles, Eccleſiaſtica communione indignos,* & *Sacerdotali Iuriſdictione priuatos* traducere, & calumniari non pertimeſcunt: Et partim vt *Sanctitas Veſtra* intelligat, tum proditores illos Sulphureos, qui omnes Romano-Catholici erant, & conſcientias ſuas Patrum Ieſuitarum, eorumve fautorum directioni concreditas habebant, in noua hac, falſaque *fide Catholica,* de poteſtate Papali Principes deponendi, & de eorum Coronis & Capitibus in ordine ad bonum ſpirituale diſponendi, falſam fictamque barbaræ & inauditæ ſuæ *Coniurationis* iuſtitiam potiſſimùm fundaſſe, & palliare conatos eſſe, tum *Coniurationem* illam adeo inſolitam, nouo huic & inſolito fidelitatis *Iuramento à Rege, Regniḡ, Ordinibus* excogitando cauſam dediſſe, eo duntaxat fine, vt ſubditos fideles, præſertim *Romano-Catholicos,* quos *Papiſtas* vocant, non à *Proteſtantibus,* ſed à *perfidis proditoribus,* cæteriſque *Romano-Catholicis,* qui impijs *Coniurationis* ſulphureæ principijs adhæreſcunt, faciliùs internoſcerent, & cognitos reprimerent.

27. *Secundò,* ſatis etiam notum eſt, quòd ſimulac

lex

lex iſta de *Iuramento* præſtando promulgata erat,
D. Georgius Blackuellus tunc *Archipresbyter*, diligenti et
matura, vti ipſe exiſtimabat, de ſingulis *Iuramenti* clau-
ſulis diſquiſitione pręhabita, illud licitum eſſe, et iuxta
verba legis, et mentem Legiſlatoris ab Anglis Catholicis tutâ conſcientiâ ſuſcipi poſſe iudicauerit, atque in
hunc finem literas ſuas ad Sacerdotes ſibi aſſiſtentes,
quò cæteris Catholicis hanc ſuam de *Iuramento* ſententiam patefacerent, illico tranſmiſerit. Huic autem
Domini *Archipresbyteri* ſententiæ quidam Sacerdotes
doctiſſimi mordicus adhærebant: quidam, præſertim
ex Patribus Ieſuitis, eorumque aſſectatoribus, vel
planè repugnabant, vel in contrariam ſententiam
propendebant: Alij (è quorum numero ego *Thomas
Preſtonus* vnus eram) rationes et fundamenta, quibus
nixus *Dominus Archipresbyter* Iuramentum iſtud licitum
eſſe arbitratus eſt, omnino improbabant, quandoquidem non ipſam Summi Pontificis Regę deponendi
poteſtatem, et authoritatem, ſed praxim tantùm, et
exequutionem eiuſmodi poteſtatis, rebus ſic ſtantibus, inficiari illi tunc temporis inſtitutum erat, (quan-
tumvìs poſtea tam praxim, quàm ipſam deponendi
poteſtatem penitus improbauerit) cùm tamen mihi
tunc manifeſtiſſimum eſſet, non poſſe *Iuramentũ* iùxta
verborum proprietatem, et Legiſlatoris mentem, tanquam licitum à quoquam defendi, niſi et *praxim ipſam*, et quamcunque *veram, realem, propriam, ſufficientẽ,*
et *legitimam* Regem deponendi *poteſtatem* Summo
Pontifici conceſſam denegare voluerit. Inter has tamen opinionum varietates nemo prorſus ſiue ex Patribus Ieſuitis, ſiue ex Presbyteris Secularibus, vel Re-
gularibus, (quantum ſcire potuimus) eo audaciæ et
temeritatis

temeritatis proceffit, vt vel Dominum Archipresbyterum, cæterofque eius fententiæ adhærentes, vel eos
Catholicos, qui tanta authoritate freti, aut Iuramentũ
fufceperunt, aut licitè fufcipi poffe exiftimarunt, de
hærefi, errore, temeritate, aliove *crimine mortifero* condemnandos, & à communione Ecclefiaftica, ac Sacramentorum perceptione, tanquam indignos, arcendos effe
affirmare tunc aufus effet.

28. Sed fœlix hæc, & Laicis præfertim Catholicis vtiliffima prædictorum omnium Sacerdotum in
vnam fententiam de licita Iuramenti fufceptione,
quod ad *praxim* attinet, confpiratio non multo pòft
tempore perdurauit. Nam quidam ex Patribus Iefuitis, & præ cæteris eorum Prouincialis, qui *Patri Gar-
netto* proximè fucceffit, & iam etiam in viuis eft, (an
forfan verentes, ne *noua* eorum *fides Catholica,* de poteftate Papali Principes deponendi, in eorum potiffimùm officina recêns cufa & formata ex hoc Iuramento penitus in Anglia concideret, an vt maiorem *Ro-
mani Pontificis,* in cuius fauorem *nouam* hanc *fidem* ex-
cogitarunt, præ cæteris Catholicis, Sacerdotibus, &
Religiofis, qui tali fidei, vtpote non *verè Catholicæ,* nec
fufficienter fundatæ, non adhuc acquiefcunt, gratiam
fibi conciliarent, vel quo alio fine, Deo, & eorum
confcientijs iudicandum relinquimus) prædictam
concordiam, & confenfionem indignè ferentes, eam
breuî fe difrupturos, & mandatum à *Summo Pontifice*
contra licitam Iuramenti fufceptionem impetratu-
ros, verbis minacibus palam affirmabant. Qui mina-
ces eorum fermones, quamprimùm ad mei, nempe
Thomæ Preftoni notitiam peruenerunt, idem ego *Thomas
Preftonus,* tunc Religioforum *Caffinenfium* in Anglia
E   Superior,

Superior, pacis & vnitatis Eccleſiaſticæ atque etiam
ciuilis conſeruandæ cupidus, & præſentiens, quantæ
perturbationes, diſcordiæ, ac diſſenſiones, non ſolùm
inter ipſos Catholicos, verùm etiam inter Regem noſtrum Sereniſſimum, Regnique Ordines, & inter ſubditos eius Catholicos ex *tali mandato* hîc in Anglia
prouenirent, ſtatim per literas Romam miſi ad *D. Ni-
colaum Fitzberbertũ* nationis noſtræ Anglicanæ Catholicum, qui tunc Romæ degebat, ipſum de toto hoc
negotio certiorem reddens, atque inſtantiſſimè deprecans, vt pro communi Catholicorum Anglorum
commodo, & *Apoſtolicæ* etiam *Sedis* honore, quibuſcunque poterat medijs ac vijs, etiam *Illuſtriſſimorum
Cardinalium* opem implorando, *Suæ Sanctitatis* animum
à *tali mandato* huc mittendo dimoueret; hancque ob-
ſecrationis meæ rationem aſſignaui, quòd Dominus
Archipresbyter, eiuſque ſententiæ adhærentes, non *ipſam* Summi Pontificis *poteſtatem* Principes deponendi, ſed illius tantùm *praxin*, rebus ſic ſtantibus, abnegare adhuc in animo habuerint. Attamen ſi *Sanctitas
Sua*, calamitoſo hoc tempore, & poſt tam *execrandam*
Catholicorum contra *Regem*, totumque *Regnum*, ſub
prætextu poteſtatis Pontificiæ de Coronis & Capitibus Principum diſponendi, Coniurationem recêns
detectam, tale mandatum huc tranſmitteret, pro certo
intelligeret, idque *mihi*, vtpote de mentibus quorundam Iuramento fauentium optimè conſcio, planè in-
dubitatum eſſe affirmaui, quòd non *praxis* tantummodò, ſed ipſa etiam *poteſtas* & authoritas Pontificia
tam in temporalibus, nempe Principes deponendi,
&c. quàm in ſpiritualibus, ſcilicet res fidei abſque
Concilio generali infallibiliter definiendi, magis nunc

&

& vehementiùs, quàm vnquam antea ab eruditis Catholicis in quæstionem adduceretur : Quod ex parte verum esse, quoad *potestatem* scilicet Principes deponendi, rei euentus comprobauit, & nisi pacificus scandalosis hisce calumniationibus, & virorum innocentium oppressionibus finis quamprimùm *vestra authoritate* imponatur, ex toto verissimum fore, quoad potestatem etiam res fidei certò definiendi, proculdubio confirmabit.

29. Veruntamen hæc mea humilis, syncera, & erga Sedem Apostolicam, Regiamque Maiestatem pietate ac zelo plena postulatio, & præmonitio, nullum planè effectum sortita est. Nam Patres Iesuitæ, eorumque fautores intra pauculos menses à Iureiurando promulgato, partim sinistris, & falsis eorum informationibus, *quòd* scilicet *potestas Summi Pontificis Regem excommunicandi in Iuramento abnegetur*, & *quòd potestas eius Principes deponendi sit res de fide certa, & ab omnibus necessariò credenda*, partim importunis sollicitationibus, & partim prægrandi *Card. Bellarmini*, illique in *Curia Romana* fauentium potentia, & authoritate præmuniti, *primum Breue Apostolicum* contra licitam Iuramenti susceptionem, datum decimo *Calendas Octobris* 1606. obtinuerunt, in quo Summus Pontifex disertè asserit, *ex ipsis Iuramenti verbis perspicuum esse debere Anglis Catholicis, quòd salua fide Catholica, & salute animarum præstari non possit, cùm multa contineat quæ fidei ac saluti apertè aduersantur.* Deinde vndecim pòst mensibus missum huc est *secundum Breue*, datum decimo *Calendas Septembris* 1607. in quo *Sanctitas Sua* primum confirmat, atque insuper ait, *illud non solùm ex proprio motu, & certa eius scientia, veruntamen etiam pòst longam, & grauem deli-*

berationem de omnibus, quæ in illo continentur adhibitam, fuiße scriptum, & ob id teneri Anglos Catholicos illud omnino obser-uare omni interpretatione secus suadente reiecta. Quæ verba solùm significant, *Breue* illud non fuiße surrep-titium, aut temere & absque maturo, & diligenti exa-mine scriptum, sed nihilominùs, non obstante longa hac, & graui deliberatione, in *falsis informationibus,* aut *suppositionibus,* sicut & librum *Card. Bellarmini* con-tra *Iuramentum,* non obstante longa eius, & graui deli-beratione in *falsis suppositionibus* fuiße fundatum *Wid-dringtonus* [y] euidenter demonstrat.   Demùm anno pòst sequenti *Calendis Februarij* 1608. datum est *tertium Breue,* in quo *Sanctitas Sua* Magistrum *Georgium Bir-kettum,* Archipresbyterum Sacerdotum Anglorum Apostolicorum Seminariorum, in locum Magistri *Georgij Blackuelli substituit, illique iniungit, & mandat, ac specialem facultatem ad hoc tribuit, vt authoritate sua omnes, & singulos Sacerdotes Anglos, qui præfatum Iuramentum præstiterunt, aut qui illud licitè præstari poße docuerunt & docent, admonere curet, vt ab huiusmodi errore resipiscant & abstineant. Quod si intra tempus (extraindicialiter tamen) arbitrio suo illis præfigendum hoc facere distulerint, illum, seu illos facultatibus, & priuilegijs omnibus ab Apostolica_, Sede, seu illius authoritate à quocunq, alio illis, vel cuiuis il-lorum conceßis, eadem authoritate priuet & priuatos eße de-claret.* Quis autem verus & genuinus horum verbo-rum sensus sit *Widdringtonus* [z] syncerè, & fideliter ex-ponit, hasque literas tum in *primo Breui* fundatas eße, tum in illis Sacerdotibus, qui Iuramentum præstant aut præstari poße docent, errorem & culpam suppo-nere, atque ex veritate ac iustitia *primi Breuis* ex toto pendere euidenter conuincit.

[y] *In Confutat. Tho. Fitzherb. part.3.cap.17.*

[z] *In Disp.Theol. cap.10.sec.2 nu. 60. & seq.*

30. Sed cumprimùm Rex noſter Sereniſſimus,pro
ſingulari eius prudentia, præuideret, quantas in toto
ſuo Regno perturbationes, & quàm graues, non ſolùm inter ipſoſmet Catholicos, verùm etiam inter
eius Maieſtatem,Regnique Ordines,& inter Catholicos eius ſubditos diſcordias, & diſſentiones prædicta
Breuia Iuramenti ſuſceptionē prohibentia excitatura
eſſent (vti reuera iam ea excitaſſe lugubri admodùm
experimento didicimus) placuit Regiæ eius Maieſtati,
vt ipſemet primus omnium, pro debito ſui, Regniq;
Ordinum honore, & communi Catholicorum illi
ſubditorum ſalute, *duo prima* ex præfatis *Breuibus* (nam
tertium tunc non extabat) quamprimùm refelleret, &
pro *Iuramento fidelitatis* ab *Ipſo,Regniq Ordinibus* in legem
publicam ſancito,*Apologiam* conficeret : In qua quidē
Apologia primò, de *imprudentia,* & *iniuſtitia* Summi Pontificis conqueritur, *Imprudentia eſt* (ait Sua Maieſtas)
me ſi reſpicias, quòd partitè, & minutatim Iuramentum non
refutauerit, nec verbulum aut ſententiolam, quam ibi repre-
hendit, aliquo detexerit indicio. Id verò ſi feciſſet, pro paterna
mea cura, quæ non ſinit, vt quenquam meorum ad extrema
tentanda adigam, quæ duriuſculè ſonare videbantur, fortaſſe
aut deleſſem planè, aut benigna interpretatione molliora reddi-
diſſem : Iniuſtitia eſt Catholicorum ſuorum reſpectu, nam ſi
mihi viſum fuiſſet in Iuramento quippiam vel mutare, vel
interpretari, omni illico labore Pontificij leuati fuiſſent ; Sin
ſecus mihi conſtitiſſet, nihil ex Iuriſiurandi conditionibus re-
mittere, prætextum ſaltem aliquem recuſandi illius Sacramenti
inveniſſent, quaſi non obſequium, fidemq; debitam abnuentes,
ſed anxijs religioſi animi ſcrupulis deterriti, in ea verba quæ
notaviſſet Pontifex, iurare vererentur. Secundò, in eadem
Apologia tum literæ *Card. Bellarmini* refelluntur, in

quibus Magiſtrum *Georgium Blackuellum* tunc Archipresbyterum, eo quòd Iuramentum ſuſceperat, de *in-
conſtantia*, & *lapſu in fide*, per iniuriam accuſat, & *S. Petro* qui CHRISTVM negauit, *Sanctoᷠ Marcellino*,
qui thus idolis immolauiṭ falſò aſsimilat, & *vnum ex
præcipuis fidei noſtræ capitibus, ac Religionis Catholicæ fundamentis*, nempe *Primatum Papæ in ſpiritualibus ob Iuramentum iſtud in diſcrimen adduci*, immeritò, & abſque vlla
prorſus probatione affirmat ; tum generalia quædam,
& firmiſsima principia, ac fundamenta in ea Apologia iaciuntur, (quod Suæ Maieſtatis inſtituto in tam
breui opuſculo ſatis erat) ex quibus magis particula-
tìm tam *Breuia* prædicta, tanquam in *falſis ſuppoſitionibus* fundata, impugnari, quàm ſingulæ etiam Iuramenti clauſulæ defendi facilè poſsint ; quorum mu-
nitus præſidio *Widdringtonus* poſtea vtrumque præſti-
tit, atque ad particularia deſcendens, tum ſingulas Iuramenti clauſulas veritati & iuſtitiæ conſonas, tum
literas etiam Summi Pontificis in *falſis informationibus*, & *ſuppoſitionibus* fundatas eſſe copioſiſsimè comprobauit.

   31. Veruntamen cùm Patres Ieſuitæ, nouæque eorum fidei defenſores iam clariſsimè cernerent, *nouam
ſuam fidem Catholicam* de poteſtate Summi Pontificis
de Principum Coronis, ac Capitibus in ordine ad bonum ſpirituale diſponendi (quam ſub ſpecioſo *Primatus Papæ in ſpiritualibus*, quem nemo Catholicorum
negat, velo palliare ſtudent, quæque nefandiſsimæ
illius Coniurationis puluerariæ radix & fundamentũ
erat) ex prædicta Regis noſtri Sereniſsimi Apologia in
extremum fere diſcrimen adduci ; omnem ſuam operam, ſtudium, artem, eruditionem, ac potentiam adhi-
buerunt,

buerunt, vt *falsam* hanc eorum *fidem Catholicam,* San-
ctisque Patribus incognitam, per fas & nefas propug-
narent: Et proinde quamplurimos Theologos, omnium hac nostra ætate celeberrimos atque doctissimos, ex eorum præsertim Societate, & inprimis Illustrissimum *Cardinalem Bellarminum,*cæterorum Ducem
ac Principem, deinde *Iacobum Gretzerum, Martinum Becanum, Leonardum Lessium,* & *Franciscum Suarez* (vt *Thomã
Fitzherbertum,* nunc Iesuitam, sed tunc Presbyterum
Secularem, & *Matthæum Kellinsonum,* qui Anglicè
scripserunt, & quædam tantùm fragmenta ex prædictis excerpserunt, nunc prætereamus) quibus contradicere, pro ea qua præditi sunt eruditione,atque etiam
Curiæ Romanæ potentia freti, nullus Catholicus (vti
Patres illi existimabant) aut valeret, aut saltem aude-
ret, præ cæteris selegerunt, qui Regis nostri Apologiam refutarent, prædicta Summi Pontificis Breuia
confirmarent, et novum fidelitatis Iuramentum, in
quo *noua* eorum *fides Catholica* abnegatur, omnibus
vijs et artificijs impugnarent; suosque, quod peius
est, emissarios incitarunt, qui eorum scriptis quàm
maximè applauderent,eosque Catholicos, qui eorum
doctrinæ aduersarentur, tanquam hæreticos, vel de
hæresi suspectos,et Romanæ Ecclesiæ hostes, Sedique
Apostolicæ rebelles, apud imperitum vulgus, *prob
nefas,*traducerent.

32. Sed *magna est veritas, & prævalet* [a]; occultari quidem *ad tempus, vinci non potest* [b]. Nam, vt *Guglielmum,*
et *Ioannem Barclaios,* cæterosque nostræ nationis Bri-
tannicæ, qui nouam hanc Patrum Iesuitarum fidem
egregiè impugnarunt, nunc taceamus, vnus *Rogerus
Widdringtonus* Anglus Catholicus, Dei Opt. Max. qui
totius

[a] 3 Esdræ 4.
[b] *S. Augustin.
in Psalm.*61.

totius veritatis Author, et defenſor eſt, (quique *perdet*
c 1 Cor. 1. *ſapientiam ſapientium, & prudentiam prudentium reprobabit* [c],
& nonnunquam *quæ ſtulta ſunt mundi eligit, ut confun-*
d ibidem. *dat ſapientes, & infirma mundi ut confundat fortia*[d]) ſingulari auxilio adiutus, omnia & ſingula eorum argu-
menta, quæ vel ex ſacris literis, vel ex Concilijs, illaque
maxima *Lateranenſi Synodo*, (de qua tantopere gloriari
ſolent) vel ex rationibus Theologicis, aut aliunde pe-
tita, ad *nouam* ſuam *fidem* corroborandam, & ad *nouum*
fidelitatis *Iuramentum* impugnandum ab ipſis allata
ſunt, adeo clarè & manifeſtè refutauit, atque Illuſtriſſimorum Cardinalium Decretis quoſdam *Widdringtoni* libros proſcribentibus, & *Breuibus* Summi Pontificis *Pauli* V. Prædeceſſoris veſtri Iuramenti ſuſcep-
tionem prohibentibus adeo perſpicuè ſatisfecit, atque
in *falſis informationibus*, & *ſuppoſitionibus* fundata eſſe
euidentiſſimè commonſtrauit, ut omnes iam videant,
ſe, *nouæ* ſuæ *fidei* pertæſos, fugam arripuiſſe, neque eam
vi diſputationis propugnare vlterius poſſe. Quod
profectò non leue viris prudentibus argumentum eſſe
poteſt, *fidem* hanc *nouam* de poteſtate Papali Principes
deponendi, quam ſtabilire totis ſuis viribus, & artibus
tentarunt, non eſſe *certam*, et *verè Catholicam*, ſed infir-
miſſimis fundamentis nixam, cùm tot, tamque celeberrimi, et ex toto Chriſtiano orbe ſelectiſſimi Theologi, eam contra paucos, et eorum comparatione
Theologorum minimos, vi argumentorũ defendere
non valeant; neque enim difficile eſt paucis optimè
armatis, quamplurimos ipſo etiam *Hercule* robuſtio-
res, ſi iuncis pugnent, ſuperare.

33. Et nihilominùs noſtrates Ieſuitæ, eorumque
fautores, cùm nullũ aliud effugium quò ſe recipiant,

iam

iam illis relinquatur, vt faltem fœdà inobedientiæ, &
contra *Sedem Apoſtolicam* rebellionis notâ *Widdringto-*
num, eiufque doctrinæ adhærentes apud plebem im-
peritam afpergant, prædicta *Breuia,* & *Decreta,* quibus tamen pleniſſimè fatisfactum eft, adhuc etiam
plenis faucibus conclamitare non definunt, ac fi
Catholicis indoctis, fed alioquin timoratæ confci-
entiæ perfuadere vellent, *obedientiam cœcam Summo*
etiam *Pontifici* in omnibus abfque vlteriori examine
exhibendam, vel à Sanctis Patribus, vel à quoquam
antiquo, aut recentiori Theologo laudatam effe, vel
vllum effe inobedientiæ crimen præcepto Prælati, et-
iamfi fit *Summus Pontifex,* in *falfis informationibus,* &
fuppofitionibus fundato, quando in *tertiæ perfonæ,* &
præcipuè *Principis fupremi,* qui in poffeffione fuæ
famæ & bonorum eft, præiudicium tendit, non acqui-
efcere; dummodo fubditus rationes ob quas dubitat,
præceptum illud iniuftum effe, & veræ obedientiæ,
Deo & *Cæfari* iure diuino debitæ repugnans, *Prælato*
humiliter proponat. Sed quàm falfò, calumniosè,
fchifmaticè, & contra etiam *Iuris Canonici* regulas
Widdringtonus, eiufque doctrinæ adhærentes, de *inobedi-*
entia, & rebellione contra *Sedem Apoſtolicam* argu-
antur, vt propterea communione Ecclefiaftica priuari
mereantur, eo quòd *Decreta* illa, & *Breuia* in *falfis fuppo-*
fitionibus fundata non admittant, infrà ᵉ manifeftiùs   ᵉ *nu. 51. & feq.*
Veſtræ Beatitudini oftendemus.

34. Interim quod ad *Decreta* attinet, meminerit,
quæfumus, *Sanctitas Veſtra,* vti in *Appellatione* noftra
ᶠ declarauimus, quòd fimulatque *Widdringtonus* Apo-   ᶠ *nu. 3, 4.*
logiam fuam *pro Iure Principum* ediderat, in qua *falfam*
Cardinalis Bellarmini fidem, de poteftate Papali Principes

ſupremos deponendi, ex ipſiuſmet *Card. Bellarmini*
principijs tum ſolidè , .tum modeſtè confutauit, &
perſpicuè commonſtrauit, eam neque in verbo Dei,
vel Traditione, aut praxi *Apoſtolica*, vel *Sanctorum Pa-*
trum teſtimonio, vel *Conciliorum*, aut *Summorum Pontifi-*
cum Decretis, vel in alia quauis authoritate, aut ratione
Theologica ſufficienter fundari, eam rem *Card. Bellar-*
minus moleſtiſſimè ferens, nimia in *Widdringtonum* in-
dignatione exarſerit, & videns prædictam ſui, ſuo-
rumq; *fidem nouam* non ſolùm à Catholicis in dubium
vocari, verùm etiam ſi forſan taceret omnino pericli-
tari, ſtatim ſeſe, quorundam etiam perſuaſionibus in-
ſtigatus (vti ex ipſiuſmet literis conſtat) ad *Widdring-*
tono reſpondendum accinxerit ; ſed timens, ne priuſquam opus-deſignatum perficeret, interim doctrina
Widdringtoni magis excreſceret, & altiores radices in
mentibus Catholicorum defixas teneret, vt omnem
planè fidem prædictæ *Apologiæ*, eiuſque *Authori*, tum
apud vulgus imperitum, tum apud viros quoſcunque
doctos, qui eam non perlegerant, detraheret, eam ex
decreto *Sacræ Congregationis* Illuſtriſſimorum *Cardina-*
lium ad Indicem deputatorum (qui, vti accepimus,
ſenarium numerum non excedunt, & è quibus ipſemet *Card. Bellarminus* vel primùs, vel vnus ex primis
erat, & ſolus ac vnicus tunc *Widdringtoni* Aduerſarius,
quique proinde in propria ſua cauſa & Accuſator, &
Teſtis, & Iudex *Widdringtoni*, qui falſam eius fidem ex-
pugnauerat, eſſe voluit) omnino prohibendam, & ac
ſi dogmata hæretica contineret, in medio librorum
quos *Proteſtantes* ſcripſerunt, collocandam, & à ne-
mine vllo vnquam tempore legendam diligentiſſimè
curauerit .

35. Hac

35. Hac autem eius ad *Widdringtoni* Apologiam Refponfione iam plenè finita, eam confeftim prælo committendam, & *Roma* typis excudendam manda- uit,fed nihilominus fub proprio eius nomine in lucem publicam prodire non permifit, quâ verò de caufa ip- fe meliùs nouerit, nos aliam coniectare non poffu- mus, nifi quòd tam falfa & horrenda crimina *Wid- dringtono* per calumniam impofuerit, vt quiuis Ca- tholicus etiam literarum, & modeftiæ Chriftianæ ru- dis, nedum eruditione & dignitate illuftriffimus tam falfa, immodefta, inuerecunda de viro Catholico, quique præfertim pro fide Catholica Romana graues ærumnas indies fuftinet, & præterea in omnibus Ca- tholicæ Ecclefiæ Romanæ iudicio fe humillimè fub- mittit, palá afferere omnino erubefceret. Veruntamen non multò poft eadem *Card. Bellarmini* Refponfio, feu *Apologia*, quod ad fubftantiam eius attinet, *Coloniæ A- grippinæ* fub nomine, non *Card. Bellarmini*, fed *Adolphi Schulckenij* Geldrienfis *Sacræ Theologiæ* Doctoris, & in ciuitate *Colonienfi* profefforis, prodijt, & cum ingenti *Patrum Iefuitarũ* applaufu magnâ Chriftiani Orbis par- té peragrauit, fed dum Chriftianiffimũ *Franciæ* Regnũ profpero etiã flatu tranfuolare, & in nobiliffima *Pari- fiorum* ciuitate dogmata fua perniciofa difpergere niti- tur,ecce derepente nominis fui, gloriæ, & honoris ia- cturã fecit, fummoq; cum dedecore flãmis vltricibus in cineres redacta eft. Atque ex hac *falfiffima fide Catho- lica*, quam *Card. Bellarminus* eiufq; fequaces orbi Chri- ftiano per vim obtrudere conati funt, mota eft *Sacra* illorũ fex *Cardinaliũ Congregatio* ad prædictã *Widdringtoni* pro Iure Principũ *Apologiam* omnino profcribendam; exiftimabant enim, (malè eos informante *Card. Bel-*

larmino)

larmino) doctrinam hanc de Principibus authoritate Papali deponendis eſſe *de fide certam*, & ab omnibus fidelibus neceſſariò credendam, & contrariam non tam *ſententiam*, quàm *hæreſim* omnino reputandam, quòd tamen falſiſſimum eſſe tum *Ioannes Barclaius*, cuius *Pietati*, ſiue *publicis pro Regibus ac Principibus*, & *priuatis pro Guilielmo Barclaio Parente contra Card. Bellarminum vindicijs* nemo adhuc reſpondit, tum etiam *Widdringtonus* euidenter commonſtrarunt.

36. Neque etiam adhuc (*Pater Beatiſſime*) nobis perſuadere vllo modo poſſumus, quod tamen quidam hîc contra nos, cæteroſque Catholicos Anglos doctrinæ *Widdringtoni* adhærentes vehementer obijciunt, nempe *Ioannem Barclaium*, nunc *Romæ* degentem, priorem ſuam, patriſque ſui *Guilielmi Barclaij* ſententiam, de poteſtate Papali principes deponendi, iam ex animo mutaſſe, & reuocaſſe, atque *nouam Card. Bellarmini*, eiuſque ſequacium de ea poteſtate *fidem* approbaſſe, cùm nihil tale vel ex relatione fide digna, vel ex ipſius ſcriptis publicis colligere adhuc poſſimus. Hoc ſolum in *Epiſtola* ſua ad *Lectorem* præfixa libro illi, quē *Paræneſim* ad *Sectarios* appellat, quod ad præſentē controuerſiam attinet, ab eo ſcriptū reperimus, *ſe in ſcriptis ſuis multa aduertiſſe, quæ vel tacentibus cunctis ipſe damnaret; quale illud, quòd Reſpublicas Eccleſiaſticam & ciuilem ita diſtingui voluit, vt non in vnum corpus miſtæ, ſed ſociæ tantùm eſſent, nec vnicam rempublicam Chriſtianam facerent, in qua illa ſpiritum referret, hæc corpus &c. Et hæc ſtrictim*, ait, *annotata aliquando fuſiùs proſequi mihi animus tempore & otio meliore. Nequeenim mihi ſatis quæ fuſè diſſerui, hîc paucis caſtigaſſe.* Veruntamen ſi *D. Ioanni Barclaio* animus ſit (quod ſanè veritatis Catholicæ inueſtigandæ & confirmandæ

firmandæ gratia plurimùm optamus) vti promittere
videtur, illam poteſtatis *politicæ* ad *Ecclefiaſticam*, quam
Widdringtonus negat, *fubordinationem*, & Reipublicæ *ciuilis*, atque *Ecclefiaſticæ* in vnam *totalem* Rempublicam
Chriſtianam, cuius ſupremus Princeps eſt *Summus
Pontifex*, coalitionem, non argumentis tantùm pro-
babilibus (hæc enim ad rem fidei demonſtrandam
non ſufficiunt) ſed demonſtratiuis, & quibus nulla
Reſponſio verè probabilis adhiberi poteſt, confirmare, * nos etiam *Veſtræ Beatitudini* ſyncerè pollice-
mur, vel nos, vel *Widdringtonum*, vel vnum aliquem
ex eius doctrinæ adhærentibus, eum, Deo adiuuante,
ex ipſiuſmet *Ioannis Barclaij* principijs, quæque verif-
ſima eſſe comprobabimus, ſtatim aut refutaturos,
aut nos in errore verſatos eſſe, & *nouam* Card. *Bellarmini*, eiuſque ſequacium *fidem*, de poteſtate Papali
Principes ſupremos deponendi, *verè Catholicam* eſſe,
quam nihilominus adhuc *falfiſſimam* eſſe credimus,
illico & abſque mora palam conceſſuros.

* Sed interim
videat D. Bar-
claius in Reſpon-
ſione Widdring-
toni ad Th. Fitz-
herbertum parte
2. huius ſubordi-
nationis, & vni-
onis refutatio-
nem, priuſquam
eam confirmare
aggrediatur, ne
aerem fruſtra
verberare, &
cum propria ipſi-
us vmbra otiosè
concertare reperi-
atur.

37. Iam vt *Veſtræ Sanctitati* paucis oſtendamus, tam
præfatum *Sacræ Congregationis* decretum, & reliqua *duo
decreta*, quorum in noſtra *Appellatione* fit mentio, quoſdam *Widdringtoni* libros proſcribentia, quàm *Veſtri*
Prædeceſſoris *Pauli V. Breuia* Iuramentum prohibentia, eò quòd *multa contineat, quæ fidei & ſaluti apertè aduerſantur*, in *falſis ſuppoſitionibus*, & præſertim in *falſa*
illa *Card. Bellarmini*, eiuſque ſequacium *fide Catholica*,
de Principibus authoritate papali deponendis fundata
eſſe, quædam *generalia indicia* ad id probandum *Veſtræ
Beatitudini*, ab ea pro ſingulari ſua prudentia diligentius examinanda, proponemus.

38. *Primum indicium* eſt, quòd *ſex* illi *Illuſtriſſimi*
Cardinales

Cardinales ad Indicem deputati, ex quibus ipſemet
Card. Bellarminus, præcipuus *Widdringtoni* Aduerſarius,
vel primus, vel vnus ex primis erat, non ſolùm *Apolo-*
giam eius *pro Iure Principum,* verùm etiam *Diſputationem*
eius *Theologicam de Iuramento Fidelitatis,* verbis tantùm
generalibus damnauerint, cùm tamen *Diſputatio* illa
Theologica humillima tantùm ad *Summum Pontificem*
Supplicatio erat, & non alium ob finem, quàm ad
eum malè à quibuſdam, præſertim *Card. Bellarmino,*
de ſtatu controuerſiæ, & de vero Iuramenti Fidelitatis
ſenſu informatum, meliùs informandum ab Authore
compoſita : In qua etiam Author nihil ex propria
ſententia aſſerit, ſed ſolùm quid Catholici Angli Iuramentum approbantes, vel improbantes, in vtramque
partem obijcere ſoleant, ſyncerè, fideliter, & cum
" omni debita ſubmiſſione, proponit : *Suam Beatitudi-*
" *nem* humiliter deprecans, vt poſtquam de rationibus,
" ob quas Catholici Angli Iuramentum illud licitum
" eſſe arbitrantur, plenè informata fuerit, illaſque dili-
" genter examinauerit, eas pro paterna eius ſolicitudine,
" & munere paſtorali, particulatim vel approbet, vel
" condemnet ; & *vnicam* ſaltem Iuramenti *clauſulam,*
" quæ fidei & ſaluti repugnans ſit, illis ſignificare velit,
" vt ipſi in hoc negotio grauiſſimo, quod Pontificiæ
" authoritatis, & Regiæ dignitatis prærogatiuam tam
" intimè attingit, tum *Sedis Apoſtolicæ* præceptis obſiſte-
" re formidantes, tum *Regio mandato,* quantum tutâ con-
" ſcientiâ poſſunt, parere cupientes, clarè perſpiciant,
" atque ab animarum ſuarum Paſtore perſpicuè &
" abſque vllis ambagibus, aut verborum integumentis
" edoceantur, quas Iuramenti clauſulas admittere,
" quaſque reijcere teneantur, neque enim omnes & ſingulas

gulas Iuramenti partes à veritate aut iuſtitia alienas
eſſe quiſquam Catholicus Anglus affirmare audet. An
autem hæc tam *humilis,* tamque *neceſſaria* ouium ad
Paſtorem, filiorum ad Patrem, diſcipulorum ad Magiſtrum, & oppreſſorum ad Iudicem *Supplicatio,* adeo
iniuſta & irrationabilis ſit, vt propterea non ſolùm
non exaudiri, ſed penitus condemnari mereatur,
nullo tamen crimine ob quod condemnetur indicato, vel potiùs vtrùm *Sanctitas Sua* tunc planè vi-
derit, *Breuia* ſua in *falſis ſuppoſitionibus* fundata eſſe,
neque quicquam in Iuramento aſſignare potu-
erit, quod fidei & ſaluti apertè aduerſetur, vti ſuis
Breuibus declarauerat, apud *Veſtram Beatitudinem* iudicium eſto.

39. *Secundũ indiciũ* eſt, quòd prędicti *ſex Cardinales Illᵐⁱ*
non ſolùm *Apologiam pro Iure Principum,* & *Diſputationem*
Theologicam de Iuramento fidelitatis,. verbis tantùm gene-
ralibᵒ damnauerint, verùm etiã, quod magis mirandũ
eſt, ipſum etiam *Authorẽ* ſeuerè admonuerint, *vt quam-*
primũ ſe purgaret, alioquin cenſuris alijſ́q poenis Eccleſiaſticis,
quæ temporalibus longè grauiores ſunt, *omnino coercen-*
dus : Et nihilominus more prorſus inſolito, & præter
omniũ tribunaliũ conſuetudinem, illum de nullo crimine, à quo ſe purgare debeat, vel ſpeciatim, vel generatim certiorem reddunt. Quid enim de illo Iudice
exiſtimaret *Sanctitas Veſtra,* qui verbis minacibus ali-
cui diceret, Ecce poenis grauiſſimis te coercebo, vt
quamprimùm te purges, nullum tamen crimen tibi
indicabo, à quo te purgare debeas.

40. *Tertium indicium* eſt, quòd tametſi *Author* illorum librorum, iuxta *Sacræ Congregationis* decretum,
ſeſe quamprimùm purgauerit, eiuſque *Purgationem* ad
Sanctiſſimum

Sanctissimum *Dominum Paulum* V. *Vestræ Sanctitatis* prædecessorem transmiserit, atque ab omni hæreseωs, et erroris suspicione sese generatim purgauerit, & *Ecclesiæ Catholicæ Romanæ* iudicio se in omnibus humilli-
" mè submiserit, *Suamque Sanctitatem* instantissimè de-
" precatus fuerit, vt *Decretum* illud *Sacræ Congregationis,* si
" post debitam examinationem ex mala informatione
" latum esse deprehenderet, vel reuocare, et *Widdringtoni*
" famam inde grauiter læsam in integrum restituendam
" curare, vel ipsum de aliqua saltem propositione in li-
" bris eius contenta, quæ fidei aut bonis moribus ad-
" uersetur, certiorem facere dignaretur, hac insuper
" protestatione ab *Authore* adhibita, vt quæ corrigenda
" sint corrigere, quæ explicanda explicare, quæ re-
" tractanda retractare, & quæ purganda purgare
" quàm primùm vellet, quam sanè *Purgationem* ad se ab
" omni crimine purgandum, & ad ora maledicorum
obstruenda abundanter sufficere iudicauit : Et quod
tametsi idem *Widdringtonus* quotidianis experimentis
persentiens, se, cæterosque eius doctrinæ adhærentes,
non obstante prædicta eius *Purgatione,* magis indignè
& iniuriosè deinceps, quàm vnquam antea à *Card.*
Bellarmini fautoribus hîc in Anglia tam verbis, quàm
factis tractari, & tanquam hæreticos, à fide Apostatas,
Sedi Apostolicæ rebelles, communione Ecclesiastica
indignos, omniq; Iurisdictione Sacerdotali priuatos,
cum non leui tum *Protestantium,* tum *Catholicorum* scan-
dalo, maximaque ipsius, cæterorumque eius doctrinæ adhærentium ignominia, apud imperitum vulgus
per iniuriam traduci, aliam prætereà *Supplicationem* ad
eundem *Summum Pontificem* conscripserit, in qua de
prædictis eorum oppressionibus plurimùm conqueritur,

ritur,& tandem *hæc tria* potiffimùm à *Sua Beatitudine*
fupplex petierit.

41. *Primò,* vt *Sanctitas fua,* quænam fintilla multa, "
vel vnum faltem è multis, quæ in Iuramento fidei & "
faluti apertè aduerfari fuis *Breuibus* declarauit, pro mu- "
nere fuo Paftorali Anglis Catholicis notum facere "
dignaretur, vt ita & proprijs confcientijs, & *Regiæ* "
Maieftati, & *Suæ* etiam *Sanctitati,* quantum in ipfis effet, "
fatisfacere poffent. "

Secundò, vt *Decretum* illud *Sacræ Congregationis* contra "
Widdringtonum, eiufque libros ex mala informatione "
editum vel reuocandum, famamque eius inde graui- "
ter læfam in integrum reftituendam curaret, vel quæ- "
nam fint illa dogmata ob quæ libri eius prohibiti "
funt, vt ea aut retractare, aut ab illis fe purgare poffit, "
Sanctitas fua pro debita eius cura Paftorali, illi fignifi- "
care quamprimùm vellet. "

Tertiò, vt *Sanctitas fua* opufculum illud *Widdringtoni,* "
cuius ftatim mentio habebitur, (in quo horrendiffimæ "
quædam calumniæ, quas *Card. Bellarminus;* fub *Adol-* "
phi Schulckenij nomine perfonatus, *Widdringtono* impo- "
fuit, perfpicuè deteguntur) ferio perlegere, & diligen- "
ter examinare non grauaretur, vt ita non ex aliorum, "
qui eius *Sanctitate,* iuftitia, ac charitate abutuntur, fug- "
geltionibus, fed ex propria fcientia grauiffimam hanc "
controuerfiam expendere, & quod rectum & iuftum "
eft, iudicare poffit. "

42. Nihilominùs, quod maximè mirandum &
ftupendum eft, præfati *fex Cardinales Illuftrifsimi,* his
omnibus non obftantibus, hanc etiam *Supplicationem*
tam iuftam & rationabilem, in qua *Widdringtonus fuam*
Sanctitatem fuppliciter obfecrat, vt iam tandem, poft

G   tot

tot humillimas *Supplicationes* illi exhibitas; ad particularia defcendere, & vnicam faltem propofitionem vel
in Iuramento, vel in eius libris contentam, quæ fidei,
faluti, aut bonis moribus repugnet, illi patefacere dignaretur, omnino condemnandam decreuerunt, & in
medio librorum, quos *Proteftantes* fcripferunt, repo-
nendam curarunt : quafi verò iniquum, aut Ecclefiæ
filio indignum effet, inftructionem in dubijs à communi fidelium Patre ac Paftore, aut iuftitiam pro in-
iurijs & calumnijs etiam contra Illuftriffimos Cardinales à fupremo omnium noftrûm in fpiritualibus
Iudice humiliter poftulare. Et certè fi *Iudex* quifpiam
Secularis, quantæcunque alioquin authoritatis, dignitatis, aut apud populum, vel Principem exiftimationis
fuerit, in filios alicuius quantumcunque pauperrimi,
aut ignobilis animaduerteret, eofque indicta caufa
nec crimine aliquo, ob quod tam dirè plectuntur,
indicato, in perpetuum exilium eijciendos, & ab omni
hominum confortio excludendos, & quod maius eft,
etiam *Patrem* ipforum, nifi fe quamprimum purgaret,
grauiffimis fupplicijs omnino coercendum palam de-
cerneret, & fi *Pater* ille à *Iudice* non femel, fed iterum
humiliter poftularet, vt vel fententiam illam reuoca-
ret, vel crimen aliquod, cuius ipfe confcius non eft, ob
quod filij eius pœna tam crudeli afficiuntur, & à quo
ipfe, alioquin etiam ex decreto Iudicis grauiffimè ca-
ftigandus, fe quamprimum purgare debeat, illi notum facere dignaretur; nihilominus *Iudex* ille, neque
crimen vllum patefacere, nec decretum fuum reuocare vellet, fed executioni omnino mandandum præciperet, nonne *Sanctitas Veftra* tam infolitam, & pene
inauditam iftius *Iudicis* fententiam fufpectam haberet,
talemque

talemque *Iudicem* de aperta iniuſtitia,& iniqua oppreſ-
ſione palam & in conſpectu totius mundi accuſa-
tum, ad rationem eiuſmodi *Decreti* reddendam, atque
vt illis, quos per violentiam, & ſuæ potentiæ, autho-
ritati, aut Principis fauori nimium confiſus, iniquè
oppreſſit, plenè ſatisfaciat, à ſupremo illius *Iudicis*
Principe omninò compellendum meritò exiſtimaret?

43. *Quartum indicium* eſt, quòd tametſi idem *Widdringtonus,* vt *Sanctitatem Suam* certiorem faceret, quàm
turpiter *Card. Bellarminus,* ſub *Adolphi Schulckenij* nomine perſonatus, tum *Suam Beatitudinem,* tum *Illuſtriſſimos
Cardinales,* totumque mundum falſis informationibus
ludificari, tum etiā ipſum *Widdringtonum* inuerecundè
admodùm ſcriptis publicis calumniari auſus fuerit,in
alio libello ſupplici quinq; abhinc annis conſcripto,
qui *Appendix ad præcedentem Supplicationem* nuncupatur, plurima nefandiſſima crimina (videlicet *hæreſeos,
erroris, temeritatis, inobedientiæ, ſummæque impudentiæ,
præſumptionis, & arrogantiæ,* & quod ridiculum eſt,
etiam *læſæ Maieſtatis, quòd ſit impoſtor, & non Eccleſiæ
Catholicæ filius, ſed Sereniſſimi Regis Magnæ Britanniæ*
Iacobi *ſtipendiarius miles, aut conductitius ſeruus, Catholicæ verò Eccleſiæ iuratus ac capitalis hoſtis, & in reprobum
ſenſum datus,* quòd *damnatam Lutheri & Caluini Hære-
ſiarcharum doctrinam propugnet,* quòd *contra ſacras literas, doctrinam Conciliorum, vnanimem conſenſum Patrum
& Doctorum hæreticis ſchiſmaticiſque in oppugnanda &
mutilanda Pontificia poteſtate ſe iungat,* quòd *iuſtificet
Caipham, Nerones, Domitianos, Diocletianos, & ſimiles
peſtes Eccleſiam Chriſti perſequentes, & condemnet Chri-
ſtum, Apoſtolos, cæteroſque pios martyres patientes,* vt cætera eiuſdem farinæ conuitia in *noua* ſua *fide Catholica,*

de Principibus author itate Papali deponendis atque
etiam occidendis, fundata nunc mittamus) ab eodem
Schulckenio per manifeſtam calumniam *Widdringtono*
impoſita *Suæ Sanctitati* patefecerit, atque clariſſimè
oſtenderit, eundem *Schulckenium*, vt *Widdringtonum*
tam execrandis criminibus verè obnoxium eſſe cum
maiori probabilitatis ſpecie commonſtraret, verba eius
vel addendo, vel detrahendo, vel in ſenſum peſſimum,
& ab Authoris mente omnino alienum, & contra verborum proprietatem inuertendo, & plerumque verum
quæſtionis ſtatum immutando, turpiter deprauaſſe; ac
proinde eundem *Schulckenium de crimine falſi*, & *de a-*
perta calumnia apud *Sedem Apoſtolicam* in iudicium vo-
cauerit, & iuſtitiam contra eum pro tam atrocibus calumnijs *Widdringtono*, & conſequenter cæteris eius
doctrinæ adhærentibus falſò illatis inſtantiſſimè po-
ſtulauerit: nihilominus neque *Card. Bellarminus*, neq;
Doctor Schulckenius, nec quiſquam alius pro ipſis præfatum *Schulckenium* à tam fœdiſſimis criminationibus,
de quibus à *Widdringtono* accuſatur, vindicare toto hoc
tempore conatus fuerit ; cùm tamen Illuſtriſſimus
Bellarminus iam morti vicinus, & exactiſſimam de
omni verbo etiam otioſo rationem ſupremo omnium
Iudici breui redditurus, melius profectò (vti nos cum
omni reuerentia debita loquentes arbitramur) & famæ & conſcientiæ ſuæ conſuleret, vt vel illis Catholicis, quos palam aut in occulto iniuria affecit, dum
tempus eſt, ſatisfaceret (*ſi enim res aliena, propter quam*
peccatum eſt, cùm reddi poſſit non redditur, non agitur pœ-
nitentia ſed fingitur, ſi autem veraciter agitur, non remitte-
tur [g] *peccatum, niſi reſtituatur ablatum cum reſtitui poteſt:*)
vel ſi innocentem ſe eſſe arbitretur, vt à tam fœdis
criminibus,

[g] *S. Auguſtin.*
epiſt. 54. ad Ma-
cedon. prope x
& c.

criminibus, de quibus à *Widdringtono* accuſatur, ad ſe
purgandum pauxillum temporis inſumeret, cùm neque ætas eius iam fere decrepita, neque negotia vel
publica vel priuata eum ab aliquo ſpirituali opuſculo
quotannis conſcribendo impediant.

44. *Quintum indicium* eſt, quòd tametſi idem *Wid-*
dringtonus etiam *Iacobum Gretzerum, Martinum Becanum,*
Leonardum Leßium, Franciſcum Suarez, & Thomam Fitz-
herbertum Societatis Ieſû religioſos, qui prædictum
Fidelitatis Iuramentum impugnandum, & *nouam ſuam*
fidem Catholicam, de poteſtate papali Principes deponendi, propugnandam ſuſceperunt, ſcriptis publicis
refutauerit, nemo tamen illorum, aut alius quiſpiam
pro illis ad prædictas refutationes hucuſque reſpon-
derit, quod ſanè viris prudentibus, & *Patrum Ieſuitarum*
mores, ingenium, eruditionem, & ſingularem ſeſe ab
omni reprehenſionis nota vindicandi curam & dili-
gentiam vel mediocriter callentibus, non leue argumentum eſſe poteſt, prædictos *Patres* iam tandem
clarè perſpicere, *nouam* illam *fidem Catholicam,* quæ præcipua horum omnium tumultuum, pulueris ſulphu-
rei Coniurationum, Breuium, Decretorum, & inter
Catholicos diſcordiarum cauſa extitit, abſque ſufficienti fundamento ab ipſis potiſſimùm adinuentam
eſſe, neque ſine maiori eorum dedecore ab ipſis defendi vlterius poſſe.

45. Quibus indicijs (vt alia plura nunc mittamus)
addi poteſt tum *Decretum* ſex *Illuſtriſſimorum* (nempe
Pauli Sfondrati, Roberti Bellarmini, Ioannis Garſiæ Mellini,
Fabricij Veralli, Fratris *Auguſtini Galamini,* & *Aloyſij Cap-*
poni) S. R. E. *Cardinalium,* à Sanctiſſimo Domino *Paulo*
Papa Quinto ſuper librorũ permiſſione, prohibitione,
G 3   expurgatione,

expurgatione, & impreſſione in vniuerſa Republica
Chriſtiana ſpecialiter deputatórum aduersùs *controuer-*
ſiam Anglicanam Martini Becani de poteſtate Regis & Ponti-
ficis, tanquam *nonnulla falſa, temeraria, ſcandaloſa, & ſedi-*
tioſa reſpeEtiuè continentem die tertia *Ianuarij* 1613.
ex mandato *Suæ SanEtitatis* ſancitum : tum quæ à *Do-*
Etoribus Pariſienſibus Calendis *Decembris* 1612. (quæque præfato *IlluſtriſſimorumCardinalium* Decreto euul-
gando cauſam præbuerunt) & 2. *Ianuarij* 1613. & die

h *Iſta AEta Do-*
Etorum Pariſien-
ſium & Cenſura
Cardinalium in-
frà in fine Sup-
plicationis noſtræ
cum alijs nonnul-
lis obſeruatu dig-
nis ad verbum
habentur.

prima *February* 1613. aEta ſunt ʰ in *Congregatione* ordinaria *Facultatis* Theologiæ *Pariſienſis,* quæq; à Magi-
ſtro *Antonio Fayet* Sacræ Theologiæ DoEtore, nomine
totius *Facultatis* in *Regis Lupara* die ſeptimo *Ianuarij*
1613. ad *Sereniſſimam Reginam* diEta ſunt contra præfatam *Becani* controuerſiam Anglicanam, & *nouas* quaſdam ac *periculoſas propoſitiones* de poteſtate *Summi Ponti-*
ficis Reges deponendi in ea contentas ; quæ omnia ſi
SanEtitas Veſtra diligenter expendere voluerit, facilè
perſpiciet, quam opinionem tum præfati *Cardinales Il-*
luſtriſſimi, tum omnes vt plurimum *Theologi Pariſienſes*
de poteſtate *Papali Principes* deponendi tanquam de
fide Catholica ab omnibus neceſſariò credenda habuerint, & vtrùm præfati *Widdringtoni* libri eò quòd noua
hæc, ſeditioſa, & Principum Capitibus periculoſa *fi-*
des Catholica in illis impugnetur, eorumque, qui
eam propugnare ſtudent, fraudes, cauilli, & ſophiſ-
mata detegantur, vlla prorſus Cenſura notari mereantur.

46. *Denique,* quod ſpeEtat ad *Breuia* Prædeceſſoris
Veſtri *Iuramentum* prohibentia, eo quòd *multa contineat,*
quæ fidei & ſaluti apertè aduerſantur, ea quoque in *falſis*
ſuppoſitionibus fundata eſſe nimis manifeſtum eſt,
quandoquidem,

quandoquidem, vti *Widdringtonus* ¹ ex aperta *Card.Bel-*   ¹ *In Disputat.*
larmini, Iacobi Gretzeri, Martini Becani, Leonardi Leſſij, &   *Theol. de Iura-*
mento cap. 3. &
Franciſci Suarez doctrina (vt *Thomam Fitzherbertum,*   4. & *in Append.*
contra Suarez
& *Matthæum Kellinſonū* Scriptores Anglicos nunc mit-   *part.* 2. *ſect.* 3.
tamus) clariſſimè comprobauit, tam *Primatum Papæ*   4. & 5.
directè in ſpiritualibus, nempe *poteſtatem* eius *excommu-*
nicandi, in *Iuramento* abnegari, quod falſiſſimum eſſe
Widdringtonus tum ex ipſius *Iuramenti* verbis propriè ac-
ceptis, tum ex expreſſa *Suæ Maieſtatis* declaratione euidenter commonſtrauit, quàm *Primatum* eius indirectè
in temporalibus, nempe *poteſtatem* Summi Pontificis
Principes ſi id meriti ſint deponendi, atque de rebus
omnibus temporalibus, & conſequenter de Coronis
& Capitibus Regum in ordine ad bonum ſpirituale
diſponendi, quæ quidem in *Iuramento* expreſſe abnegatur, eſſe rem *de fide certam,* neque apud Catholicos
eruditos in controuerſia poſitam, quod non minus
falſum eſſe tum *Widdringtonus* demonſtrauit, tum
ex ijs quæ ſuperius ᵏ à nobis dicta ſunt, manifeſtè   ᵏ *Nu.* 19. &
ſeq.
elucescit.

47. Vnde perſpicuè conſequitur, tum prædicta
Breuia, cùm in *falſis rationibus fundamentalibus,* & *ſuppo-*
ſitionibus fundentur, ad ea obſeruanda neminem obli-
gare, quandoquidem iuxta veriſſimam *Franciſci Suarez*   ˡ *Lib.* 3. *de Le-*
ˡ doctrinam ſatis conſtat, nullum *præceptum,* ſeu *Breue*   *gibus cap.* 14.
Pontificis *declaratiuum* maiorem obligandi vim habe-
re, quàm valeat *ratio fundamentalis,* quæ in præcepto
illa, ſeu *Breui* ſupponitur, & declaratur: tum etiam
nouum fidelitatis *Iuramentum* nihil in ſe continere, quod
fidei, aut *ſaluti* aduerſetur. Si enim ſemel admittatur,
quod proculdubio veriſſimum eſt, non eſſe doctrinam de *fide certam,* & ab omnibus neceſſariò credendam,

dam, sed ad summum *speculatiuè* probabilem, quòd Papa Principes supremos deponendi, & de rebus omnibus temporalibus, & consequenter tam de Capitibus, quàm Coronis Regum in ordine ad bonum spirituale disponendi potestatem habeat, hinc perspicuum est *primò*, licitum esse iureiurando interposito *agnoscere & profiteri* (quæ est *secunda* Iuramenti *clausula* contra quam omnes nostri Aduersarij adeo vociferantur, nam *primam Clausulā*, nempe quòd *supremus Dominus noster Rex Iacobus sit legitimus & verus Rex huius Regni*, & *omnium aliarum Maiestatis Suæ Dominiorum, & Terrarum*, omnes nostræ nationis Catholici libenter admittunt, tametsi exteri quidam *Iesuitæ*, veluti *Gretzerus*, *Suarez*, atque etiam *Becanus* in controuersia eius Anglicana recognita contra hanc etiam *Clausulam* partim friuolè ac imperitè, partem seditiosè & scandalosè cauillentur) quòd *Papa non habeat vllam* veram, realem, propriam, sufficientem, & legitimā *potestatem vel authoritatem Regem deponēdi* &c. cùm clarum sit (vti supra ostendimus) *potestatem, quæ non omnino certa, sed probabilis, non posse esse fundamentum, quo immediatè aliquis puniatur, & iure suo ac dominio priuetur, & generales Canones pœnales statuantur,* &c. *sed talis potestas certissimè, non dubiè debet competere* [m].

[m] *Sunt verba ipsius Lessii in suo Singletono, pag. 71. 72.*

48. *Secundò* perspicuum est, licitum etiam esse cuivis Regis subdito *promittere* & *polliceri*, quæ est *Tertia Iuramenti Clausula*, quòd *non obstante quacunque sententia Excommunicationis, Depriuationis,* aut *Absolutionis subditorum ab eorum fidelitate, obedientia, & subiectione per Papam, vel Successores suos facta aut facienda contra prædictum Regem, Hæredes & Successores suos, fidelitatem tamen & veram obedientiam suæ Maiestati, Hæredibus & Successoribus suis præstabit, Ipsumque & ipsos contra omnes proditorias conspirationes*

tiones totis suis viribus defendet, omnemque operam impendet,
vt omnes proditiones, & proditorias conspirationes contra ip-
sum, aut aliquos eorum,quæ ad eius notitiam,vel auditum per-
venient, Suæ Maiestati, Hæredibus, & Successoribus suis re-
uelet & manifestas faciat : quandoquidem *Summus Pon-*
tifex nullam veram, realem, propriam, sufficientem, &
legitimam potestatem quantumcunque *probabilis* esse
supponatur, habet Principes supremos deponendi,seu
depriuandi, ac proinde nec eorum subditos à temporali fidelitate,illis ex lege Christi,& naturæ debita, ab-
soluendi, & consequenter neque licentiam subditis
concedendi, vt Principes suos supremos contra omnes proditiones, & proditorias conspirationes totis
suis viribus non defendant, easve, quando ad eorum
notitiam peruenient, manifestas non faciant. Illud
verò, quod *Card.Bellarminus*, cæterique Iesuitæ suprà
citati eius vestigia sequuti asserunt, illis verbis [*non ob-*
stante quacunq, Excommunicationis sententia] apertè negari
Summo Pontifici potestatē. Reges etiam hæreticos excommuni-
*candi,*falsissimū esse *Rex* noster *Serenissim'* [n] tū palam, &
scriptis publicis totius Christiani Orbis Monarchis,
ac Principibus declarauit,tum *Widdringtonus* [o] solidissi-
mè comprobauit; nam per illa verba [*non obstante qua-*
cunq, sententia Excommunicationis] potestas Regem ex-
cōmunicandi supponitur potiùs, quàm negatur,(licet
revera neque *asseratur*, neque *negetur, sed quæstio de tali*
potestate omnino declinetur) & hoc solùm ex illis verbis
colligitur, Excommunicationem neque iure diuino,
cùm ex lege Christi spiritualis tantùm Censura sit, &
Christianos, si in peccatis obstinati sint, tanquam
Ethnicos duntaxat, & Publicanos faciat, neque iure
Pontificio, aut Ecclesiastico (cùm neque Summo

Bell. in Resp. ad
Apologiā Coloniæ
1610. *pag.*9. *&*
in Apologia cap.
15. *in primo*
mendacio.

[n] *Tum in Apo-*
logia,tum in præ-
fatione Monito-
ria non longe à
principio : & in
Catalogo menda-
ciorū Torti §. 1.
[o] *In Disputat.*
Theol.ca.4.sec.1.

Pontifici, neque totæ Chriſti Eccleſiæ ſpirituali vlla *vera, realis, propria, ſufficiens,* & *legitima,* quamdiu *probabilis* tantùm manet, neque tanquam certa, & de fide Catholica ab omnibus neceſſariò credenda, ab *Eccleſia,* quæ *columna,* & *firmamentum veritatis eſt* P, declaratur, poteſtas competat Reges deſtituendi) hunc effectum habere, vt ex Regibus non Reges efficiat, aut Principes ſupremos Regnis, quæ poſſident, etiam per ſententiam priuet.

P *2 Tim. 3.*

49. *Tertiò* perſpicuum eſt, poſſe quemuis tutâ conſcientia *abhorrere, deteſtari,* & *abiurare* (quæ eſt *quarta* Iuramenti *Clauſula*) hanc doctrinam ſeu poſitionem, tanquam falſam, impiam, Principibus ſupremis iniurioſam, damnabilem, & Verbo Dei, ſaltem per neceſſariam conſequentiam repugnantem, & proinde *hæreticam* (accipiendo *hæreticam* propoſitionem pro ea, quæ vel in ſacris literis expreſsè continetur, vel per neceſſariam conſequentiam ex ijs deducitur; prout à noſtris Theologis ⁹, & Proteſtantibus etiam plerūnque accipi ſolet) quæ aſſerit, *poſſe ſubditos, vel alium quemcunq; Principes per Papam excommunicatos, vel depriuatos deponere,* ſeu è ſuis dominijs per vim extrudere, & multo minùs *occidere.* Si enim certiſſimum non ſit (vti proculdubio non eſſe paulò antè oſtendimus) ſed apud Catholicos controuerſum, quòd Papa Principes depriuandi poteſtatem non habeat, & inſuper ſi veriſſimum ſit, quòd *poteſtas, quæ non omnino certa, ſed probabilis, non poſſit eſſe fundamentum quo immediatè aliquis puniatur, & iure ſuo ac dominio* (vt rectè dixit *Leonardus Leſſius* ʳ) *priuetur,* & proinde non ſit *vera, realis, propria, ſufficiens,* ac *legitima* depriuandi *poteſtas,* & quòd *aperta ſit iniuſtitia in Papa,* & conſequenter crimen læſæ Maieſtatis in ſubdito,

⁹ *S. Thom. 2ª. 2æ. q. 11. ar. 2. Bannes ibidem. Turrecremata in Summa de Eccl. lib. 4. part. 2. cap. 10. Canus lib. 12. de locis, cap. 7. Directorium Inquiſitorum part. 2. comment. 27. Franciſcus de Chriſto in lib. 3. ſent. diſt. 25. in q. de hæreſi, in Excurſu de Catholica veritate. Alphonſ. de Caſtro lib. 1. aduerſus hæreſes, cap. 8. Couerruuias lib. 4. variarum reſolut. cap. 14. Molina 1. part. q. 1. ar. 2. diſp. 1.* ʳ *In cius Singetoto part. 2, nu. 38.*

Regem

Regem aliquem *fua Corona & Regno priuare,qui ius probabile,*
& fimul poffeßionem habet, vt optimè afferit *Matthæus*
Kellinfonus[f]*,* & proinde quòd nulla fententia etiam
depriuationis per Papam facta contra quemcunque
Regem, qui antea verus & legitimus Rex erat (quantumcunque quoad *fpeculationem* probabile fit effe in
Pontifice poteftatè Principes depriuâdi)poffit efficere,
quin Rex ille per Papâ priuatus,non obftante tali depriuationis fententia, ius faltem *probabile* ad Regnum,
& fimul *poffefsionem* habeat, ex prædictis *duobus princi-*
pijs, quæ fanè veriffima funt, manifeftè confequitur,
effe *apertam iniuftitiam in Papa,*& perduellionem in fub-
dito, & confequenter *impium, damnabile,* atque illis Sacræ Scripturæ verbis, *Non furtum facies, Non occides*[t]*,*
Quis extendet manum fuam in Chriftum Domini, & innocens
erit[u]*? Reddite quæ funt Cæfaris Cæfari*[x]*,* indirectè faltem,
& per neceffariam confequentiam repugnans, *Princi-*
pes per Papam depriuatos deponere aut occidere.

50. Atque hinc fatis perfpicuum eft,in iftis *tribus*
Iuramenti *Claufulis,* quas præ cæteris præfati *Societatis*
Iefu Doctores celeberrimi, *Card. Bellarminum* fequuti,
tanquam fidei & faluti repugnantes impugnandas
fufceperunt,et contra quas magno verborum ftrepitu,
fed exigua aut nulla argumentorum efficacitate inue-
huntur,nihil *fidei,* aut *faluti repugnans* contineri, & confequenter reliquas omnes quæ fubfequuntur *claufulas,*
& quarum veritas ex præcedentium *veritate ac iuftitia*
omnino pendet, (nempe *quòd nec Papa, nec vlla alia per-*
fona poteftatem habeat me ab *hoc Iuramento, aut aliqua eius*
parte abfoluendi, quòd *fit recta ac plena authoritate mihi legi-*
timè miniftratum, & omnibus indulgentijs & difpenfationibus
in contrarium, renunciem, & quòd *voluntariè, cordialiter,*

H 2 *fyncerè,*

[f] *In Tractatu de*
Ecclefiaftica &
Regia poteftate,
cap.11.pag.235.

[t] *Exod.20.*

[u] *1 Reg. 26.*
[x] *Matth.22.*

ſyncerè, abſque vlla æquiuocatione, aut mentali reſeruatione,
iuxta hæc expreſſa verba à me prolata, & iuxta planum &
communem ſenſum eorundem verborum illud ſuſcipiam)
adeo manifeſtas eſſe, vt nihil momenti contra illas
obijci poſſit : Quas omnes *clauſulas*, quæque contra
eas, totumque Iuramentum vel generatim, vel ſpeciatim obijci ſolent, *Sanctitas Veſtra*, ſi vel pauculum
temporis ad grauiſſimam hanc controuerſiam exami-
nandam inſumere velit, à *Widdringtono* fuſiùs, ſed in
Strena Catholica preſſiùs & dilucidè explicatas videbit.

51. Quæ cùm ita ſint, *Veſtræ Beatitudinis* prudentiæ,
charitati, ac iuſtitiæ iudicandum relinquimus, vtrùm
prædicta *Breuia,* & *Decreta,* in tam *falſis ſuppoſitionibus*
fundata, iuſta vel iniuſta ſint, Angloſque Catholicos
ad ea cum maximo eorum præiudicio obſeruanda
obligare queant, quàmq; iniurioſum, calumnioſum;
& à charitate Chriſtiana prorſus alienum, atque notiſſimis *Theologiæ, Iuriſque Pontificij* principijs diſſenta-
neum ſit, nos, cæteroſque Catholicos doctrinæ *Wid-*
dringtoni adhærentes, de culpabilis *inobedientia*, & *rebel-*
lionis contra Sedem Apoſtolicam noxa arguere, eò quòd
declaratiuis Veſtri Prædeceſſoris *Breuibus* Iuramentum
prohibentibus non adhuc acquieſcamus, cùm idem
Widdringtonus per plures literas, & Supplicationes typis
etiam excuſas, *Suæ Sanctitati* rationes humiliter pro-
poſuerit, ob quas Catholici Angli non ſolùm dubi-
tant, ſed firmiter ſibi perſuadent, prædicta *Breuia* iniuſta eſſe, atque in prædictis *duabus*, quas ſuprà retuli-
mus, *falſis ſuppoſitionibus* fundata, & proinde ad ea
cum extrema fortunarũ ruina, *Proteſtantium* ſcandalo,
Suæque Maieſtatis iniuria ſtrictè obſeruanda, donec
Sanctitas Sua eorum rationibus ſatisfacere dignetur

(quibus

(quibus tamen non adhuc fatisfecit) eos obligare nequaquam poſſe. Conſtat enim ex veriſſimis *Theologiæ,* *Iuriſq̄ Canonici* principijs, non teneri ſubditum *Prælati* ſui mandato, quod in tertiæ perſonæ præiudicium tendit, obedire, quando dubitat ſubditus, & à fortiori quando certiſſimè exiſtimat, iniuſtum eſſe illud, quod à *Prælato* præcipitur, dummodo rationes ſui dubij *Prælato* humiliter proponat.

52. Nam *Prælati & Iudices,* ait doctiſsimus *Soto, non ſunt in poſſeſſione reſpectu ſubditorum, niſi quatenus iuſta præcipiunt; & ideo quando dubium eſt, an præcipiant iuſtum, tunc ſi ſit in præiudicium tertij, quia ille tertius eſt etiam in poſſeſſione ſuæ famæ & bonorum, in eã partem inclinandum eſt, vbi eſt minus periculi. Neque Prælati, qui præcipiunt vnde nullum periculum Religioni, aut Reipublicæ, aut tertiæ perſonæ timetur, conſtringuntur rationem reddere, ſed ſimpliciter parendum eſt illis etiam in dubijs, vt ſuprà dictum eſt, quia tunc nullum eſt periculum, ſi Iudex præſumatur iuſtè præcipere. Quando verò eiuſmodi periculum imminet, tunc ſi ſubditus dubitat, nihil facit contra obedientiam, ſi exigat à Prælato rationem præcepti, proponens humiliter rationes dubitandi.* Ita *Sotus.*

Sotus de deteg. ſecreto memb. 3. *q.* 2. *in reſp. ad* 1.^m

53. Atque hæc eius doctrina non ſolùm Theologiæ principijs, ipſique rationis naturalis lumini, ſed etiam *Iuri Canonico* eſt quàm maximè conſentanea, & ab *Alexandro* Papa Tertio circa *Breuia,* ſeu *Reſcripta Apoſtolica* verbis expreſſis tradita: *Si quando,* ait *Pontifex* ad Archiepiſcopum Rauennatem ſcribens, ᵞ *aliqua tuæ Fraternitati dirigimus, quæ animum tuum exaſperare videntur, turbari non debes. Qualitatem negotij pro quo tibi ſcribitur diligenter conſiderans, aut mandatum noſtrũ reuerenter adimpleas, aut per literas tuas quarè adimplere*

ᵞ *Extrà de Reſcriptis, cap. Si quando.*

non

non possis rationabilem causam prætendas , quia patienter
sustinebimus, si non feceris, quod praua fuerit nobis insinua-
tione suggestum. Vnde *Glossa,* Ioannes *Andreas,* Petrus
de Ancharono, Panormitanus, Felinus, & omnes communiter Canonistæ illum *Alexandri* Papæ *canonem* expo-
nentes, hanc regulam generalem tradunt, quòd *manda-*
tum Superioris vel debeat adimpleri, vel ratio reddi quare
non adimpleatur.

54. Quibus omnibus rite perpensis, quis timoratæ
conscientiæ Catholicus, & vel *Sacram Theologiam,* vel
Ius Canonicum mediocriter callens, audeat in Anglos
Catholicos vllum *inobedientiæ,* aut *rebellionis* contra *Se-*
dem Apostolicam crimen conijcere, eosque tanquam
Ethnicos & Publicanos, ac Sacramentorum perceptione & communione Ecclesiastica indignos, omni-
busque suis facultatibus, & Sacerdotali Iurisdictione
priuatos traducere, eò quòd prædictis *Breuibus,* tam
Suam Maiestatem, quàm *seipsos, totumq́ Regnum* adeo ex-
asperantibus obedire hucusque refugerint, quandoquidem, iuxta prædictam *Alexandri* Papæ, omniumque
Canonistarum regulam, rationes tam manifestas, quibus adhuc satisfactũ non est, humiliter reddiderunt,
ob quas arbitrantur, *Breuia* illa *declaratiua* omnino iniusta esse, & praua quorundam, præsertim *Card. Bellar-*
mini, insinuatione *Summo Pontifici* suggesta, atque manifestè *falsis suppositionibus,* & *rationibus fundamentalibus*
innixa, quæque proinde maiorem vim obligandi ha-
bere non possunt, iuxta verissimam *Francisci Suarez*
a Num. 47. doctrinam supra relatam, quàm habeat *ratio fundamen-*
talis, quam supponunt & declarant.

55. Iudicet iam *Sanctitas Vestra,* quàm indignè, ir-
religiosè, parumque Christianè nos Angli Catholici
doctrinæ

doctrinæ *Widdringtoni* adhærentes, (quam ſtatim retractare, ſi *Sedes Apoſtolica* aliquam particularem propoſitionem in libris eius contentam, quæ fidei, aut
ſanæ doctrinæ repugnet, nobis notam faceret, para-
tiſſimi ſumus, quod etiam ipſemet *Widdringtonus* ſæpiùs ſcriptis publicis proteſtatus eſt)*Veſtræ Beatitudinis,*
Sanctæque Sedis Apoſtolicæ filij obſeruantiſſimi, quique
pro fide Catholica Romana palam agnoſcenda ipſam
etiam mortem ſubire non pertimeſcimus͜ ab Anglis
quibuſdam, præſertim *Ieſuitis,* per plurimos iam annos oppreſſi fuerimus,magiſque indies opprimamur,
eò quòd *falſæ* eorum *fidei Catholicæ,* de Principibus authoritate Papali deponendis, atque etiam, ſi opus ſit,
interimendis, *Veſtrique Prædeceſſoris Breuibus* Iuramentum prohibentibus, in *falſa* illa *fide* potiſſimùm fundatis, tutâ conſcientiâ,& ſalua fide Catholica,ac temporali noſtra fidelitate *Regi* noſtro *Sereniſsimo* ex lege
Chriſti debita (ob rationes tam ſolidas,quas *Suæ San-*
ctitati notas fecimus, quæque, iuxta *Iuris Canonici* præ-
ſcriptum, ab omni *inobedientiæ* nota nos liberare ſufficiunt) acquieſcere non adhuc poſſimus. Et certè ſi
Sanctiſsima veſtra *Paternitas* ſeriò ſecum cogitaret,
quàm intolerandas perſequutiones & calumnias,nos
Ecclefiæ Romanæ filij obſequentiſſimi (ob doctrinam,
quæ apud eruditos Catholicos controuertitur, propugnandam, quæque à *Senatu Pariſienſi* pluribus *Ar-*
reſtis ſub pœna læſæ Maieſtatis condemnata eſt, &
quæ ab *ipſomet Domino Papa in Francia toleratur, nec impe-*
dire debet, teſte *Card. Perono, reunionem eorum, qui Ecclefiæ*
reconciliari deſiderant) longo iam tempore hîc in Anglia, cum maximo *Ecclefiæ Romanæ* ſcandalo, perpeſſi
fuerimus, nequaquam profectò ambigimus, quin

ſeria

feria tam grauium noftrarum, & fcandalofarum op-
preffionum recogitatio, ad nobis tam iniquè oppref-
fis tandem aliquando commiferandum, ad pacem in
Ecclefia Anglicana ob opiniones tantùm in controuerfia pofitas, à *Pàtribus* præfertim *Iefuitis*, eorumque fequacibus tam miferè diftracta, quamprimùm conci-
liandam, atque ad eos, qui præcipui tantarum pertur-
bationum Authores extiterunt, *falfamque fidem Catholicam* in re tam graui, qualis eft debita noftra Deo aut
Cæfari fidelitas, confingere & propugnare per fas &
nefas præfumpferunt, grauiffimè caftigandos, tener-
rima *paternæ* veftræ *charitatis* (cuius fingulare fpecimen
in ipfomet Pontificatus fui primordio iam dediffe
Chriftiani omnes gaudent, laudant, & mirantur)
vifcera commoueret.

56. Hactenus enim opprobria & calumnias non
ferendas animo tranquillo tulimus, nofq; tanquam
hæreticos, à fide Apoftatas, Ecclefiæ Romanæ hoftes,
in Sedem Apoftolicam rebelles, communione Ecclefiaftica indignos, & facultatibus priuatos à *Patribus
Iefuitis*, eorumque fequacibus, & potiffimùm ab indoctis quibufdam fœminis [a] (quæ *Patribus Iefuitis* fe
totas deuouerunt) falsò & per calumniam traduci,
& tanquam *purgamenta huius mundi omnium peripfema fa-
ctos*, à communibus etiam eleemofynis excludi patienter & pacificè fuftinuimus, neque tam eos, qui
nos falsò & iniquè calumniati funt, offendere, quàm

[a] *Iftæ fœminæ à plurimis noftrati-
bus tam Catholi-
cis quàm Prote-
ftantibus* Iefui-
tiffæ, *& Ambu-
latoriæ* Monia-
les *appellantur:
de quaxum nouo
& ante hæc fæ-
cula planè inau-
dito vitæ inftituto,* Anglis quidem Iefuitis *pro tempore fatis commodo, fed quamplurium prudentum & exper-
torum iudicio, tum fœminis ipfis, earumque Sodalitati periculofo, tum toti* Iefuitarum Ordini *portentofo & malè
ominofo, nihil amplius inpræfentiarum dicemus; confifi, eas in pofterum cautiores futuras, & linguis fuis male-
dicis frænum impofituras, neque deinceps fub fuco zeli, & fpeciofo* Patres *fuos* Iefuitas *fuper fydera extollendi,
prætextu (vt ita omnes vtriufque fexus Catholicos ad eos facilius alliciant) aliorum Sacerdotum tam Secularium quàm Regularium famam, fubdolè & malis artibus, quas nunc tacebimus, denigraturas: Quod in
præfenti* Veftræ Sanctitati, Reuerendoque admodum Patrum Iefuitarum Generali *tantùm infinuaffe, quò
futura fcandala præcaueantur, fatis erit.*

nofmetipfos,

nósmetipfos, noftramque innocentiam folidis, mol-
libufque refponfis defendere hucufque conati fumus:
plurimùm confifi, quòd patientia, & fyncera noftra
tum pacis & vnitatis inter Catholicos conferuandæ,
tum veritatis Catholicæ inueftigandæ, & cognita
propugnandæ auiditas, eorum animos temporis pro-
greffu emolliret, iftudque faltem efficeret, vt, poftquam ipfi manifeftè perfpicerent, *nouam* hanc *fidem*
Catholicam, de poteftate Papali Principes deponendi,
quæ horum omnium tumultuum radix & origo extitit, non effe in veris & antiquis fidei Catholicæ re-
gulis atque principijs fufficienter fundatam, & proinde neque nos in ea abneganda, fed femetipfos in ea
tam acriter & turbulentè propugnanda egregiè allu-
cinatos effe, à nobis vlteriùs ea de caufa maledicendis,
& iniuriosè opprimendis, ob pacis Ecclefiafticæ &
fraternæ charitatis bonum tandem abftinerent.

57. Veruntamen cùm longa hac noftra patientia
abuti, nofque ad extrema quæque tentanda, innocentiæ noftræ defendendæ gratia, compellere noftrates
Iefuitâ, eorumque hac in re affectatores gratum habere
videantur, haud indignè ferant, fi nos deinceps non
per modum *defenfionis* tantùm, fed *iuridicæ* etiam *accu-*
fationis contra eos procedamus, neque *reorum,* fed *acto-*
rum perfonas pofthac induamus. Nam certè, fi ab
iniquis fuis obtrectationibus, & irreligiofis machinationibus quamprimùm non defiftant, fed nos, cæ-
terofue doctrinæ *Widdringtoni* adhærentes, à communione Ecclefiaftica, & Sacramentorum participatione
tanquam Ethnicos, aut Publicanos excludere in futurum præfumant, nos breuî præcipuos eorum, qui
nos tam dire perfequuntur, non verbis tantùm gene-

I   ralibus,

ralibus, fed nominatim de grauiffimis criminibus
apud *Veftram Beatitudinem, Sanctamq́ Sedem Apoftolicam*
accufabimus, et falua femper pace ac vnitate Ecclefiaftica, eorumque confcientijs folius Dei, qui corda et
renes fcrutatur, iudicio relictis, eos in iudicium ad-
ducemus;

58. *Inprimis* de *Schifmate*, eo quòd Ecclefiæ Anglicanæ pacem ac vnitatem difcindere, virofquè Catholicos, et qui Ecclefiæ Catholicæ Romanæ iudicio fe
in omnibus fubmittunt, ob opiniones, quas *ipfemet
Dominus Papa in Francia tolerat, quæque impedire non debent
revnionem eorum*, qui extra Ecclefiam funt, et *Ecclefiæ
reconciliari defiderant*, à communione Ecclefiaftica, et
participatione Sacramentorum excludere non vereantur. *Secundò*, de calumnia, eo quòd viros Catholicos, et qui Ecclefiæ Romanæ filios obfequentiffi-
mos fe effe palam, fyncerè, et coram Deo profitentur,
tanquam hæreticos, à fide Apoftatas, Pfeudo-Catholicos, in Sedem Apoftolicam rebelles, Ecclefiaftica
communione indignos, et vel excommunicatos, vel
Iurifdictione Sacerdotali priuatos, contra veras, antiquas, et indubitatas *fidei Catholicæ*, et *Iuris* etiam *Canonici*
regulas traducere non pertimefcant. *Tertiò*, de *crimine
falfi*, ac *impofturæ*, eo quòd *falfam fidem Catholicam*, contra
veriffimas *fidei Catholicæ*, et *Sacræ Theologiæ* regulas, procudere, propugnare, et cæteris omnibus Catholicis
contra fentientibus per vim obtrudere non reformident. *Quartò*, de *fcandalo* non tantùm *accepto*, fed mul-
tifariam *dato*; eo quòd in rebus maximi ponderis, vtpote ad debitum noftrum ex lege Chrifti Deo et Cæfari obfequium fpectantibus, *falfam fidem Catholicam*
vijs indebitis, per fas et nefas, vi et potentia humana
ftabilire

ſtabilire conantes, atque ita vera et antiqua fidei Catholicæ fundamenta,regulas et principia quantum in
ipſis eſt ſubuertentes, multiplicem non vni vel alteri,
ſed vniuerſo fermè humano generi,Pontificibus, Regibus,ſubditis, Catholicis,hæreticis,atque infidelibus
ruinæ occaſionem præbeant. Quòd autem *neceſſaria*
veritatis Catholicæ defenſio, et falſæ fidei in rebus
præſertim quæ ad fidelitatem ſpectant, impugnatio
non niſi *paſsiuè* ſcandaloſa eſſe queat, et proinde doctrinam *Widdringtoni,*vel*falſam fidem Catholicam,*de poteſtate Papali Principes deponendi et occidendi, à *Ieſuitis* potiſſimùm adinuentam et ſuſtentatam impug-
nantis,vel*Breuia* Summi Pontificis Iuramenti ſuſcep-
tionem prohibentia in falſis ſuppoſitionibus, et in
prædicta illa *falſa fide Catholica* præcipuè fundata non
admittentis, (eo modo quo *Widdringtonus* eas quæſti-
ones tractat) non eſſe *actiuè* ſcandaloſam, aut vllam
dati ſcandali occaſionem præbere poſſe, tum ipſemet
Widdringtonus ^b clariſſimè commonſtrauit,tum quiuis
vir eruditus, qui *ſcandali* naturam, definitionem, et
conditiones à Theologis traditas expendet,luce meri-
diana clariùs perſpicere poteſt. *Quintò,* de *proditióne*
& *læſa Maieſtate* in Sacro-ſanctam Chriſti Eccleſiam :
nam ſicut cuſor falſæ monetæ proditor eſt in Regnũ,
ita qui falſam fidem Catholicam cudit, in Eccleſiam
perduellis cenſetur. *Sextò,* de *læſa Maieſtate* in Principes Chriſtianos, eo quòd *falſamfidem Catholicam,* &
doctrinam non *neceſſariam,* quæ Principum Coronis
iniuriam, eorumque Capitibus periculum affert,& in
Francia pluribus Arreſtis ſub pœna *læſa Maieſtatis* condemnata eſt,tueri,atque factionibus ſtabilire non per-
horreſcant. De iſtis ſex criminibus niſi Aduerſarij

^b *In Præfat.
Reſp. Apolog. &
nu.21. & ſeq. &
in Diſput. Theol.
cap.10.ſec.3.*

pacem *Eccleſia Anglicana,* quam iniquè abſtulerunt, confeſtim reddant, eorum præcipuos apud *Veſtram Beatitudinem* nominatim accuſabimus, & contra eos cœlũ & terram, Deum, Angelos, Sanctos, Pontifices, Reges, totumque Chriſtianum orbem pro iuſtitia inuocabimus.

59. Itaque falſum, ſcandaloſum, atque tam *Sedi Apoſtolicæ,* quàm *Principibus ſupremis* iniurioſum illud eſt, in quo quidam ex noſtris Aduerſarijs plurimùm gloriantur, quodq; maiorem nobis indies inſultandi, & in ſolitis ſuis calumniationibus perſeuerandi illis animum addit, nempe *Widdringtonum,* cæteroſque eius doctrinæ adhærentes, non *Sedis Apoſtolicæ,* quam tanquam matrem venerari deberent, ſed contra *Sedem Apoſtolicam* Principum etiam hæreticorum cauſam agere, & *Sedis Apoſtolicæ* authoritaté cum hæreticis, & Eccleſiæ Romanæ hoſtibus, *Caluino, Luthero,* & *Marſilio Patauino* impugnare: at verò *Card. Bellarminum,* cæteroſque eius doctrinæ adhærentes, *Sedis Apoſtolicæ* patrocinium ſuſcipere, & contra hæreticos, & iniquos Principes poteſtatem Eccleſiaſticam ſeu Pontificiam propugnare, & proinde nobis ſperandum non eſſe, quòd vllus *Summus Pontifex* vel *Breuia* & *Decreta* in fauorem ſuæ poteſtatis ſemel facta vnquam reuocare, vel eos, qui in eius authoritate promouenda quantumuis plùs nimio efferueſcant, duriùs increpare, vel aliquod remedium contra eos, qui nos perſequuntur, nobis adhibere, quin potiùs nos pœnis & cenſuris Eccleſiaſticis, quamdiu cum *hæreticis,* & *Eccleſiæ hoſtibus* eius poteſtatem abnegamus, caſtigare voluerit.

60. Neque enim nos (*Pater Sanctiſſime*) doctrinæ *Widdringtoni* (ſeu potiùs veterum Eccleſiæ primitiuæ

Patrum,

Patrum, quamque *Francia* femper vti certam tenuit,
& *Widdringtonus* præ cæteris horum temporum Theologis neruofiùs defendit, quam idcirco doctrinam
Widdringtoni vocamus) adhærentes, vllum fidei verè
Catholicæ dogma, fed folummodò *falfam fidem Catho-*
licam, à quibufdam recentioribus Theologis, in maximum *Romanæ Ecclefiæ* fcandalum, & fummam *pote-*
ftatis Regiæ derogationem, contra approbatas fidei
Catholicæ regulas nuper adinuentam reijcimus, neq;
vllam planè *Sedis Apoftolicæ* poteftatem, quam illi
competere certò conftat improbamus, fed folùm
certa ab incertis, vera à falfis, & Catholica dogmata
ab opinionibus feparamus, illamque duntaxat *Summi*
Pontificis authoritatem, quæ dubia & incerta eft, &
apud eruditos Catholicos, Sedique Apoftolicæ addi-
ctiffimos in controuerfia pofita, non effe pro certa,
indubitata,& ab omnibus fub pœna hærefis,aut æternæ damnationis neceffariò admittendam contendi-
mus. Neque etiam nos cum *hæreticis, fchifmaticis*, aut
Ecclefiæ hoftibus (vti *D. Schulckenius* ^c *Widdringtono* per ca-   ^c *Cap.* I. *fuæ*
lumniam imponit) fed cum doctiffimis Catholicis,   *Apolog.*
& deuotiffimis Ecclefiæ Romanæ filijs in hac Summi
Pontificis poteftate Principes deponendi, tanquam
re de fide certa & ab omnibus neceffariò credenda,
impugnanda coniungimur: Neque *Caluinus, Luthe-*
rus, Marfilius Patauinus idcirco hæretici vel Ecclefiæ
hoftes reputati funt ab ijs, qui de hærefibus fcripferunt, eo quòd hanc Summi Pontificis poteftatem
Principes deponendi improbare aufi fuerint: Neque
etiam eos Catholicos, qui omnem illam authoritatem, quam quidam Summorum Pontificum po-
fterioribus hifce feculis vel fibi arrogarunt, vel plu-

rimi

rim i Doctores Catholici illis competere arbitrantur, non admittunt, quando alij contrà pugnant Catholici perdocti, idcirco tanquam *Ecclesiæ Romanæ, Sedisq̃; Apostolicæ hostes* traducendos quisquam vir pius & eruditus affirmabit.

61. Quis enim Catholicus pius, ac eruditus illum insolentissimæ, & scandalosæ admodùm temeritatis & calumniæ meritò condemnandum, & grauissimè castigandum non iudicaret, qui vel Illustrissimum *Cardinalem Bellarminum*, aliosque doctissimos Theologos, eo quòd cum *hæreticis & Romanæ Ecclesiæ hostibus, Caluino, Luthero, Marsilio Patauino* directum Summi Pontificis in temporalibus dominium, seu temporalem eius iure diuino Monarchiam vehementer impugnent; vel *doctissimum Soto*, aliosque Thologos quamplurimos, eo quòd cum *ysdem Ecclesiæ Romanæ hostibus* potestatem Summi Pontificis in matrimonio rato non consummato dispensandi (non obstantibus tot Summorū Pontificum ea in re dispensationibus pluribus eorum Bullis & Breuibus confirmatis) acerrimè refellant, vel *Theologos Parisienses*, quorum doctrinam doctissimus *Victoria* probabilem esse affirmat [d], eò quòd superioritatem Summi Pontificis supra Concilium generale, & infallibilem eius res fidei certò definiendi potestatem, non obstante *Lateranensi Concilio* vltimo, quod rem istam teste *Card. Bellarmino*, [*] *expressissimè definiuit,* cum prædictis Ecclesiæ Romanę hostibus reijcere & refutare non vereantur, *Caluino, Luthero, Marsilio Patauino* assimilare, & tanquam hæreticorum fautores, aut Ecclesiæ Romanæ hostes per calumniam traducere, neque eos, quantumcunque per iniuriam opprimantur, à *Sede Apostolica* vnquam audiendos,

[d] *Relect.4. de potest. Pape, & Cōcil. propos. 3.*

[*] *Lib. 2. de Cōcil. cap. 13.*

audiendos, quin potiùs quamdium hæreticis, & Ecclefiæ Romanæ hoftibus in impugnanda poteftate
Pontificia fe iungant, grauiter puniendos affirmare
non pertimefceret? Qui autem palam afferere non
verentur, nolle *Romanos Pontifices* Ecclefiæ Romanæ
filijs iuftitiam facere, neque *Breuia*, & Decreta vel fua,
vel Prædecefforum, vel *Illuftrifsimorum* S. R. E. *Cardina-*
lium, poftquam ea iniufta effe, & in falfis informationibus, aut fuppofitionibus fundata, atque in tertiæ
perfonæ, præfertim *Regiæ Maieftatis,* præiudicium con-
dita perfpexerint, eò quòd in Pontificiæ poteftatis fauorem tendant, refcindere & reuocare, quin potiùs
eos Catholicos, qui optimis rationibus moti eiufmodi iniuftis, & *Regiæ Maieftati* iniuriofis *Breuibus,* &
Decretis obfiftunt, pœnis & Cenfuris Ecclefiafticis
caftigare velle, *Sedem Apoftolicam*, Regibus, ac Principibus, quorum *ad exemplum totus componitur orbis*, quantum in ipfis eft, exofam reddunt, atque hæreticis in
hærefi fua perfiftendi, neque ad Ecclefiæ gremium
reuertendi, & Catholicis præfertim infirmioribus ab
Ecclefiæ *Romanæ* vnitate difcedendi, atque ad *Turcifmū,*
Paganifmum, vel planè *Atheifmum* deflectendi non exiguam occafionem fubminiftrant.

62. *Denique* falluntur *Aduerfarij* fi exiftiment, nos
minis, terroribus, pœnis, aut Cenfuris Ecclefiafticis,
quas ipfi nobis minitantur, ab innocentia noftra vijs
licitis defendenda, & à *falfa fide Catholica,* in rebus præfertim, quæ ad debitam noftram fidelitatem *Deo* &
Cæfari exhibendam fpectant, impugnanda vnquam,
Deo volente, abfterrendos. Neque enim æternæ fa-
lutis noftræ tam negligentes fumus, vt *Cenfuras Eccle-*
fiafticas, quæ, tefte *S. Auguftino* ^e, pœnis quibufcunque

e *Lib.* 1. *contra*
Aduerfarium le-
gis & *prophet.*
cap. 17.

tempo-

temporalibus grauiores funt, fi iuſtæ fint, & ob verũ crimen nobis inflictæ, non plurimùm timeamus; Neque tam timidi, & puſillanimes, vt Cenſuræ iniuſtæ, & ob crimen non verum, ſed duntaxat præſumptum, à *doctrina neceſſaria* propugnanda, & à *falſa fide_ Catholica* in rebus præſertim maximi ponderis (qualis hæc eſt de Principibus authoritate Papali deponendis & occidendis) refutanda nos dimouere poſſint: Neq; *Sacræ Theologiæ, Iuriſque Canonici* tam ignari ſumus, vt neſciamus, *Cenſuras Eccleſiaſticas,* iuxta approbatam *Theologorum,* & *Iuriſprudentium* doctrinam [f], fi iniuſtæ fint, & non pro vera culpa infligantur, *in conſcientia_ non obligare,* nec coram Deo, & in foro animæ, ſeu interno *Iuriſdictionem tollere,* aut *ſuſpendere,* ſed *parum plus nihilo valere niſi in foro externo,* ſeu contentioſo, *& ad ſcandalum vitandum;* neque *animam* ſeu conſcientiam *lædere* (niſi forſan eorum qui eas iniuſtè infligunt) ſed *læſam ſupponere,* & in peccati commiſſi *pœnam,* ſeu potiùs *medelam* infligendas eſſe; ideoque *interdum contingere,* [g] *vt qui ligatus eſt apud Deum, apud Eccleſiam ſit ſolutus, & qui liber eſt apud Deum, Eccleſiaſtica ſit ſententia innodatus.* Et proinde in hac cauſa noſtra, quam iuſtiſſimam eſſe coram *Deo,* & in conſcientia nobis perſuademus, illud *Chriſti Domini* monitum aſſiduè meditamur, *Nolite timere eos, qui occidunt corpus, animam autem non poſſunt occidere, ſed potiùs timete eum, qui poteſt & animam & corpus perdere in gehennam.* Quapropter ſicut pro *vera fide_* Catholica Romana palam agnoſcenda ipſam etiam mortem ſubire, Dei gratia adiuti, non pertimeſcimus, ita pro *falſa fide* Catholica Romana, quæque præſertim tum Eccleſiæ Catholicæ Romanæ tam ſcandaloſa eſt, vti diximus, tum Principibus Chriſtianis tam iniurioſa

[f] *Vide Nauarrum in Enchiridio cap. 27. nu. 3. Sayrum lib. 1. de Cenſuris cap. 17. Suarez diſp. 4. de Cenſuris ſec. 12. nu. 6. & alios, qui de Cenſuris ſcribunt.*

[g] *Innocentius 3° extra in cap. A nobis de ſentent. Excom.*

Matth. 10.

iniuriofa & periculofa, palam abneganda, nec minas,
nec terrores, nec Cenfuras Ecclefiafticas, aut alias
quafcunque perfequutiones, Deo nos adiuuante, for-
midabimus ; fed aureum illud doctiffimi, & deuo-
tiffimi *Ioannis Gerfonis* documentum, quo Romanæ
Ecclefiæ filios inftruit, quando, & in quo cafu licitum
fit *dogmatizare contra fententiam Papæ* (funt enim *Gerfonis* verba) non obftante *profequutione fententiarum, &
pœnarum contra ipfos,* ante oculos mentis noftræ pofitũ
femper habemus, & confolamur nos inuicem in ver-
bis iftis, *Beati, qui* (fiue in Anglia, fiue in Francia, Hi- Matth.5.
fpania, Germania, Italia, Curia Romana, aut vfpiam
alibi) *perfequutionem patiuntur propter iuftitiam, quoniam ipforum eft regnum cœlorum.*

63. Vt igitur huic noftræ *Supplicationi, Appellationi,*
eiufdemque *profequutioni* finem imponamus, *Veftram
Beatitudinem* (ad quam de nouo, ob rationes fuprà &
in noftra *Apellatione* memoratas, ab Illuftriffimis *Dominis Cardinalibus* ad Indicem deputatis, alijfque quibufcunque, & à quacunque fententia fiue definitiua,
fiue interlocutoria, aut alio quouis nomine nuncupetur, ab ipfis, aut alijs quibufcunque intuitu prefatæ
Widdringtoni doctrinæ, aut vllo ad eam refpectu habito,
vel iam lata & denunciata, vel deinceps ferenda &
denuncianda immediatè appellamus & prouocamus)
per vifcera Chrifti fuppliciter deprecamur ; *Primò,* vt
non grauetur hanc noftrã, quinetiã *Veftrã,* & omnium
Principum præfertim *Chriftianorum* caufam diligenter expendere, neque Ill^{mi} *Cardinalis Bellarmini,* eiufq; fequacium (quorũ plurimos nobis infenfiffimos & impla-
cabiles Aduerfarios reputamus) informationibũs nimiùm confidere, fed quod rectum & iuftum eft, poft

K maturam

maturam cauſæ noſtræ diſcuſſionem, abſque vlla ac
ceptione perſonarum iudicare, neque contra nos, cæteroſque *Anglos Catholicos* doctrinæ *Widdringtoni* adhærentes (quorum hîc in Anglia copioſus eſt numerus)
niſi ordine iuris ſaltem naturalis ſeruato, & de parti-
culari aliquo crimine à nobis commiſſo iuridicè admonitos, citatos, auditos, atque defenſos procedere,
ſed vel nos à *Card. Bellarmino,* alijſque pluribus præſertim *Ieſuitis falſam* eius *fidem Catholicam* vijs indębitis
propugnantibus, vi oppreſſos de manibus calumniantium eruere, noſque omnino innocentes, nullique
crimini eo nomine obnoxios declarare, noſtræque famæ ab illis per ſummam iniuriam grauiter læſæ omni meliori modo conſulere velit ; vel ſi fortaſſe (quod
nó credimus) *Sanctitas Veſtra* vel proprio ſuo iudicio,
vel aliorũ ſuggeſtionibus nos alicuius criminis (cuius
adhuc conſcij non ſumus) eo nomine reos eſſe iudicauerit, vt crimen illud non verbis tantùm generalibus, ſed ſpeciatim & particulatim, quò *Sanctitas Veſtra*
quid ad illud reſpondere poſſimus intelligat, nobis
manifeſtum facere non dedignetur : nam omnia &
ſingula à nobis dicta, ſcripta, aut commiſſa, quæ corrigenda ſunt corrigendi, quæ retractanda retractandi,
quæ purganda purgandi, & quæ explicanda explican-
di, quamprimùm nobis nota fuerint, nos animum
paratiſſimum habere, ſyncerè & coram Deo proteſtamur.

64. *Secundò,* vt vel *vnicam* ſaltem noui fidelitatis *Iu-*
ramenti per *declaratiua* Prædeceſſoris veſtri *Breuia* prohibiti *Clauſulam,* quæ fidei aut ſaluti apertè, aut etiam
tacitè repugnet, & *vnicam* ſaltem *propoſitionem* in *Wid-*
dringtoni libris, à Sacra *Illuſtriſſimorum Cardinalium* ad
Indicem

Indicem deputatorum Congregatione proscriptis contentam, quæ fanæ doctrinæ, aut bonis moribus verè aduerfetur, nobis, cæterifque Catholicis Anglis doctrinæ *Widdringtoni* adhærentibus, vt eaʃ deteftari, *poʃʃimʒ* abhorrere, & quantùm opus fuerit, retractare, nobis patefacere non dedignetur; vel vt *Breuia* illa Iuramentum prohibentia, eò quòd *multa contineat, quæ fidei & faluti apertè aduerfantur,* & *Decreta* illa quofdam *Widdringtoni* libros verbis tantùm generalibus proscribentia (quorum vtraque in manifeftè falfis suppofitionibus fundata effe nobis certiffimè perfuademus) refcindere, abrogare, & planè irrita & non obferuanda (faluo, quantum fieri poteft, *Summi Pontificis* honore, & totâ vel præcipuâ in eos, qui eum malè informarunt, culpâ meritò coniecta) declarare quamprimùm velit. Neque enim probro, fed laudi et honori vertendum eft *illi Summo Pontifici,* qui *Decreta,* vel fua vel Prædecefforum, quæ in prauis fuggeftionibus, ac falfis suppofitionibus fundantur, et in tertiæ perfonæ præfertim *Regiæ Maieftatis* præiudicium tendunt, refcindit, et non adimplenda declarat : Nam *patienter fuftinere debet Summus Pontifex,* (vt *Alexander* Papa tertius ʰ fuprà citatus ⁱ non minùs doctè quàm religiosè obferuauit) *fi non adimpleatur, quod praua infinuatione illi fuerit fuggeftum.*

65. *Tertiò* demùm, vt d~~octrinam~~ hanc falfam, feditiofam, antiquis Patribus incognitam, ab Ecclefiæ primitiuæ praxi alienam, Sedi Apoftolicæ atque Ecclefiæ Romanæ fcandalofam, Principum fupremorũ Coronis iniuriofam, eorumque Capitibus periculofam *doctrinam,* atque à *Card. Bellarmino,* alijfque nonnullis recentiorib' præfertim *Societatis Iefu* Theologis,

K 2   viris

ʰ *In cap.* Si quãdo *de Refcriptis.* ⁱ *Num.* 53.

viris alioquin eruditis, prudentibus, ac Religiofis, nec
tamen eruditè, prudenter, modeftè, aut religiosè, fed
contra veras, et antiquas tum fidei Catholicæ, tum
prudentiæ, modeftiæ, charitatis et iuftitiæ Chriftianæ
regulas per plurimos iam annos, proh dolor, propug-
natam, *de poteftate Papali Principes fupremos in ordine ad bonum fpirituale deponendi, &,* fi opus fuerit, *occidendi,* tanquam *de fide Catholica* certam, *aut fub pœna æternæ damnationis ab omnibus neceffariò credendam* (in qua tam *Breuia,*
quàm *Decreta* prædicta potiffimùm fundantur) penit⁹
extirpandandam, atque è Chriftianorum Scholis omnino explodendam curet. Ita enim tum *pax* et *vnitas
Ecclefiaftica,* quæ à prædictis præfertim *Iefuitis,* eorumq;
affeclis per plurimos iam annos hîc in Anglia *ob hanc
potiffimù doctrinam* miferè difciffa eft, in integrum re-
ftitui, et perniciofiffimi *Schifmatis* flamma, quam ijdē
hîc in Anglia *ob hanc potiffimùm doctrinam* iam accende-
runt, et in *Francia* etiam accendere, fed fruftra et cum
non leui eorum dedecore & periculo tentarunt, faciliùs extingui, tum concordia ftabilis inter *Regnum* &
Sacerdotium perfectiùs conferuari, & noftra, aliorumq;
plurium Catholicorum *falfam* hanc *fidem Catholicam*
impugnantium, et vfque ad mortem, Dei auxilio, impugnare volentium fama, à prædictis per fummam
iniuriam *ob hanc potiffimù doctrinam* grauiter læfa, re-
cuperari vtcunque poteft.

66. Neque aliam viam commodiorem, et facilio-
rem, rebus fic ftantibus, ad fcandalofam hanc controuerfiam componendam, ad pacem in Ecclefia Anglicana reftaurandam, ad firmam inter Regnum et Sacerdotium concordiam ftabiliendam, ad prædicta
Breuia et *Decreta* in falfis fuppofitionibus fundata
tacitè

tacitè faltem refcindenda, ad iuftitiæ Chriftianæ, omniumque, quantum fieri poteft, famæ et honori pro-
fpiciendum, atque ad maiora fcandala deinceps fe-
quutura, nifi controuerfia hæc pacificè componatur,
eo modo quo aliæ quæftiones inter Theologos con-
trouerfæ componi folent, deuitanda, Nos cum omni
fubmiffione debita loquentes arbitramur, quàm vt
Veftra authoritate Anglis Catholicis ftrictè iniungatur,
vt paci ac vnitati Ecclefiafticæ conciliandæ et conferuandæ fummopere ftudeant, neque ob *hanc præfertim,*
aut vllam aliam controuerfiam in difputatione pofi-
tam, quam *ipfemet Dominus Papa in Francia tolerat, quæque* *Card. Peronius*
impedire non debet reunionem eorum, qui Ecclefiæ reconciliari *fuprà nu. 3.*
defiderant, inuicem mordeant, pacem et vnitatem Ec-
clefiafticam fcindant, Schifma nutriant, aut quenquá
à communione Ecclefiaftica, vel Sacramentis, vel
communibus piorum eleemofynis percipiendis ex-
cludant, fed omnes fe mutuò diligant, eademque Chriftianæ charitatis officia, ac fi controuerfia hæc nūquá
nata fuiffet, fibi inuicem exhibeant.

67. Nihilominùs quæ via magis idonea fit, faluo
honore, & confcientia *Sedis Apoftolicæ,* ad fcandalofam
hanc controuerfiam componendam, atque adeo ad
Schifma deuitandum, Ecclefiæ pacem ac vnitatem
conferuandam, Catholicos vi oppreffos de manu calumniantium liberandos, *Veftræ Sanctitatis* prudentiæ,
charitati, ac iuftitiæ iudicandum relinquimus.

Deus Opt. Max. *Veftram Beatitudinem* gratia fua
cœlefti illuminet, dirigat & confirmet, vt abfque vllo
humani refpectus intuitu, nec ᴾ *confiderans perfoná pau=* ᴾ *Leuit. 19. &*
peris, nec honorans vultum potentis, fed *ita parum audiens* *Deuteron. 1.*
vt magnum, nec accipiens cuiufq; perfonam iuftè iudicet proximo

K 3   *fuo,*

ſuo, omnique proſpera fortuna in hac vita fruens, ita *Chriſti Domini*, cuius vices gerit, charitatem ac iuſtitiam imitetur, & *Veterum Sanctorum Pontificum* veſtigijs inhæreat, vt poſtea cœleſtis vitæ gaudijs perfrui mereatur æternis.   *Datum* & *Actum* Londini in *Carcere Clinkenſi* die 29. Maij 1621.

Veſtræ Beatitudinis, Sanctæq̃; Sedis Apoſtolicæ

Filij & Serui humillimi,

D. Thomas Preſtonus Congregationis Caſſinenſis Ordinis
S. Benedicti Presbyter Religioſus.

Fr. Thomas Greenæus Congregationis Hiſpanicæ Ordinis
S. Benedicti Presbyter Religioſus.

Et quoniam *Sanctiſſimum Dominum Papam*, ad quem immediatè appellamus, perſonaliter adire non poſſumus, cùm in cuſtodia detenti ſimus, neque perſonam aliquam authenticam, & in dignitate Eccleſiaſtica conſtitutam hîc manentem nouimus, cui hanc noſtrâ *Appellationem*, eiuſdemque *proſequutionem* intimemus, notificemus, & ab ea cum inſtantia & reuerentia debita Apoſtolos petamus ac requiramus, neque *Procuratorem* ad *Curiam Romanam* mittendi media nobis ſuppetant, cùm ad victum & veſtitum vix neceſſaria ipſimet habeamus, eam idcirco, vt omnibus nota fieret, & citiùs ac ſecuriùs ad *Suæ Sanctitatis* notitiam perueniret, typis imprimendam, & coram idoneis teſtibus, probis & honeſtis Catholicis nobiſcum in eodem

Carcere

Carcere detentis, & ad teſtificandum, nos hanc noſtrã *Supplicationem, Appellationem,* eiuſdemque *proſequutionem* illis notificaſſe rogatis, quorum nomina ſubſcripta ſunt, publicandam curauimus die proxime ſequenti eiuſdem Menſis, et anni.

Robert⁹ Charnock Sacrę Theo-
    logiæ Baccalaureus.
Rodulphus Stanford.
Richardus White.
Chriſtopherus Thulis.
Ioannes Barker.
Ioannes White.

Thomas Leke.
Edmundus Canon.
Ioannes Tomſon.
Ioannes Brian.
Ioannes Farmer.
Gulielmus Dauis.

Et ego *Rogerus Widdringtonus* Anglus Catholicus nunc *Londini* præſens, in teſtimonium debiti mei erga *Sedem Apoſtolicam* in ſpiritualibus, et *Regiam Maieſtatem* in temporalibus obſequij, atque in confirmationem veritatis à mę per plurimos iam annos palam agnitæ et propugnatæ, huic prædictorum *Reuerendorum Pa-trum Supplicationi, Appellationi,* eiuſdemque *proſequutioni* aſſentior, ſubſcribo, et iuſtitiam à *Sede Apoſtolica* inſtanter poſtulo ; Sicut etiam abſens priori eorundem *Ap-pellationi,* nomine etiam meo ad *Romanum Summumque Pontificem* menſe *Decembris* anni præteriti factæ, ex-preſſum meum aſſenſum et approbationem in ſcriptis præbui. *Datum Londini* die vltimo Maij 1621. et manu mea propria ſcriptum, et ſignatum.

Rogerus Widdringtonus Anglus Catholicus.

*Excerptum ex Conclufione Facultatis Theolo-
giæ Parifienfis facta 2. Ianuarij 1613.*

HONORANDI Magiftri noftri Antonius Fayet, Iacobus Hennequin, Hieronymus Parent, & Nicolaus de
Paris, Doctores Facultatis, nominati funt à Facultate
vt adeant Sereniffimam Reginam, Illuftriffimum
Franciæ Cancellarium, & Illuftriffimum Cardinalem Bonzium
nomine Facultatis, die 2. Ianuarij 1613.

De mandato D. Domini Decani & Facultatis.

P. COTEREAV.

SVMMA ACTORVM FACVLTATIS THEO-
logiæ Parifienfis contra librum infcriptum, *Controuerfia Anglicana de poteftate Regis & Pontificis, &c. auctore R. Martino
Becano Societatis IESV, Theologiæ Doctore & Profeffore ordinario. Moguntiæ, Ex officina Ioh. Albini. an. Domini 1612.*

ANno Domini 1613. die prima Februarij in Congregatione ordinaria facræ Facultatis Theologiæ Parifienfis,
Magifter Antonius Fayet, Doctor eiufdem Facultatis, retulit die
lunæ, feptima Ianuarij fe ex decreto eiufdem Facultatis vna cum
Magiftris Hieronymo Parent, Nicolao de Paris, & Huberto
Tranchant (quem in locum Magiftri Iacobi Hennequin, fuis ordinarijs prælectionibus occupati, affumpferat) fereniffimam Reginam, & Dominum Cancellarium Franciæ, conueniffe : huic
autem fummatim narraffe, quæ acta fuiffent in congregatione ordinaria Facultatis, die prima Decembr. 1612. & 2. Ianuarij 1613.
fuper quibufdam nefarijs propofitionibus collectis ex libro in-
fcripto *Controuerfia Anglicana de poteftate Regis & Pontificis,* &
Magiftrum Ioannem Fillefac Syndicum, ac Magiftrum & Fratrem Rogerium Gerard Auguftinenfem Doctorem eiufdem Facultatis, dixiffe Facultati Illuftriffimum Cardinalem Bonzium

L   mandato

mandato Reginæ fibi præcipiffe, fignificarent eidem Facultati, vt omnino abftineret à difcuffione illius libri, quoniam Regina ftatuiffet alia ratione huic malo prouidere. Sed quoniam hoc negotium permaximi effet momenti, vifum fuiffe ordini Theologico, vt prædictus Magifter Antonius Fayet, cum tribus alijs Doctoribus fupra memoratis Sereniffimam Reginam & Dominum Cancellarium adirent, eamque ob caufam fefe ad illum contuliffe, vtque de re controuerfa accuratius poffet iudicare, eidem prædictas propofitiones cum poftulatione & inductionibus factis & propofitis à Magiftro Nicolao de Paris, in Congregatione primi Decembris 1612. & 2. Ianuarij 1613. ad hunc modum exfcriptas obtuliffe.

In comitijs facræ Theologiæ Facultatis in aula Sorbonæ habitis, more folito, Calendis Decembris 1612. honorandus Magifter Nicolaus de Paris Doctor eiufdem Facultatis narrauit fe nuper accepiffe à viris pijs & doctis, peffimos rumores exire inter Catholicos, ex quodā libello admodū nefario & fcandalofo, qui infcribitur, *Controuerfia Anglicana de poteftate Regis & Pontificis, &c. Autore R. Martino Becano Societatis* I E S V, *Theologiæ Doctore & profeffore ordinario, Moguntiæ. Ex officina* Ioannis Albini, *anno Domini* M.DC.XII. *propterea quod hæ nouæ & periculofæ affertiones in ipfo continentur.*

1. *Pag.*108. Eft ergo quæftio, an Pontifex qui poteft Reges & Imperatores excommunicare, vt dictum eft, poffit etiam deponere, fi id meriti fint: negant auctor Iuramenti Fidelitatis, Sacellanus, Barclaius: affirmant C A T H O L I C I, E T M E R I T O, &c.

2. *Pag.*115. Poterat ergo (Pontifex) mandare, vt (Reges leprofi) feorfim habitarent, etfi nollent obedire, vt V I T A priuarentur, nihil certius. Hinc colligimus Pontificem duplici titulo potuiffe Reges priuare fuo Regno. Primo, quia poterat eos, fi contumaces effent, priuare V I T A, ergo & Regno: de hoc N E M O D V B I T A T, &c.

3. *Pag.*120. Plus dicam, in hac re tantum valuit confenfus Populi, etiam fi fupereffet L E G I T I M V S H A E R E S, cui Regnum deberetur, & hoc palam omnibus conftaret, tamen fi Populus prætermiffo L E G I T I M O H A E R E D E *alium delegiffet,* ille alius fuiffet V E R V S R E x, &c.

4. *Ibid.* Quæres, An Pontifex propria auctoritate Athaliam Regno priuauerit, &c. Refpondeo, & propria auctoritate fecit, & tamen

tamen opus erat CONSPIRATIONE, &c. *Et paulò poſt*, ſub-
rogato nouo Rege Athaliam Regno ſpoliauit,&c.

5. · *Pag.* 123. dices, Iojada Pontifex non ſolùm Regno, ſed
etiam VITA priuauit Athaliam, ergo ſi poteſtate Pontificis id fecit, ſequitur Pontifices veteris Teſtamenti habuiſſe poteſtatem
non ſolùm deponendi,ſed etiam INTERFICIENDI Reges,&c.
Reſpondeo, Iojada Pontifex priùs priuauit Athaliam Regno,de-
inde VITA. Itaque priuauit illam Regno, vt Reginam & Publicam perſonam: Priuauit autem VITA, vt Priuatam perſonam, &c.

6. *Pag.* 125. ex eodem ergo ſic argumentor, quicquid poteſtatis ac Iuriſdictionis permiſſum fuit Pontifici in Veteri Teſta-
mento, hoc etiam in NOVO permiſſum illi eſt: at in Veteri permiſſum illi fuit vt deponeret Reges,ſi id meriti eſſent: ergo etiam
in NOVO permiſſum illi hoc eſt, &c.

7. *Pag.*127. Reges & Principes qui violauerint priuilegia Mo-
naſterijs à Pontifice conceſſa,excommunicandos & ſua DIGNI-
TATE AC HONORE priuandos eſſe.

8. *Pag.* 130. & 131. Tertio, quia vnuſquiſque id iure facit,
quod ex officio facit: at Pontifex quando deponit Reges contumaces,ex officio id facit, ergo IVRE id facit,&c. quia Pontifex
eſt vniuerſalis Paſtor Eccleſiæ, cui à Chriſto dictum eſt, PASCE
OVES MEAS,&c. Per CANES intelliguntur, partim Reges &
Imperatores,&c. Igitur hi CANES quandiu FIDI *& excitati
ſunt*, Paſtori ad manum eſſe debent; at *ſi languidi & otioſi, &c.*
mox à Paſtore ſubmouendi,& ab officio repellendi ſunt. Hoc di-
ctat RECTA RATIO.

9. *Pag.* 133. Quæres,quomodo fiat hæc Depoſitio? Reſpondeo,varijs modis fieri poteſt. Vſitatus modus eſt hic, vt Pontifex
abſoluat ſubditos à debito ſeu vinculo ſubiectionis, quo obligati
ſunt ſuis Regibus &c.& quidem POTESTATEM ABSOLVENDI
accepit Pontifex à Chriſto his verbis, *Quicquid ſolueris ſuper terram erit ſolutum & in cœlis:* Eſt autem legitima cauſa ex parte
ſubditorum, quando Reges, vel non defendunt ſubditos à vio-
lenta incurſione hæreticorum,vel &c.

10. *Pag.* 134. Pontifex poteſt & alio modo id facere,nempe per
viam COMPENSATIONIS, quod ſic declaro; inter Reges &
eorum ſubditos eſt mutua quædam promiſſio & obligatio, &c. ſi
ergo Reges non præſtent fidelitatem, ad quam iure obligantur,

digni funt, vt nec fubditi præftent ipfis fidelitatem, iuxta illud *Frangenti fidem fides frangatur eidem, &c.* Nihil certivs apvd Catholicos.

11. *Pag.*136. Igitur prima eft, vt Rex meritus fit depofitionem: nam fi meritus non eft, deponi non debet. An autem meritus fit, Ex prvdenti Doctorvm ac Piorvm hominvm Ivdicio æftimandum eft,&c.

Quas Propofitiones dictus de Paris, mendacijs æque ac impofturis exundare, fibi quidem, cum bona venia Facultatis, videri dixit: nouorum errorum ac criminum defenfionem Catholicis affingere: inducere periculofa fchifmata: deprauare fcripturas facras: atque ex interpretatione falfa & erronea, dominos temporales iuribus fuis iniufte fpoliare: execrabilem Regum & Principum cædem, tanquam rem licitam & gloriofam Chriftianis proponere: fubindeque publicæ pacis extinctionem, proditiones horrendas, & innumeras populorum ftrages, rebelliones ac feditiones varias, in regna omnia importare, denique ius diuinum & humanum penitus euertere. Quapropter ne tam peftilens venenorum colluuies fit detrimento Reipubl.Chriftianæ; præfertim vero, ne regno huic Gallicano caufam fui luctus renouet, iam duobus maximis optimis & clementiffimis Regibus, ex ipfius finu Vno eodemque parricidij genere funeftiffimo & prorfus horribili,abreptis; ipfe de Paris, dictæ Facultati fupplicauit; vt quid ipfa de eiufmodi propofitionibus fentiret nunc quoque palam facere dignaretur. Poftquam quidem fupplicationem, honorandus Magifter Ioannes Fillefac etiam Doctor & Syndicus eiufdem Facultatis dixit fe etiam legiffe prædictum libellum, nec alium quidem à fe peftilentiorem vnquam vifum: tamen paucis abhinc diebus hoc mandatum habuiffe,ab Illuftriffimo Cardinali Bonzio nomine Sereniffimæ Reginæ, vt fignificaret ac renunciaret omnibus honorandis Magiftris noftris, ipfam prohibere ne quidquam de libello ifto noftris in comitijs deliberaretur, nifi aliter edixerit. Quo audito præfatus de Paris,petijt de omnibus & quæ ipfe propofuit, & quæ Dominus Fillefac Syndicus refpondit,extare monumentum perpetuum in libro ac regiftro Facultatis, & fibi exemplar hodiernæ Conclufionis in bonum publicum concedi,cui petitioni Vniuerfa Facultas annuit.]

Infuper quoque fe (Antonium Fayet) addidiffe, Facultatem more & inftituto maiorum confueuiffe in rebus etiam leuiffimis

&

& ad difciplinam Scholæ pertinentibus, vbi de Regis voluntate
agereretur, nunquam litetis parui figilli, nedum priuatorum relatio-
nibus & teftimonijs, fed tantum patentibus magno figillo inftru-
ctis, fidé habere : Veruntamen in teftimonium fui obfequij erga
Regem & Reginam matrem, omnem cohibuiffe deliberationem
fuper memoratis propofitionibus quoad amplius de Reginæ voluntate liqueret ; Facultatem magnopere vereri, ne pofteri in
controuerfia follicitata à Becano filentium aut remiffionem fuam
in eam partem accipiant, vt arbitrentur Theologos Parifi-
enfes, eandem feditiofiffimam doctrinam approbare, & maioru
placita, quibus Regum Chriftianiffimorum vt & aloru omnium
vita & fuprema autoritas fulcitur, damnare : quanti autem id ad
publicam tranquillitatem referat, admirabili prudentiæ ipfius
Domini Cancellarij relinquere : interea facrum ordinem Theologorum omnino percupere, fuam fidem atque religionem in tu-
tanda fuorum Regum vita & dignitate, nec non etiam in reti-
nenda maiorum doctrina, omnibus perfpectam atque explora-
tam effe.

Dominum Cancellarium vultu maxime beneuolo & humano
refpondiffe, gratiffimum fe habere Facultatis ftudium erga perfonas Regum fuorum Chriftianiffimorum, fe ordinem Theologorum Parifienfium & Vniuerfam Academiam, cui primam fuam
eruditionem acceptam referebat, femper magni feciffe ; Legiffe
integrum Becani libellum, & valde perniciofum iudicaffe, non folum expedire, verumetiam perneceffarium effe ; tum vt pofteri
cognofcant doctrinam Facultatis ab ifta noua & periculofa doctrina longe differentem effe ; tum vt prefentiffimum remedium
contra illam quando in dies glifcit vehementius, reperiatur. Porro
Facultatem Theologicam prudenter feciffe, quod priuatorum
obnuntiationibus & teftimonijs præfertim in re tanti momenti
non credidiffet : Viderent vt circa horam vndecimam fe in Regis Lupara fifterent, quoniam eos ad Sereniffimam Reginam in-
tromittere, eique ftudium Facultatis commendare vellet, vt reuera fecit.

Prædictum vero Magiftrum Antonium Fayet apud Reginam
præfente Domino Principe Condeo, Dominis Cancellario, Villa
regio, Illuftriffimo Cardinali Bonzio, cum permultis alijs viris
nobilibus facri Confiftorij, hanc orationem habuiffe ; Facultatem
Theologicam humillime fuam Maieftatem obfecrare, diceret

quid

quid vellet, iuberetq; fieri de pestilentissimo libro inscripto, *Controuersia Anglicana*, Illustrissimum Cardinalem Bonzium nomine suæ Maiestatis quibusdam Doctoribus Theologiæ priuatim dixisse, suam Maiestatem minime gratum habere Facultatem de memorato libro sententiam dicere: sed si placeret suæ Maiestati prouidendum esse, ne posteri silentium Facultatis hac in parte capiant pro consensu & approbatione tam pestilentis doctrinæ quæ Reges & Principes omni potestate & suprema auctoritate spoliat, subditos ad rebellionem & nefarios quosque ad Parricidia patranda solicitat. Tum Serenissimam Reginam dixisse, vna cum Concilio se de hac re acturam ac per Dominū Cancellarium voluntatem suam Facultati Theologiæ declaraturam.

Quocirca die Sabbathi 12. Ianuarij prædictos Magistros Antonium Fayet, Parent, de Paris, & Tranchant, circa horam secundam pomeridianam D. Cancellarium iterato conuenisse, vt de Serenissimæ Reginæ voluntate certiores fierent: illū eis dixisse; Reginam cùm antea duceret librum Becani non ita communem esse, sed vnum aut alterum exemplum illius extare in Gallijs, prudenter quidem eum potiùs silentio obrui, quàm Censura notari voluisse, idque Do. Cardinali Bonzio significasse; veruntamen postquam exploratum habuit eiusmodi librum in multorū hominum manibus versari, tandem censuisse malo huic medendum esse & permittendum Facultati vt pro sua fide, religione & conscientia de eo libro quæ viderentur, ageret, & decretum quod super ea re faceret, in acta Facultatis referret, vt posteri similibus occurrentibus controuersijs libros Facultatis Theologiæ consulerent: Magnopere dolendū esse sacrū Theologicū ordinem à quo totū regnū Franciæ in rebus ad religionem spectantibus, pendere debet, hodie in varia diuortia partium ire, Facultatē igitur paci & concordiæ salutari omni studio inuigilare debere. Ad hæc prædictum Fayet respondisse, diuisionem, si quæ est inter Doctores Facultatis, non aliunde oriri, quam ex dissidio istius doctrinæ nouæ & exoticæ. Interea scire percupere, an D. Cancellarius velit sibi adferri decretum Facultatis quod super hoc negotio fiet: illum dixisse, oportere quidem maiorum doctrinam sartam tectam à Facultate omni adhibita moderatione retineri ac gratissimum esse, imo rogare eosdem Magistros sibi decretum quod conflaretur adferre, ac præterea renunciare Facultati, quoties aliquid negotij emergeret, ipsum conuenirent, nunquam ab eo sine consilio & ope certa recessuram.

Vltimo ijdem Magiftri Antonius Fayet, Hieronymus Parent, Nicolaus de Paris, & Hubertus Trenchant, hanc fuam relatione Magiftro Petro Cottereau apparitori Facultatis in publicis comitijs legendam & recitandam tradiderunt, atque in acta referri, & vna cum decreto Facultatis quod fuper dicta relatione interueniet, fibi dari petierunt, vt iuxta mandatum fibi factum, ad D. Cancellariu omnia deferant, in cuius rei fidem & teftimonium præfentem relationem propria manu in dicta congregatione obfignarunt die & anno fupra dictis, Subfcriptum Fayet, Parent, de Paris, Tranchant : verum prædictus Fillefac Syndicus, perlecto quodam exemplo decreti Pontificij continente Cenfuram præfati libelli factam Romæ in Congregatione Dominorum Cardinalium die 3. Ianuarij anni præfentis, eo quòd nonnulla falfa, temeraria, fcandalofa & feditiofa refpectiuè, in eo reperta fuiffent ; atque ad maiorem rei fidem lectis etiam quibufdam literis teftimonialibus Domini Ruperti Epifcopi Politiani, Sanctiffimi Domini noftri Papæ in Galiijs Nuncij, prædictam Doctorum relationem recipi, & in acta referri, atque novum aliquod decretum à Facultate fuper nefarijs propofitionibus in ipfa relatione notatis, fieri impediuit ; idque prohibere Dominum Franciæ Cancellarium affeuerauit, & tanquam Syndicus ne fuper ea re deliberaretur, interceffit.

Cenfura libri Becani Soc. I E S V à S. D. N. Paulo diuina prouidentia Papa V. facta.

CVm nuper in lucem editus fuerit Libellus fermone Latino confcriptus, cuius titulus eft, *Controuerfia Anglicana de poteftate Regis & Pontificis contra Lancelotum Andream Sacellanum Regis Angliæ, qui fe Epifcopum Elienfem vocat, pro defenfione Illuftriffimi Cardinalis Bellarmini, auctore R.P. Martino Becano Societatis Iefu Theologo ; & Profeffore ordinario, Moguntiæ, ex officina Ioannis Albini anno 1612.* in quo nonnulla falfa, temeraria, fcandalofa, & feditiofa *refpectiuè* continentur. Hâc re ad S. D. N. diuina prouidentia Paulum Quintum delata ; idem Sanctiffimus præhabita dicti libelli matura difcuffione, ægrè ferens pro paftorali follicitudine fua atque vigilantia, eiufmodi libros, ex quibus

graue

graue aliquod fcandalum aliquando oriri poffet, à viris Catholicis in lucem emitti,præfatum libellum omnino prohiberi manda-
uit, donec corrigatur. Nos igitur Paulus Sfondratus Epifcopus
Albanenfis Sanctæ Ceciliæ, Robertus Bellarminus Sanctæ Mariæ in via, Ioannes Garzia Mellinus Sanctorum quatuor, Fabri-
cius Verallus Sancti Auguftini, Frater Auguftinus Galaminus
Aræ Cœli titulorum presbyteri, necnon Aloyfius Capponus
Sanctæ Agathæ diaconus S.R.E.nuncupati Cardinales à S.D.N.
Paulo diuina prouidentia Papa V. Sanctaque Sede Apoftolica
fuper librorum permiffione, prohibitione, expurgatione, & im-
preffione in vniuerfa republica Chriftiana fpecialiter deputati,
prædictum libellum præfenti decreto, iuxta S.D.N. mandatum
quocunque idiomate, vbicunque impreffum, prohibemus, & in
feeunda Claffe Indicis reponendū cenfemus, donec correctione
approbata,iuxta regulas Indicis denuo imprimatur, decernentes
quod nullus deinceps cuiufuis gradus, & conditionis, fub pœnis
in facro Concilio Tridentino & in Indice librorum prohibitorum
contentis, audeat imprimere, aut imprimi curare, vel quomodo-
cunque apud fe retinere aut legere præfatum libellum,& fub eifdē
pœnis quicunque nunc illum habent, vel habuerint in futurum,
locorum ordinarijs, feu inquifitoribus ftatim à præfentis decreti
notitia exhibere teneantur. In quorum fidem præfens decretum
fubfcriptum & munitū fuit figillo Illuftriffimi & Reuerendiffimi
Domini Cardinalis Sanctæ Ceciliæ Epifcopi Albanenfis, die
tertia Ianuarij 1613.

P.Epifcopus Albanenfis Cardinalis Sanctæ Ceciliæ
Frater Paulus Picus Secretarius.

Excerptum

Excerptum ex literis Claudij Aquavivæ *Præpositi Generalis Societatis* I E S V, *datis* Romæ 2. Januarij, anno 1613. ad R. P. Christophorum Baltazarem Prouincialem *eiusdem Societatis in Prouincia Franciæ super prædicto* Becani *libello.*

CV M primum huc liber ille peruenit, idque in eo deprehensum est quod aliter dictū aut omnino prætermissum oportuit, Censuræ notas illuc remisimus, vt iuxta eas liber emendaretur: atque hoc solum nobis superfuit remedium, vnde speramus Patrem illum cautiorem futurū in posterum, & instrui posse eos qui turbas moliuntur, resque nostras aliter ac par est, interpretantur; non ideo redarguendam Societatem, aut vniuerso corpori adscribendum, quod vnus aliquis quouis modo peccauerit: quando id non modo Societas non admittit, sed etiam manifestè improbat, atque emendare studet, vt à nobis factum est circa opinionem Marianæ de Tyrannicidio.

Item ex literis eiusdem Generalis eodem die scriptis ad R. P. Petrum Cotonum.

ERRORE factum est, quod vehementer doluimus, vt huc liber ille *Becani* non mitteretur recognoscendus. Quod ergo superfuit remedij minime neglexîmus: quamprimum enim hic liber comparuit, ea notanda curauimus, atque ad eundem Patrem remittenda; quæ vel deleri omnino, vel corrigi oportere deprehensa sunt, vt, quoad licebit emendentur, constetque vnius errorē non esse toti Societati adscribendum, quando eum Societas non adprobat. Deinceps autem speramus fore vt ille Pater sit cautior in scribendo, & præcaueantur omnes eiusmodi offensiones diligentius.

M. Georgij Frogerij Doctoris Sorbonici & Parochi Sancti Nicolai de Cardineto, Iudicium de libro inscripto, *Controuersia Anglicana* auctore *R. P. Martino Becano, Societatis* Iesv *Theologo, &c.*

Excerptum ex eiusdem Frogerij notis in librum de Ecclesiastica & Politica potestate, num. 18.

POSTREMO hoc numero ad finem vsque libelli sui producto author explicat quo modo & sensu Ecclesia vendicare possit sibi potestatem indirectam in temporalia Regum & Principum.

Quinimo etiamsi Summus Pontifex possit de iure ferire peculiari excommunicationis fulmine Reges, etiam Franciæ (vt ne amplius probem, indicant priuilegia à summis Pontificibus indulta Regibus Christianissimis, ne sibi, suisue liberis, aut coniugibus vnquam metuere debeant ab ictu excommunicationis fulmineo) nulla tamen ratione potest aut Reges deponere, suoue deturbare solio, multo minus subditos eorum absoluere à iuramento fidelitatis, aut in Reges permittere, iusue cuiquam facere sæuiendi aut mortem intentandi : *etenim effectus excommunicationis maioris sunt merè spirituales,* puta, priuare excommunicatum sacramentorum Ecclesiæ participatione & vsu, fidelium suffragijs, Ecclesiastica sepultura, & consuetudine vitæ cum alijs, nisi excusent casus concepti, & contenti hocce versiculo,

Vtile, lex, humile, &c.

Neque momentũ habent rationes in contrarium adductæ, nempe, quod sicut spiritus habet imperium in corpus, vt illud castiget, si seditiose secedat & detrectet obsequi spiritui : Ita Ecclesia Summusque Pontifex, qui est per religionem quasi anima status politici, possit animaduertere in Principes seculares. Item quod ille cui datur Facultas aliquid perficiendi, etiam detur eorum sine quibus illud fieri non potest : at Christus Dominus dedit suæ

Ecclesiæ

Ecclefiæ auctoritatem fefe propagandi toto orbe, ergo & amo-
uendi impedimenta aduerfantia, inter quæ fi reperiatur proter-
uus Princeps, qui aut cuniculis aut machinis aperto opertoue
marte prohibeat Ecclefiæ liberæ diffufionem & libertatem, è gra-
du dimoueri, deponi, & è medio tolli poterit auctoritate Summi
Pontificis.

Verum ad priorem rationem refpondeo, non licere fpiritui
quodcunque genus correptionis in corpus, neque in iftud habere
merum vitæ & necis Imperium, tefte Apoftolo 2 Corinth.6. qui
hortatur, *Simus vt caftigati & non vt mortificati,* ὡς παιδδόμψοι ϰ̀ μὴ
θανατέμψοι : enimuero voluntas noftra, quamuis architectonice, &
Regina Facultas totius fuppofiti noftri, non gaudet iam iure in
appetitū animalem defpotico (Ariftot.in ethi. & D.Thom.1.2)

Ad alteram quoque refpondeo, non quodlibet medium effe
aut idoneum, aut honeftum, aut licitum ad finem aliquem obti-
nendum ; deinde iftud eget maturrima, & longiffima deliberatione : & vt olim Areopagitæ de muliere veneficij rea confultatio-
nem & iudicium remiferunt in centum annos : ita poftulanda
effet merito annorum centuria vt videretur, expediatne Ecclefiæ
Dei, fidem & religionem orthodoxam fpargere & diffeminare vi
Principibus terrenis illata. Certè *virga Regni Ecclefiæ, virga eft
directionis, & pro columna ignis,* quæ prælucebat antiquo Mofaico
populo: iam tegit nos & protegit columna nubis, id eft gratia,
quæ neque naturam, neque naturalia, aut gentilitia Principū iura
deftruit, fed perficit : Quapropter non exiftimo Summum Pontificem Romæ fedentem ad clauum Ecclefiæ, vnquam proba-
turum, *fpermologos iftos nouatores,* fanctiffimæ Sedi Apoftolicæ
affingentes id quod antea nefciuit : Quinetiam non dubito paterna tanti Pontificis vifcera plurimum commoueri erga chariffi-
mos Principes filios fuos, quos non amat ad iracundiam prouo-
care, imo quibus metuit, & inuigilat quotidie lachrimabundus,
vt malit quidlibet ab ijs pati, quam de exhæredando illos cogi-
tare, prodigi fuerint fupra modum, attamen cito profert illis fto-
lam primam, & annulo fiduciæ & bonæ fpei reddito, procumbet
in eorum colla, matrem fe meminit, matrem fe cogitat, non minus
deficientium quam proficientium, & compatitur fuper contriti- S. *Bernard.*
one Iofeph, expreffo illis lacte etiam exhortationis de vbere com-
paffionis, vnde fi quando laceretur ipfa, & fibi vngues infigant fui,
non conqueritur, propterea quod mater eft.

Denique

Denique tametsi omnia ista suspiria, lachrimæ, labores, mole-stiæ, orationes, & beneficia non emollirent Principes malos, fa-tius multo foret expectare & comparare se ad martyrium quam iugum excutere subiectionis ; sic enim sanguis sub gladio gemen-tium, foret iterum semen & germen Christianorum, sicut segetes falce demessæ & tribulâ excussæ è spicis, denuo in terram reiectæ, moriendo refundunt adauctam spicarum granis onustarum co-piam, scilicet minus multo est, quod bellicus labor parit Ecclesiæ, quam quod pax Christiana subijcit : Quoniam igitur non video partem oppugnantium niti vllo fidei orthodoxæ articulo, ea de re edito, (neque *Patres* me arguent temeritatis) nondum com-pellor à sententia hac recedere, cui dum inhæreo, nolo vel tantillâ obseruantiæ erga communem omnium nostrū Patrem Sanctissi-mum Dominū Papam partem minuere, vel auctoritati supremæ atque plenitudini in Ecclesia potestatis, quam supra demonstraui, accepisse à Christo Domino non ab Ecclesia ipsa, detrahere, aut labem inspergere.

Quantus enim ego sum vt succensere & æmulari debeam, aut inquirere patrios & auitos in vsus Summi Pontificis, eosque pro-babiles, hoc est nemini hactenus inuidiosos, ergo non possum in-terea non offendi magnopere & exacerbari aduersus dirum & pessimè feriatum hominem *Becanum*, eiusque ominosum & por-tentosum valde libellum, non repudiare & proculcare, quem nu-per inscripsit & edidit sub titulo, *Controuersiæ Anglicanæ*, sed plane maniaco & dæmoniaco, & mente impia, atque sacrilega : atque aduersus istam pestilentissimam, furiosissimamque *Becani buccam*, & scripturam oppono, vt compendio dicam, *Barclaium, & Ioannem Barclaÿ, & Rogerum Vindrictonum* Catholicum An-glum, qui firmissimis argumentorum machinis arietant & extur-bant propugnacula *Becani, Bellarmini Cardinalis alioqui Illustrissi-mi, & de Ecclesia sancta optimè meriti, Marianæ & similium*. Quod autem postremo loco hic attexo, exhomologesis mea est, quà meas hasce animaduersiunculas, ni valde fallor, Sanctorum Patrū, Conciliorum œcumenicorum, adeoque ipsius Scripturæ sacræ doctrinis & decretis omnino consentientes, vna cum totius vitæ meæ ratione & serie melioribus iudicio, censuræ, ἡ δικῆ ἡ ἐκδικήσει Ecclesiæ Catholicæ Apostolicæ & Romanæ matris meæ expono & subijcio, ita me Deus Optimus Maximus, salua Academia aris & focis, incolumen seruet sospitetque.

I. Ex

1. Ex his perſpicuum eſt (*Pater Sanctiſsime*) *doctrinam* hanc *nouam* de poteſtate Papali Principes ſupremos deponendi, & de rebus omnibus temporalibus, & conſequenter de *Coronis* & *Capitibus* Principum, in ordine ad bonum ſpirituale diſponendi, tanquam de *fide Catholica certâ*, & ab omnibus fidelibus *neceſſariò*, & ſub pœna æternæ damnationis *credendam* (in qua tum *Breuia* Veſtri Prædeceſſoris *Pauli* V. Iuramentum fidelitatis prohibentia, tum *Decreta* Illuſtriſſimorum *Cardinalium* quoſdam *Widdringtoni* libros verbis tantùm generaliſſimis proſcribentia potiſſimùm fundantur, & ob quam impugnandam idem *Widdringtonus*, cæterique Angli Catholici eius doctrinæ adhærentes à Card. *Bellarmino*, eiuſque ſequacibus tanquâ Pſeudo-Catholici, à fide Catholica Apoſtatæ, & *Sedi Apoſtolicæ* rebelles per ſummam iniuriam traducuntur, et varijs oppreſſionibus iniuſtè affliguntur) non ſolùm *Senatui Pariſienſi* ex probis, doctis, et prudentibus Catholicis maxima ex parte conflatæ, quæ pluribus *Arreſtis* [a] contra libros *Card. Bellarmini, Franciſci Suarez*, et aliorum editis, *doctrinam* hanc *nouam*, tanquam *falſam, ſcandaloſam, ſeditioſam*, et *Principum Coronis iniurioſam*, eorumque *Capitibus periculoſam*, ſub *pœna læſæ Maieſtatis* condemnauit, verùm etiam ipſi Doctorum Pariſienſium *Vniuerſitati*, aut plurimis ad minimum illius *Academiæ* Doctoribus (vti *Acta* ſuperiùs relata commonſtrant) quàm maximè diſplicere, et exoſam eſſe.

a *Hæc Arreſta habentur in fine Strenæ Catholicæ.*

2. Adeo vt *Cardinalis Peronus* nationis *Gallicanæ* Catholicus celeberrimus, et non dignitate tantùm *Cardinalitia*, ſed eruditione etiam *Theologica* illuſtriſſimus, atque in hac controuerſia optimè verſatus, neq; *doctrinæ*, quam *Regnum Franciæ* (teſte *Petro Pithæo* [b] viro

b *Suprà nu. 21.*

etiam

ᶜtiam doctiſſimo) vti *certam* ſemper tenuit,ignarus,aut
ᶜorum quæ tum à *Senatu,* tum à *Facultate Pariſienſi* acta
ſunt inſcius,affirmare non dubitauerit, (quod ſæpe ſæpiùs inculcare neceſſarium ducimus) *non debere hanc
Diſputationem impedire revnionem eorum,qui Eccleſiæ reconci-*

ᶜ *Nu.23.ſuprà.* *liari deſiderant* ᶜ: Vnde manifeſtè conſequitur,impug-
nationem huius *nouæ doctrinæ* quæ *Eccleſiæ Romanæ* tam
ſcandaloſa eſt,vti diximus, & *supremæ* Regum *poteſtati*
tam iniurioſa, eorumque *Capitibus* periculoſa, non
poſſe à quoquam timoratæ conſcientiæ Catholico
vti illicitam reprehendi, neque iuſtâ præbere cauſam
Patribus Ieſuitis, aut alijſque quibuſcunque eorum
ſectatoribus, pacem ac vnitatem Eccleſiaſticam in
Anglia diſrumpendi, Schiſma fouendi, vel eos Catholicos, qui eam impugnant, à communione Eccleſiaſtica tanquam *Ethnicos, Publicanos,*aut *manifeſtè criminoſos* ſeparandi, aut Illuſtriſſimis *Dominis Cardinalibus* ad
Indicem deputatis eorum Catholicorum libros, qui
eam refutant,hoc duntaxat nomine prohibendi,& in
librorum prohibitorum Catalogo reponendi.

3. Eapropter *Veſtram Beatitudinem* iterum atque
iterum ſuppliciter obſecramus & obteſtamur, vt vel
prædicta *Illuſtriſſimorum* Cardinalium *Decreta,*& Veſtri
Prædeceſſoris *Breuia,*reſcindat & irrita declaret, vel vt
Illuſtriſsimos Cardinales, qui *Decreta* illa condiderunt,&
Veſtrum *Prædeceſſorem* ad *Breuia* ſua huc mittenda,vti
credibile eſt, incitarunt,ad particularia deſcendere, &
vel *vnicam propoſitionem* aut in Iuramento,aut in libris
Widdringtoni contentam, quæ fidei, ſaluti, ſanæ doctrinæ,aut bonis moribus repugnet, quò eam deteſtari,
retractare, aut ab ea nos purgare quamprimùm poſſimus, nobis notam facere ſua authoritate compellat.

Quòd

Quòd si post tot humillimas *Supplicationes* prædicti *Cardinales Illustrissimi* ad particularia descendere abnuerint, neque *Widdringtono*, nobisque eius doctrinæ adhærentibus vllam *particularem propositionem* Censura dignam palam facere voluerint, quid *Sanctitas Vestra*, totusque Christianus orbis de eiusmodi Illustrissimorum Cardinalium Decretis meritò iudicare possit, tum *Vestræ Beatitudinis* prudentiæ, ac iustitiæ, tum eorum conscientijs iudicandum relinquimus.

4. Etenim si quispiam hæreticus toties *Vestram Beatitudinem* humillimè deprecaretur, vt si forsan aliquis illius liber authoritate *Sedis Apostolicæ* verbis tantùm generalibus proscriptus esset, propositiones illæ particulares, ob quas proscriptus est, illi indicarentur, atq; palam & in conspectu mundi coram Deo protestans, se quæ purgandæ sint, purgaturum, quæ explicandæ explicaturum, quæ corrigendæ correcturum, & quæ retractandæ confestim retractaturum, quoties *Widdringtonus* idem, & cum eadem protestatione à *Vestro Prædecessore* suppliciter postulauit, non dubitamus, quin *Sanctitas Vestra*, pro Pastoralis sui officij debito, & tam in priuatam illius hæretici, quàm in publicam totius mundi, in cuius conspectu *Supplicatio* tam humilis facta est, satisfactionem, ad particularem aliquam propositionem ab eo vel omnino retractandam, vel saltem melius explicandam descendere dignaretur: Et nunquid forsan haud æquum & dignum est, vt viri Catholici, & qui pro fide *Catholica Romana* palam agnoscenda varias ærumnas sustinuerunt, & mortem ipsam subire parati sunt, quique *Ecclesiæ Catholicæ Romanæ* iudicio se in omnibus humillimè submittunt, eandē gratiam, quin potiùs iustitiam à *Sede Apostolica*,

&

& fupremo animarum Paftore poft tot humillimas
Supplicationes obtineant ? Non ita egerunt Patres Concilij *Constantienfis* cum *Wicleffo, Ioanne Hus,* & *Hieronimo*
de *Praga,* nec *Leo* Papa decimus cum *Luthero,* nec *Vni-*
uerfitas Parifienfis & *Colonienfis* cum *Marco Antonio de*
Dominis, nec Doctores *Sorbonici* cum *Becano,* aut *Parlia-*
mentū Parifienfe cum *Card. Bellarmino,* & *Francifco Suarez,*
fed *particulares propofitiones* Cenfura dignas, quamuis
haud rogati, annotarunt. Et nonne idem viris Catholicis fi non eò quòd Catholici funt, faltem propter
importunitatem rogantium concedi debuiffet ? Adeo
vt hæc ipfa *Prædecefforis* Veftri, & *Illuftrifsimorum Cardi-*
ualium poft tot *Supplicationes,* vt ad particularia defcen-
dant, reticentia non leue tum *Veftræ Beatitudini,* tum
alijs quibufcunque viris prudentibus argumentum
effe poffit, prædicta *Breuia,* et *Decreta* in falfis fuppofitionibus, quas præfati *Cardinales Illuftrifsimi* iuftificare
non poffunt, fundata effe; quæque proinde vt veftra
authoritate refcindantur, et irrita declarentur, à *Veftra*
charitate et iuftitia inftantiffimè poftulamus, atque
vt vel nos innocentes declararemur, ijque qui nos
tam iniquè calumniati funt, coerceantur, et repriman-
tur, vel crimen aliquod *particulare,* cuius adhuc con-
fcij non fumus, quod emendare tenemur, nobis pate-
fiat, à *Sanctitate Veftra* iterum atque iterum obnixè ac
humiliter poftulare innocentiæ noftræ defendendæ
gratia nunquam, Deo volente, defiftemus.

5. *Denique,* de pluribus alijs obferuatione dignis
circa præfatam *Illuftrifsimorum Cardinalium* contra librū
Becani Cenfuram, et Reuerendi admodum Patris *Clau-*
dij Aquaviuæ Societatis Iefu Præpofiti generalis contra eundem librum *literas,* et circa *recognitam* et expur-
gatam

gatam, feu potiùs magis fædè, quàm antea confpurca-
tam eiufdem *Becani* Controuerfiæ Anglicanæ *Editionê*
paulò pòft in lucem emiffam, Summoque Pontifici
Paulo V. dedicatam, atque à Patribus fuæ *Societatis* ap-
probatâ; & quàm artificiosè *Becanus* tum *Sereniſſimæ*
Franciæ Reginæ, tum *Doctoribus Pariſienbus* fub fuco
Recognitionis, feu Expurgationis illuferit (cùm *vnicam*
ᶜ tantùm ex illis propofitionibus, quas præfati *Doctores*
tanquâ *Cenfura* dignas annotarunt, expunxerit, quam
tamen ftatim poftea Illuftriffimus *Card. Bellarminus* in
fuo *Schulckenio* ᵈ, tametfi non adeo affertiuè ficut *Beca-*
nus, fed tantùm, *cùm credibile eſt,* palam propugnare non
eft veritus) & quàm iniuriosè idem *Becanus* vocabula
illa *legitimus,* & *fupremus,* quæ in priori *Editione* pag.
102. idque pro *certo* affirmans pofuerat, in *Controuerfia,*
vti prætendit, *recognita* expungens, ᵉ *Regem* noftrum
Sereniſſimum, totumque *Angliæ* Regnum tractauerit,
nihil ampliùs ob pacis Ecclefiafticæ bonum in præfenti dicemus; plurimùm confifi, *Veſtram Beatitudinem,*
pro fingulari fua prudentia, charitate, iuftitia, & pacis
ac vnitatis Ecclefiafticæ conferuandæ zelo, *fcandalofæ*
huic *controuerfiæ,* ob quam Angli Catholici grauiffi-
mas tribulationes & perfequutiones iam per plurimos annos à fuis præfertim fratribus, eiufdemque fidei Catholicæ domefticis paffi funt, finem quietum,
tranquillum, & pacificum breuî impofituram, nofque
vi oppreffos, & à viris in *Curia Romana* potentibus plurimùm tribulatos & vexatos, de manibus calumniantium & tribulantium citò liberaturam, vt ita *Sanctitas*
Veſtra iuxta elogium illud, [*In tribulatione pacis* ᶠ] quod
Sanctus *Malachias* ᵍ Ordinis *S. Benedicti* monachus, &
Archiepifcopus *Ardinacenſis,* quingentis ferme abhinc

N   annis

ᶜ *nempe, tertiam*
in ordine.

ᵈ *pag. 558. Edi-*
tionis Colonienſis.

ᵉ *pag. 116.*

ᶠ *Habetur apud*
Arnoldum Wion
in ligno vitæ lib.
2. pag. 307. vbi
recitat prophetias
S. Malachiæ de
Summis Pontifi-
cibus.
ᵍ *Eius vitam de-*
fcribit S. Bernar-
dus.

annis de *Veſtra Beatitudine* ſpeciatim vaticinatus eſt, *Vir pacificus in tempore tribulationis,* tum à nobis, tum ab omnibus qui pacis & concordiæ non ſolùm inter ipſoſmet *Eccleſiaſticos,* ſed inter etiam *Regnum, & Sacerdotium* conſeruandæ ſtudioſi ſunt, veriſſimè dici, & palam prædicari queat.

VESTRÆ SANCTITATIS
Filij & Serui quàm humillimi

D. Thomas Preſtonus
Fr. Thomas Greenæus } qui ſupra.

ᵏ *Num. 43.*

Et ego *Rogerus Widdringtonus* huic iuſtiſſimæ prædictorũ Patrũ poſtulationi aſſentior, ſubſcribo, & pro tot atrociſſimis calumnijs ſuprà ᵏ relatis, quæ mihi falſè et per ſummam iniuriam impoſita ſunt, iuſtitiam à *Sanctitate Veſtra* inſtantiſſimè poſtulo.

Rogerus Widdringtonus Anglus Catholicus.

Pag.	Lin.	Errata.	Corrig.
33.	32.	veruntamen.	verùm etiam.
36.	5.	immolauit falsò, aſſimilat.	immolauit, falsò aſſimilat.
75.	19.	vnquam	nunquam.
93.	5.	noluerint.	voluerint.
83.			